2002 EDITION

Economic portrait
of the European Union 2002

Data up to 2001

EUROPEAN COMMISSION

THEME 2
Economy and finance

.... Immediate access to **harmonised statistical data**

Eurostat Data Shops

A personalised data retrieval service

In order to provide the greatest possible number of people with access to high-quality statistical information, Eurostat has developed an extensive network of Data Shops ([1]).

Data Shops provide a wide range of **tailor-made services:**

- ★ immediate information searches undertaken by a team of experts in European statistics,
- ★ rapid and personalised response that takes account of the specified search requirements and intended use,
- ★ a choice of data carrier depending on the type of information required.

Information can be requested by phone, mail, fax or e-mail.

([1]) See the list of Eurostat Data Shops at the end of this publication.

Internet

Essentials on Community statistical news

- ★ Euro indicators: more than 100 indicators on the euro zone; harmonised, comparable, and free of charge.
- ★ About Eurostat: what it does and how it works.
- ★ Products and databases: a detailed description of what Eurostat has to offer.
- ★ Indicators on the European Union: convergence criteria; euro yield curve and further main indicators on the European Union at your disposal.
- ★ Press releases: direct access to all Eurostat press releases.

For further information, visit us on the Internet: **www.europa.eu.int/comm/eurostat/**

A great deal of additional information on the European Union is available on the Internet.
It can be accessed through the Europa server (http://europa.eu.int).

Cataloguing data can be found at the end of this publication.

Luxembourg: Office for Official Publications of the European Communities, 2002

ISSN 1680-1687
ISBN 92-894-3771-5

© European Communities, 2002

Printed in France

PRINTED ON WHITE CHLORINE-FREE PAPER

PREFACE

The purpose of this annual review — which has now become a traditional part of Eurostat's publications programme — is to bring together for analysis in a single work a wide range of mainly macroeconomic data on the European Union and its Member States.

Although this review refers to specific national circumstances, the idea is to use the main economic variables to present a profile of the Fifteen and of the euro-zone. Where possible, the comparison is extended to the various economic areas of the world as well as to the Union's main economic partners. Again this year, special importance is attached to the macroeconomic data of the candidate countries.

As always, the bulk of the information is taken from the national accounts, but this edition also makes extensive use of data from other sectors of Eurostat activity, such as social statistics, business statistics and agricultural accounts. We are convinced that this combination of information from different sources offers additional insight to the reader.

Compared with the economic analyses and forecasts prepared by other services of the European Commission, this report provides only a descriptive analysis of the facts. While the emphasis is primarily on the latest available data, retrospective series also figure prominently.

In an age when up-to-the-minute information is crucial to understanding socioeconomic events, it may seem inappropriate to publish and comment on relatively old data. However, these data have certain advantages:

— most of them have been compiled according to the harmonised and comparable concepts and methods of the European system of accounts (ESA 95);
— most of them come from the national statistical institutes of the Member States;
— a knowledge of recent trends helps in understanding information about the present.

By presenting and analysing in a single report the main macroeconomic data of the Union and the Member States, this publication will make the information more accessible to users and will contribute significantly to an understanding of the economic phenomena of our time.

Yves FRANCHET
Director General
Eurostat

Under the responsibility of Marco De March, Eurostat Unit B.2 "Economic accounts and international markets: production and analysis" benefited for the production of the present summary report from the precious expertise of Units B.3, B.4, B.5, C.4, D.2, D.3, E.1, E4, F1 and F.4. Unit C.1 and the Translation Service of the Commission also provided their essential logistic support.

Overall coordination
Ingo Kuhnert (Unit B.2)

Writing team
Roberto Barcellan, Wayne Codd, Marco De March, Ingo Kuhnert, Jarko Pasanen and Peter Ritzmann (Economic accounts), Jean Lienhardt, Jenny Runesson and Gunter Schäfer (Entreprises), Ulrich Eidmann (Agricultural accounts), Eduardo Barredo-Capelot, Anne Berthomieu-Cristallo and Luis Biedma (External trade), Paolo Passerini (Balance of payments), Axel Behrens and Volker Stabernak (Regions), Aarno Laihonen (Population), Ana Franco and Sylvain Jouhette (Labour market), Gérard Abramovici and Flavio Bianconi (Social protection), Gesina Dierickx, Olivier Delobbe and Sheldon Warton-Woods (Interest rates, euro and exchange rates), Eckhard Borchert and Silke Stapel (Prices).

Layout and desktop publishing
Cindy Brockly and Madeleine Larue

Manuscript completed in August 2002

For further information or any suggestions, please contact:

Eurostat — Unit B.2
5, rue Alphonse Weicker
L-2721 Luxembourg
Tel. (352) 43 01-33207
Fax (352) 43 01-33879
marco.demarch@cec.eu.int
ingo.kuhnert@cec.eu.int

All data requests should be addressed to
one of the Eurostat Data Shops listed on the last but one page.

CONTENTS

Introduction — 7

1. Economy of the Union

    1.1. Gross domestic product — 9

    1.2. Expenditure breakdown of GDP — 20

    1.3. Production breakdown of GDP: the economy by branch — 28

    1.4. National income and the distribution breakdown of GDP — 41

    1.5. The economic situation of the regions — 49

2. The Union in the international framework

    2.1. The EU in the world — 53

    2.2. The candidate countries — 56

    2.3. External trade — 66

    2.4. International trade in services — 74

    2.5. Foreign direct investment — 77

3. Enterprises in the Union

    3.1. Structural business development — 87

    3.2. Short-term business developments — 95

    3.3. Developments in agriculture — 102

4. Household consumption expenditure

    4.1. Overview — 109

    4.2. Analysis by purpose — 112

5. General government in the Union

    5.1. Major aggregates of general government — 119

    5.2. General government revenue and expenditure — 120

    5.3. Public deficit and debt — 124

6. Population, labour market and social protection in the Union

    6.1. Population — 127

    6.2. Employment — 131

    6.3. Unemployment — 133

    6.4. Social protection and pensions — 136

7. Money, interest rates and prices in the Union

    7.1. Exchange rates, the euro and EMU — 149

    7.2. Interest rates — 152

    7.3. Consumer prices — 155

    7.4. Purchasing power parities — 160

Symbols and abbreviations — 166

INTRODUCTION

In terms of economic performance, 2001 was a year marked by a significant slowdown. Gross domestic product (GDP) grew by + 1.5 % in the European Union and by + 1.4 % in the euro zone, which in both cases meant a reduction by around two percentage points in comparison with 2000, when the highest growth rates of the decade were recorded.

However, in the international context, most of the world's economies also experienced a slowdown, and some of them even showed negative growth rates, i.e. real GDP actually declined. The US economy, after years of vigorous growth well ahead of the figures registered in the European Union, encountered near-stagnation in 2001, its GDP rising by only + 0.3 %. Japan, which had hardly recovered from the weak years before, reported a negative result of - 0.6 % annual change. Thus, the reduction in growth was three percentage points or more for both the United States and Japan.

Of the four major European economies, three registered mediocre results of + 1.9 % (United Kingdom) and + 1.8 % (Italy and France), while the German result of + 0.6 % was significantly lower. The smaller economies of Ireland and Luxembourg again showed the best results among Member States, but for them, too, the slowdown was evident. Results in the candidate countries for accession to Union membership were more varied, but exhibited the same overall trend.

Measuring economic performance simply on the basis of GDP growth is however too simple an approach given the complexity of the European economy. To enable a deeper analysis, this publication gives thus a large series of macroeconomic indicators which are essential for the understanding of the economy of the Union and its Member States, presenting data, wherever appropriate or feasible, in a wider geographic context, including in particular the United States, Japan and the candidate countries.

Even if, at the end of 2001, the big aggregates of national accounts gave a rather bleak picture, several other indicators exhibited more positive features: for the Fifteen as a whole, employment rose by 1.2 %, bringing unemployment down to 7.4 %. Interest rates remained at a low level, with an average 2001 long-term interest rate of only 5.0 %. With respect to public finances, the weak economic development did not allow a general government surplus as in 2000. The deficit, however, was limited, and general government debt as a % of GDP sank by almost one percentage point in 2001, to 63 % of GDP for the Union. Inflation finally stayed more or less at its 2000 levels.

All data presented as averages for the Union as a whole may sometimes disguise significant differences between Member States. Even if we exclude Luxembourg due to the rather atypical nature of its economy, GDP per head varies from 27 700 PPS in Ireland to 15 500 PPS in Greece, and the unemployment rate still exceeds 10 % in Spain and Greece while only reaching 2.4 % in the Netherlands. Italy and Belgium have a public debt in excess of 100 % of GDP, while some others are far below the 60 % threshold contained in the Maastricht convergence criteria. Nevertheless, in most areas, including the examples just cited, a converging tendency between Member States could be observed.

This publication intends to give the reader, mainly in the form of simple and easily understandable tables and graphs, the basic information necessary for a better understanding of the European economy. Confronted with the figures, certainties can quickly waver, intuitions be confirmed or invalidated, judgements be revised.

1. Economy of the Union

1.1. Gross domestic product

In 2001, the gross domestic product of the European Union amounted to EUR 8 815 billion at current prices; while GDP in the euro-zone was EUR 6 811 billion, which is about 23 % less than the EU total. Comparing the result for the European Union with the figures for its main trading partners shows that the GDP of the United States (EUR 11 257 billion) exceeds that of the EU by almost 28 %, whereas Japan's (EUR 4 631 billion) is about 53 % that of EU-15. It should be kept in mind that these relations are effected by exchange rate movements.

Germany alone (EUR 2 063.0 billion) accounts for more than 23 % of the EU's GDP; it is followed by the United Kingdom (EUR 1 588.8 billion in 2001, about 18 % of EU-15 GDP), followed in turn by France (EUR 1 463.7 billion, or 16.6 % of the total). In 2001, Italy's GDP was EUR 1 216.7 billion, or 13.8 % of the total for EU-15. These four countries together account for 74.1 % of the Union's gross domestic product. If we add Spain, whose EUR 650.2 billion GDP contributes 7.4 % of the EU total, and the Netherlands, which, at EUR 424.8 billion, accounts for 4.8 %, we see that just six countries account for roughly 87 % of the European Union's GDP, the other nine Member States making up the remaining 13 %.

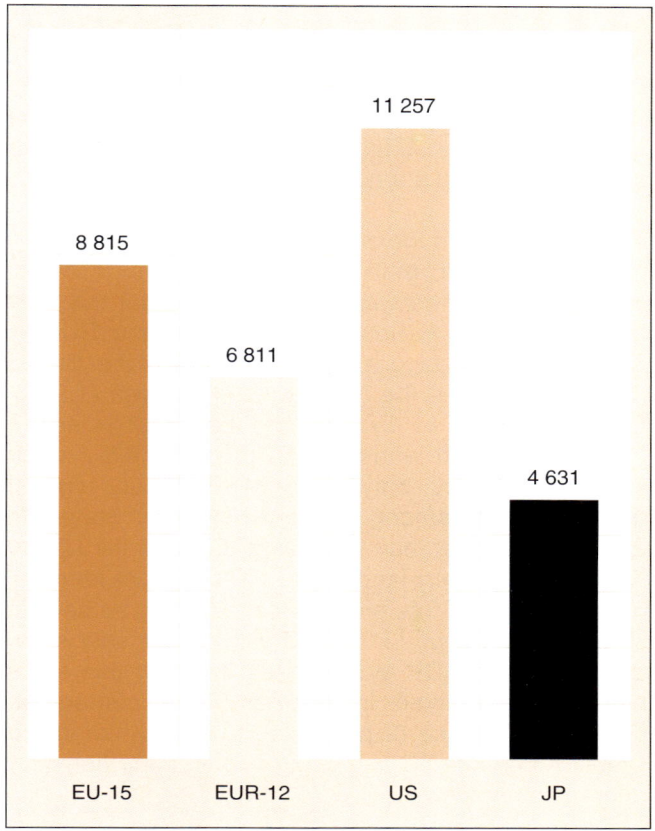

Figure 1.1.1. Gross domestic product at current prices, 2001 (billion EUR)

Source: Eurostat.

Figure 1.1.2. Gross domestic product at current prices, 2001

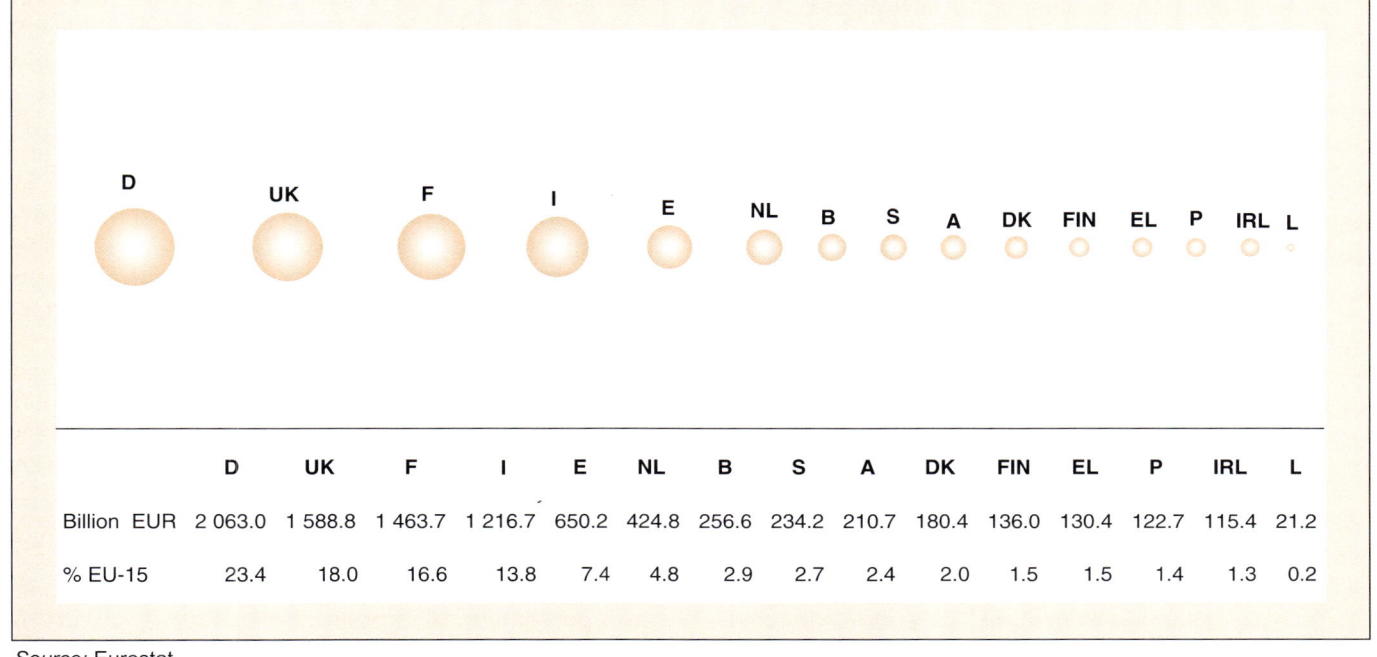

	D	UK	F	I	E	NL	B	S	A	DK	FIN	EL	P	IRL	L
Billion EUR	2 063.0	1 588.8	1 463.7	1 216.7	650.2	424.8	256.6	234.2	210.7	180.4	136.0	130.4	122.7	115.4	21.2
% EU-15	23.4	18.0	16.6	13.8	7.4	4.8	2.9	2.7	2.4	2.0	1.5	1.5	1.4	1.3	0.2

Source: Eurostat.

ECONOMY OF THE UNION

GDP growth rates

In 2001, the European Union's gross domestic product rose by 1.5 %, which means a significant slowdown compared to the previous years (3.5 % in 2000). Compared with its main trading partners however, the EU's growth rate compared favourably with that of the United States (+ 0.3 %) and of Japan (– 0.6 %), both of which recorded stronger slowdowns.

The growth rate in the euro-zone in 2001 was at 1.4 % marginally lower than in the Union as a whole (+ 1.5 %), while the two had been identical the year before (+ 3.5 % in both the euro-zone and EU-15). Among the four biggest Member States, the United Kingdom recorded the highest rate of growth (1.9 %), followed closely by France and Italy (1.8 % each). Germany showed weak growth of only 0.6 %, which was lowest not only among the four biggest economies, but among all the 15 Member States. In 2000, the situation had been different, with the United Kingdom, Germany and Italy having almost identical growth of around 3 % and France recording somewhat stronger growth of 3.8 %. Thus, all four saw slowdowns in their GDP growth rates in 2001; this effect being more marked in Germany (2.4 percentage points) and France (2 percentage points) than in the United Kingdom (1.2 percentage points) and Italy (1.1 percentage points).

As in the year before, Ireland recorded growth rates well above those in the other Member States in 2001: Ireland's GDP expanded by 5.9 %, followed by Greece at 4.1% and Luxembourg at 3.5 %. Among these three, Ireland and Luxembourg saw significant slowdowns when compared to the growth rates of 2000. Behind the three countries mentioned, but still ahead of the average came Spain with 2.8 % growth in 2001. All other Member States are grouped together in a quite narrow range, with Germany and Finland marking the lower end at 0.6 % and 0.7 % growth, respectively. All EU Member States with the exception of Greece recorded growth rates below those of 2000: the biggest slowdowns were recorded in Ireland (by – 5.6 percentage points), Finland (by – 5.4 % points) and Luxembourg (by – 4.0 points). In Italy (– 1.1 points) and Spain (– 1.3 points), the slowdown was comparatively modest in size, and only Greece managed to maintain its economic growth at an unchanged annual rate of 4.1 %.

In both the euro-zone and EU-15, the contribution of household consumption to GDP growth in 2001 was much larger than in 2000 and thus turned out to be — just as in the three preceding years — the biggest of all GDP components at 78.0 % of total growth in EU-15 and, markedly lower, at 66.9 % in the euro-zone. The contribution of government consumption was more

Table 1.1.1. GDP growth rates (as a %)

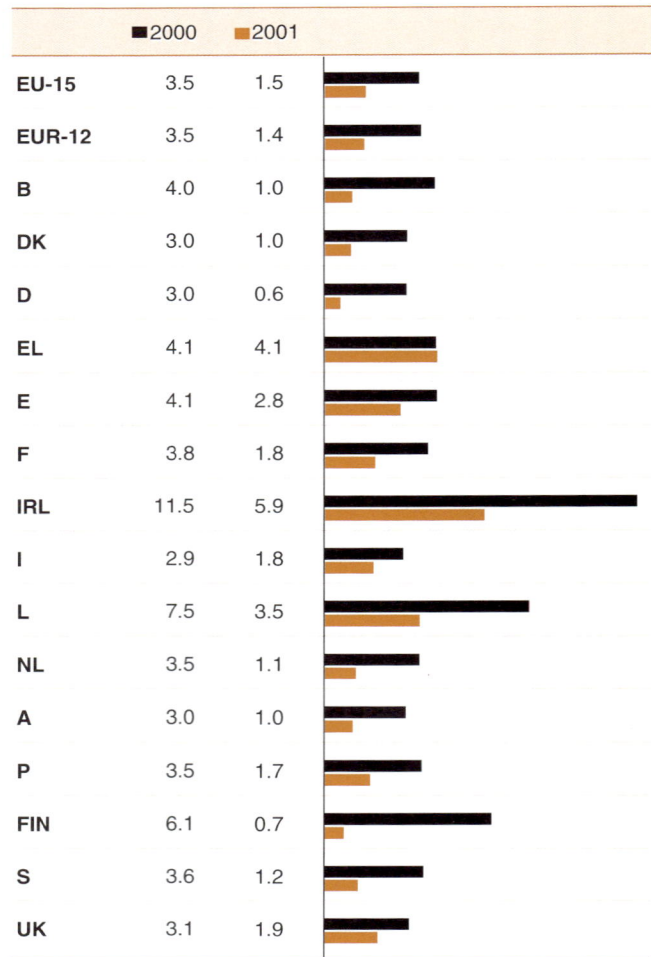

	2000	2001
EU-15	3.5	1.5
EUR-12	3.5	1.4
B	4.0	1.0
DK	3.0	1.0
D	3.0	0.6
EL	4.1	4.1
E	4.1	2.8
F	3.8	1.8
IRL	11.5	5.9
I	2.9	1.8
L	7.5	3.5
NL	3.5	1.1
A	3.0	1.0
P	3.5	1.7
FIN	6.1	0.7
S	3.6	1.2
UK	3.1	1.9

Source: Eurostat.

substantial than in the previous years as well and came second, amounting to about 28 % of total growth in the EU as a whole and almost 30 % in the euro-zone. These two consumption components were in fact the only ones contributing positively to GDP growth. Gross fixed capital formation had rivalled private consumption as a growth motor in 2000, but in 2001 however, it reduced GDP growth by 6.0 % (percentage of total growth) for EU-15 and by 7.6 % for the euro-zone. The biggest difference in comparison with the previous year was again the contribution of external trade, which was strongly negative again after a positive impact in 2000. The contribution pattern was thus significantly different from the preceding year; and different also from 1998 and 1999 especially with respect to the negative contribution of investment in 2001.

When analysing the growth contributions by country, it should be remembered that these are expressed as a percentage of total growth, so that at periods of low GDP growth, component contributions may take on

ECONOMY OF THE UNION

Figure 1.1.3. GDP growth rates in the EU, the euro-zone, the US, Japan and the four biggest EU economies (as a %)

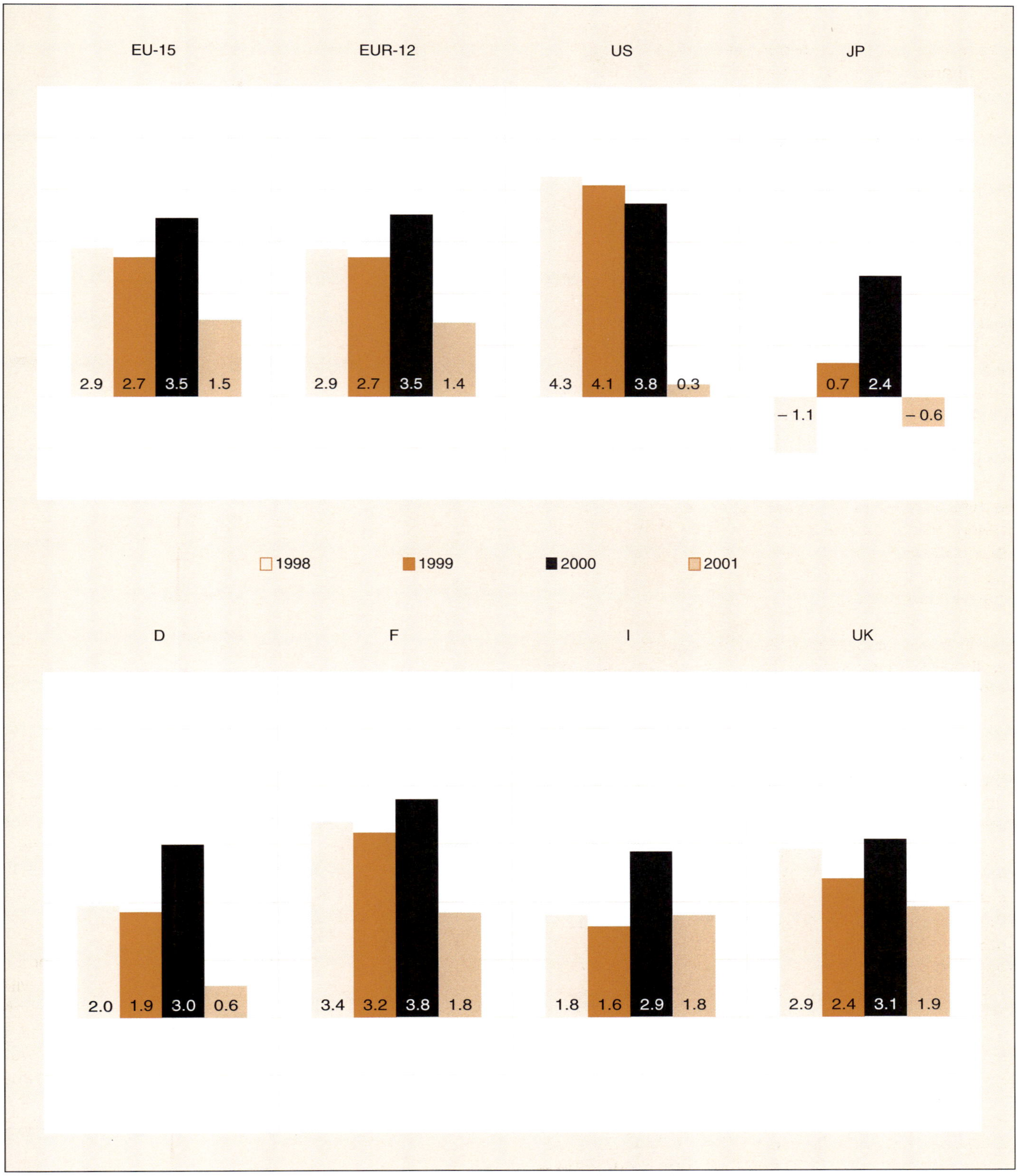

	1998	1999	2000	2001
EU-15	2.9	2.7	3.5	1.5
EUR-12	2.9	2.7	3.5	1.4
US	4.3	4.1	3.8	0.3
JP	−1.1	0.7	2.4	−0.6
D	2.0	1.9	3.0	0.6
F	3.4	3.2	3.8	1.8
I	1.8	1.6	2.9	1.8
UK	2.9	2.4	3.1	1.9

Source: Eurostat.

ECONOMY OF THE UNION

Map 1.1.1. Annual GDP growth rates, 2001 (as a %)

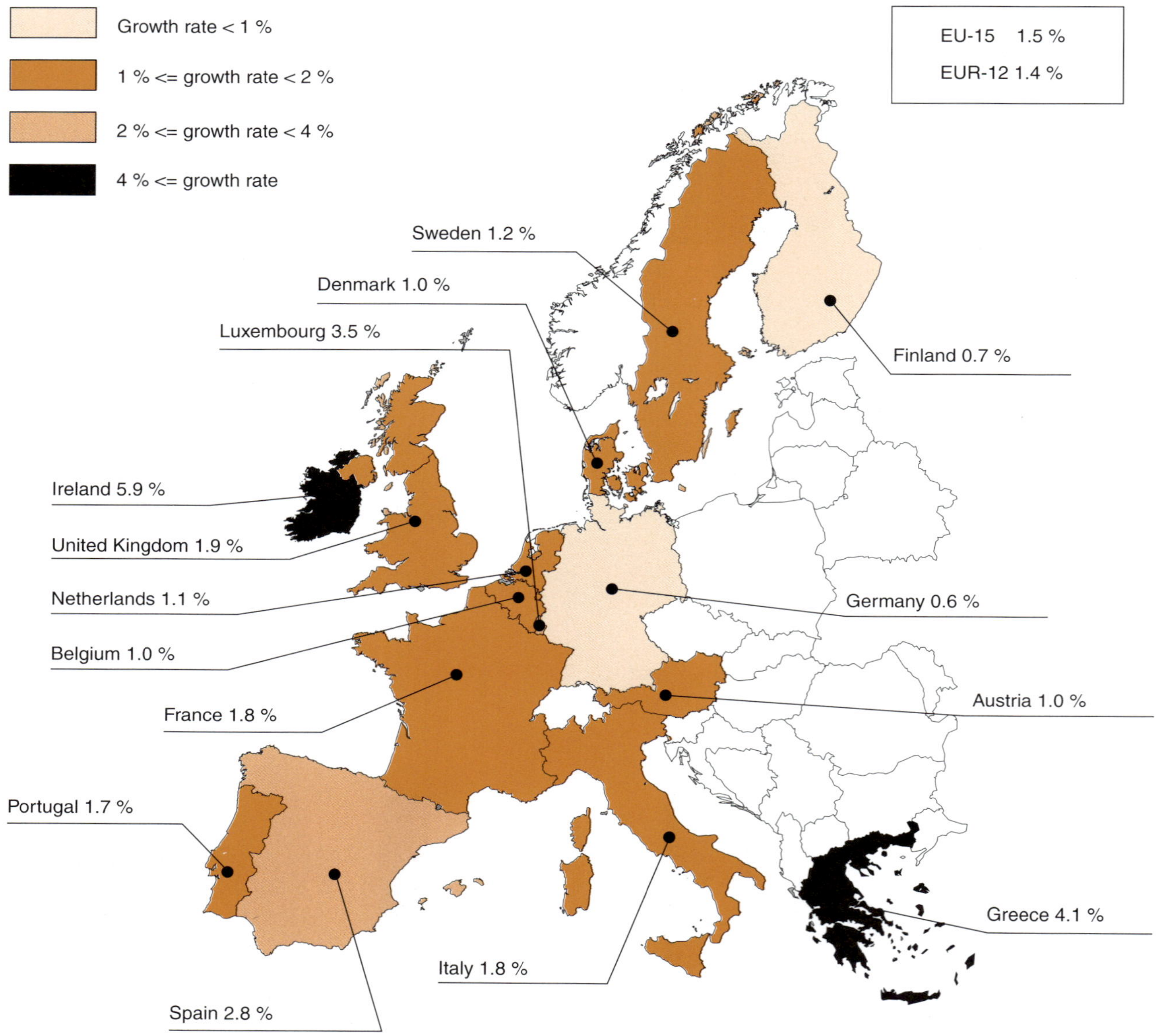

Growth rate < 1 %
1 % <= growth rate < 2 %
2 % <= growth rate < 4 %
4 % <= growth rate

EU-15   1.5 %
EUR-12 1.4 %

Sweden 1.2 %
Denmark 1.0 %
Luxembourg 3.5 %
Finland 0.7 %
Ireland 5.9 %
United Kingdom 1.9 %
Netherlands 1.1 %
Belgium 1.0 %
Germany 0.6 %
France 1.8 %
Austria 1.0 %
Portugal 1.7 %
Italy 1.8 %
Greece 4.1 %
Spain 2.8 %

ECONOMY OF THE UNION

extremely large values in relation to GDP growth, without necessarily being extreme in absolute size. It is thus Germany that shows the most extreme contribution pattern: the overall 0.6 % GDP growth recorded in 2001 was the net result of a major boost provided by the external balance (+ 276.2 % contribution to GDP growth) and persistent household consumption (+ 114.1 % contribution) combined with strong counter-effects from investment (− 192.7 % contribution) and changes in inventories (− 154.4 % contribution). In France, the main factor behind GDP growth in 2001 was household consumption (+ 77.2 % contribution), with all other components except stocks also contributing positively. In Italy, all components supported GDP growth, none of them dominating the others. In the United Kingdom, on the other hand, economic growth was due exclusively to the development of consumption, in particular household consumption (+ 143.6 % contribution), while investment and external trade acted as a brake. For most of the other countries, too, household consumption was the main driving force for GDP growth, particular exceptions being Austria and Sweden and, to a lesser extent, Portugal, where the external balance was the major contributor in 2001, and Finland, where the external balance gave a contribution of − 155.3 % to growth and the biggest positive contribution came from gross fixed capital formation rather than household consumption.

Table 1.1.2. Components' contribution to GDP growth in 2001 (as a % of total GDP growth)

	Household consumption	Government consumption	Gross fixed capital formation	External balance	Stock		GDP growth rate
EU-15	78.3	28.4	− 6.2	30.9	− 31.4	→	1.5
EUR-12	66.8	30.0	− 7.5	43.4	− 32.7	→	1.4
B	87.2	47.4	5.4	25.1	− 65.1	→	1.0
DK	39.1	31.9	− 0.5	− 8.6	38.0	→	1.0
D	114.1	56.8	− 192.7	276.2	− 154.4	→	0.6
EL	56.1	6.1	41.6	− 1.5	− 2.3	→	4.1
E	58.6	20.0	22.0	− 5.1	4.5	→	2.8
F	77.2	30.4	25.7	7.0	− 40.4	→	1.8
IRL	40.4	12.1	1.6	33.8	12.2	→	5.9
I	38.2	21.3	28.0	10.6	1.8	→	1.8
L	58.0	37.8	21.2	9.3	− 26.3	→	3.5
NL	54.1	68.1	− 22.1	8.5	− 8.5	→	1.1
A	70.5	− 3.2	− 35.2	94.0	− 26.1	→	1.0
P	34.2	27.2	1.4	38.1	− 0.8	→	1.7
FIN	77.9	58.6	104.6	− 155.3	14.2	→	0.7
S	8.8	27.1	20.9	79.6	− 36.4	→	1.2
UK	143.6	20.9	− 4.1	− 30.1	− 30.4	→	1.9

NB: Negative contributions do not indicate a slowdown in the component growth.
Source: Eurostat.

GDP per head

If gross domestic product indicates the size of a country's economy in absolute terms, calculating per capita GDP, that is GDP in relation to the population, provides an indication, albeit somewhat simplistic, of a country's wealth. No statement about the (in-)equality of the distribution of wealth can, however, be derived from GDP per head. To allow simple cross-country comparisons, the data presented in this chapter have been calculated in purchasing power standards (PPS). PPS are an "artificial currency unit" that take into account price level differences. Figures expressed in PPS are derived from figures in current price national currency units using conversion factors called purchasing power parities (PPP) that assess the purchasing power of a currency with respect to the EU average. More details on these concepts are given in Section 7.4. of this publication.

In 2001, the per capita figure for each citizen in the European Union amounted to 23 200 PPS, slightly above the figure for the euro-zone (23 100 PPS). The highest figures occurred in Luxembourg (44 300 PPS), Ireland (27 700 PPS) and Denmark (27 600 PPS). The four largest EU economies are very close together in terms of GDP per head, ranging between 24 400 PPS in Italy and 23 200 PPS in the United Kingdom, with Germany (24 100 PPS) and France (23 300 PPS) lying in between.

ECONOMY OF THE UNION

Figure 1.1.4. Components' contribution to GDP growth (as a % of total GDP growth)

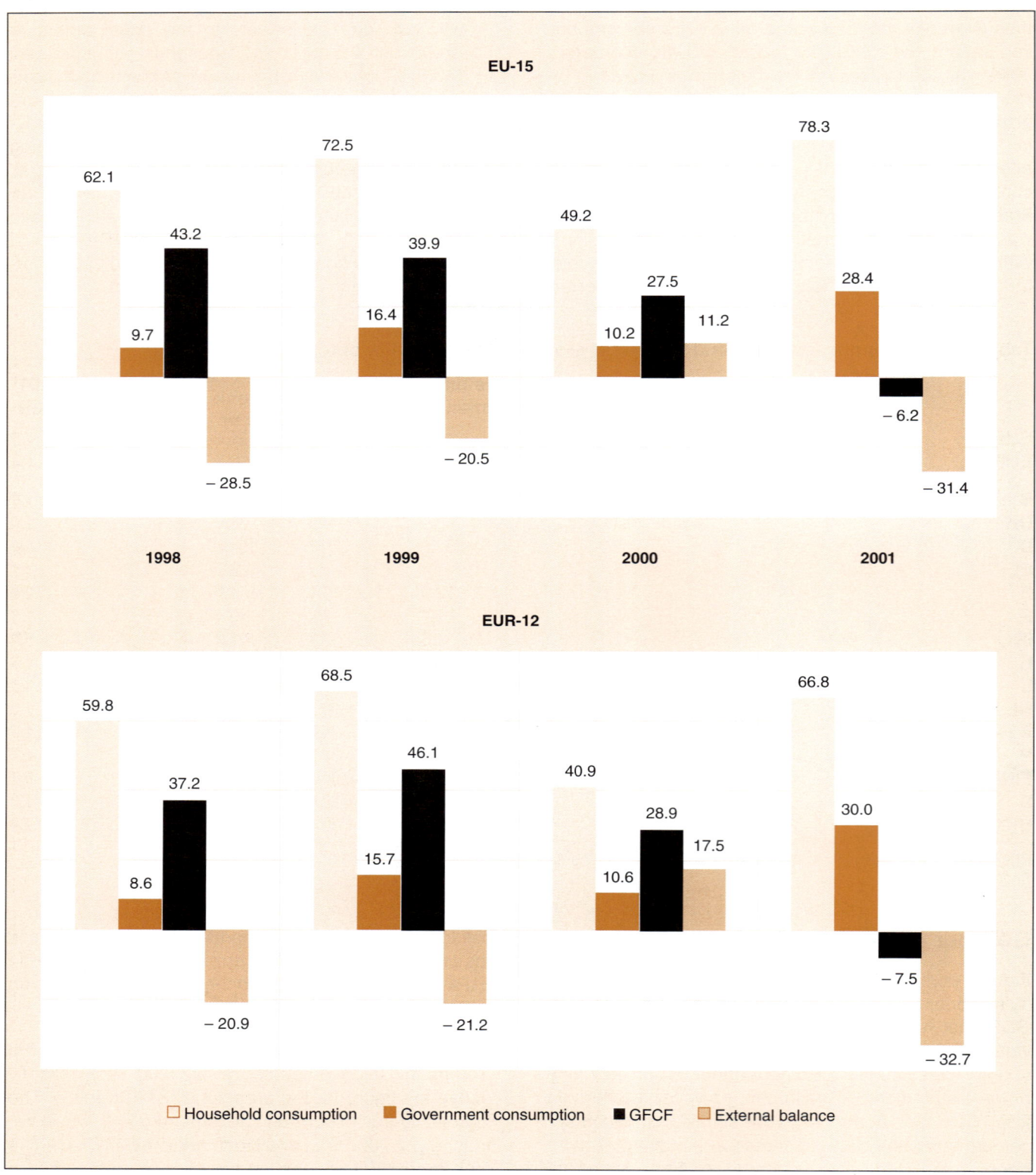

NB: To make the reading easier, the contributions of change in stocks have not been included.
Source: Eurostat.

ECONOMY OF THE UNION

Figure 1.1.5. Components' contribution to GDP growth in 2001 (as a % of total GDP growth)

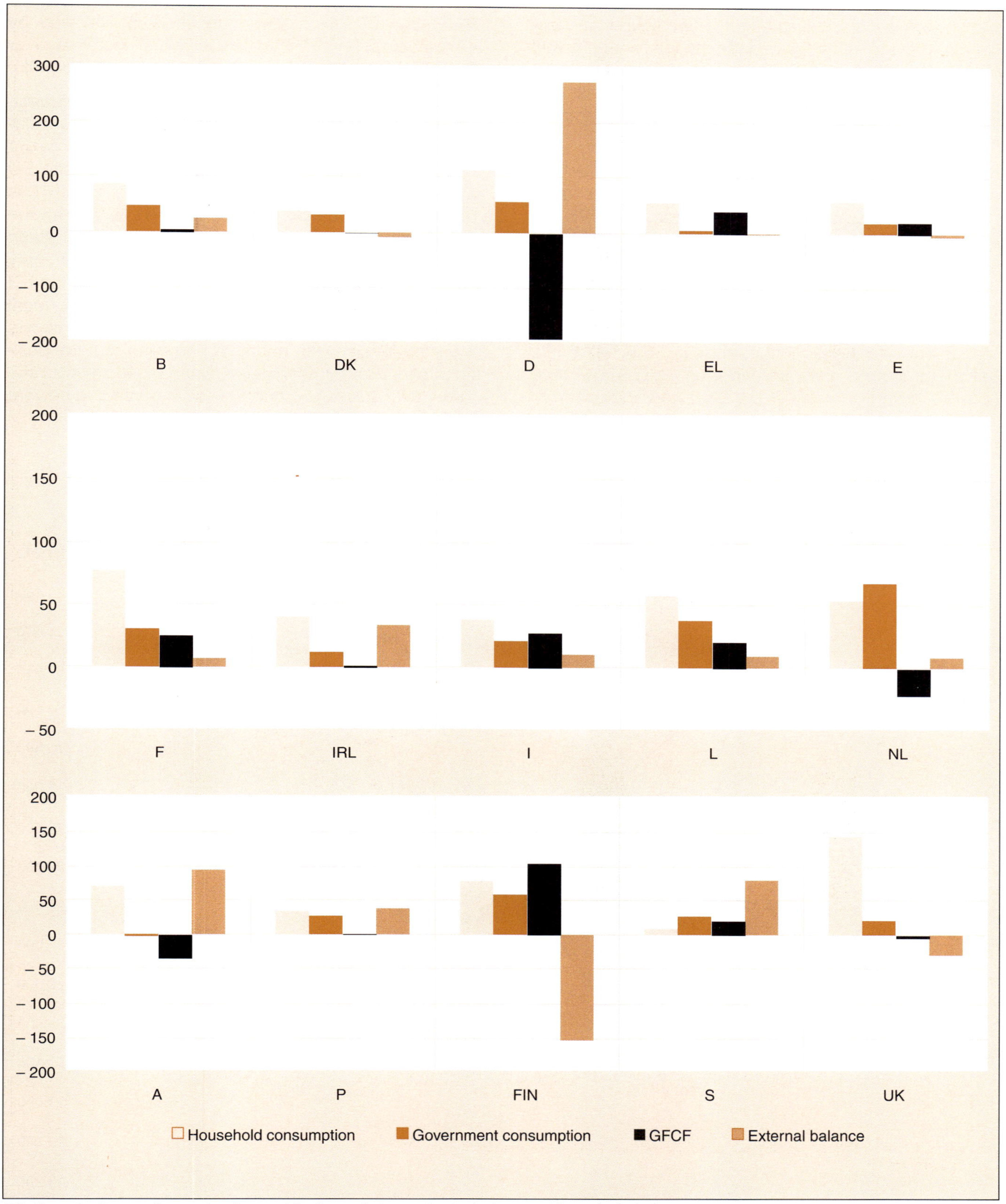

□ Household consumption   ■ Government consumption   ■ GFCF   ■ External balance

NB: To make the reading easier, the contributions of change in stocks have not been included.
Source: Eurostat.

ECONOMY OF THE UNION

Figure 1.1.6 shows per capita GDP for all the EU countries. The web figure has the advantage of providing a visual overview of the distribution of the figures: if every country had the same figure, then the final shape would be a circle. The figures for 1995 are also shown, but it must be remembered that the PPS figures are at current prices and have been calculated primarily for comparison in terms of space and not time.

However, in order to show how per capita GDP has developed over time, Table 1.1.3 shows the value growth index (1995 = 100) derived from the PPS figures. It is apparent from this that per capita GDP expressed in PPS in the EU in 2001 was 31.8 % higher than in the reference year; the corresponding figure for the euro-zone was somewhat lower at + 30.5 %. Among the four largest countries, the United Kingdom stands out with the biggest change (+ 36.5 %). While Italy was not too far behind at + 33.3 %, France (27.3 %) and Germany (+ 24.2 %) had significantly smaller increases. The biggest change by far among the Fifteen was recorded in Ireland, where per capita GDP was 67.9 % higher than in 1995, followed by Luxembourg (+ 46.7 %). The smallest increase over the period considered was that in Belgium (+ 23.6 %).

To make it easier to compare the Member States, Figure 1.1.7 shows the GDP per capita figures in relation to the EU average (EU-15 = 100). It is thus easier to observe and measure the big gap between the EU average and the figure for Luxembourg, which has moved further ahead and is now 91 % above the EU average. The second highest figures are for Ireland and Denmark, but here the difference is only 19 %. The biggest differences for figures below the EU average are in Greece (33 % below average), Portugal (– 26 %) and Spain (– 17 %). Figure 1.1.7 also shows the situation in 1995, and it can be seen that the positions at the extremes remain unchanged, even if the three lowest ranking countries have moved somewhat

Figure 1.1.6. Gross domestic product per head, (in PPS)

	1995			2001
EU-15	17 600		EU-15	23 200
EUR-12	17 700		EUR-12	23 100
B	19 900		B	24 600
DK	20 800		DK	27 600
D	19 400		D	24 100
EL	11 600		EL	15 500
E	13 800		E	19 200
F	18 300		F	23 300
IRL	16 500		IRL	27 700
I	18 300		I	24 400
L	30 200		L	44 300
NL	19 300		NL	26 000
A	19 500		A	25 900
P	12 400		P	17 100
FIN	17 100		FIN	24 000
S	18 100		S	23 200
UK	17 000		UK	23 200

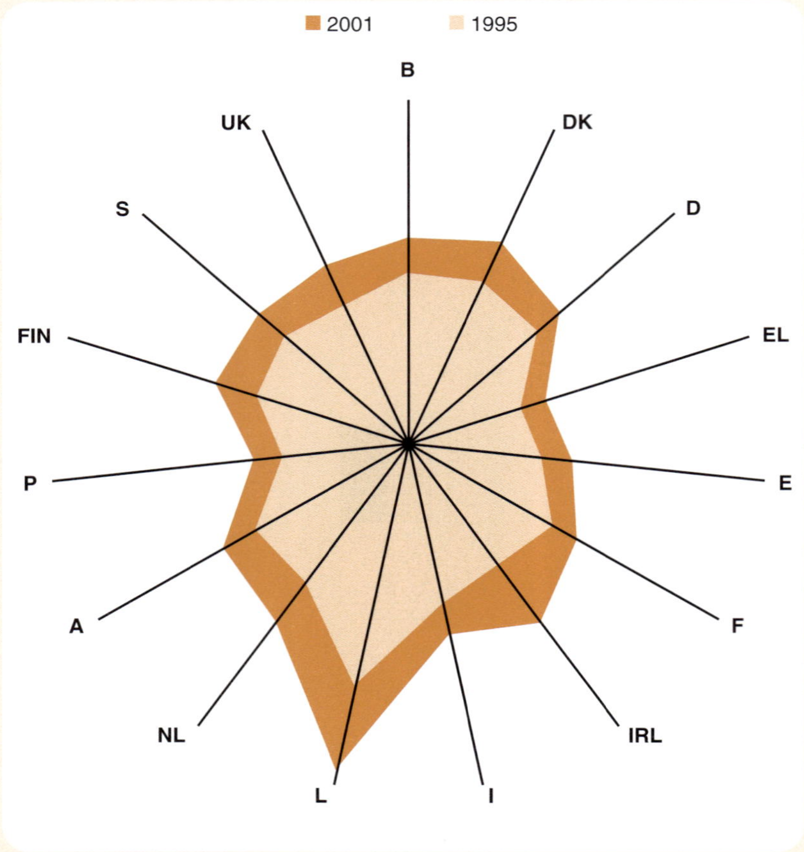

Source: Eurostat.

ECONOMY OF THE UNION

Map 1.1.2. GDP per head, 2001 (EU-15=100)

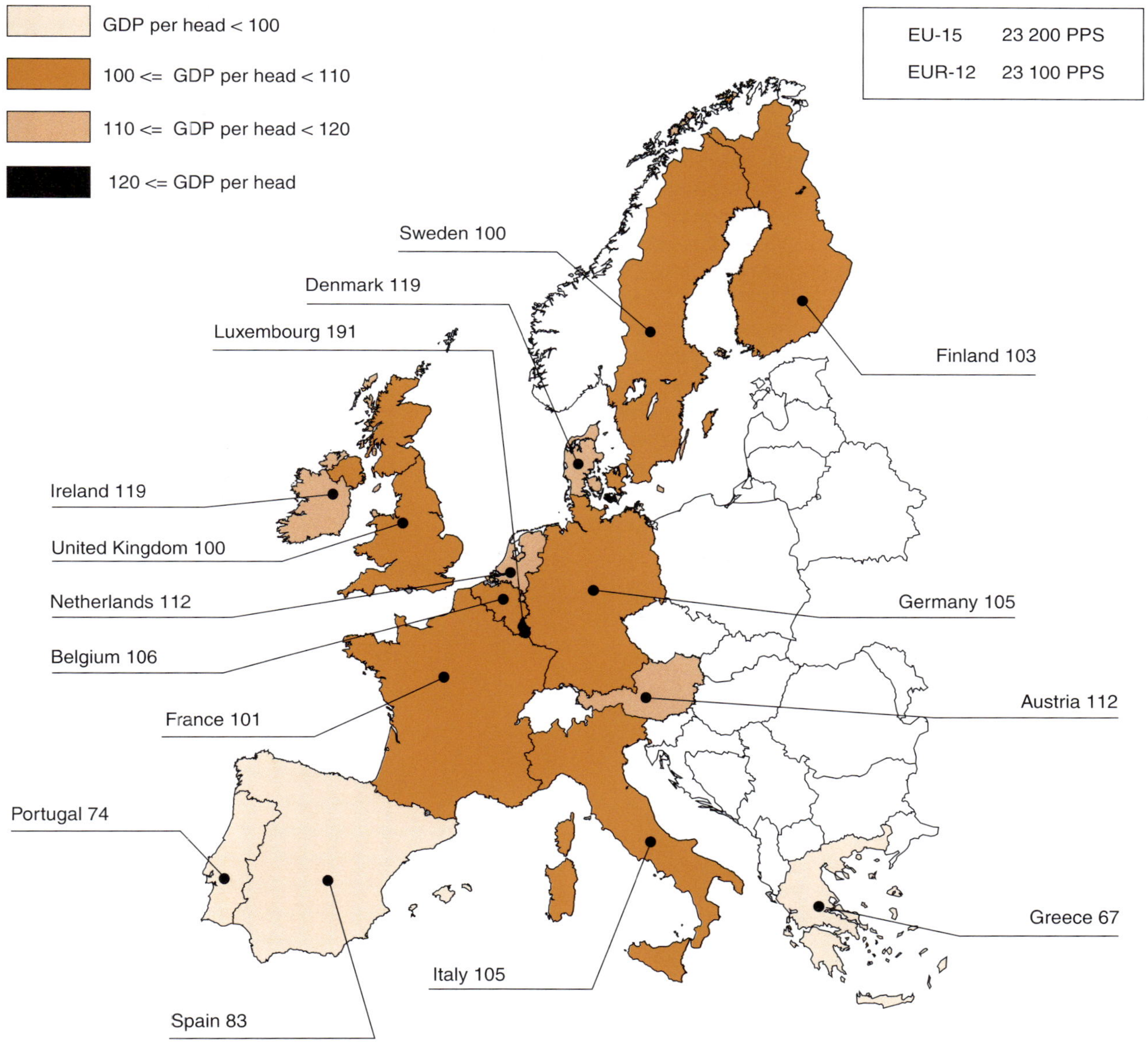

GDP per head < 100
100 <= GDP per head < 110
110 <= GDP per head < 120
120 <= GDP per head

EU-15   23 200 PPS
EUR-12   23 100 PPS

Sweden 100
Denmark 119
Luxembourg 191
Finland 103
Ireland 119
United Kingdom 100
Netherlands 112
Belgium 106
Germany 105
France 101
Austria 112
Portugal 74
Greece 67
Italy 105
Spain 83

ECONOMY OF THE UNION

closer to the EU average. The most obvious change was for Ireland, which recorded a figure for per capita GDP that was lower than the EU average at the beginning of the period under review (1995 to 2001), while in 2001 it was 19 % above average, placing Ireland second among all EU Member States. The same type of change, though less pronounced, took place in Finland, which was slightly above the EU average in 2001 while starting slightly below in 1995.

Figure 1.1.8 shows a set of data intended to show the level of similarity, or difference, between the Member State figures with respect to GDP per head, and how these have evolved over the last five years. Firstly, the top figure shows the highest figures (Luxembourg again first, followed by Denmark and, in 2001, Ireland), the lowest figure (always Greece) and the EU average. The line that links these points shows the range, or the distance between the highest and lowest figures and their position in relation to the average (in this case EU-15). In 2001, the range between the highest and lowest per capita GDP recorded in the Union was 28 800 PPS. In other words, per capita GDP in Luxembourg was 2.9 times the figure for Greece. If we exclude Luxembourg, the gap between the figures for Ireland and Denmark and Greece was slightly more than 12 000 PPS, meaning that the per capita GDP of the Irish and Danes was 1.8 times that of the Greeks.

Table 1.1.3. Gross domestic product per head, 2001

	PPS	Value growth index 1995=100
EU-15	23 200	131.8
EUR-12	23 100	130.5
B	24 600	123.6
DK	27 600	132.7
D	24 100	124.2
EL	15 500	133.6
E	19 200	139.1
F	23 300	127.3
IRL	27 700	167.9
I	24 400	133.3
L	44 300	146.7
NL	26 000	134.7
A	25 900	132.8
P	17 100	137.9
FIN	24 000	140.4
S	23 200	128.2
UK	23 200	136.5

Source: Eurostat.

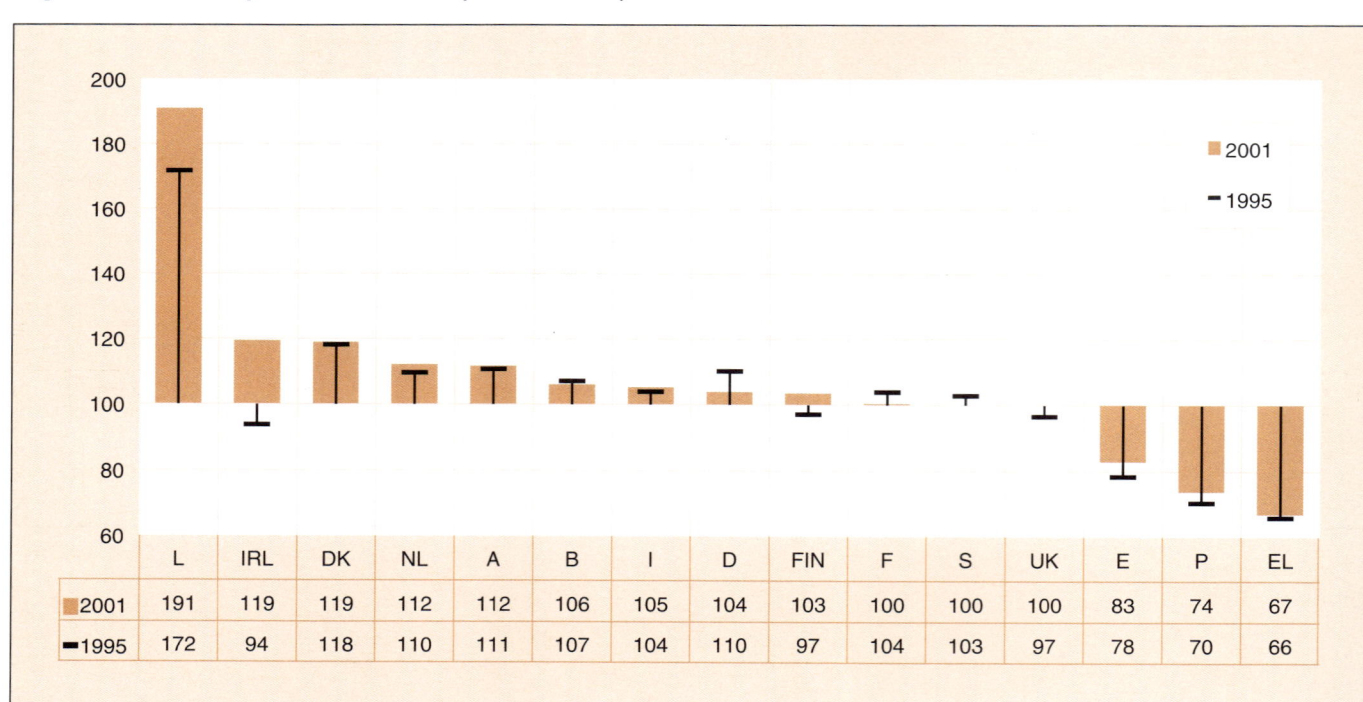

Figure 1.1.7. GDP per head in PPS (EU-15 = 100)

	L	IRL	DK	NL	A	B	I	D	FIN	F	S	UK	E	P	EL
2001	191	119	119	112	112	106	105	104	103	100	100	100	83	74	67
1995	172	94	118	110	111	107	104	110	97	104	103	97	78	70	66

Source: Eurostat.

ECONOMY OF THE UNION

To give an overall indication of the range of values for all the EU countries, the relative standard deviation has been calculated, that is, a measure for the average "distance" of the figures from their average ([4]), expressed as a percentage of the average. Thus, in 2001, per capita GDP figures for the 15 Member States had a standard deviation of 25.3 % around their (unweighted) average, a figure higher than in 1997 but slightly down from the previous year. If again Luxembourg, as a sort of "outlier", is excluded from the calculation, the relative standard deviation is considerably lower at 15.1 % of the average, and the figure for 2001 turns out to be largely unchanged compared both to 1997 and to 2000.

Figure 1.1.8. Variation of GDP per head

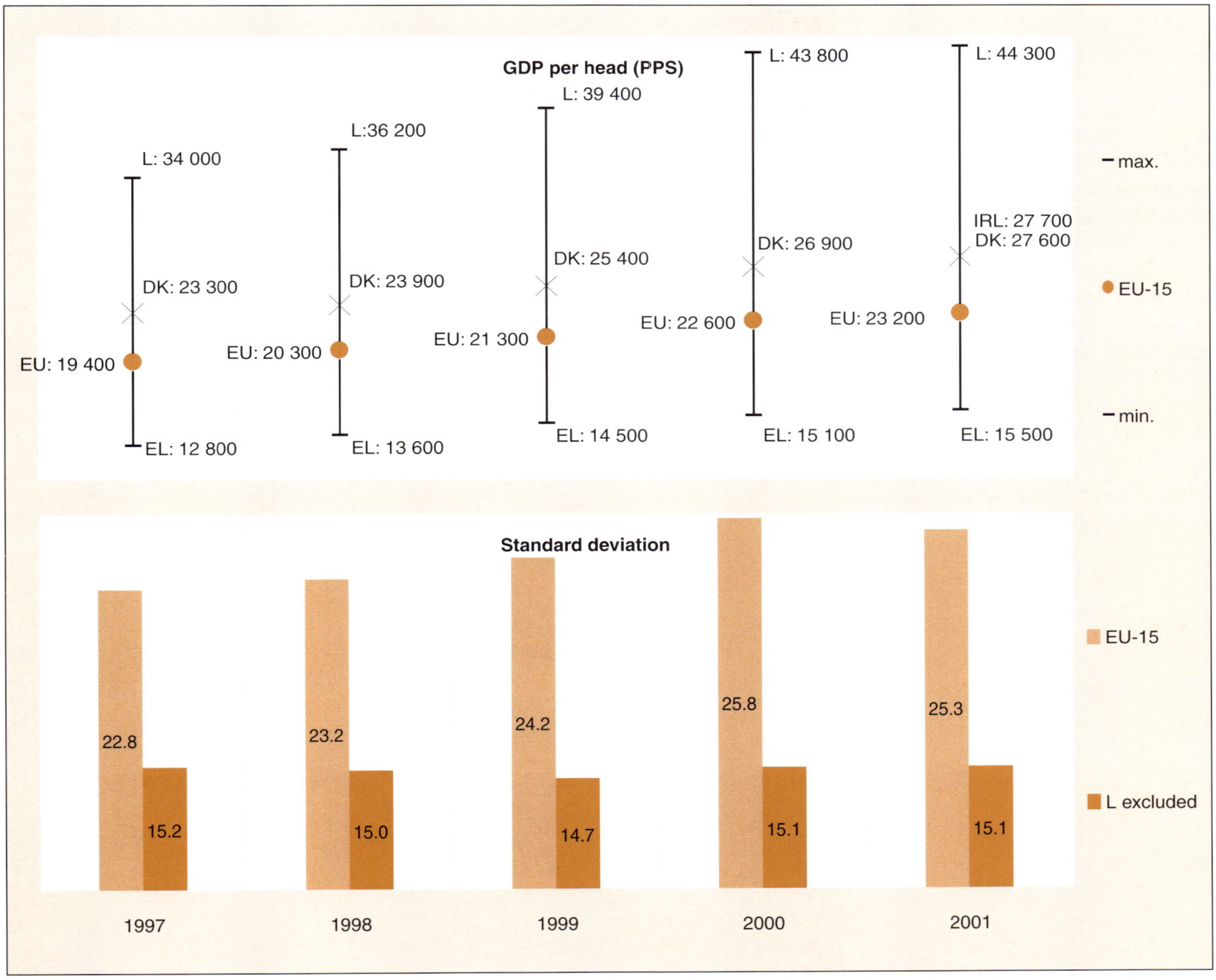

NB: As all maximum figures have been recorded for Luxembourg, we also added the second largest figures. During the period considered, these were those of Denmark and, in 2001, Ireland.
Source: Eurostat.

([4]) In this case, the simple arithmetic average and not the EU value, which is a weighted average.

ECONOMY OF THE UNION

1.2. Expenditure breakdown of GDP

Table 1.2.1 shows the absolute values ([2]) of the main expenditure components of GDP: household final consumption expenditure, government final consumption expenditure and gross fixed capital formation. Other components of GDP are imports and exports ([3]) and changes in stocks, but these are left out of consideration in this chapter, for the sake of simplicity.

In 2001, household final consumption in the European Union amounted to EUR 5 161 billion, a level well above those recorded for investments (EUR 1 774 billion) and government final consumption (EUR 1 774 billion). It should be noted, though, that household consumption as used here also includes the consumption expenditure of non-profit institutions serving households such as churches, trade unions, political parties, sports clubs, etc. It is also true for all Member States that household consumption is the most important expenditure component, bigger in size than government consumption and investments combined. While for EU-15 as a whole, the latter two are of almost equal size, the situation varies between Member States: for a first group, consisting of Belgium, Germany, Italy, the Netherlands and Finland, government consumption is of broadly the same size as gross fixed capital formation. For a second group, investments are dominating: Greece, Spain, Ireland, Luxembourg, Austria and Portugal. For Denmark, France, Sweden and the United Kingdom, finally, government consumption is the more important expenditure component.

Consumption per head

To permit comparisons between countries, the per capita values for household consumption and government consumption have been calculated and expressed in terms of EU value (EU-15 = 100) (see Table 1.2.2 and Figure 1.2.1). As with GDP, Luxembourg stands out from the other Member States by having, per capita, a much higher household consumption (35 % higher than the EU as a whole) as well as government consumption (+ 66 %). This is in contrast with Ireland and Denmark, the Member States with the second-highest per capita GDP: in Ireland, both private and public consumption are actually below the EU average (– 4 % and – 21 %, respectively), while in Denmark, government consumption is above the EU average (+ 51 %) as is the

Table 1.2.1. Main components of GDP, 2001 (billion EUR, current prices)

	Household consumption	Government consumption	GFCF
EU-15	5 160.7	1 773.5	1 774.1
EUR-12	3 905.6	1 358.5	1 434.4
B	139.6	55.3	53.6
DK	84.7	46.0	37.9
D	1 218.1	393.2	417.8
EL	90.3	20.1	30.3
E	381.9	112.3	162.9
F	805.6	340.6	295.6
IRL	54.8	15.5	26.6
I	732.3	224.7	241.0
L	8.8	3.7	4.5
NL	210.7	98.7	93.4
A	121.1	40.6	48.1
P	74.7	25.2	33.7
FIN	67.9	28.6	26.9
S	116.7	62.4	41.0
UK	1 053.7	306.6	260.9

Source: Eurostat.

Table 1.2.2. Consumption per head, 2001

	Household consumption PPS	Household consumption EU-15 = 100	Government consumption PPS	Government consumption EU-15 = 100
EU-15	13 600	100	4 700	100
EUR-12	13 300	98	4 600	98
B	13 400	99	5 300	113
DK	13 000	96	7 100	151
D	14 200	104	4 600	98
EL	10 700	79	2 400	51
E	11 300	83	3 300	70
F	12 800	94	5 500	117
IRL	13 100	96	3 700	79
I	14 700	108	4 500	96
L	18 300	135	7 800	166
NL	12 900	95	6 100	130
A	14 900	110	5 000	106
P	10 400	76	3 500	74
FIN	12 000	88	5 100	109
S	11 600	85	6 200	132
UK	15 400	113	4 500	96

Source: Eurostat.

---

[2] The absolute values are measured at current prices, rates of growth are calculated at constant prices, and per capita PPS values are based on current prices.

[3] A more detailed analysis of external trade is given in Chapter 2.3, using data obtained from Comext. The data reproduced in this chapter, however, were obtained from the national accounts, and are not adjusted for intra-Community trade.

case in Luxembourg, but household consumption is lower than the average of the other Member States (– 4 %). Germany, Italy and the United Kingdom are those Member States where household consumption is above but government consumption is below the EU average. The situation is inversed, i.e. household consumption is below but government consumption above the EU average for Belgium, Denmark, France, the Netherlands, Finland and especially so for Sweden.

As regards household consumption, the United Kingdom and Austria, alongside Luxembourg, stand out as having a per capita figure well above the average (+ 13 % and + 10 %, respectively) for all Member States. The lowest figures for per capita household consumption are those for Portugal (24 % below the EU average), Greece (21 % below the average) and Spain (17 % below the average). The countries with the lowest figures for government consumption are the same, albeit in a different order: Greece has the lowest figure (49 % below the EU average), while Spain is 30 % below the average and Portugal 26 % below. Next comes Ireland, where per capita government consumption is 21 % below the average despite the relatively high GDP per capita. In addition to Luxembourg and Denmark, which, it has already been seen, have the highest figures, Sweden and the Netherlands recorded values which were much higher (32 % and 30 % respectively) than the EU average.

As with per capita GDP, the scatter around the average may be compared across GDP components and time by using the relative standard deviation. Without giving a full set of figures, we state that the scatter between the per capita values for household consumption in the Member States in 2001 is well below that for government consumption: in the case of household consumption, the (unweighted) relative standard deviation in 2001 was 15 % of the average, whereas the figures for government consumption displayed a scatter of more than 28 % with respect to the average. If we examine this indicator for the last five years, we see that the scatter for both consumption items has slightly increased with respect to 1997, but neither is showing a clear trend.

Growth rates of main GDP components

Turning to rates of growth in 2001, government consumption in the European Union had the fastest growth of the main components, increasing by 2.2 % compared with the previous year. Household consumption grew by 2.0 % and gross fixed capital formation fell by 0.4 %. Over the last five years (1997 to 2001), the components show quite different behaviour: investment growth peaked in 1998, and while it had been superior to the other two components from 1997 to 2000, the huge slowdown experienced in 2001 made it fall behind the consumption items. Growth of household consumption peaked one year later, in 1999,

Figure 1.2.1. Household consumption (HC) and government consumption (GC) per head, 2001 (in PPS – EU-15 = 100)

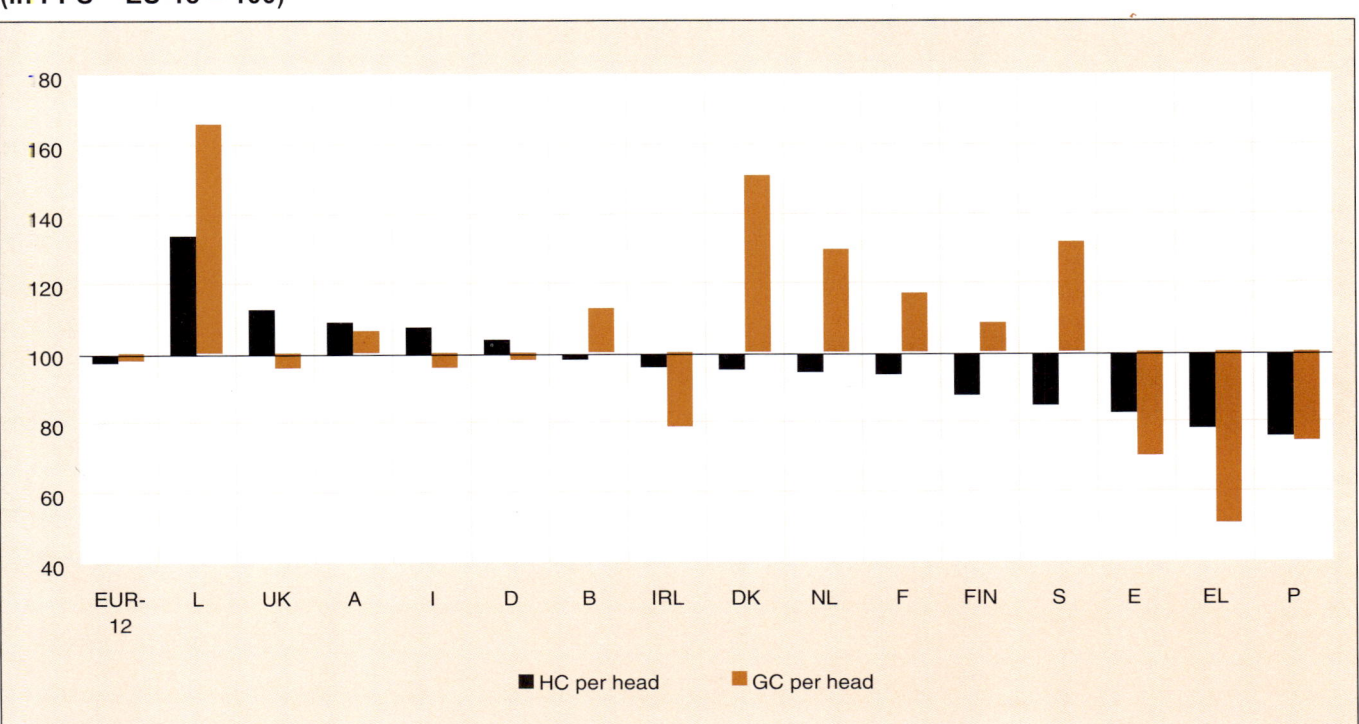

NB: Member States are shown by HC data in descending order.
Source: Eurostat.

ECONOMY OF THE UNION

and the decline since then has been rather moderate. In the case of government consumption, last year's slowdown was not repeated, growth accelerated in fact and attained the 1999 peak level again, making it the fastest growing among the three expenditure components considered here. The trends in the euro-zone ran in parallel, the only differences being that the growth of investments was more modest in 1998 (+ 5.1 % compared to 6.2 % in EU-15), and that the growth rates for household consumption were generally somewhat lower (see Figure 1.2.2 and Table 1.2.3).

Household consumption grew fastest in Ireland and Luxembourg (+ 4.8 % for both) and in the United Kingdom (+ 4.1 %). The worst growth rates were recorded in Sweden (+ 0.2 %), Denmark (+ 0.8 %) and Portugal (+ 0.9 %), thus unlike the previous year, no country recorded negative growth.

Luxembourg also stands out for having the fastest-growing government consumption (+ 7.8 % in 2001), more than two percentage points ahead of the country with the second fastest growth: Ireland in this case with 5.3 %. Government consumption showed only modest growth in Denmark (+ 1.2 %) and Sweden (+ 1.4 %), but the lowest growth rate in 2001, and effectively the only negative one, was found to be at − 0.2 % in Austria.

Investments had been the fastest growing component of domestic demand in 2000, but showed weak results in 2001: a significant drop in Germany (− 4.8 %), together with declining investments in Austria (− 1.5 %), the Netherlands (− 1.1 %) and the United Kingdom (− 0.4 %) caused the EU-15 total to decline as well, despite rather strong results in Greece (+ 7.4 %) and Finland (+ 4.0 %).

Table 1.2.3. Growth of main GDP components, 2001 (as a %)

	Household consumption	Government consumption	GFCF
EU-15	2.0	2.2	− 0.4
EUR-12	1.7	2.2	− 0.5
B	1.6	2.3	0.3
DK	0.8	1.2	0.0
D	1.1	1.7	− 4.8
EL	3.2	1.8	7.4
E	2.7	3.1	2.5
F	2.6	2.5	2.3
IRL	4.8	5.3	0.4
I	1.1	2.2	2.4
L	4.8	7.8	3.3
NL	1.2	3.4	− 1.1
A	1.3	− 0.2	− 1.5
P	0.9	2.4	0.1
FIN	1.1	2.1	4.0
S	0.2	1.4	1.5
UK	4.1	2.2	− 0.4

Source: Eurostat.

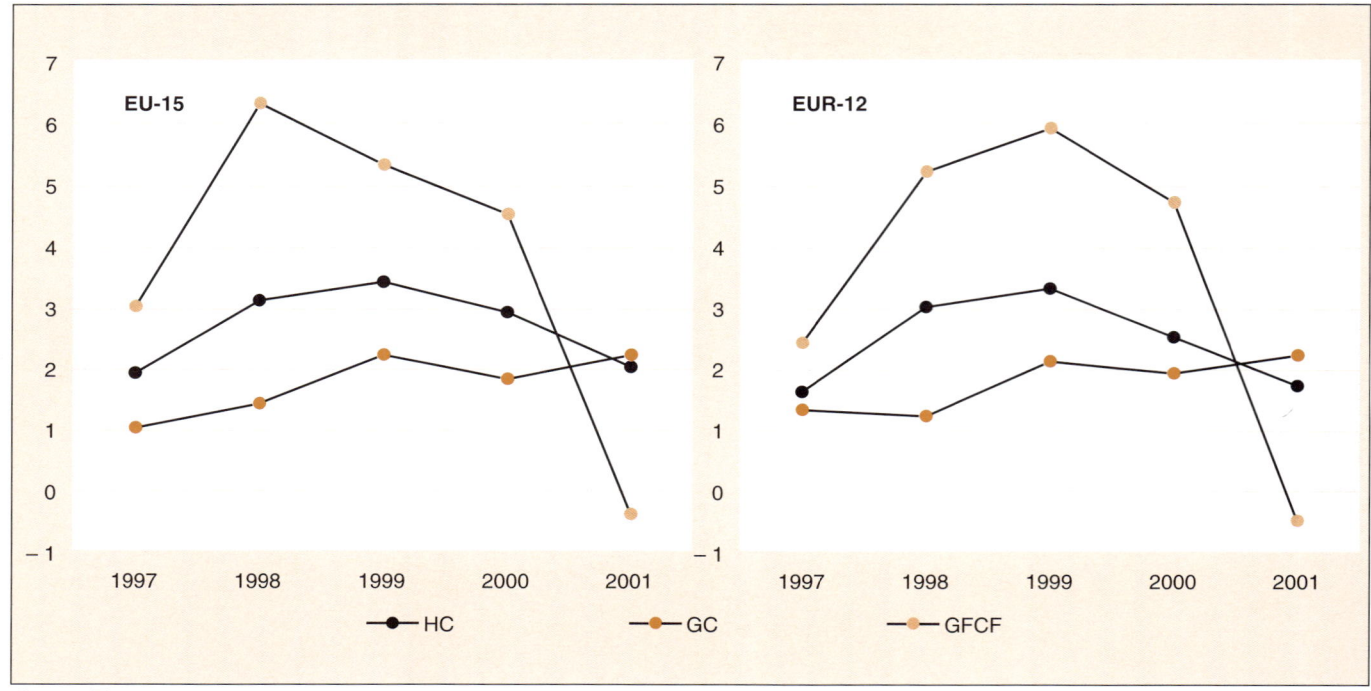

Figure 1.2.2. Growth of main GDP components, 1997-2001 (as a %)

Source: Eurostat.

ECONOMY OF THE UNION

Figure 1.2.3. Growth of main GDP components, 2001 (as a %)

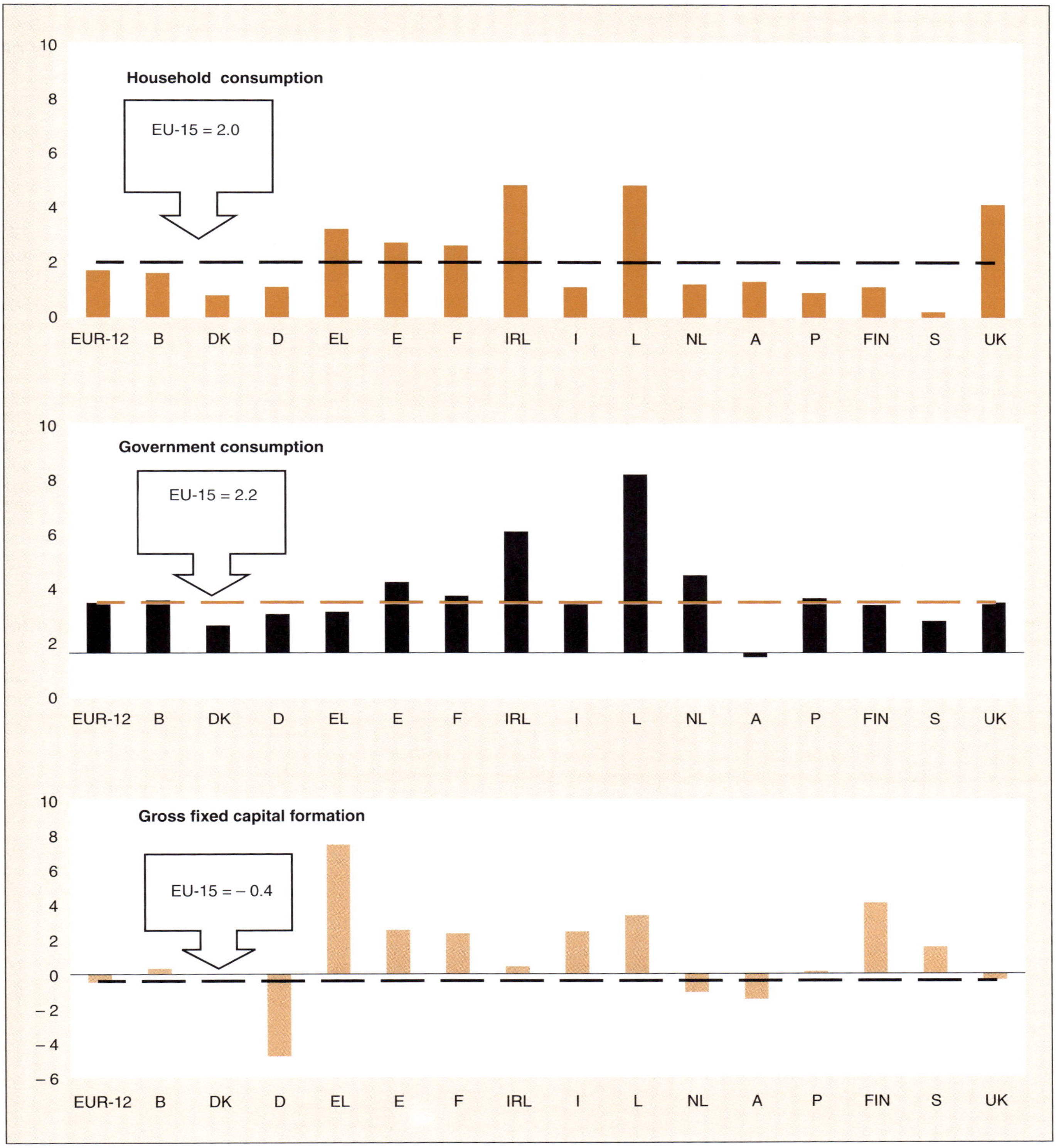

Source: Eurostat.

ECONOMY OF THE UNION

Structure of GDP

The main component of current price gross domestic product (GDP) in the European Union is household final consumption expenditure, which in 2001 accounted for 58.6 % of GDP, followed by gross fixed capital formation and government final consumption expenditure with identical shares of 20.1 % for both. Together, these three components accounted for practically all of the Union's GDP (98.8 %).

Figure 1.2.4. Structure of gross domestic product in the EU, 2001 (as a % of GDP)

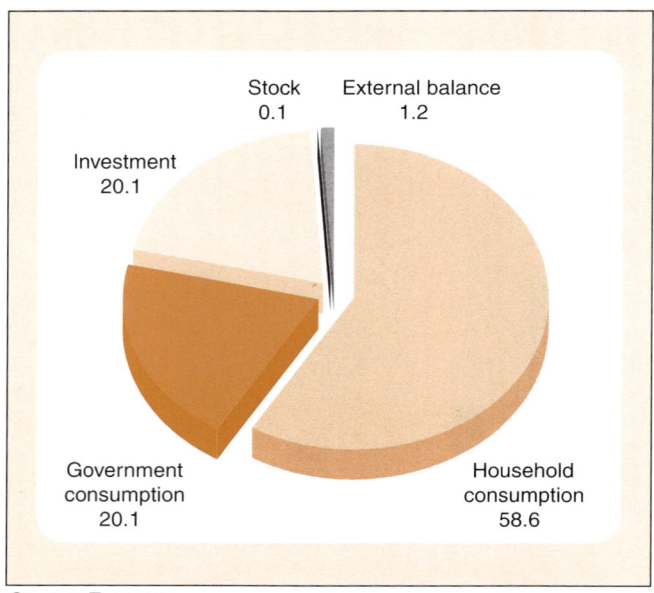

Source: Eurostat.

Due mainly to a specific structure of GDP in the United Kingdom, the structure in the euro-zone was somewhat different from that for the Union as a whole; with gross fixed capital formation and external balance gaining share, mainly at the expense of household consumption (see Table 1.2.4).

The structure of GDP in the United Kingdom was particularly dominated by household consumption, which, with a figure of 66.3 %, was one of the highest amongst all Member States of the Union. The shares for government consumption and investment, on the other hand, were both below average, especially so for investment. The structure of GDP in Germany and Italy are quite similar, for both, household consumption was the major component, too, though with lower shares than in the United Kingdom (59.1 % and 60.2 % respectively). The breakdown between government consumption and investment was fairly even, with investment making up slightly bigger shares. In France, however, while household consumption accounted for the largest share of GDP (55.0 %), government consumption (23.3 %) was ahead of investment (20.2 %). In contrast to the United Kingdom, the three economies mentioned had a positive external balance between 1.6 % of GDP in France and Italy and 1.9 % of GDP in Germany.

Household final consumption expenditure was the biggest component of GDP in every Member State, with figures ranging from 69.2 % in Greece to 41.3 % in Luxembourg. With respect to the other two main components, investment ranked second in eight of the

Table 1.2.4. Structure of gross domestic product, 2001 (as a % of GDP)

	Household consumption	Government consumption	GFCF	Stock change	External balance		Imports	Exports
EU-15	58.6	20.1	20.1	0.1	1.2	→	34.7	35.9
EUR-12	57.3	19.9	21.1	0.0	1.7	→	35.6	37.3
B	54.4	21.6	20.9	− 0.2	3.3	→	81.1	84.4
DK	47.0	25.5	21.0	0.1	6.4	→	39.2	45.6
D	59.1	19.1	20.3	− 0.3	1.9	→	33.1	35.0
EL	69.2	15.4	23.2	− 0.1	− 7.8	→	32.2	24.5
E	58.7	17.3	25.1	0.4	− 1.5	→	31.4	29.9
F	55.0	23.3	20.2	− 0.1	1.6	→	26.4	27.9
IRL	47.5	13.4	23.1	1.1	14.9	→	80.5	95.4
I	60.2	18.5	19.8	− 0.1	1.6	→	26.7	28.3
L	41.3	17.4	21.3	1.0	19.0	→	133.0	152.0
NL	49.6	23.2	22.0	− 0.2	5.3	→	59.7	65.1
A	57.5	19.3	22.8	0.8	− 0.4	→	52.6	52.2
P	60.9	20.5	27.5	0.8	− 9.6	→	41.2	31.6
FIN	49.9	21.0	19.8	0.9	8.4	→	31.7	40.1
S	49.8	26.7	17.5	0.1	5.9	→	40.6	46.5
UK	66.3	19.3	16.4	0.2	− 2.3	→	29.4	27.2

Source: Eurostat.

ECONOMY OF THE UNION

15 Member States, while in the remaining seven, government consumption expenditure figured more prominently.

Figure 1.2.5. Structure of domestic demand, 2001 (as a % of GDP)

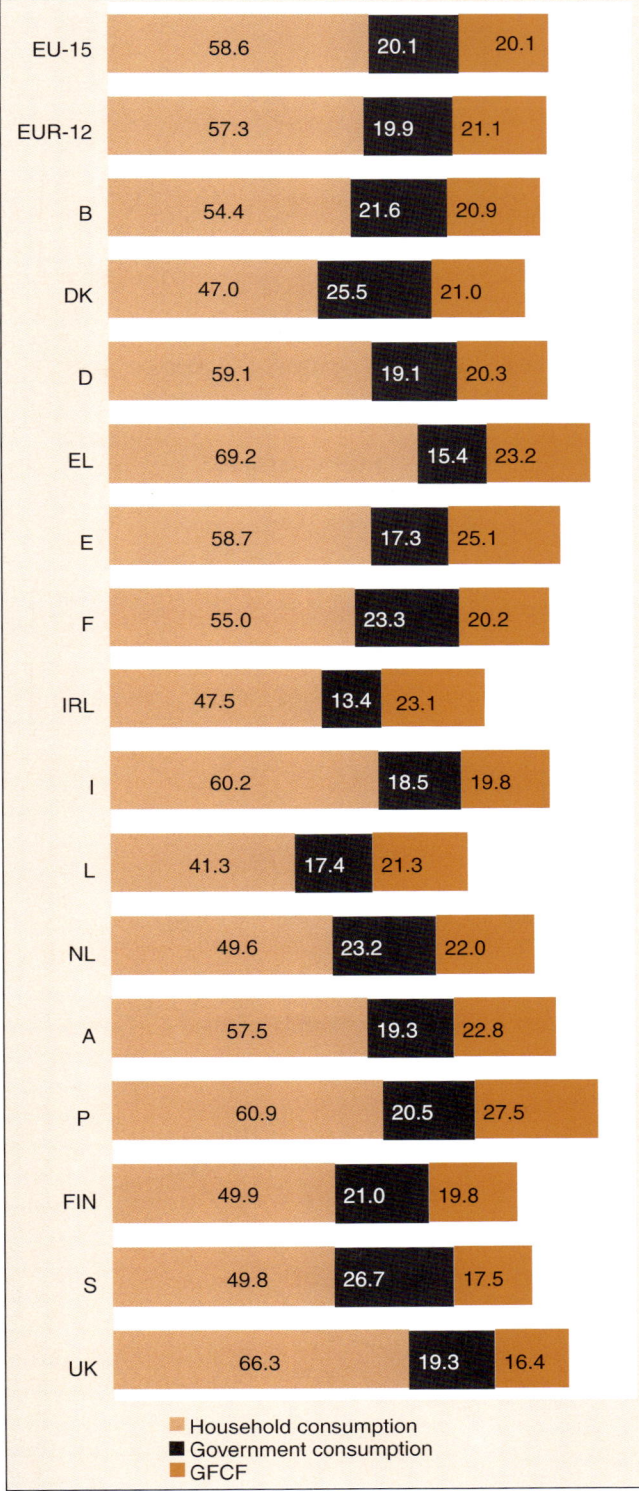

Source: Eurostat.

Changes in the expenditure structure between 1997 and 2001

A look at the breakdown of GDP into its components in the last five years shows that GDP structure in the European Union did not change dramatically, though some fluctuations could be observed. Household consumption (+ 0.7 percentage points) and investment (+ 0.7 points) went up, while government consumption (− 0.1 points) and the external balance (− 1.1 points) declined. As for trade [4] in particular, the figures for imports and exports both recorded upward changes: up by 5.0 percentage points for imports and by 3.9 points for exports, giving rise to the 1.1 points drop in the share of the external balance (see Figure 1.2.5).

The structural changes were only slightly different in the euro-zone over the period under review. The increase in the share of household consumption expenditure (+ 0.4 points) was smaller, that in the share of investment (+ 0.9 points) was bigger than in EU-15, while on the other hand the decline in the share of government consumption expenditure (− 0.3 points) was stronger and that for the external balance (− 0.8 points) weaker. Import and export shares figures were both marked by significant increases: + 6.0 points for imports and + 5.2 for exports. The fact that the drop in the share of the external balance was more pronounced in EU-15 is attributable to above-average downward variations in the United Kingdom and Sweden.

Regarding the four biggest economies of the European Union, it is remarkable that no two have exhibited the same pattern of change over the last five years: all four have seen a rise in the relative importance of household consumption, but this was much weaker in France compared to the other three. For government consumption, France and Germany recorded declining shares, Italy and the United Kingdom rising ones. For gross fixed capital formation, only Germany registered a significant decrease in the share of GDP while Italy and France saw the importance of investments grow. For the external balance, the decline in importance ranged between − 1.4 percentage points in France via − 2.3 points in the United Kingdom to − 2.5 points in Italy, Germany standing out for the only growth in relative size (+ 0.5 points) for this item. Another peculiarity is that, while the share of the external balance declined for several countries, the United Kingdom was the only Member State for which this was not due to a stronger rise in the share of imports than of imports, but to the share of exports actually declining while that of imports rose. It should be noted, though, that a declining share of GDP does not necessarily mean that this particular component was actually declining itself.

---

[4] Trade balance figures in this section refer to national accounts and therefore do not include intra-Community trade. They might differ from figures shown in Chapter 2.3.

ECONOMY OF THE UNION

Figure 1.2.6. GDP Structure in the EU, 1997-2001 (as a % of GDP)

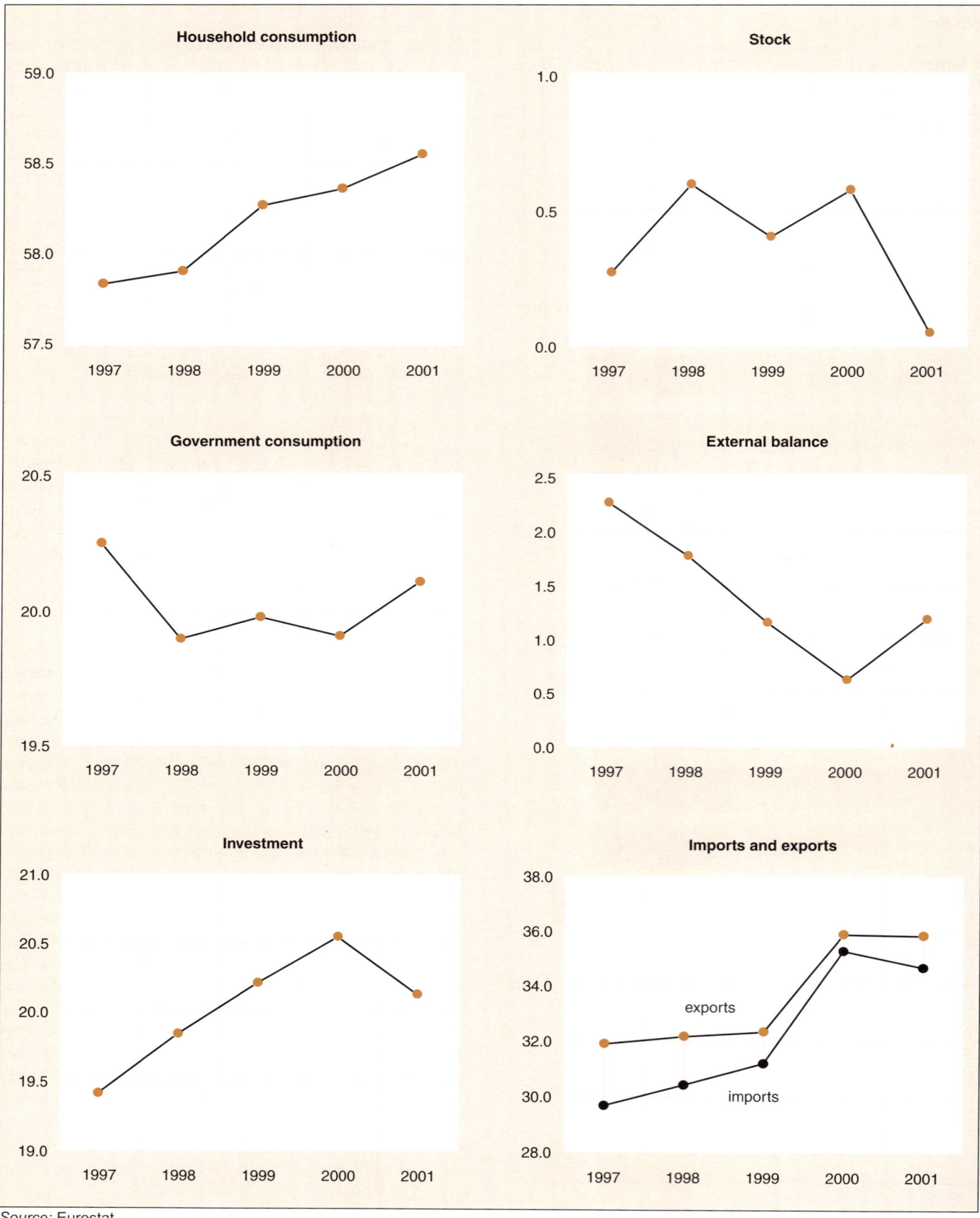

Source: Eurostat.

ECONOMY OF THE UNION

Apart from the four big economies already mentioned, the share of household consumption expenditure showed a slight increase only in Belgium and the Netherlands (+ 0.2 percentage points each). All other Member States recorded reductions, some of them quite substantial, as in Ireland (– 4.0 points) and Luxembourg and Denmark (– 3.3 points for both). In the case of Ireland and Denmark, this reduction in household consumption was offset by increases in the percentage shares of investment and the external balance. In Luxembourg, on the other hand, the reduction in private consumption was countered solely by the contribution of the external balance, which went up by 4.6 points.

Apart from Italy and the United Kingdom, the share of government consumption increased in Belgium, Greece, the Netherlands, Portugal and Sweden, Portugal being the only country where this rise was substantial (+ 1.5 percentage points). In the rest of the Member States the trend was negative. The biggest reductions were observed in Ireland (– 1.7 points) and Finland (– 1.4 points). Gross fixed capital formation has increased its share over the last five years in 12 out of the 15 Member States, the exception added to Germany and the United Kingdom being Austria. The biggest increases where those in Greece (+ 3.4 points) and Spain (+ 3.2 points).

The variations in the external balance call for some explanation: if the balance is negative, a change with a "minus" sign does not indicate a lower percentage but an increase in the share. For example, the – 2.5 percentage points change for Italy meant passing from a 4.1 % share of the positive external balance in 1997 to a 1.6 % share in 2001, while the – 2.3 points change for the United Kingdom are the result of a balanced external trade (+ 0.0 points) in 1997 passing to – 2.3 % of GDP in 2001. For the purpose at hand, this means an increase in the significance of the external balance as a component of GDP for the United Kingdom, even if the effect is negative (deficit). This applies in the case of Greece, Spain, Portugal and the United Kingdom. In Austria, which also has a negative external balance, its share of GDP improved from – 1.6 % to – 0.4 % of GDP. Among the Member States with a positive external balance, its share increased in Denmark, Germany, Ireland, Luxembourg and Finland. In particular, the relatively large variation for Spain (– 2.5 percentage points) indicates a worsening of the trade deficit, while the 4.6 points change for Luxembourg indicates a growing trade surplus. Yet both mean a bigger significance of trade as a component of GDP. For further analysis, Table 1.2.5 shows variations in GDP percentage not only for the external balance but also for imports and exports separately.

Table 1.2.5. Change in GDP structure between 1997 and 2001 (in percentage points)

	Household consumption	Government consumption	GFCF	External balance	Imports	Exports
EU-15	0.7 ↑	– 0.1 ↘	0.7 ↑	– 1.1 ↓	5.0 ⬆	3.9 ⬆
EUR-12	0.4 ↗	– 0.3 ↘	0.9 ↑	– 0.8 ↓	6.0 ⬆	5.2 ⬆
B	0.2 ↗	0.4 ↗	0.5 ↗	– 1.1 ↓	10.9 ⬆	9.8 ⬆
DK	– 3.3 ⬇	0.0 ↗	1.4 ↑	2.9 ⬆	6.2 ⬆	9.1 ⬆
D	1.4 ↑	– 0.4 ↘	– 1.2 ↓	0.5 ↗	6.5 ⬆	7.1 ⬆
EL	– 2.9 ⬇	0.3 ↗	3.4 ⬆	– 0.4 ↘	5.2 ⬆	4.8 ⬆
E	– 0.6 ↓	– 0.3 ↘	3.2 ⬆	– 2.5 ↓	5.7 ⬆	3.2 ⬆
F	0.1 ↗	– 0.9 ↓	2.2 ↑	– 1.4 ↓	3.8 ⬆	2.4 ↑
IRL	– 4.0 ⬇	– 1.7 ↓	2.8 ⬆	2.3 ↑	13.3 ⬆	15.6 ⬆
I	1.3 ↑	0.3 ↗	1.6 ↑	– 2.5 ↓	4.3 ⬆	1.9 ↑
L	– 3.3 ⬇	– 0.3 ↘	– 0.9 ↓	4.6 ⬆	29.1 ⬆	33.6 ⬆
NL	0.2 ↗	0.3 ↗	0.5 ↗	– 0.6 ↓	4.6 ⬆	4.0 ⬆
A	– 0.1 ↘	– 0.4 ↘	– 0.7 ↓	1.2 ↑	9.2 ⬆	10.4 ⬆
P	– 1.7 ↓	1.5 ↑	1.9 ↑	– 1.9 ↓	3.1 ⬆	1.2 ↑
FIN	– 1.0 ↓	– 1.4 ↓	1.8 ↑	0.3 ↗	0.7 ↑	1.0 ↑
S	– 0.7 ↓	0.1 ↗	2.3 ↑	– 1.4 ↓	5.2 ⬆	3.8 ⬆
UK	1.8 ↑	0.9 ↑	– 0.1 ↘	– 2.3 ↓	0.9 ↑	-1.4 ↓

Reading note:
Stable: 0≤x≤0.5 : ↗   Small change: 0.5<x≤1.5 : ↑
– 0.5≤x<0 : ↘   – 1.5≤x<-0.5 : ↓

Medium change : 1.5<x≤2.5 : ↑   Strong change: x>2.5 : ⬆
– 2.5≤x<1.5 : ↓   x<-2.5 : ⬇

Source: Eurostat.

ECONOMY OF THE UNION

1.3. Production breakdown of GDP: the economy by branch

Gross value added growth by branch of production

The analysis of GDP so far has been limited to the expenditure side. In this chapter, we set out to investigate in which parts of the economy gross value added (GVA) was created. We use a breakdown of six branches here in order to keep the presentation readable.

> **Branches of production**
> — Agriculture, hunting, forestry and fishing.
> — Mining and quarrying; manufacturing; electricity, gas and water supply.
> — Construction.
> — Wholesale and retail trade, repair of motor vehicles, motorcycles and personal and household goods; hotels and restaurants; transport, storage and communication.
> — Financial intermediation, real estate, renting and business activities.
> — Other services: public administration and defence; compulsory social security; education; health and social work; other community, social and personal service activities; private households with employed persons.
>
> This breakdown is specified as 'A6, in the European system of accounts 1995 (ESA 95) and derived from the European classification of economic activities NACE Rev.1.

The most vigorous growth in GVA in the European Union in 2001 occurred in financial services and business activities (+ 3.3 % compared with the previous year) followed by trade, transport and communication (+ 2.7 %). Somewhat behind came the public services (+ 1.2 %). Manufacturing recorded only a slight growth (+ 0.3 %) and construction (+ 0.0 %) actually stagnated. Agriculture was in last place again, with the only negative growth rate among all branches: – 1.5 % (see Figure 1.3.1). A look at the results in relation to the average for the reference period (1997-2001) shows that all branches grew slower than the average of the last five years, and some, especially agriculture and manufacturing, even markedly so. Only the other services recorded growth close to the five-year average: GVA in this branch increased by 1.2 %, while during the reference period, it had been growing by an average of 1.4 % each year (see Figure 1.3.2).

The euro-zone figures were slightly below those of the Union for the services branches. In agriculture and manufacturing, the euro-zone fared significantly better, in construction significantly worse than the Union. Three of the four larger EU economies, namely Germany, France and the United Kingdom recorded the highest growth rates in 2001 in financial services and business activities: 5.1 % for the United Kingdom, 3.0 % for France and 2.9 % for Germany. For all three of them, the second place was held by trade, transport and communication with growth rates of + 3.8 % for the United Kingdom, + 2.4 % for France and + 2.3 % for Germany. In Italy, construction was the fastest growing branch with a 4.4 % increase over the previous year, and trade, transport and communication tied for second

Figure 1.3.1. GVA growth rates by branch of production, 2001 (as a %)

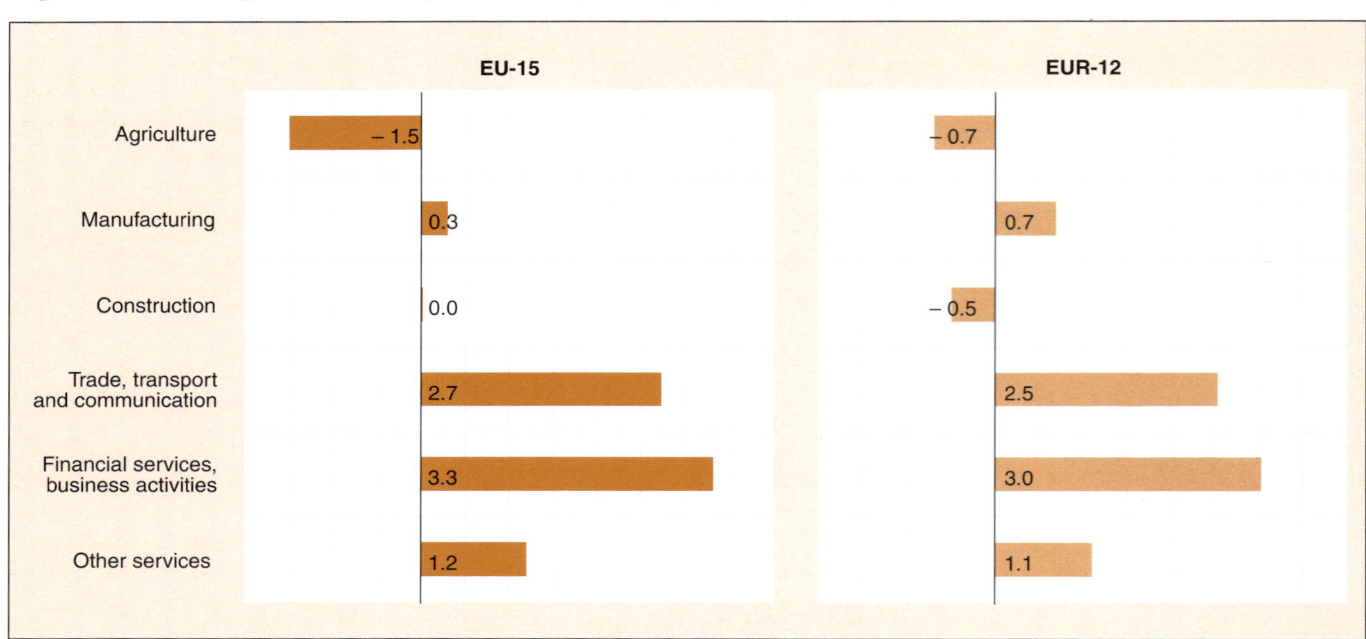

Source: Eurostat.

ECONOMY OF THE UNION

place with financial services and business activities (+ 3.0 % for both). Agriculture showed the weakest results of all branches in the United Kingdom (– 11.6 %), Italy (– 1.0 %) and France (– 0.7 %), while Germany was exceptional again not only by a positive growth rate in agriculture (+ 1.2 %), but also by a significant negative growth in construction (– 6.6 %).

For those Member States for which data are available ([5]), the majority showed relatively high GVA growth in financial services and business activities, though only Belgium, Spain and France managed to beat the five-year average. The highest growth rates were recorded in Portugal (+ 5.7 %) and Belgium (+ 5.4 %). The lowest result was a + 0.7 % growth in Finland, making this branch the only one for which all Member States experienced positive growth.

Trade, transport and communication were also relatively strong, even if only a single country (Italy) recorded above average growth. Among the other Member States, the best performance by far was registered in Luxembourg (+ 6.9 %), the lowest in Belgium (– 0.1 %).

Growth in other services usually shows a lower level of variation among Member States, and this also applies to 2001. A high growth rate was recorded in Luxembourg (+ 5.3%), with Spain (+ 3.3 %) and the Netherlands (+ 3.2 %) following two percentage points behind, while the other end of the scale was marked by Denmark (– 0.1 %).

The results achieved for GVA in manufacturing were generally weak. For all Member States, growth was lower than the average of the last five years. The best result achieved was a modest + 2.9 % in Greece, the worst a sizeable decline in the United Kingdom (– 2.1 %) which explains the difference between EU-15 and the euro-zone figures.

Results in construction varied widely between Member States, with Greece (+ 10.4 %) and Luxembourg (+ 6.3 %) topping the league. The weak EU-15 and euro-zone results are connected to the – 6.6 % recorded in Germany, but Austria, Denmark and Finland also saw declines in value added for construction.

Gross value added in 2001 for agriculture showed negative results in most Member States, the strongest declines by far being observed in the United Kingdom (– 11.6 %) and Luxembourg (– 9.6 %). Only three countries, namely Denmark (+ 1.3 %), Germany (+ 1.2 %) and Austria (+ 1.1 %) had positive agricultural growth rates, making Austria the only country to surpass the average growth of the last five years.

Figure 1.3.2 shows the growth rates per branch and Member State for 2001 and the average growth rates for the period 1997 to 2001. Given the quantity of data, it has been presented graphically to allow comparisons both in time and between countries.

Structure of GVA in 2001

The structure of production in the European Union (see Figure 1.3.3) is based mainly on the three service sector headings. Financial services and business activities (27.2 %) accounted for the largest proportion of gross value added (GVA) produced by the 15 Member States in 2001, followed by other services (21.6 %) and trade, transport and communications (21.5 %) with almost identical shares. Combined, these three branches accounted for more than 70 % of total GVA in the Union's economy. Of the remaining part, the lion's share is accounted for by manufacturing (22.3 % of total GVA). In fact, if the GVA produced by manufacturing and services is disregarded, the remaining contributions made by agriculture and construction are only of secondary importance: 2.1 % and 5.4 % respectively. In the euro-zone, the structure of production was essentially the same as that in the Union as a whole, with slightly larger shares for agriculture and manufacturing and slightly smaller shares for services.

As in the EU as a whole, in all four larger Member States financial services and business activities played a major role as a source of GVA. In France, GVA in this branch contributed 30.1 % to the total economy, while in Germany, the figure was 30.0 %, in the United Kingdom 28.0 % and in Italy 26.3 %. As for the other branches, Germany derived a particularly high contribution from manufacturing (25.2 %), as did France from other (i.e. mainly public) services (23.1 %). The figures for Italy and the United Kingdom reveal relatively balanced structures, with manufacturing (22.9 % for Italy, 21.3 % for the United Kingdom) and trade, transport and communications (24.0 % for Italy, 22.6 % for the United Kingdom) of roughly equal importance. In Italy, other services (19.2 %) were somewhat less important than in the other three big economies.

A closer look at the structures in individual Member States ([6]) (see Table 1.3.1) shows that in most cases production in the EU countries is concentrated in one of the service branches. There is one group of countries, namely Belgium, Luxembourg and the Netherlands in addition to Germany, France, Italy and the United Kingdom as mentioned before, where financial services and business activities make the biggest contribution to GVA, with Luxembourg standing out for having a 39.8 % share of total GVA concentrated in this branch. Other services play the main role in Sweden (26.6 %), Denmark (25.7 %) and Portugal (25.6 %), while trade, transport and communication is

---

[5] Constant price data for 2001 are lacking for Ireland.

[6] The structure has been calculated at current prices.

29

Figure 1.3.2. GVA growth rates, 2001 and average 1997-2001 (as a %)

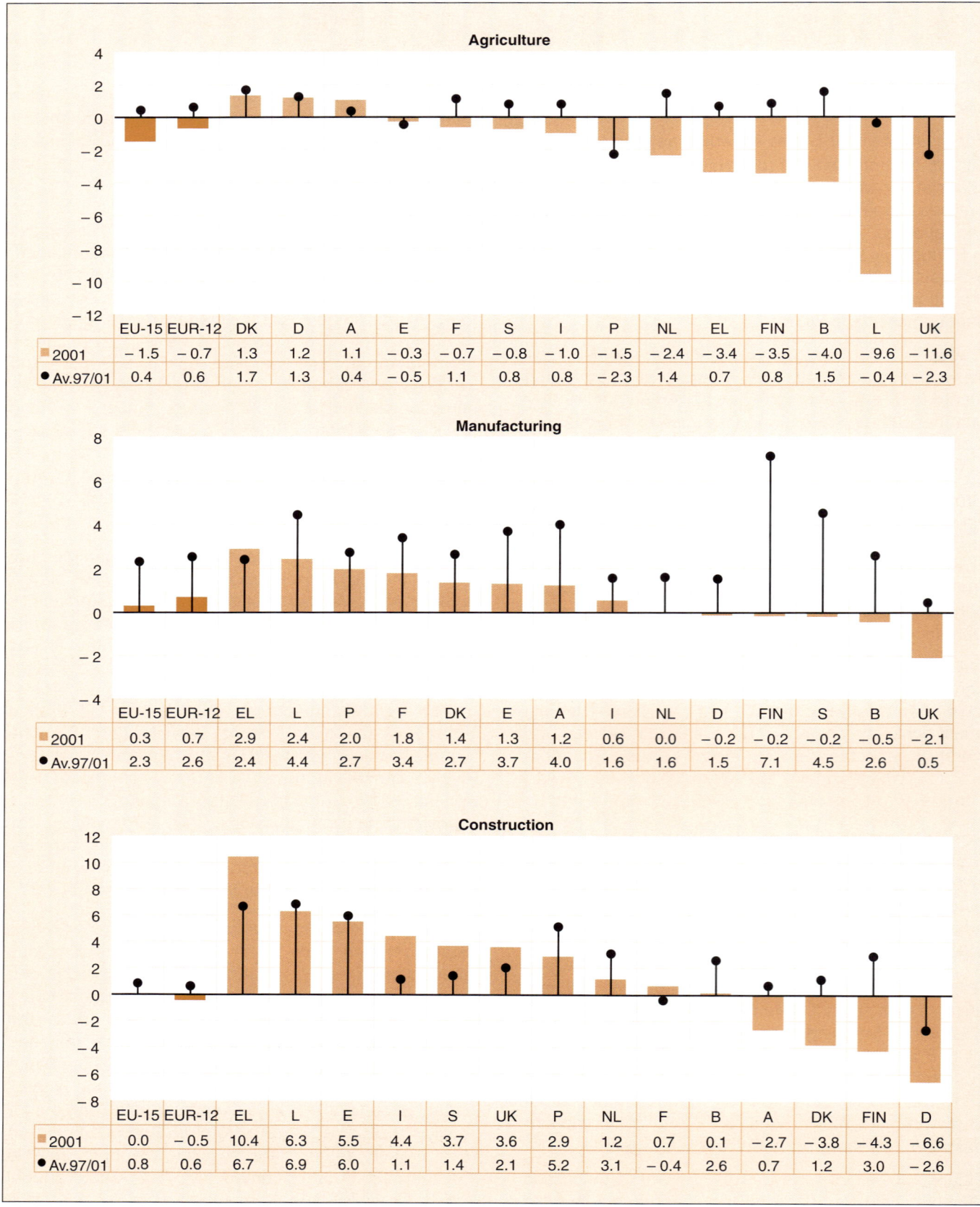

ECONOMY OF THE UNION

Trade, transport and communication

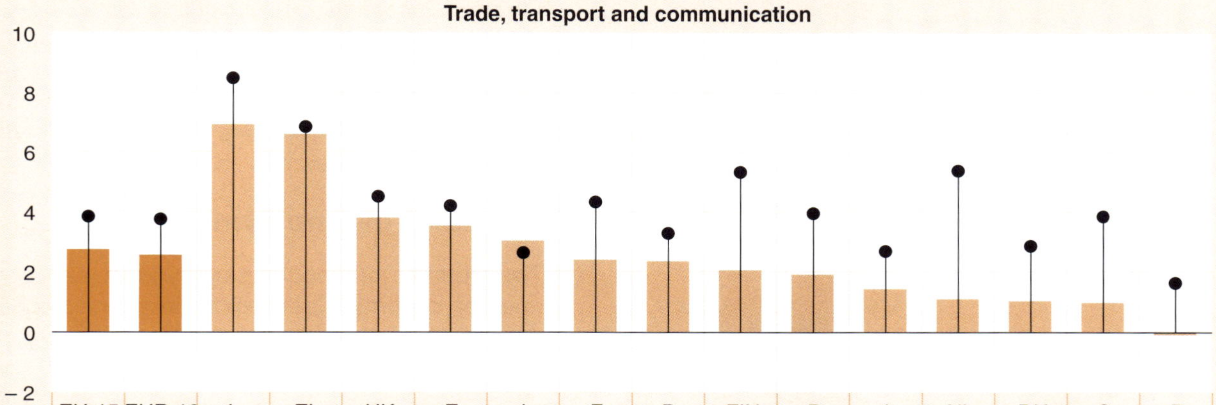

	EU-15	EUR-12	L	EL	UK	E	I	F	D	FIN	P	A	NL	DK	S	B
2001	2.7	2.5	6.9	6.6	3.8	3.5	3.0	2.4	2.3	2.0	1.9	1.4	1.1	1.0	1.0	−0.1
Av.97/01	3.8	3.8	8.5	6.9	4.5	4.2	2.6	4.3	3.3	5.3	4.0	2.7	5.4	2.9	3.9	1.7

Financial services and business activities

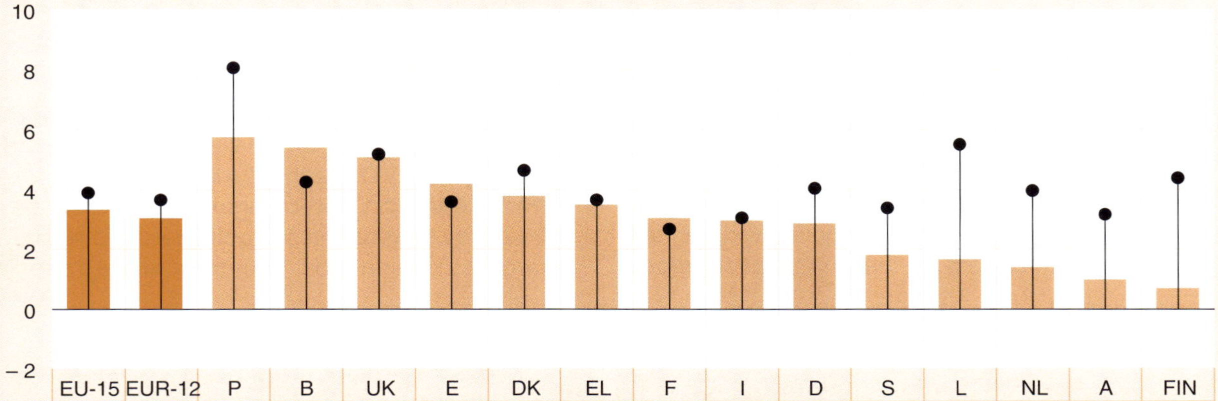

	EU-15	EUR-12	P	B	UK	E	DK	EL	F	I	D	S	L	NL	A	FIN
2001	3.3	3.0	5.7	5.4	5.1	4.2	3.8	3.5	3.0	3.0	2.9	1.8	1.7	1.4	1.0	0.7
Av.97/01	3.9	3.7	8.1	4.3	5.2	3.6	4.6	3.7	2.7	3.1	4.1	3.4	5.5	4.0	3.2	4.4

Other services

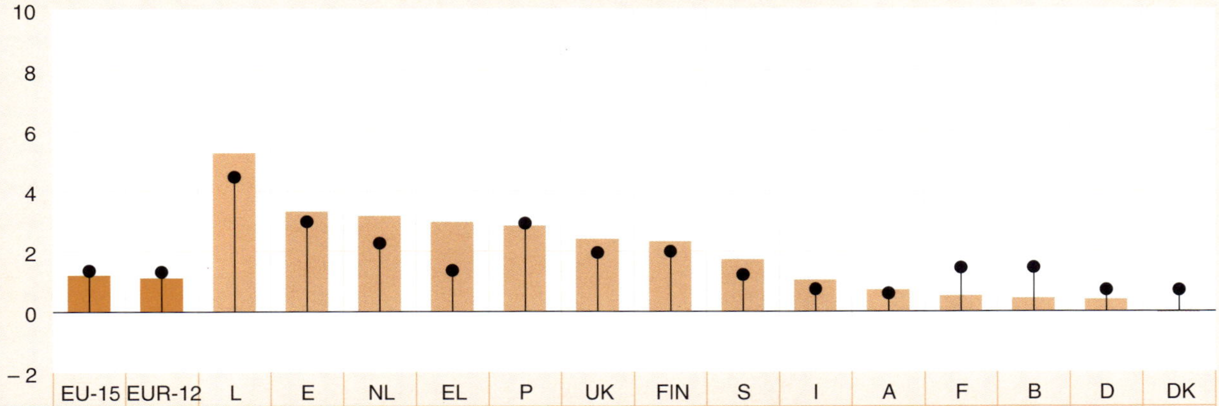

	EU-15	EUR-12	L	E	NL	EL	P	UK	FIN	S	I	A	F	B	D	DK
2001	1.2	1.1	5.3	3.3	3.2	3.0	2.8	2.4	2.3	1.7	1.0	0.7	0.5	0.4	0.4	−0.1
Av.97/01	1.4	1.3	4.5	3.0	2.3	1.4	2.9	1.9	2.0	1.2	0.7	0.6	1.4	1.4	0.7	0.7

NB: No constant price data for 2001 are available for Ireland.
Source: Eurostat.

ECONOMY OF THE UNION

Figure 1.3.3. Structure of GVA in the EU, 2001 (as a % of total economy)

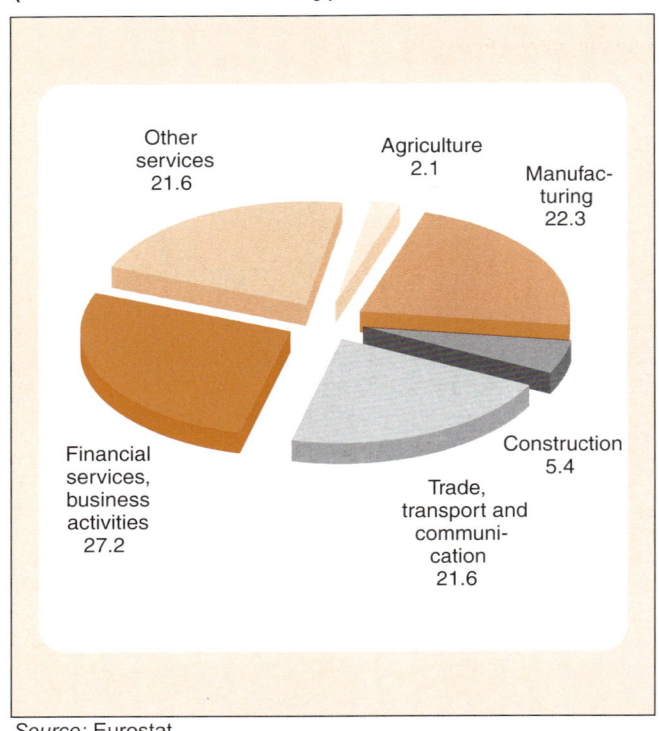

Source: Eurostat.

the branch that is the biggest contributor in Greece (30.4 %) and Spain (28.1 %). Finally, Ireland, Finland and Austria are exceptions, in that the biggest proportion of GVA comes from manufacturing (34.8 %, 27.1 % and 24.0 %, respectively).

Figure 1.3.4 shows the structure of GVA by branch, together with the structure of employment. GVA and employment are two fundamental indicators for analysing the branches of the economy, and the web diagrams allow the relations between these two factors to be seen at a glance.

Structure of employment by branch

The number of people employed in each branch is another important factor in defining the importance of the branch in the economy. A look at the structure of employment in the European Union in 2001 shows that other (i.e. mainly public) services provided the most jobs (29.6 % of total employment), followed by trade, transport and communication (25.4 %), while only 14.3 % of the workforce was employed in financial services and business activities. The latter branch produced more than a quarter of the value added produced in the EU, while employing a much smaller proportion of the workforce.

Among the Member States for which data are available ([7]), there are some broad similarities in the structure of employment. Throughout the EU, public services and trade, transport and communication are the branches that provide most jobs. Public services account for the largest share in most countries, while trade, transport

Table 1.3.1. Structure of GVA in 2001 (as a % of total economy)

	Agriculture	Manufacturing	Construction	Trade, transport, communication	Financial services, business activities	Other services
EU-15	2.1	22.3	5.4	21.5	27.2	21.6
EUR-12	2.4	22.6	5.5	21.2	27.1	21.2
B	1.5	21.3	4.9	19.7	29.2	23.4
DK	2.7	20.8	4.5	23.3	23.0	25.7
D	1.2	25.2	4.7	17.8	30.0	21.1
EL	7.0	13.1	7.2	30.4	22.4	19.8
E	3.4	20.3	8.8	28.1	19.2	20.2
F	2.8	20.1	4.7	19.3	30.1	23.1
IRL	3.6	34.8	6.6	19.1	19.9	16.0
I	2.7	22.9	4.9	24.0	26.3	19.2
L	0.7	12.8	6.4	23.5	39.8	16.7
NL	2.6	20.1	5.9	22.1	26.2	23.0
A	2.2	24.0	7.5	23.7	22.2	20.4
P	3.6	21.0	7.6	23.7	18.4	25.6
FIN	3.3	27.1	5.7	21.3	21.5	21.0
S	1.7	22.4	4.3	20.1	24.9	26.6
UK	0.9	21.3	5.2	22.6	28.0	22.0

NB: 2000 data for Ireland.
Source: Eurostat.

([7]) For Portugal the structure illustrated refers to 1998 and for Ireland and Luxembourg to 2000. Please note that the unavailability of more recent employment data for Portugal renders comparisons difficult. There are no national accounts data available on employment by branch for the United Kingdom.

ECONOMY OF THE UNION

Figure 1.3.4. Structure of GVA and employment by main branch, 2001 (as a % of total economy)

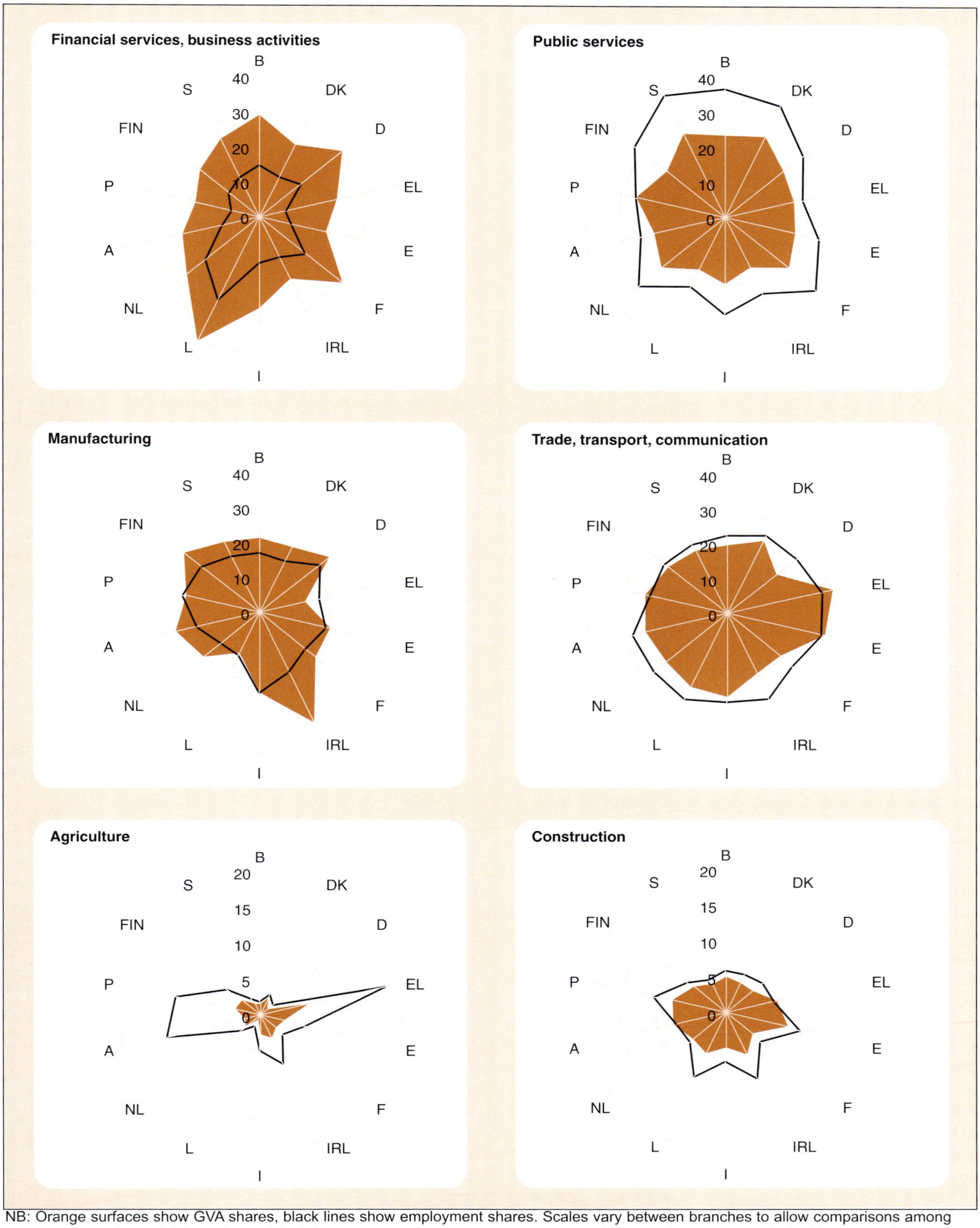

NB: Orange surfaces show GVA shares, black lines show employment shares. Scales vary between branches to allow comparisons among countries, although this makes it difficult to compare branches. No data are available on employment in the United Kingdom. 1998 employment data for Portugal, 2000 for Ireland and Luxembourg, 2000 GVA data for Ireland.
Source: Eurostat.

ECONOMY OF THE UNION

and communication is the largest provider of employment in Greece, Spain, Luxembourg, Austria, and Ireland.

Sweden is the Member State which has the biggest share of employment in public services (38.9 %). Next comes Belgium (36.9 %), followed by Denmark (35.6 %). There were relatively fewer jobs in this branch in Luxembourg (21.9 % of total employment) and Greece (22.4 %). As mentioned earlier, trade, transport and communication accounted for the largest share of employment in Greece (27.6 %), Spain, Luxembourg Austria and Ireland (all close around 27 %). In the case of employment in financial services, Luxembourg (26.4 %) and the Netherlands (19.4 %) stood out with figures markedly higher than those recorded in other EU countries, while Spain, Portugal and Greece recorded employment shares of less than 10 % in this branch. Italy (22.7 %), Germany (22.0 %), Portugal (21.9 %) and Finland (20.9 %) were remarkable for the importance that employment in manufacturing has in their economies. High percentages for employment in construction are recorded for Spain (10.6 %), Portugal (10.2 %) and Ireland (10.1 %). Echoing the situation observed for GVA, Greece (18.0 %) also recorded the largest share of employment in agriculture among Member States. Austria (13.2 %) and Portugal (12.0 %) were also ahead of the other Member States in this respect.

Figure 1.3.5. Structure of employment in the EU, 2001 (as a % of total economy)

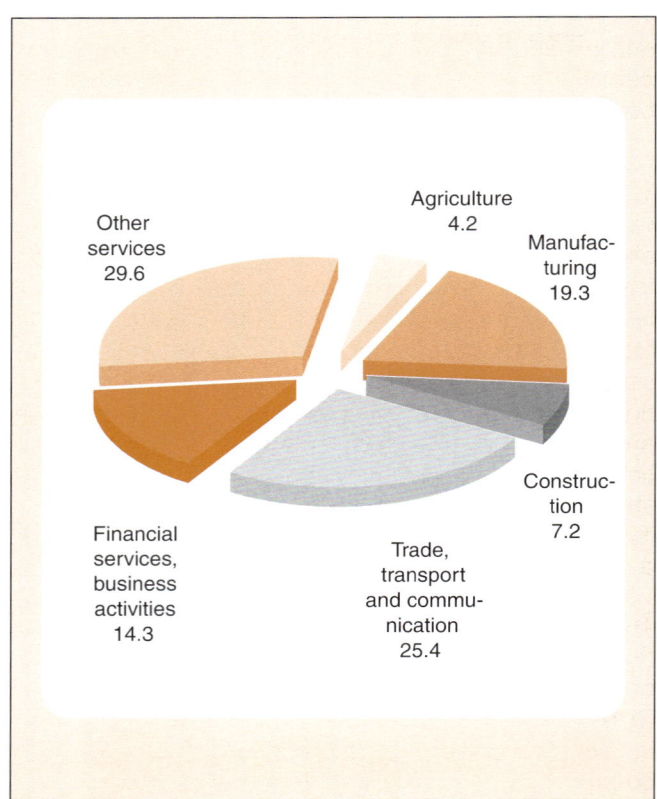

Source: Eurostat.

Table 1.3.2. Structure of employment in 2001 (as a % of total economy)

	Agriculture	Manufacturing	Construction	Trade, transport, communication	Financial services, business activities	Other services
EU-15	4.2	19.3	7.2	25.4	14.3	29.6
EUR-12	4.9	19.7	7.2	25.2	14.0	28.9
B	2.0	17.3	5.9	22.8	15.1	36.9
DK	3.3	16.6	6.0	25.4	13.0	35.6
D	2.4	22.0	6.7	25.4	15.2	28.3
EL	18.0	17.3	7.0	27.6	7.7	22.4
E	6.5	19.1	10.6	27.2	9.5	27.1
F	4.1	16.5	6.2	23.7	16.7	32.9
IRL	7.5	18.8	10.1	26.9	12.7	24.0
I	4.8	22.7	6.7	25.1	13.1	27.5
L	1.6	13.2	9.8	27.1	26.4	21.9
NL	3.3	13.6	6.3	26.4	19.4	31.1
A	13.2	17.8	6.9	27.1	10.7	24.2
P	12.0	21.9	10.2	22.3	8.0	25.7
FIN	5.8	20.9	6.8	22.8	11.0	32.6
S	2.6	18.1	5.2	22.4	12.8	38.9
UK	:	:	:	:	:	:

NB: 1998 data for Portugal, 2000 data for Ireland and Luxembourg.
Source: Eurostat.

Productivity

To give an overview of the relationship between production and employment in each branch, labour productivity has been calculated as a simple ratio between gross value added and total employment.

Labour productivity, or rather a general productivity indicator of output per unit of labour, allows the branches to be considered in terms of labour and employment and, obviously, also allows the comparison of data from different-sized productive systems. This indicator is, of course, very simplified. Firstly, the ratio should rather be based on hours actually worked ([8]) and not simply on the number of those employed. Secondly, no account is taken of the efficient use of resources and technical progress. Given the rather simple definition of the labour productivity indicator used here, it should be borne in mind that an increase in productivity may be due to an increase in gross value added or a reduction in employment or both.

The highest productivity level in the European Union ([9]) in 2001 was achieved in financial services and business activities, where each worker produced EUR 92 100 of value added. Next came manufacturing with EUR 56 300, followed by trade, transport and communications (EUR 41 200) and, quite close together, construction (EUR 36 200) and other services (EUR 35 300). Productivity in agriculture, however, was significantly lower than in the other branches: EUR 24 400 in 2001 (see Figure 1.3.6).

The figures for the euro-zone were more or less in line with those of the EU, albeit a little higher for financial services and business activities (EUR 92 600) and somewhat lower for trade, transport and communication (EUR 40 100) and agriculture (EUR 23 300).

Data are available for only three of the four larger Member States, since there are no national accounts data on employment by branch in the United Kingdom. Productivity figures in the branches are essentially similar, with the highest figures being recorded for financial services and business activities in France (EUR 98 500), Germany (EUR 97 500) and Italy (EUR 97 100). Manufacturing came next for all three countries: EUR 66 800 in France, EUR 56 800 in Germany and EUR 48 600 in Italy. France also stands out with a relatively high figure for productivity in agriculture (EUR 37 300), while for Germany, productivity in trade, transport and communications is relatively low at EUR 34 800.

A clearer comparison of the Member States can be seen in Table 1.3.3, where the productivity figures for the six branches of the economy are shown in relation to the average for the Union as a whole (EU-15 = 100).

A closer look at these figures shows that the highest productivity in agriculture was achieved in Denmark (EUR 47 300) and Belgium (EUR 44 300), where the

Figure 1.3.6. Productivity by branch in 2001 (EUR, current prices)

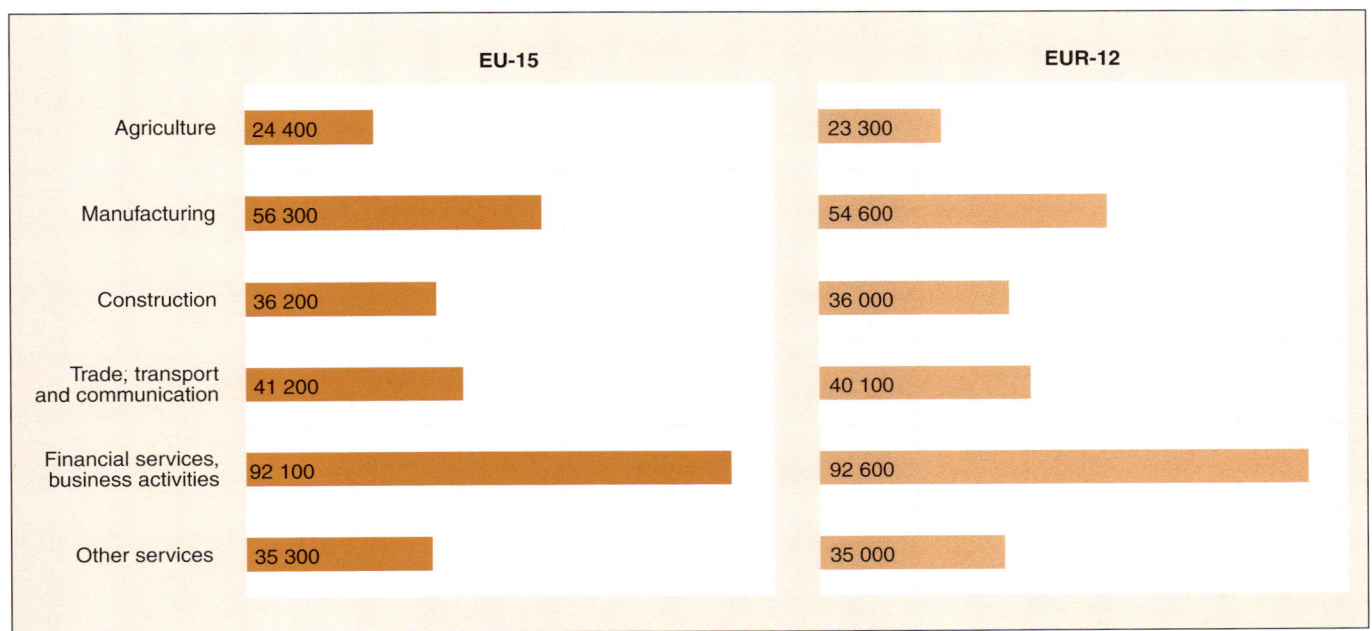

Source: Eurostat.

([8]) In quantifying the labour effectively employed in a productive process, hours worked would avoid distortions resulting from the inequality between the number of people employed and the number of jobs.

([9]) Productivity levels have been calculated at current prices; in the calculation of the growth index, GVA is at constant prices.

ECONOMY OF THE UNION

Table 1.3.3. Productivity by branch in 2001 (EUR, current prices)

	Agriculture		Manufacturing		Construction		Trade transport, and communication		Financial services, business activities		Other services		Total	
	EUR	EU = 100	EUR	EU = 100	EUR	EU = 100	EUR	EU = 100	EUR	EU = 100	EUR	EU = 100	EUR	EU = 100
EU-15	24 400	100	56 300	100	36 200	100	41 200	100	92 100	100	35 300	100	48 700	100
EUR-12	23 300	95	54 600	97	36 000	99	40 100	97	92 600	101	35 000	99	47 700	98
B	44 300	182	73 800	131	49 900	138	52 000	126	116 700	127	38 100	108	60 100	123
DK	47 300	194	72 300	128	43 600	120	53 100	129	102 700	112	41 700	118	57 900	119
D	24 700	101	56 800	101	35 200	97	34 800	84	97 500	106	36 900	105	49 500	102
EL	13 100	54	23 600	42	30 200	83	33 000	80	82 300	89	26 300	75	30 500	63
E	20 300	83	40 600	72	31 500	87	39 600	96	77 900	85	28 500	81	38 300	79
F	37 300	153	66 800	119	41 200	114	44 500	108	98 500	107	38 400	109	54 700	112
IRL	29 200	120	112 700	200	39 500	109	41 400	100	93 900	102	38 500	109	59 800	123
I	27 000	111	48 600	86	35 400	98	46 100	112	97 100	105	33 700	95	48 300	99
L	32 700	134	72 900	129	48 900	135	65 300	158	113 500	123	57 400	163	75 200	154
NL	37 400	153	69 700	124	44 600	123	39 600	96	63 700	69	34 900	99	47 200	97
A	8 100	33	66 200	118	53 600	148	42 900	104	101 800	111	41 500	118	49 200	101
P	7 100	29	21 800	39	15 900	44	23 400	57	49 100	53	21 900	62	22 200	46
FIN	29 800	122	67 800	120	44 000	122	49 000	119	102 500	111	33 800	96	52 400	108
S	31 500	129	61 400	109	40 500	112	44 500	108	96 500	105	33 800	96	49 500	102
UK	:	:	:	:	:	:	:	:	:	:	:	:	52 700	108

NB: Data for Ireland, Luxembourg and Portugal are Eurostat estimates.
Source: Eurostat.

figures were 94 % and 82 %, respectively, above the EU average. The top figure in manufacturing was that of Ireland (estimated at EUR 112 700), with Belgium (EUR 73 800), Luxembourg (EUR 72 900) and Denmark (72 300) following closely grouped together.

In addition to Greece, Spain and Portugal, where productivity was lower than the EU average in every branch, Italy was also below the EU-15 average for manufacturing, with a figure of EUR 48 600 in 2001. The Member States with the highest productivity in construction were

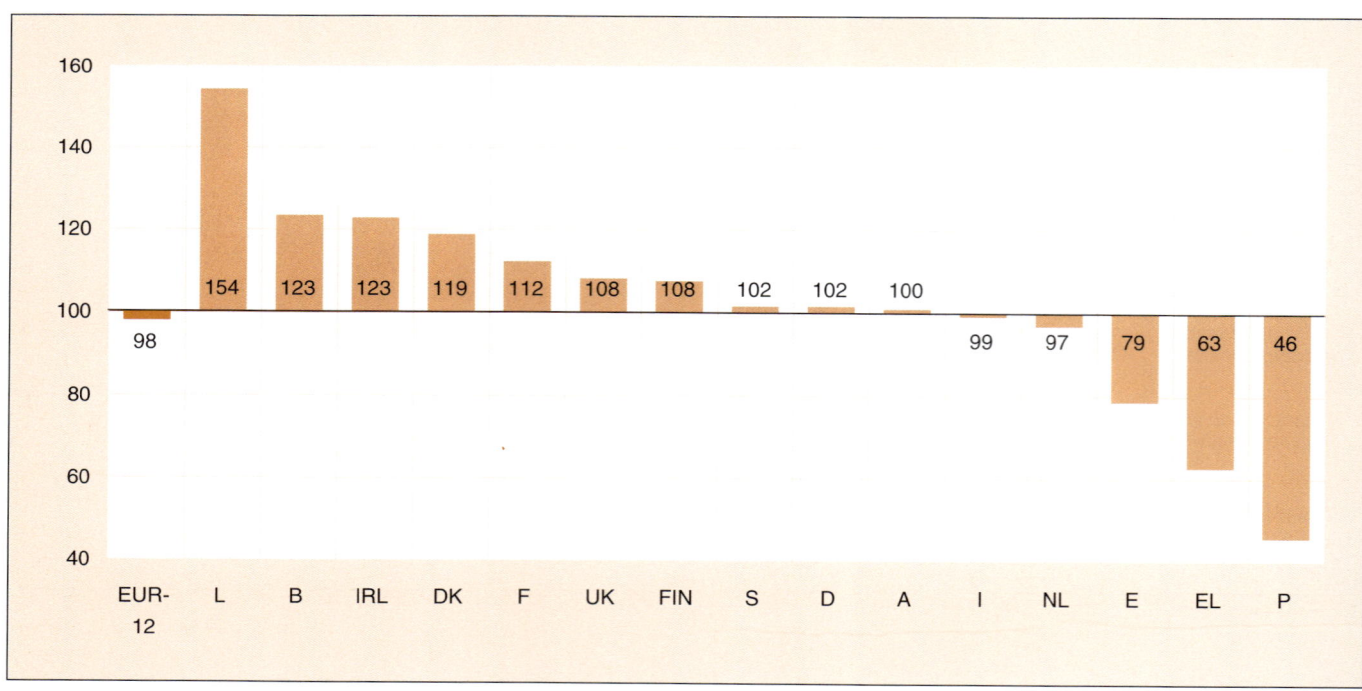

Figure 1.3.7. Productivity in 2001, total economy (EU-15 = 100)

NB: Data for Ireland, Luxembourg and Portugal are Eurostat estimates.
Source: Eurostat.

ECONOMY OF THE UNION

Austria (EUR 53 600 per person employed), Belgium (EUR 49 900) and Luxembourg (EUR 48 900), these figures exceeding the EU average by 48 %, 38 % and 35 %, respectively.

In trade, transport and communication, Luxembourg (EUR 65 300) ranked highest, with Denmark (EUR 53 100) and Belgium (EUR 52 000) somewhat behind. Productivity in financial services and business activities was particularly high in Belgium (EUR 116 700) and Luxembourg (EUR 113 500), which means 27 % and 23 %, respectively, above the EU average. Relatively strong values were also recorded in Denmark, Finland and Austria. Lastly, Luxembourg with EUR 57 400 was the only country where productivity in other services was greatly superior to the overall average, i.e. by + 63 %. Denmark (EUR 41 700) and Austria (EUR 41 500) and + 18 % each also exceeded the average significantly.

We now take a look at the development of productivity over time. Contrary to the productivity figures presented so far, the growth indices (see Table 1.3.4) are calculated on the basis of constant price gross value added in order to compensate for changes in the price levels. When these figures are considered, it must be remembered that productivity, however simple, is nevertheless a ratio that is the result of two components (gross value added and employment) that work in opposite directions: if value added goes up and employment goes down, productivity is increased, and vice versa. On the other hand, if both components go up — or down — the increase or reduction in productivity that this causes will depend on the difference in the variations. In the unlikely event that value added and employment show exactly the same variation, productivity would remain the same — even though both components had increased or decreased.

In the European Union in 2001, the highest growth rate in terms of volume (1995 = 100) was in agriculture, where productivity increased by 21 % in comparison with the reference year. This increase in productivity was a result of growth in GVA (+ 6 %), together with a significant decrease in employment in this branch (– 12 %). Productivity also increased sizeably in manufacturing (+ 13 % compared to 1995) and in trade, transport and communication (+ 12 %), but with different underlying causes. In manufacturing, the increase in productivity was due almost entirely to an increase in GVA supported by a small decrease in employment; while in trade, transport and communication both GVA and employment increased, but GVA did so at greater speed, resulting in increasing productivity. In the other branches productivity remained essentially unchanged in comparison with the benchmark year: in financial services and business activities, GVA and employment both experienced large and matching variations (respectively + 26 % and + 29 %), with the result that

Table 1.3.4. Volume growth index of productivity in 2001, total economy (1995 = 100)

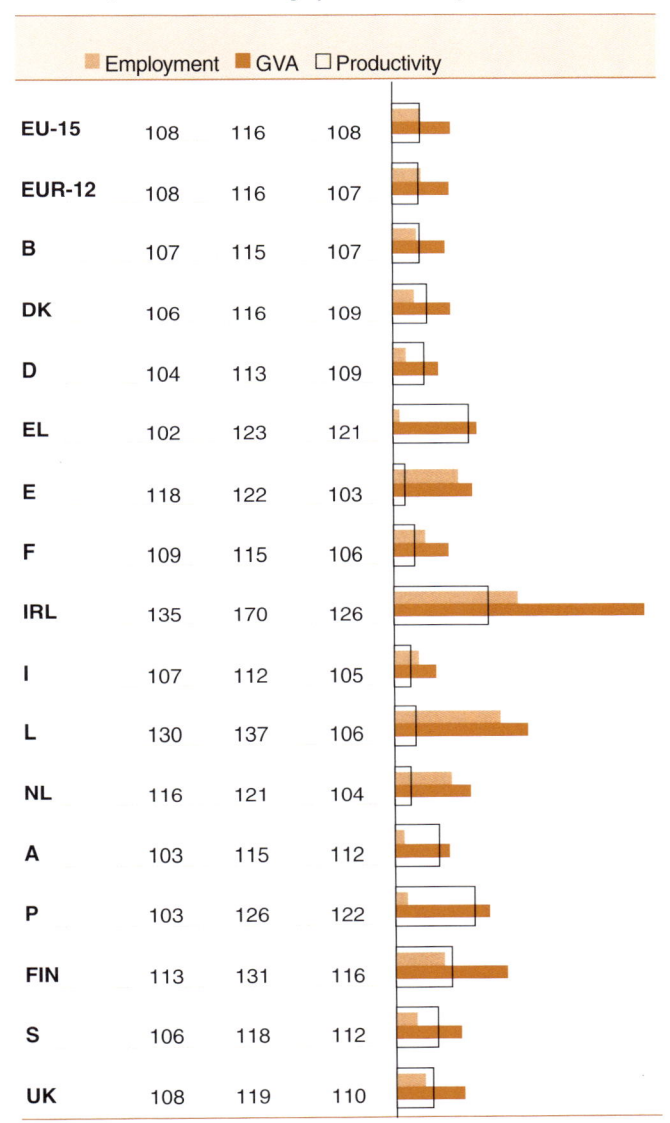

	Employment	GVA	Productivity
EU-15	108	116	108
EUR-12	108	116	107
B	107	115	107
DK	106	116	109
D	104	113	109
EL	102	123	121
E	118	122	103
F	109	115	106
IRL	135	170	126
I	107	112	105
L	130	137	106
NL	116	121	104
A	103	115	112
P	103	126	122
FIN	113	131	116
S	106	118	112
UK	108	119	110

NB: Employment growth data for Ireland, Luxembourg and Portugal are Eurostat estimates, as are GVA growth data for Ireland.
Source: Eurostat.

productivity decreased slightly. Basically the same applied to construction, although the variations were on a smaller scale. In other services, which mainly comprises public services, GVA and employment were growing at the same speed, leaving productivity at 100 % of the base year value.

Variations in productivity in the larger EU countries — although for only three of them, since no data are available for the United Kingdom — showed largely coinciding trends, the exception being construction, for which increased productivity in Germany was due to both GVA and employment decreasing while in Italy, productivity was up due to both components growing, and in France finally, productivity was lower as GVA

ECONOMY OF THE UNION

Figure 1.3.8. Growth index of productivity, 2001 (1995 = 100)

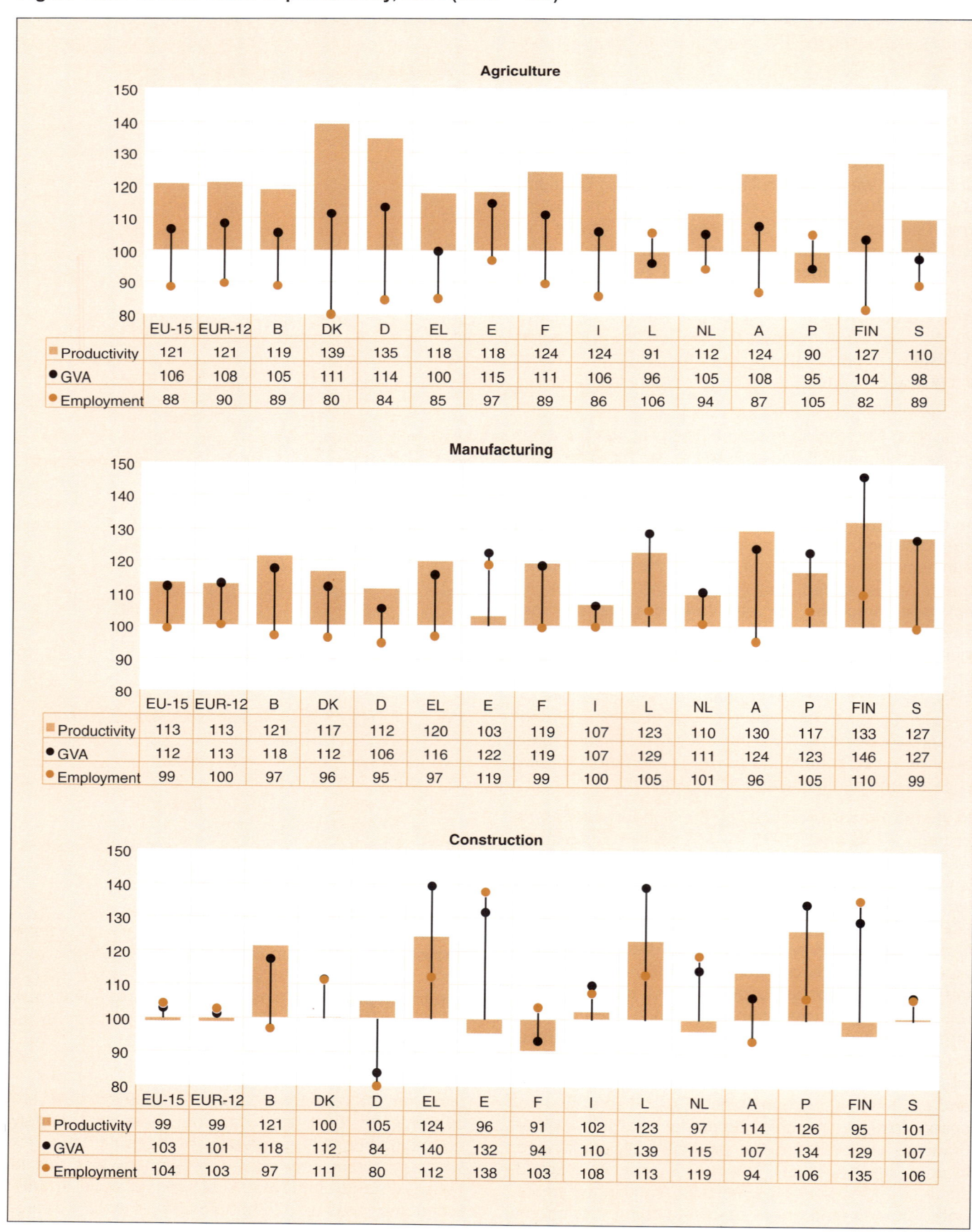

Agriculture

	EU-15	EUR-12	B	DK	D	EL	E	F	I	L	NL	A	P	FIN	S
Productivity	121	121	119	139	135	118	118	124	124	91	112	124	90	127	110
GVA	106	108	105	111	114	100	115	111	106	96	105	108	95	104	98
Employment	88	90	89	80	84	85	97	89	86	106	94	87	105	82	89

Manufacturing

	EU-15	EUR-12	B	DK	D	EL	E	F	I	L	NL	A	P	FIN	S
Productivity	113	113	121	117	112	120	103	119	107	123	110	130	117	133	127
GVA	112	113	118	112	106	116	122	119	107	129	111	124	123	146	127
Employment	99	100	97	96	95	97	119	99	100	105	101	96	105	110	99

Construction

	EU-15	EUR-12	B	DK	D	EL	E	F	I	L	NL	A	P	FIN	S
Productivity	99	99	121	100	105	124	96	91	102	123	97	114	126	95	101
GVA	103	101	118	112	84	140	132	94	110	139	115	107	134	129	107
Employment	104	103	97	111	80	112	138	103	108	113	119	94	106	135	106

ECONOMY OF THE UNION

Trade, transport and communication

	EU-15	EUR-12	B	DK	D	EL	E	F	I	L	NL	A	P	FIN	S
Productivity	112	110	107	115	112	136	106	109	104	124	115	113	120	118	116
GVA	123	121	111	124	119	143	125	123	115	157	135	118	124	136	126
Employment	110	110	104	107	106	118	112	110	126	118	104	103	115	108	

Financial services and business activities

	EU-15	EUR-12	B	DK	D	EL	E	F	I	L	NL	A	P	FIN	S
Productivity	98	95	101	98	95	102	91	93	91	80	95	91	149	96	94
GVA	126	124	105	126	128	123	119	117	120	133	130	118	150	132	121
Employment	129	130	104	129	134	121	131	127	133	167	136	130	100	137	129

Other services

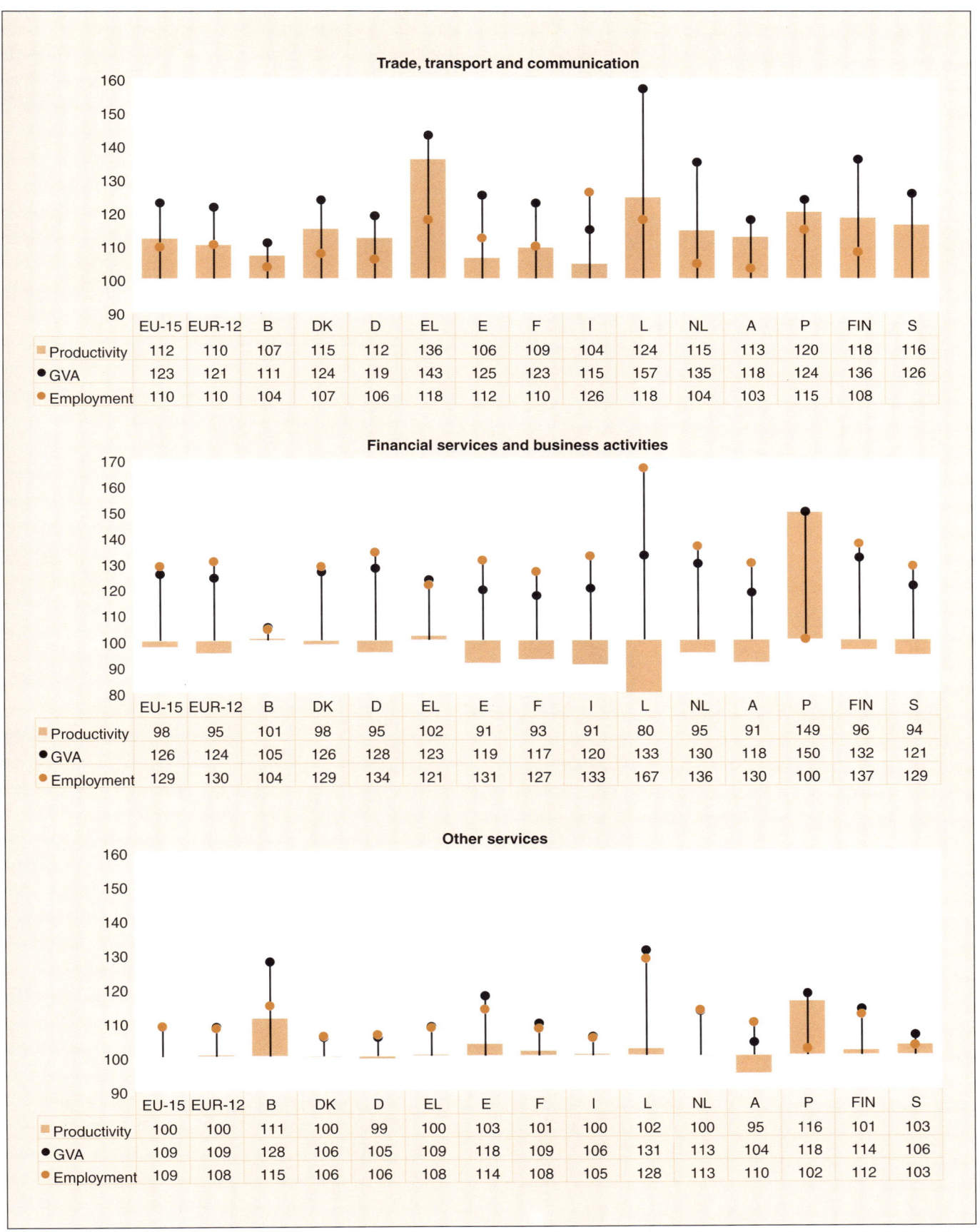

	EU-15	EUR-12	B	DK	D	EL	E	F	I	L	NL	A	P	FIN	S
Productivity	100	100	111	100	99	100	103	101	100	102	100	95	116	101	103
GVA	109	109	128	106	105	109	118	109	106	131	113	104	118	114	106
Employment	109	108	115	106	106	108	114	108	105	128	113	110	102	112	103

NB: Productivity growth was not calculated for the United Kingdom due to lack of data on employment per branch, in Ireland due to lack of data on GVA at constant prices per branch. Data for Luxembourg and Portugal are Eurostat estimates in part.
Source: Eurostat.

was down and employment up. Regarding the figures for the whole economy in 2001, productivity rose in all Member States, resulting from increases in GVA larger than those in employment. Among the biggest four economies, productivity growth from 1995 to 2001 was highest in the United Kingdom (+ 10 %), followed by Germany (+ 9 %), France (+ 6 %) and Italy (+ 5 %).

As observed, analysing variations in productivity is somewhat complex because it involves two factors and therefore two variations. Figure 1.3.8 illustrates the growth indices in terms of volume for productivity and its components (GVA and employment) both graphically and numerically. The data that are provided can thus be used to compare variations in productivity over the six branches and over the available Member States.

1.4. National income and the distribution breakdown of GDP

Distribution of GDP — income side

Section 1.2 looked at GDP as the sum of the end uses of goods and services, i.e. from the demand (or expenditure) side, while Section 1.3 was devoted to the analysis of the production (or output) side, expressing total GVA by adding up the value added over the branch of the economy that created it. Yet another definition, and another way of calculating GDP, is to look at the income produced and how that income is divided among the various recipients. To use the terminology of ESA 95, this is the primary distribution of income, i.e. distribution among the factors of production and general government. For the factors of production, labour is remunerated by compensation of employees and capital by operating surplus and mixed income. General government, however, receives income in the form of taxes.

GDP as the sum of primary incomes generated is thus broken down in ESA 95 as follows:

1. compensation of employees;
2. operating surplus or mixed income;
3. net taxes (taxes less subsidies) on production and imports.

It should be noted that income aggregates are compiled in current prices only, since it is conceptually difficult to define a "volume" component. All value growth indices are based on evaluations in euro.

In 2001, compensation of employees in the European Union accounted for more than half (51.3 %) of all generated income, with operating surplus and taxes accounting for 36.3 % and 12.3 % respectively. The structure of the income distribution has only changed slightly over the last years: compared with 1997, compensation of employees accounted for a bigger share of GDP in 2001, with a figure that was 0.5 percentage points up on the previous year. Operating surplus was down (– 1.1 points), while taxes increased their share by 0.5 points. When the changes are considered in absolute terms (value growth index), this time with 1995 as the benchmark year (1995 = 100), incomes in 2001 showed a broadly similar rise for both compensation of employees (+ 33.2 %) and for gross operating surplus and mixed income (+ 31.0 %). Taxes, on the other hand, showed a more pronounced rise of 45.4 % (see Figure 1.4.1).

With regard to the structure of GDP in the euro-zone, the percentage share of compensation of employees actually fell from 1997 to 2001 (– 0.2 percentage points), the difference to EU-15 being largely due to the relative importance of this component going up

Figure 1.4.1. Gross domestic product in EU-15: income side

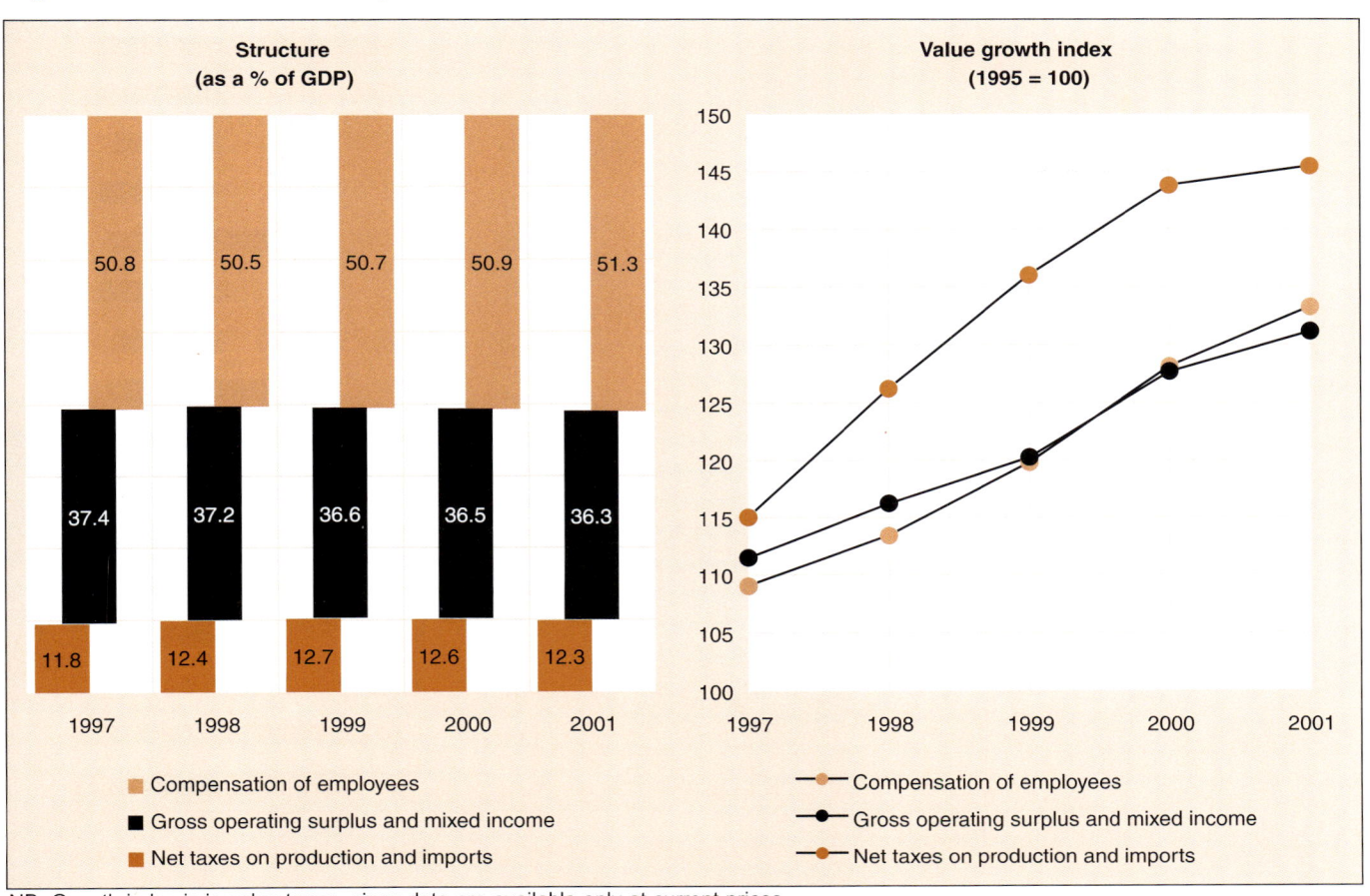

NB: Growth index is in value terms, since data are available only at current prices.
Source: Eurostat.

ECONOMY OF THE UNION

sizeably in the United Kingdom and Sweden. The share of gross operating surplus and mixed income was down by 0.3 points, while the compensating rise in taxes on production and imports (+ 0.5 points) matched the EU-15 figure (see Figure 1.4.2). A look at the value growth index (1995 = 100) presented in Table 1.4.2 shows that the figures for the three components were consistently lower in the euro-zone than in the Community as a whole: + 23.1 % against + 33.2 % for compensation of employees, + 27.1 % against + 31.0 % for gross operating surplus and mixed income and + 36.8 % against + 45.4 % for net taxes. Here, again, a major factor in these differences was the performance of the United Kingdom, where growth figures for every variable were among the highest in the Union.

Regarding the four biggest economies of the European Union, compensation of employees showed a decreasing importance as a component of GDP in Italy, while remaining virtually unchanged in Germany and increasing its percentage share in France and particularly in the United Kingdom. For gross operating surplus and mixed income, this component's share of GDP went down slightly in Italy, France and Germany and strongly so in the United Kingdom. Lastly, taxes increased their percentage share in all four countries except France, with Italy showing a particularly strong increase. Among these four countries, the smallest overall changes in the composition of GDP since 1997 were those for Germany.

As for the absolute variation (value growth index 1995 = 100, see Table 1.4.2) of income components in the biggest Member States, the United Kingdom stood out in 2001 for the size of its increases for all components of income: + 91.7 % for compensation of employees, + 68.7 % for gross operating surplus and mixed income and + 89.4 % for net taxes on production and imports. The increases were noticeable in Italy as well, especially for taxes, which showed an increase of + 80.0 % compared with 1995. In France the variations were more contained, while the value growth in Germany was one of the weakest amongst all Member States for each of the three components.

Table 1.4.1. Structure of GDP — income side, 2001 (as a % of GDP)

	Compensation of employees	Gross operating surplus and mixed income	Net taxes on production and imports
EU-15	51.3	36.3	12.3
EUR-12	49.8	38.2	12.0
B	52.3	35.9	11.8
DK	53.4	32.0	14.6
D	53.8	35.6	10.5
EL	32.5	54.6	12.9
E	50.0	40.1	9.9
F	52.9	33.3	13.8
IRL	39.9	48.7	11.5
I	40.9	45.6	13.5
L	53.0	34.1	12.9
NL	52.0	36.6	11.4
A	52.4	35.0	12.6
P	45.0	42.1	12.9
FIN	48.4	40.0	11.6
S	59.5	27.4	13.1
UK	56.3	30.6	13.4

NB: Eurostat estimation for Ireland and Portugal.
Source: Eurostat.

A more detailed look at the structure of GDP shows that compensation of employees was the major component in most Member States in 2001, with the highest figures occurring in Sweden (59.5 %) and the United Kingdom (56.3 %). In Greece, Ireland and Italy, however, it was gross operating surplus that was the single largest contributor to GDP. Greece clearly stood out as having the lowest percentage share for compensation of employees (32.5 %) of all Member States and the highest for gross operating surplus and mixed income (54.6 %) (see Table 1.4.1).

When comparing the situation in 2001 with that of 1997 in Figure 1.4.2, there is a significant tendency towards growing shares of compensation of employees as a component of GDP only for Sweden and the United Kingdom, while the opposite is true for three members of the euro-zone, namely Ireland, Italy and Portugal, thus explaining the difference observed between EU-15 and the euro-zone. In the case of gross operating surplus and mixed income, markedly falling shares were seen in Luxembourg, the Netherlands, Sweden and the United Kingdom, while the opposite was true for Ireland and Portugal. The share in GDP of taxes on production and imports went up in the majority of Member States, notable exceptions being France and Finland, where the downward changes were rather small, though. The biggest increase in the percentage share of taxes on GDP was recorded in Italy (see Figure 1.4.2).

A look at the absolute variation (value growth index 1995 =100) shows that the Member States which recorded the biggest variations for every component were the United Kingdom and Ireland. Compensation of employees showed only quite modest increases in Germany (+ 6.8 %) and Austria (+ 13.6 %). Gross operating surplus and mixed income more than doubled in Ireland (+ 152.2 %) over the period under review, while at the other extreme Sweden recorded virtually no rise at all (+ 0.3 %). The component that tended to produce the biggest increases was taxes on products and imports: apart from Ireland (+ 144.0 %) and the United Kingdom (+ 89.4 %), there were significant increases also in a number of other Member States, notably Italy (+ 80.0 %), Greece (+ 75.7 %) and Luxembourg (+ 69.4 %) (see Table 1.4.2).

Table 1.4.2. Value growth index of GDP components — income side, 2001 (1995 = 100)

	Compensation of employees	Gross operating surplus and mixed income	Net taxes on production and imports
EU-15	133.2	131.0	145.4
EUR-12	123.1	127.1	136.8
B	122.0	118.3	127.0
DK	132.2	125.3	139.9
D	106.8	112.4	117.0
EL	146.3	138.7	175.7
E	145.8	140.8	165.9
F	125.0	120.9	122.0
IRL	199.9	252.2	244.0
I	139.2	142.1	180.0
L	152.2	149.9	169.4
NL	136.8	125.7	150.5
A	113.6	121.5	121.0
P	140.1	158.7	148.3
FIN	133.5	140.9	143.6
S	138.6	100.3	160.5
UK	191.7	168.7	189.4

NB: Eurostat estimation for Ireland and Portugal.
Source: Eurostat.

ECONOMY OF THE UNION

Figure 1.4.2. GDP components — income side — in 1997 and 2001 (as a % of GDP)

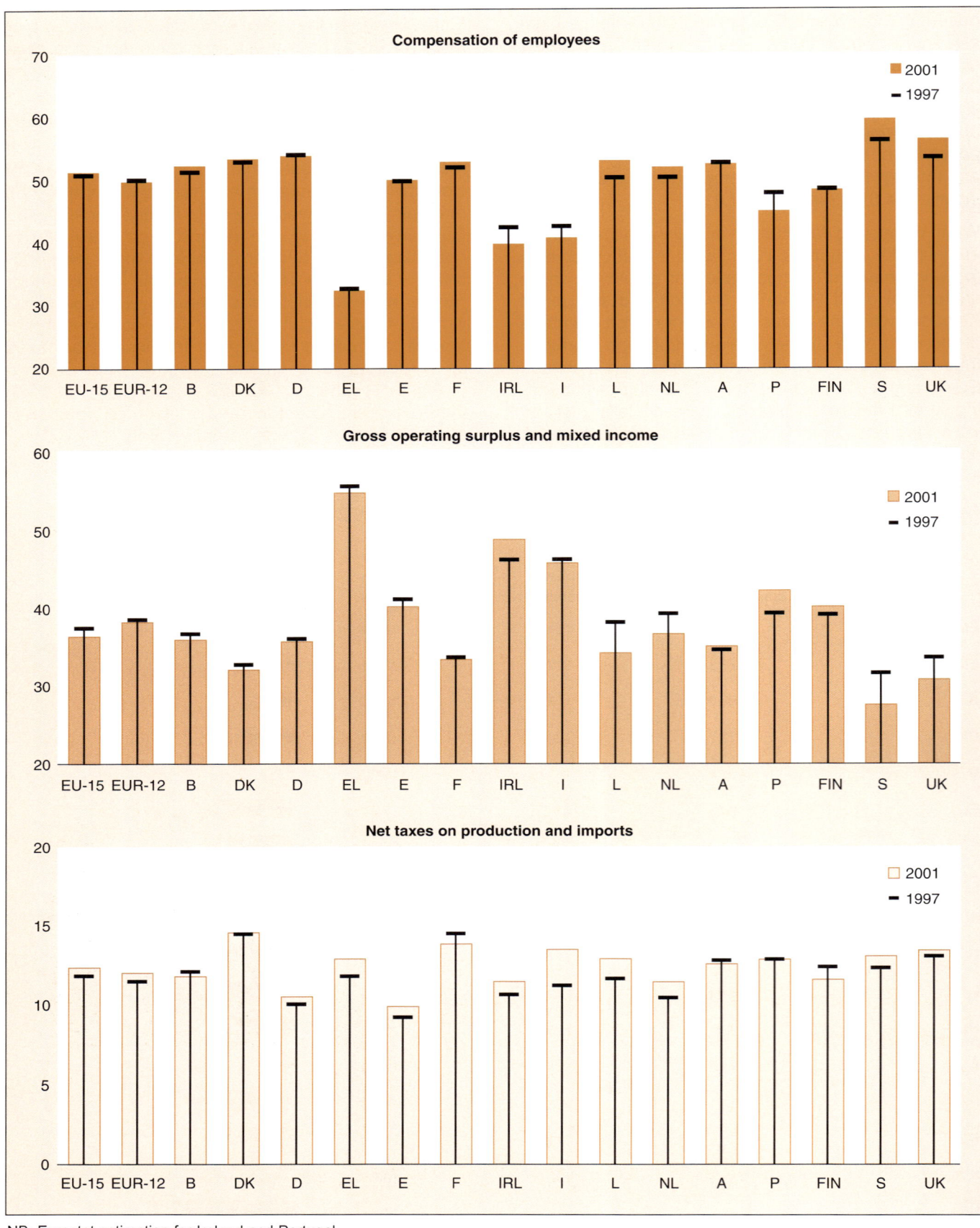

NB: Eurostat estimation for Ireland and Portugal.
Source: Eurostat.

ECONOMY OF THE UNION

Disposable income: breakdown between consumption and saving

Still on the income side, when net primary income abroad (i.e. the balance between transfers to and from other countries related to direct participation in productive processes) is deducted from GDP, the result is a figure for national income. When current transfers ([10]) are excluded from national income, what is left is national disposable income, or the resources that a country has at its disposal. These resources are divided between consumption and saving.

The disposable income of the European Union in 2001 amounted to EUR 8 733 billion, with EUR 6 934 billion going into both private and public consumption and EUR 1 799 billion earmarked for saving. In percentage terms, consumption accounted for 79.4 % of disposable income, and saving for the remaining 20.6 %. In absolute growth terms, disposable income in 2001 was 34.0 % higher than in the reference year (1995). The corresponding figure for consumption was 34.8 %, with saving showing a slightly lower increase of 30.7 % (see Figure 1.4.3).

Figure 1.4.3. Use of gross disposable income in EU-15

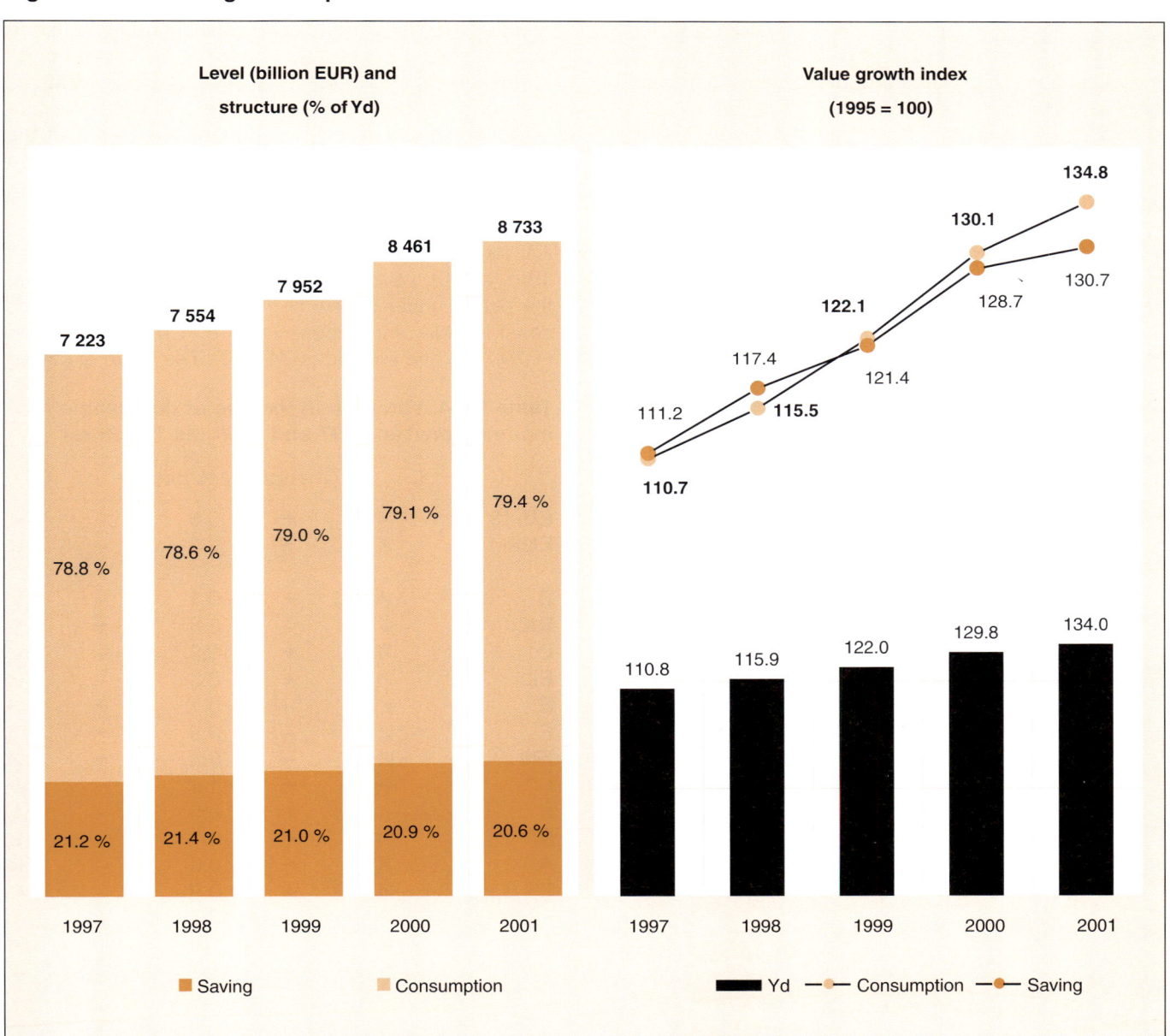

NB: Yd = disposable income; growth index is in value terms, since data are available only at current prices.
Source: Eurostat.

([10]) Current taxes on income, capital, etc., social contributions, social benefits and other current transfers.

ECONOMY OF THE UNION

In the euro-zone the division between consumption and saving is marked by a higher proportion devoted to saving; at 21.8 %, it is more than one percentage point higher than for the Union as a whole. The main reason for this is the situation in the United Kingdom, which stands out from all the other Member States with the lowest percentage of disposable income earmarked for saving (15.2 % in 2001). Among the biggest economies of the Union, there is a much greater propensity for saving in Italy (20.6 %), Germany (20.8 %) and France (21.4 %) (see Table 1.4.3). When these figures are compared with the benchmark figures for 1997, it shows that consumption was increasing its share at the expense of saving in Germany, in Italy and in the United Kingdom, the shift ranging between + 0.9 percentage points in Germany to + 1.7 % points in the United Kingdom. In France, on the other hand, saving as a percentage of disposable income went up by 0.9 points, and consequently consumption went down (see Table 1.4.4). As for the absolute variation in value terms compared to 1995, saving in France increased by 34.9 %, compared with only 21.5 % for consumption, whereas the increases in Germany were fairly contained (+ 3.1 % for saving and + 11.7 % for consumption). The variations in Italy were much larger in scale, with consumption (+ 48.9 %) ahead of saving (+ 36.9 %). Even bigger increases occurred in the United Kingdom, where saving increased by 79.7 % and consumption by 87.6 % between 1995 and 2001 (see Table 1.4.5).

Among all Member States, those most inclined to save rather than consume are Luxembourg (30.5 % of disposable income), Finland (27.9 %), the Netherlands (27.2 %) and Ireland (27.1 %). At the other extreme, consumption is highest — and saving lowest, of course — in the United Kingdom (84.8 %), Greece (83.2 %) and Portugal (81.1 %) (see Table 1.4.3).

When the composition of disposable income for 1997 and 2001 is compared, the biggest changes appear in Luxembourg, Finland and Denmark. In Luxembourg, alongside the United Kingdom, Italy, Germany, Portugal, the Netherlands, Greece and Belgium, consumption gained in relative importance, while over the same period, saving became more prominent as a use of disposable income in Finland, Denmark, Sweden, France, Ireland and Greece (see Table 1.4.4).

As for the absolute variation (value growth index 1995 = 100), saving in Ireland more than doubled over the period under review (+ 150.3 %). There were also considerable increases in the United Kingdom (+ 79.7 %) and Finland (+ 74.4 %). The value of saving

Table 1.4.3. Use of disposable income, 2001

	Disposable income (billion EUR)		Redistribution C / S	
EU-15	8 733	79.4		20.6
EUR-12	6 735	78.2		21.8
B	260	74.8		25.2
DK	173	75.4		24.6
D	2 035	79.2		20.8
EL	133	83.2		16.8
E	641	77.2		22.8
F	1 459	78.6		21.4
IRL	97	72.9		27.1
I	1 205	79.4		20.6
L	18	69.5		30.5
NL	425	72.8		27.2
A	207	78.1		21.9
P	123	81.1		18.9
FIN	134	72.1		27.9
S	228	78.5		21.5
UK	1 605	84.8		15.2

NB: Eurostat estimation for Spain, Ireland and Luxembourg.
Source: Eurostat.

Table 1.4.4. Variation in the use of disposable income between 1997 and 2001 (as % points)

	C	Change as % points		S
EU-15	↗	+	0.6	–	↙
EUR-12	↗	+	0.3	–	↙
B	↗	+	0.1	–	↙
DK	↓	–	2.8	+	↑
D	↗	+	0.9	–	↙
EL	↗	+	0.3	–	↙
E	↙	–	0.1	+	↗
F	↙	–	0.9	+	↗
IRL	↙	–	0.8	+	↗
I	↑	+	1.3	–	↓
L	↑	+	8.5	–	↓
NL	↗	+	0.7	–	↙
A	↗	+	0.0	–	↙
P	↗	+	0.9	–	↙
FIN	↓	–	3.2	+	↑
S	↙	–	1.0	+	↗
UK	↑	+	1.7	–	↓

NB:

↗ ↙ slight variation: below 1 percentage point.
↑ ↓ moderate variation: 1-3 percentage points.
↑ ↓ strong variation: over 3 percentage points

NB: Eurostat estimation for Greece, Ireland and Austria.
Source: Eurostat.

increased by only 3.1 % since 1995 in Germany, and in Luxembourg, this value even declined by 5 %. Ireland (+ 95.1 %) and the United Kingdom (+ 87.6 %) also were the countries with the largest increases in the value of consumption in comparison to the reference year 1995 (see Table 1.4.5).

Table 1.4.5. Value growth index for the uses of disposable income, 2001 (1995 = 100)

	Saving	Consumption
EU-15	130.7	134.8
EUR-12	125.2	126.2
B	121.8	121.8
DK	152.1	124.4
D	103.1	111.7
EL	137.4	139.0
E	146.9	142.0
F	134.9	121.5
IRL	250.3	195.1
I	136.9	148.9
L	95.0	136.4
NL	133.0	133.4
A	115.8	117.3
P	131.4	147.5
FIN	174.7	130.8
S	131.3	127.4
UK	179.7	187.6

NB: Eurostat estimation for Spain, Ireland and Luxembourg.
Source: Eurostat.

Net lending/borrowing

In a final step, a country's resources that are not consumed are either saved or invested or transferred to or from the country. The balance between saving, investment (capital formation) and net capital transactions with other countries therefore provides a summary of the country's lending/borrowing in relation to the rest of the world.

In 2001, the European Union's lending position amounted to about EUR 38.9 billion. This position remained steadily in the black in the period under review, with the highest value attained in 1997, when EUR 112.0 billion was lent to the rest of the world. The figures for the euro-zone were a little below the EU-15 figures until 1998, when the EUR-12 figure of EUR 73.3 billion almost coincided with the figure for the Union as a whole (EUR 74.2 billion) and passed it one year later. This gap widened in 2000, when the euro-zone lent EUR 25.7 billion to the rest of the world, well ahead of the EU-15 figure of only EUR 2.0 billion. In 2001, the downward trend was reversed: the euro-zone's net lending amounted to EUR 49.3 billion and EU-15's to EUR 38.9 billion. The main reason for this difference is the borrowing position of the United Kingdom, where in 2001 the net borrowing figure reached EUR 25.7 billion. France and Italy produced net lending figures throughout the period under review (1997-2001), though with a tendency of diminishing in size. Germany, on the other hand, consistently generated borrowing positions until 2000, while in 2001, Germany lent EUR 10 billion to the rest of the world (see Table 1.4.6).

Apart from the United Kingdom, the other Member States known to be in a position of net borrowing in 2001 were Greece, Spain, Austria and Portugal, of which all except Spain had been so for the whole period covered. Besides France, Germany and Italy, other important net lenders were the Netherlands, Belgium, Finland, Sweden and Denmark.

Table 1.4.6. Net lending and borrowing (billion EUR, current prices)

	1997	1998	1999	2000	2001
EU-15	112.0	74.2	33.1	2.0	38.9
EUR-12	103.1	73.3	50.3	25.7	49.3
B	11.5	11.3	12.5	11.2	12.3
DK	0.7	− 1.4	3.7	2.8	4.6
D	− 1.7	− 5.2	− 15.4	− 3.9	10.0
EL	− 0.4	− 1.5	− 1.2	− 2.7	− 5.1
E	7.9	2.5	− 6.4	− 15.1	− 12.2
F	31.5	30.5	33.5	17.6	17.2
IRL	2.6	2.2	1.5	1.5	0.5
I	31.5	22.8	13.7	1.3	8.6
L	:	:	:	:	:
NL	19.2	9.9	14.7	18.9	21.6
A	− 4.8	− 4.1	− 6.3	− 6.1	− 4.6
P	− 2.8	− 4.5	− 6.5	− 9.9	− 9.6
FIN	6.2	6.1	7.7	10.4	10.1
S	8.2	8.1	6.2	8.6	7.4
UK	− 1.3	− 6.4	− 27.8	− 25.2	− 25.7

NB: Eurostat estimation for Ireland. For Luxembourg, no ESA 95 data are available. The ESA 79 net lending/borrowing had been EUR 3.5 billion in 1997.
Source: Eurostat.

ECONOMY OF THE UNION

Figure 1.4.4. Net lending/borrowing

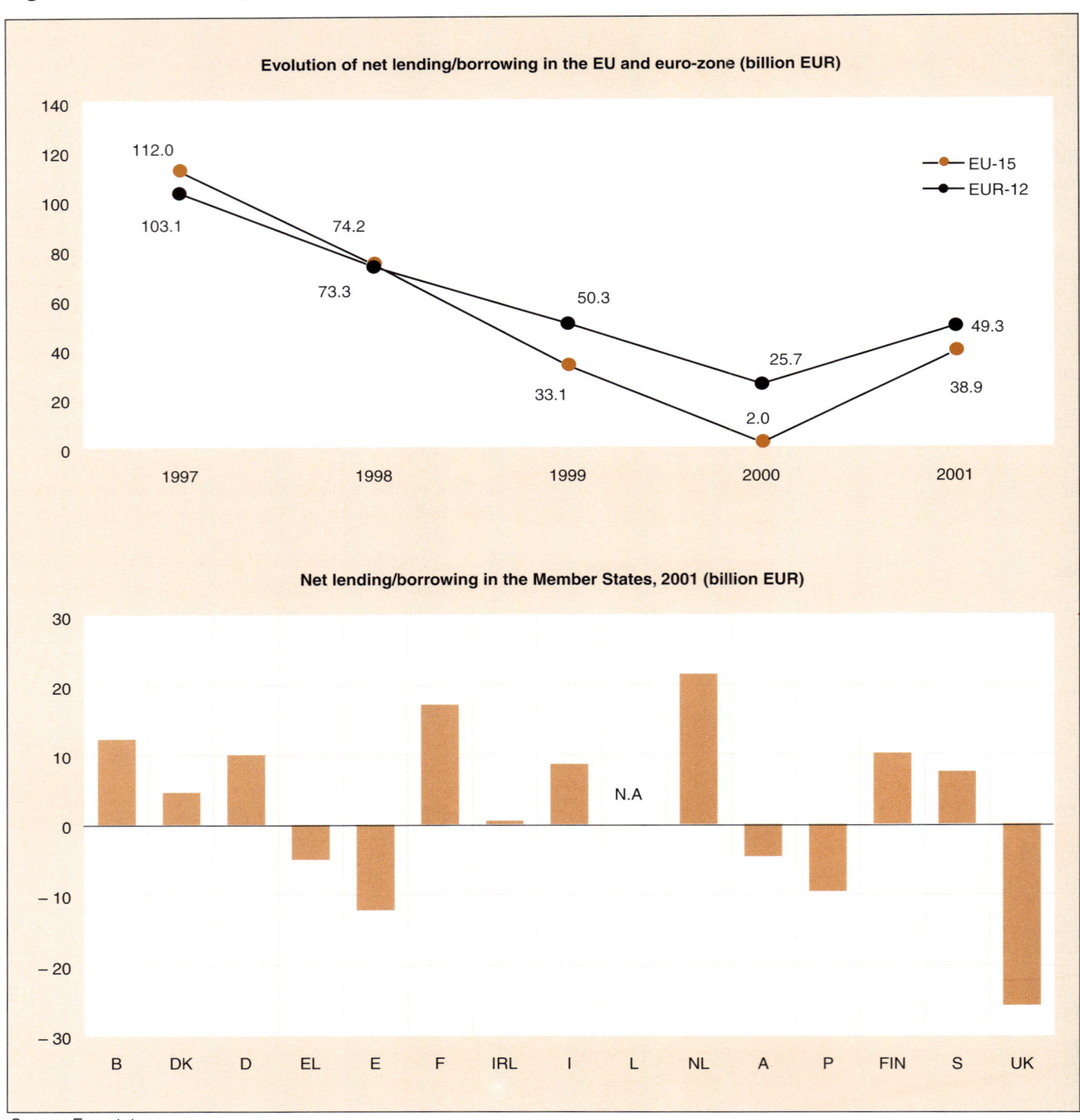

Evolution of net lending/borrowing in the EU and euro-zone (billion EUR)

Year	EU-15	EUR-12
1997	112.0	103.1
1998	74.2	73.3
1999	33.1	50.3
2000	2.0	25.7
2001	38.9	49.3

Net lending/borrowing in the Member States, 2001 (billion EUR)

L: N.A

Source: Eurostat.

ECONOMY OF THE UNION

1.5. The economic situation of the regions

Per capita GDP in the EU regions in 1999

The gross domestic product at market prices per inhabitant — one of the key indicators for the EU's structural and regional policies — had a smaller range of values in 1999 than in 1998. In 1999 it varied between 10 846 PPS in the French overseas department of Réunion and 51 392 PPS in Inner London. When expressed as a percentage of the EU average, the values thus ranged between 51 % and 242 % of the EU value.

Table 1.5.1 shows that regions with relatively high per capita GDP values in PPS are located more or less in the centre of the EU. The situation is quite different for the regions with the lowest per capita GDP values: they are either in the Mediterranean area — four in Greece, two in Portugal and one in Spain — or are French overseas departments (three regions). The gap between the regions with the highest and lowest per capita GDP values in PPS and the EU average became smaller in 1999. Inner London still leads followed by Région Bruxelles-Capitale. The next eight regions of the 10 best, however, moved closer to the top two in 1999. This also applies to the regions with the lowest per capita GDP. They, too, moved closer together. The Greek region of Ipeiros, which in 1998 still had the lowest value by far, managed to close the gap in 1999 and move up to the regions ahead of it.

Table 1.5.1. The regions of the EU with the highest/lowest per capita GDP in PPS, EU-15 =100

Regions	1998	1999
Inner London	252	242
Région Bruxelles-Capitale	227	217
Luxembourg (Grand Duchy)	178	186
Hamburg	183	183
Île de France	153	154
Oberbayern	150	151
Wien	149	150
Darmstadt	147	147
Utrecht	145	146
Bremen	142	142
EU-15	**100**	**100**
Centro (P)	57	57
Anatoliki Makedonia, Thraki	55	56
Guadeloupe	56	56
Peloponnisos	56	55
Dytiki Ellada	51	53
Açores	52	53
Extremadura	49	52
Guyane	51	51
Ipeiros	46	51
Réunion	51	51

Source: Eurostat.

It is striking that all regions with high per capita GDP values in PPS are relatively small in area. They benefit from high net commuter inflows which take the production activity in these regions beyond the level possible with working residents alone.

Comparison between 1995 and 1999 per capita GDP values

In this comparison it should be noted that the relative changes reflect not only developments in production activity: they are also influenced by changes in the size and structure of the population and the purchasing power parities.

A comparison of the situations in 1995 and 1999 shows clear differences between the EU regions. In only 39 of the 211 regions for which basically comparable data are available there was hardly any change in the per capita GDP value as a percentage of the EU average from 1995 to 1999 (ranging between 1.0 and − 1.0 percentage points). In 83 regions, however, the value rose by more than one percentage point and in 89 regions it fell by more than one percentage point.

The sharpest relative rise in the reference period was in the Irish region of Southern and Eastern, where per capita GDP as a percentage of the EU average over this period rose from just under 102 % to over 122 %: more than 20 percentage points.

Table 1.5.2. The regions of the EU with the highest increase and decrease in percentage points of the per capita GDP in PPS relative to EU-15 per capita GDP in PPS from 1995 to 1999

Regions	Relative increase/decrease
Southern and eastern	20.5
Åland	18.8
Utrecht	15.8
Luxembourg (Grand Duchy)	15.1
Hampshire and the Isle of Wight	14.1
Border, Midland and Western	12.2
Inner London	11.9
Surrey, East and West Sussex	11.4
Berkshire, Buckinghamshire and Oxfordshire	11.0
Uusimaa	10.8
EU-15	**0.0**
Koblenz	− 7.3
Detmold	− 7.5
Lüneburg	− 7.8
Réunion	− 7.8
Trier	− 7.9
Région Bruxelles-Capitale	− 8.0
Västsverige	− 8.7
Antwerpen	− 9.0
Valle d'Aosta	− 10.5
Berlin	− 11.8

Source: Eurostat.

Table 1.5.2. shows further regions with particularly sharp relative increases or decreases in per capita GDP in PPS. A point of particular note regarding the 10 regions with the sharpest increases is that three of them in 1995 still lay below the EU average for absolute per capita GDP. These were the English regions of "Hampshire and the Isle of Wight" and "Berkshire, Buckinghamshire and Oxfordshire", and the Irish region "Border, Midland and Western". The latter is the only one of these three which did not reach the EU average per capita GDP in 1999 either. The top 10 regions are all in the northern part of the EU. Four are in the United Kingdom, two are in Ireland and two in Finland. In addition we have Utrecht in the Netherlands and the Grand Duchy of Luxembourg. The group of the top 10 regions with the sharpest declines include five German, two Belgian and one French, Italian and Swedish region. Of these 10 regions, five had an absolute per capita GDP lower than the EU average both in 1995 and 1999. Four regions had values above the absolute EU average in both years. In the Berlin region, the per capita GDP was above it in 1995 and below it in 1999.

Regional unemployment in 2001

The unemployment rate, i.e. the ratio of unemployed persons to the labour force, was 7.6 % in the European Union in April 2001. If we only look at the NUTS II regions, the unemployment rate ranged between 1.2 % in the Dutch region of Utrecht and 33.3 % in the French region of Réunion. As a result, for every 100 members of the active population in each case, there were about 28 times as many people unemployed in Réunion as in the Utrecht region.

In 2001, the difference between the positive and negative extreme values was similar to that of the year 2000. Of the 208 ([11]) regions considered, in April 2001, 54 had a maximum unemployment rate of 3.8 % and thus lay some 50 % or more below the EU average. These 54 NUTS II regions were spread over 11 Member States. Only Greece, Spain and France had no NUTS II region with an unemployment rate as low as or below 3.8 %. This also applies to Denmark. Compared with the situation in 2000, the group of 10 regions with the lowest unemployment rates has now been joined by the regions of Flevoland, Noord-Holland, Zuid-Holland and Açores. The negative end of the scale is formed by a total of 16 regions: five from Italy, three each from France and Germany, four from Spain and one from Greece have an unemployment rate of over 15.2 %, which is at least twice as high as the average for the European Union as a whole. On the other hand, no region left the group of 10 with the highest rates compared with the list for the year 2000.

Table 1.5.3. The regions of the EU with the highest/lowest unemployment rates in April 2001 (as a %)

Regions	Unemployment rate
Utrecht	1.2
Åland	1.3
Berkshire, Buckinghamshire and Oxfordshire	1.6
Flevoland	1.9
Surrey, East and West Sussex	2.0
Noord-Brabant	2.0
Noord-Holland	2.0
Oberösterreich	2.1
Zuid-Holland	2.1
Açores	2.2
EU-15	**7.6**
Guyane	20.5
Sicilia	20.8
Ceuta y Melilla	21.9
Extremadura	22.1
Andalucia	22.3
Campania	22.4
Calabria	24.8
Martinique	26.3
Guadeloupe	29.0
Réunion	33.3

Source: Eurostat.

Change in the unemployment rate from 1997 to 2001

The unemployment rate fell by 2.9 percentage points for the EU as a whole between April 1997 and April 2001. Over 40 % of all regions show a better trend than the EU average. The others — just under 60 % — have either the EU average or worse results. In a total of 189 regions of the 201 ([12]) regions considered for which data are available, a decline was recorded in this period, the highest value of 9.9 percentage points being registered in the Comunidad Valenciana region (E). Of the 10 regions where the unemployment rate had the sharpest decline between April 1997 and April 2001, eight are located in Spain and one in Ireland and Italy respectively.

([11]) For the German regions of Koblenz, Trier and Rheinhessen-Pfalz, no data are available for 2001.

([12]) For the French overseas departments and the German regions of Koblenz, Trier and Rheinhessen-Pfalz, Chemnitz, Dresden and Leipzig there are no data available either for 1997 or for 2001.

Table 1.5.4. The regions in the EU with the highest increase and decrease of unemployment rates from 1997 to 2001 (in percentage points)

Regions	Decrease/increase
Comunidad Valenciana	– 9.9
Andalucia	– 9.4
Cataluña	– 8.5
Comunidad de Madrid	– 8.4
Canarias	– 7.6
Cantabria	– 7.6
Castilla y León	– 7.5
Pais Vasco	– 7.5
Extremadura	– 7.2
Southern and Eastern	– 6.9
EU-15	– 2.9
Anatoliki Makedonia, Thraki	0.7
Calabria	0.9
Sterea Ellada	1.3
Kriti	1.4
Ipeiros	1.5
Kentriki Makedonia	1.5
Dytiki Makedonia	2.0
Dytiki Ellada	2.0
Thessalia	4.1
Notio Aigaio	5.4

Source: Eurostat.

An increase in the unemployment rate was recorded in only 12 regions, the highest increase — of 5.4 percentage points — being recorded in the region Notio Aigaio (EL). Eleven of these regions lie in Greece and one in Italy. Compared with the previous five-year period, the regions of Berlin, Voreio Aigaio, Peloponnisos and Sicilia have moved out of this group. They have all been replaced by Greek regions.

2. The Union in the international framework

2.1. The EU in the world

In 2001, most of the world's economies experienced growth well below that of the previous year and also lower than the average of the last five years (see Table 2.1.1). The US economy experienced a significant decline of GDP growth after having grown vigorously during the preceding years: GDP rose by an annual rate of only 0.3 %. Domestic demand showed mixed results: – 2.7 % for investment, but + 2.5 % for private consumption and + 3.7 % for government consumption. External trade was very weak, exports declined by 5.4 % and imports by 2.9 %. The US is notable for its large share of private consumption, which accounted for 68 % of GDP in 2001 (see Table 2.1.2).

Canada also registered much lower growth than in the previous year, with a 2001 annual rate of 1.4 %. Investment growth was strongly reduced, but the 2001 growth rate of 1.7 % still compared favourably to the decreases recorded in the EU, the United States and Japan. Private consumption increased by 2.7 % and government consumption accelerated to 3.4 %.

The Japanese economy was weak, not only compared to its trading partners, but also in absolute terms: GDP actually declined by 0.6 %. As in the previous years, government consumption was the most buoyant component with an annual growth rate of 3.1 %, while private consumption slowed down to an annual rate of increase of 0.3 %. Investment diminished by 1.9 %, and while both exports and imports were sinking, exports did so at a much faster rate of 6.6%, thus contributing to the decline in GDP.

All of the G7 countries saw significantly reduced growth. The EU-15's 1.5 %, achieved despite poor growth in Germany, now marks the top of the range, together with Canada. The United States could not maintain its growth advantage over the European economies, and the recovery of growth observed in Japan was reversed. The slowdown in growth was, however, an almost global phenomenon.

Growth was down by 4 percentage points to 5.0 % in 2001 in the Russian Federation, but well above the average growth during the last five years. In Australia, the loss of pace was smaller, continuing the downward growth trend of the previous years.

In Asia, the newly industrialised countries that had seen strong growth in 2000, recorded very strong drops in GDP growth. Among the group of the four most developed Asian countries, the strongest deceleration and the lowest overall growth was recorded in Singapore, where real GDP fell by 2.1 %, down more than 12 percentage points from 2000. For Hong Kong, too, the growth reduction was more than 10 percentage points, even if overall growth was still slightly positive at 0.1 %. In South Korea, GDP slowed down to 3.0 % growth, which does not seem too bad in comparison. In Taiwan, where growth in 2000 had been below that of the other countries mentioned, GDP declined by 1.9 %, i.e. almost at the same pace as in Singapore. All four countries mentioned have comparatively high shares of exports and imports in GDP, and this is especially true for Hong Kong and Singapore. Among the other south-east Asian countries, Malaysia, the Philippines and Thailand were also seen to reduce economic growth, albeit to a different degree. While Malaysia experienced a drop of almost 8 percentage points in the growth rate, from 8.3 % in 2000 to 0.4 % in 2001, growth of GDP in the Philippines was only slightly reduced to 3.4 %. However, both the Philippines and Thailand showed growth rates above the five-year average.

Table 2.1.1. Real GDP growth rates (as a %)

	2000	2001	Average 1997/2001
EU-15	3.5	1.5	2.6
EUR-12	3.5	1.4	2.6
US	3.8	0.3	3.4
Canada	4.7	1.4	4.0
JP	2.4	– 0.6	0.6
Australia	3.2	2.4	3.9
Russian Federation	9.0	5.0	3.0
Argentina	– 0.8	– 3.7	0.7
Brazil	4.4	1.5	2.0
Chile	4.4	2.8	3.2
Mexico	6.6	– 0.3	4.3
Hong Kong	10.5	0.1	2.5
Taiwan	5.9	– 1.9	4.1
South Korea	9.3	3.0	4.1
Singapore	10.3	– 2.1	4.6
Malaysia	8.3	0.4	2.8
Philippines	4.0	3.4	3.1
Thailand	4.6	1.8	-0.4
China	8.0	7.3	7.8
India	5.4	4.3	5.4
Israel	6.4	– 0.6	2.9
Saudi Arabia	4.5	2.2	1.9
South Africa	3.4	2.2	2.2
Nigeria	3.8	4.0	2.8
Algeria	2.4	3.5	3.1

Source: IMF, Eurostat.

THE UNION IN THE INTERNATIONAL FRAMEWORK

With a growth of 7.3 % in 2001, China almost maintained the pace of economic expansion, which had been fast during all the preceding years, with an average annual increase of 7.8 % over the last five years. For India, the decrease in the annual growth rate was slightly bigger, but the 4.3 % rate observed in 2001 was still one of the highest listed in Table 2.1.1. Regarding the growth rates for expenditure components one year earlier, i.e. for 2000 in Table 2.1.2, a remarkable even growth among components is displayed, while the majority of countries had reported much higher growth in foreign trade than in domestic demand for that year.

The countries of Latin America, too, could not evade the global decrease of GDP growth rates. Argentina fared worst of the countries considered, the decline in GDP already experienced in 2000 (– 0.8 %) aggravating to – 3.7 %. Growth was substantially down in Mexico as well, and GDP was actually even declining

Table 2.1.2. GDP main components, 2001/2000

		Growth rates (as a %)					Structure (as a % of GDP)				
	Year	PC	GC	GFCF	EXP	IMP	PC	GC	GFCF	EXP	IMP
EU-15	2001	2.0	2.2	– 0.4	2.2	1.0	58.4	19.9	20.6	35.9	35.3
	2000	2.9	1.8	4.5	11.9	11.1	58.5	20.1	20.1	35.9	34.7
EUR-12	2001	1.7	2.2	– 0.5	2.4	0.8	57.1	19.8	21.6	37.2	36.3
	2000	2.5	1.9	4.7	12.3	10.9	57.3	19.9	21.1	37.3	35.6
US	2001	2.5	3.7	– 2.7	– 5.4	– 2.9	68.0	14.6	20.5	11.2	14.9
	2000	4.3	2.8	5.5	9.7	13.2	69.3	15.1	19.7	10.3	13.7
Canada	2001	2.7	3.4	1.7	– 4.0	– 5.7	55.8	18.4	19.7	100.5	40.3
	2000	3.8	2.4	7.5	8.4	8.7	56.8	18.7	19.8	43.3	38.1
JP	2001	0.3	3.1	– 1.9	– 6.6	– 0.6	55.9	16.7	26.3	10.8	9.3
	2000	0.6	4.6	3.2	12.4	9.6	56.4	17.5	25.8	10.4	9.8
Australia	2000	2.7	4.8	0.5	10.9	7.4	59.3	18.8	22.5	21.8	22.9
Russian Federation	2000	16.9	1.6	17.7	4.3	17.5	45.6	16.1	18.3	45.9	24.8
Argentina	2000	1.3	– 0.4	– 8.6	2.0	– 0.5	70.9	13.8	15.9	10.8	11.4
Brazil	2000	9.9	– 5.4	8.2	11.0	13.8	62.6	18.2	20.3	10.9	12.1
Chile	2000	4.1	3.5	4.3	7.5	10.1	63.3	12.2	22.3	31.8	30.8
Mexico	2000	9.5	3.5	10.0	16.0	21.4	67.5	11.0	20.9	31.4	33.2
Hong Kong	2000	5.5	2.1	9.8	16.7	16.7	58.1	9.6	26.3	150.0	145.3
Taiwan	2000	4.9	0.6	8.6	17.6	14.5	61.9	12.9	23.5	54.4	52.1
South Korea	2000	7.1	1.3	11.0	21.6	20.0	58.3	10.2	28.7	45.0	42.2
Singapore	2000	9.4	13.7	5.9	:	:	39.8	10.5	29.5	179.9	161.4
Malaysia	2000	– 20.9	6.1	6.1	26.2	16.3	42.7	10.6	25.6	125.5	104.4
Philippines	2000	3.1	– 1.1	– 5.0	6.6	0.2	63.2	12.8	20.5	56.3	50.2
Thailand	2000	4.5	6.5	5.7	15.4	20.4	59.8	9.4	21.3	67.0	59.0
China	2000	6.3	12.0	8.3	32.0	24.8	47.0	13.1	36.1	25.9	23.2
India	2000	4.2	6.5	4.7	5.0	5.0	65.4	13.2	21.9	14.0	16.6
Israel	2000	5.8	1.2	-1.3	23.3	11.4	59.1	28.5	17.8	40.0	46.9
Saudi Arabia	2000	:	:	:	:	:	32.8	27.0	15.7	49.6	25.7
South Africa	2000	3.2	– 2.5	1.3	8.2	7.4	63.6	18.4	14.9	29.1	26.1
Nigeria	2000	– 51.8	86.2	39.7	– 1.6	16.0	45.4	20.5	22.7	52.3	41.0
Algeria	2000	1.8	2.8	1.9	7.4	7.0	41.7	14.1	21.5	42.4	22.0

NB: PC : private consumption; GC: government consumption; GFCF: gross fixed capital formation; EXP: export of goods and services; IMP: import of goods and services.
Source: Eurostat, World Bank.

THE UNION IN THE INTERNATIONAL FRAMEWORK

slightly (– 0.3 %). Results in Brazil and Chile were somewhat better. Table 2.1.2 shows that the countries of Latin America all have relatively high proportions of GDP used for private consumption expenditure. Components growth rates in 2000, however, were quite disparate, with Argentina showing weak results across the board.

In order to give a more detailed picture of economic results, in addition to Table 2.1.1, illustrating GDP growth, Table 2.1.2 indicates the growth rates of the main components of GDP and their share of GDP. These figures refer mainly to 2000. Only for the biggest advanced economies are both 2000 and 2001 indicated.

In order to compare different countries and regions, the population and GDP have been selected to give an indication of size, whilst per capita GDP gives a measure of wealth (see Figure 2.1.1).

When compared with other major countries and regions, the population of the EU (6.3 %) as a share of the world's population is well above that of the United States (4.6 %) and three times Japan's (2.1 %). China's population, on the other hand, is more than three times bigger.

If we consider its economic weight in the world, the EU's share of world GDP is roughly a quarter (25.0 %) when expressed in current prices — the purchasing power equivalent would, of course, take a lesser part of the world total. In other words, the EU's share of GDP is four times larger than its share of world population, which translates into a GDP per head four times that of the total world average. Though their share of world population is higher, the GDP generated in the 15 European countries is lower than that produced in the United States (31.2 % of world total), but it is more than 3 000 billion USD higher than Japan's GDP (15.4 % of world total). Compared with some less well-off countries, while the EU's population is less than a third of that of China, its current USD GDP is more than seven times higher. These relations are even more extreme when comparing the EU to South Asia (including India as the biggest economy) or sub-Saharan Africa (including South Africa).

Figure 2.1.1. Size of world's main economies, 2000

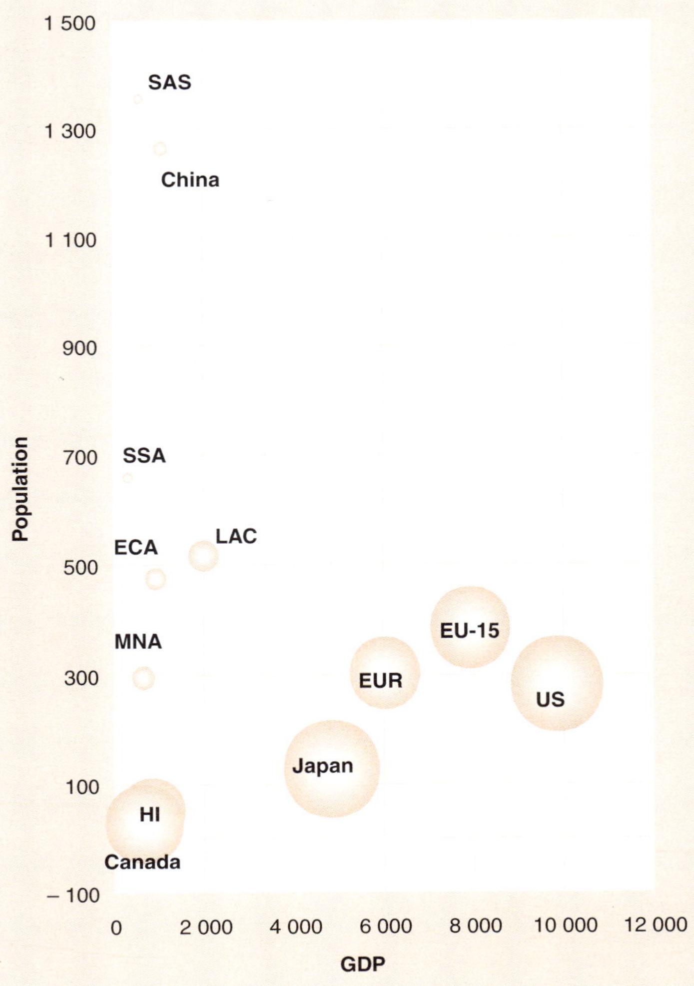

	GDP (billion of USD)	Population (million)	GDP per head (in USD)
EU-15	7 874.8	378.7	20 800
EUR-12	6 048.4	304.0	19 900
US	9 837.4	281.6	34 900
Japan	4 841.6	126.9	38 200
Canada	687.9	30.8	22 300
China	1 079.9	1 262.5	860
Non-EU-Europe and Central Asia (ECA)	942.1	474.3	2 000
Latin America and Caribbean (LAC)	2 000.5	515.7	3 900
Middle East and North Africa (MNA)	659.7	295.2	2 200
South Asia incl. India (SAS)	596.8	1 355.1	440
Sub-Saharan Africa (SSA)	322.7	658.9	490
High income non-OECD countries (HI)	857.3	50.8	16 900
--- World in total ---	31 492.8	6 057.3	5 200

NB: The countries included in the groupings are as specified in the World Bank's WDI 2002. It might be noted that the Russian Federation is included in non-EU-Europe and Central Asia.

Source: World Bank World Development Indicators 2002, Eurostat.

2.2. The candidate countries

Annual GDP growth

2001 — a year of diverging growth rates

This section sets out the most important national accounts data of the candidate countries (CCs) for membership of the European Union. The candidate countries are Bulgaria, Cyprus, the Czech Republic, Estonia, Hungary, Latvia, Lithuania, Malta, Poland, Romania, the Slovak Republic, Slovenia and Turkey.

The CCs do not comprise an economic area but a group of different countries having the same objective to join the Union. Economic performance has been, however, rather varied. In 2001 the growth of current price GDP ranged from − 7.4 to + 7.7 % in comparison with the previous year, as shown in Table 2.2.1. This differs significantly with the figures in 2000 when no country recorded negative growth. Furthermore, the fastest growing nation then went on to show the greatest decline in 2001. Consequently, the year-on-year growth of the group of 13 nations as a whole slipped into negative.

The economic situation in many of the individual countries was not as bleak as the aggregate figure. The growth was higher than the EU-15 average in nine countries out of 13, ranging from + 3.0 % in Slovenia to the + 7.7 % in Latvia. Of the four countries

Figure 2.2.1. Annual GDP growth rates (as a %)

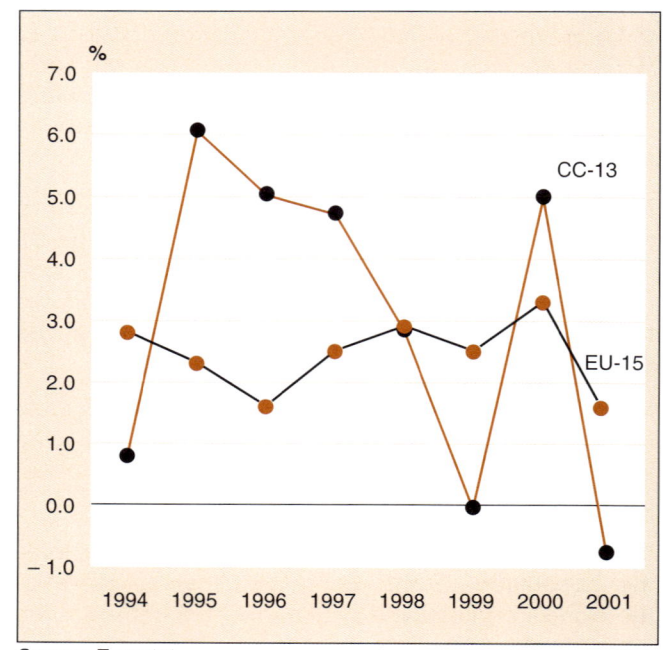

Source: Eurostat.

below the EU-15 average growth in 2001 the situation was most alarming in Turkey. The previous year's growth was undone with economic contraction of − 7.4 %. Malta also slipped into negative GDP growth but to a much more moderate degree (− 0.8 %). The economy

Table 2.2.1. GDP growth rates, percentage change on previous year

	1994	1995	1996	1997	1998	1999	2000	2001
Bulgaria (BG)	1.8	2.9	− 9.4	− 5.6	4.0	2.3	5.4	4.0
Cyprus (CY)	5.9	6.2	1.9	2.4	5.0	4.6	5.1	4.0
Czech Republic (CZ)	2.2	5.9	4.3	− 0.8	− 1.0	0.5	3.3	3.3
Estonia (EE)	− 2.0	4.3	3.9	9.8	4.6	− 0.6	7.1	5.0
Hungary (HU)	2.9	1.5	1.3	4.6	4.9	4.2	5.2	3.8
Latvia (LV)	0.7	− 1.7	3.7	8.4	4.8	2.8	6.8	7.7
Lithuania (LT)	− 9.8	3.3	4.7	7.3	5.1	− 3.9	3.8	5.9
Malta (MT)	5.7	6.2	4.0	4.9	3.4	4.1	5.5	− 0.8
Poland (PL)	5.8	7.0	6.0	6.8	4.8	4.1	4.0	1.1
Romania (RO)	3.9	7.1	4.0	− 6.1	− 4.8	− 1.2	1.8	5.3
Slovak Republic (SK)	5.2	6.5	5.8	5.6	4.0	1.3	2.2	3.3
Slovenia (SI)	5.3	4.1	3.5	4.6	3.8	5.2	4.6	3.0
Turkey (TR)	− 5.5	7.2	7.0	7.5	3.1	− 4.7	7.4	− 7.4
Total (CC-13)	0.3	6.1	5.0	4.8	3.0	0.1	5.1	− 0.7
EU-15 ([1])	2.8	2.4	1.6	2.5	2.9	2.7	3.5	1.5
EU-minimum ([1])	1.0	1.6	0.8	1.4	1.8	1.6	2.9	0.6
	P	A	D	D	I	I	I	D
EU-maximum ([1])	5.8	10.0	7.8	10.8	8.6	10.8	11.5	5.9
	IRL	IRL	IRL	IRL	IRL	IRL	IRL	IRL

([1]) Based on ESA 79 up to 1995, ESA 95 from 1996 onwards.
Source: Eurostat.

of the Slovak Republic slowed down to a moderate + 0.7 %. The fourth country below the EU-15 level was Poland (+ 1.1 %), which experienced a slowdown after seven years of stable growth.

GDP in euro

Total CC-13 GDP 7.1 % of the EU

The combined size of the economies of the CC-13 in terms of GDP in current prices was EUR 627.7 billion in 2001. Even with the inclusion of relatively large countries such as Poland and Turkey, the CC-13 corresponds to a very small economic area compared to the European Union: in 2001, its GDP was 7.1 % of that of the EU.

Candidate countries' economies are very diverse in size, ranging from EUR 4.0 billion in Malta to EUR 196.7 billion in Poland. The Maltese economy, in euro terms, is five times smaller than that of Luxembourg, the smallest EU Member State. Adding together the six smallest CC GDPs still gives a total of only EUR 57.5 billion, less than 0.7 % of the EU-15 total.

CCs GDP per head less than one-fifth of EU figure, in euro terms

The CCs display equally wide-ranging figures in terms of "GDP per head", from EUR 1 900 in Bulgaria to EUR 15 100 in Cyprus. Most of the CCs are far below those of the EU but this is partly a symptom of higher price levels in the EU. More meaningful comparisons can be made by expressing figures in purchasing power standards (PPS) instead of euro, as shown in the following section.

Table 2.2.2. GDP at current prices and exchange rates, in billion EUR

	1996	1997	1998	1999	2000	2001
BG	7.8	9.2	11.4	12.2	13.7	15.2
CY	7.0	7.5	8.1	8.7	9.6	10.2
CZ	45.5	46.8	50.6	51.6	55.8	63.3
EE	3.4	4.1	4.7	4.9	5.6	6.2
HU	35.6	40.4	41.9	45.1	50.6	58.0
LV	4.0	5.0	5.4	6.2	7.8	8.5
LT	6.2	8.5	9.6	10.0	12.2	13.4
MT	2.6	2.9	3.1	3.4	3.9	4.0
PL	113.3	127.1	141.3	145.5	170.9	196.7
RO	27.8	31.2	37.4	33.4	40.2	44.4
SK	16.1	18.6	19.6	18.9	21.3	22.8
SI	14.9	16.1	17.5	18.8	19.5	20.9
TR	143.1	167.8	177.8	173.1	216.7	164.6
CC-13	427	485	529	532	628	628
EU-15	6 920	7 288	7 630	8 024	8 545	8 815
% of EU-15	6.2	6.7	6.9	6.6	7.3	7.1
Minimum EU-15						
L	13.8	14.3	15.6	16.9	18.4	20.5

Source: Eurostat.

GDP in real terms

Cyprus and Slovenia consolidate growth

Figure 2.2.2 summarises the current position of the CCs in 2001 using the three key indicators of "annual growth", "GDP per head in PPS" and "economic size" (total GDP in PPS).

Table 2.2.3. GDP per head at current prices and exchange rates

	EUR						EU-15 = 100					
	1996	1997	1998	1999	2000	2001	1996	1997	1998	1999	2000	2001
BG	900	1 100	1 400	1 500	1 700	1 900	5	6	7	7	7	8
CY	10 800	11 500	12 300	13 000	14 300	15 100	59	59	61	61	63	65
CZ	4 400	4 500	4 900	5 000	5 400	6 200	24	23	24	24	24	27
EE	2 400	2 900	3 400	3 600	4 100	4 500	13	15	17	17	18	19
HU	3 500	4 000	4 200	4 500	5 100	5 700	19	20	20	21	22	25
LV	1 600	2 000	2 200	2 600	3 300	3 600	9	10	11	12	15	16
LT	1 700	2 400	2 700	2 800	3 500	3 800	9	12	13	13	15	17
MT	6 900	7 700	8 100	8 800	9 900	10 300	37	40	40	41	44	44
PL	2 900	3 300	3 700	3 800	4 400	5 100	16	17	18	18	20	22
RO	1 200	1 400	1 700	1 500	1 800	2 000	7	7	8	7	8	9
SK	3 000	3 500	3 600	3 500	4 000	4 200	16	18	18	16	17	18
SI	7 500	8 100	8 800	9 500	9 800	10 500	40	42	43	44	43	45
TR	2 300	2 700	2 800	2 700	3 200	2 400	12	14	14	13	14	10
CC-13	3 000	3 400	3 600	3 800	4 200	4 600	16	17	18	18	19	20

NB: For the calculation of per capita GDP, the data for the total population is taken from national accounts; it may be different from that obtained via demographic statistics.
Source: Eurostat.

THE UNION IN THE INTERNATIONAL FRAMEWORK

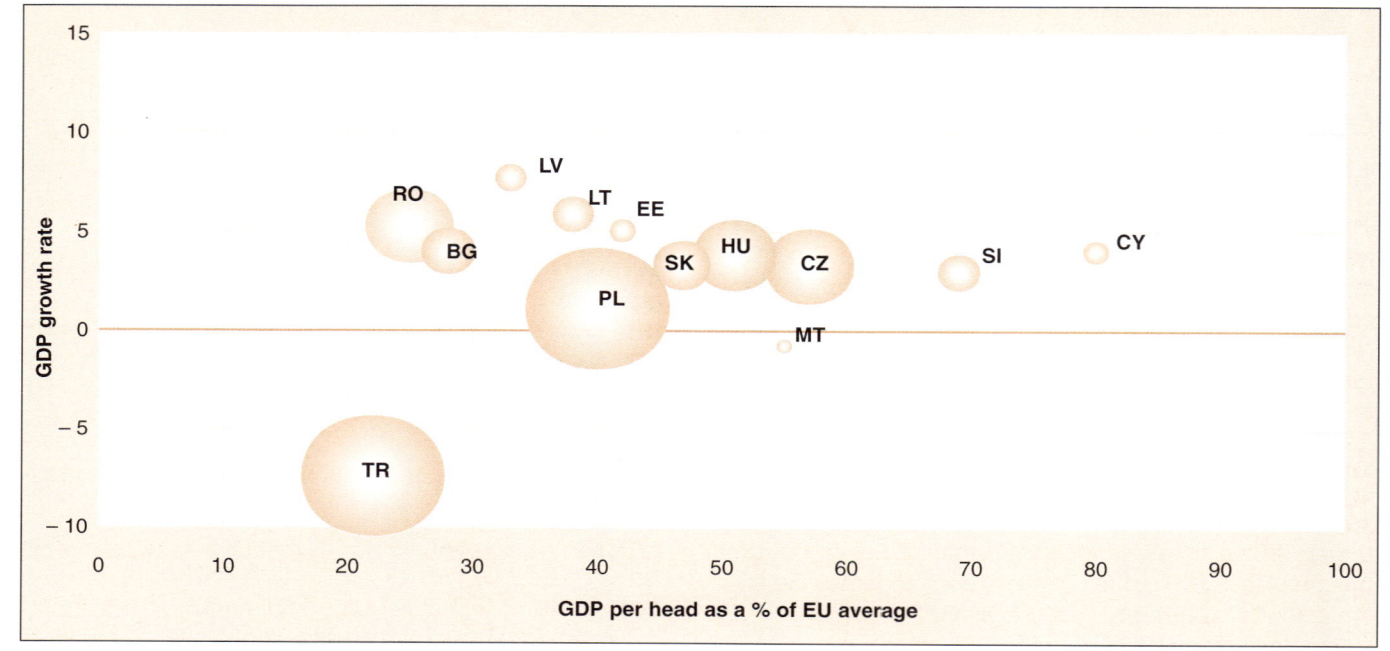

Figure 2.2.2. Growth, size of GDP and GDP per head (as a % of EU average), in PPS, in 2001

NB: The size (area) of the bubbles indicates the level of GDP in PPS.
Except for GDP growth, 1999 data are used for Malta.
Source: Eurostat.

The most widely used indicator of economic prosperity, GDP per head, is displayed on the horizontal axis and shows Cyprus and Slovenia ahead of the CC pack. With respective 2001 growth rates of 4 % and 3 % following the healthy growth rates of the past decade, they are positioned near the advantageous top-right-hand portion of the graph.

Turkey is positioned in a less favourable area of the graph, with low GDP per head and a contracting economy. Other countries with low GDP per head recorded positive GDP growth rates in 2001.

Candidate countries smaller than most Member States, in real terms

When making comparisons between the GDP of different countries, it is better to express figures in an artificial currency unit called PPS (purchasing power standard, see Section 7.4). This makes allowances for the varying price levels in different countries and makes the comparisons of GDP, both in absolute terms and "per head", more meaningful.

Table 2.2.4 shows that the CC-13 group is not as small compared to EU-15 as it appeared in euro terms (see Table 2.2.2). It amounts to 15.3 % of the EU total in 2001, compared to just 7.1 % when using the euro figures.

With certain exceptions, most of the candidate countries have small economies compared to the EU Member States. Turkey and Poland, on the other hand, appear in seventh and eighth place in a league table of the 28 Member States and candidate countries. All but four of the candidate countries are larger than Luxembourg.

Cyprus and Slovenia closest to EU in real GDP per head

Table 2.2.5 shows Cyprus and Slovenia maintaining their position as leading CCs in terms of GDP per head in PPS (80 % and 70 % of EU-average, respectively), both above the EU minimum, Greece (67 %), and with Cyprus also exceeding Portugal and Spain.

Many of the CCs have made progress towards the EU average between 1996 and 2001 with Estonia (35 to 42 %), Slovenia (64 to 70 %) and Latvia (26 to 32 %) making the largest strides in percentage point terms. Conversely, Romania and Turkey, at the foot of the table, slipped 5 and 3 percentage points respectively while the Czech Republic, one of the leading CCs, dropped from 64 % of the EU average to 60 % in 2001.

Table 2.2.4. GDP at current prices in billion PPS

	1996	1997	1998	1999	2000	2001
D	1 630.5	1 716.9	1 765.2	1 853.6	1 952.4	1 989.8
F	1 115.2	1 149.7	1 203.8	1 278.3	1 375.4	1 421.4
I	1 107.8	1 138.6	1 208.2	1 267.3	1 362.5	1 411.5
UK	1 090.8	1 173.9	1 241.9	1 273.3	1 347.1	1 392.6
E	575.6	610.3	633.8	692.7	736.7	773.3
NL	312.9	340.6	367.1	384.3	405.6	417.4
TR	318.8	352.3	369.6	360.4	379.1	357.3
PL	256.3	281.3	300.1	319.6	345.9	355.9
B	209.1	220.4	229.6	231.5	247.7	253.1
A	166.3	173.9	179.4	190.9	206.3	210.4
S	167.3	175.5	182.2	190.9	202.2	206.6
P	130.2	143.7	148.2	155.8	165.7	172.2
EL	129.0	134.3	142.6	153.0	159.4	170.0
DK	117.4	123.0	126.9	135.1	143.7	148.0
CZ	122.1	124.5	125.4	128.9	129.6	136.2
RO	120.0	115.8	112.2	113.5	122.6	131.3
FIN	91.7	99.0	105.8	111.0	121.7	124.5
HU	87.0	93.4	99.7	106.3	114.5	121.0
IRL	62.7	73.6	79.4	88.9	99.3	106.2
SK	47.5	51.6	54.6	56.6	56.6	59.5
BG	45.9	44.5	47.1	49.3	48.9	51.8
SI	23.6	25.3	26.8	28.8	30.4	31.8
LT	22.2	24.5	26.2	25.8	28.3	30.5
L	13.1	14.4	15.5	17.2	19.3	19.8
LV	11.6	12.9	13.8	14.5	16.6	18.2
EE	9.2	10.4	11.1	11.3	12.5	13.4
CY	10.0	10.5	11.2	12.0	11.8	12.5
MT	3.8	4.1	4.3	4.5	:	:
CC-13 ([1])	1 074	1 147	1 198	1 227	1 297	1 319
EU-15	6 920	7 288	7 630	8 024	8 545	8 817
% of EU-15	15.5	15.7	15.7	15.3	15.2	15.0

([1]) Not including Malta.
Source: Eurostat, OECD.

GDP main aggregates

Expenditure components

According to Table 2.2.6, the share of 2001 GDP accounted for by final consumption of households and NPISH, where data were available, varied amongst the CCs from 52.5 % in Hungary to 72.0 % in Turkey. Historically, Romania posted the highest share, but was unable to provide up-to-date figures. There is a general tendency for the poorer countries (low GDP per head) to use a higher share of their GDP for this component, in order to satisfy basic needs from limited incomes. The Czech Republic, Estonia, Hungary, and the Slovak Republic displayed shares smaller than the EU-15 total.

Concerning final consumption of general government, CC figures range from just 14.2 % in Bulgaria and Turkey to 22.4 % in Hungary. The highest value of gross fixed capital formation, as a % of GDP, in 2001 was 28.3 % in the Czech Republic. CC investment rates are generally higher than those in the EU, though comparable with the levels seen in Greece, Ireland, Portugal and Spain.

In 2001, Estonia took over Malta's position as the heaviest trader, relative to their economic size, with exports amounting to 90.6 % of GDP, and imports 94.4 %, much larger figures than in 1999. Turkey and Poland, the largest CC economies, posted the lowest trade figures, as a percentage of their total GDP.

Whilst seven of the 12 available countries saw their trade deficit decrease between 1999 and 2001, only Turkey's broke into surplus (+ 2.4 %). Lithuania continued to record the most severe deficit (− 11.3 %).

Figure 2.2.3. GDP per head, in thousands of PPS, 2001

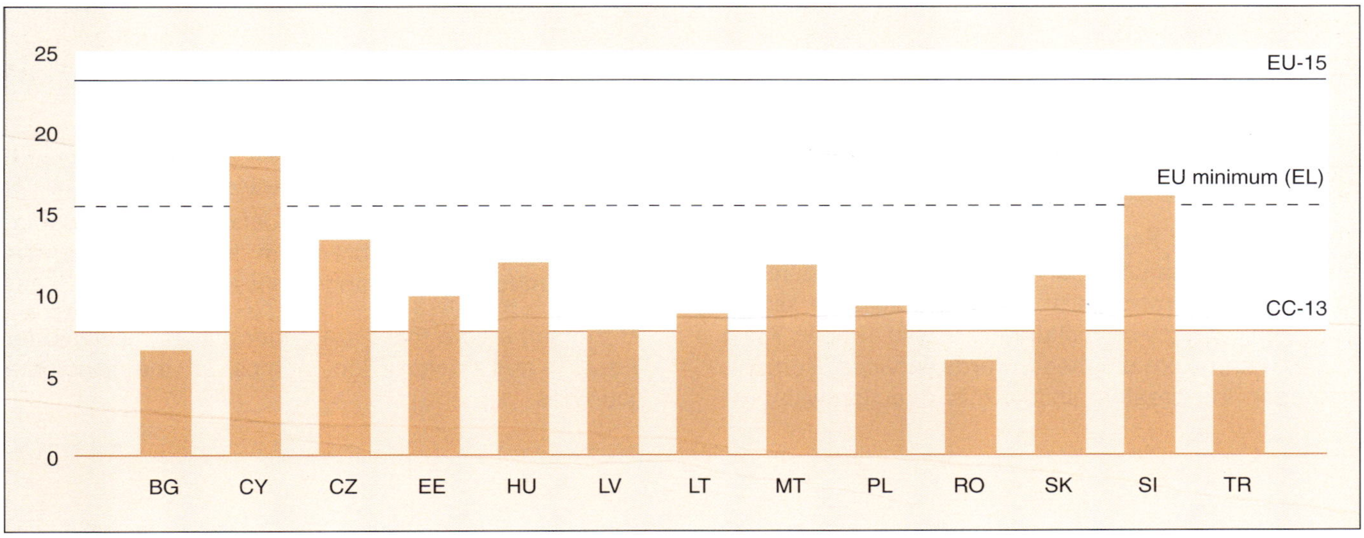

NB: For Malta 1999 figure is used.
Source: Eurostat.

THE UNION IN THE INTERNATIONAL FRAMEWORK

Table 2.2.5. GDP per head at current prices in PPS

	In PPS						EU-15 = 100					
	1996	1997	1998	1999	2000	2001	1996	1997	1998	1999	2000	2001
L	31 200	34 000	36 200	39 400	43 800	44 300	169	175	178	185	194	191
IRL	17 300	20 100	21 400	23 800	26 200	27 700	94	104	105	112	116	119
DK	22 300	23 300	23 900	25 400	26 900	27 600	121	120	118	119	119	119
NL	20 200	21 800	23 400	24 300	25 500	26 000	109	112	115	114	113	112
A	20 600	21 500	22 200	23 600	25 400	25 900	111	111	109	111	112	112
B	20 600	21 700	22 500	22 600	24 200	24 600	111	112	111	106	107	106
I	19 300	19 800	21 000	22 000	23 600	24 400	104	102	103	103	104	105
D	19 900	20 900	21 500	22 600	23 800	24 100	108	108	106	106	105	104
FIN	17 900	19 300	20 500	21 500	23 500	24 000	97	99	101	101	104	103
F	18 700	19 200	20 000	21 200	22 700	23 300	101	99	99	100	100	100
UK	18 600	19 900	21 000	21 400	22 500	23 200	101	103	103	100	100	100
S	18 900	19 800	20 600	21 500	22 800	23 200	102	102	101	101	101	100
E	14 700	15 500	16 100	17 500	18 500	19 200	79	80	79	82	82	83
CY	15 400	16 100	17 000	18 100	17 600	18 500	83	83	84	85	78	80
P	13 100	14 400	14 900	15 600	16 600	17 100	71	74	73	73	73	74
SI	11 900	12 800	13 500	14 500	15 300	16 000	64	66	67	68	67	69
EL	12 300	12 800	13 600	14 500	15 100	15 500	66	66	67	68	67	67
CZ	11 800	12 100	12 200	12 500	12 600	13 300	64	62	60	59	56	57
HU	8 500	9 200	9 900	10 600	11 400	11 900	46	47	49	50	51	51
SK	8 800	9 600	10 100	10 500	10 500	11 100	48	49	50	49	46	48
EE	6 500	7 500	8 000	8 200	9 200	9 800	35	38	39	38	40	42
PL	6 600	7 300	7 800	8 300	9 000	9 200	36	38	38	39	40	40
LT	6 200	6 900	7 400	7 300	8 100	8 700	33	35	36	34	36	38
LV	4 700	5 200	5 600	6 100	7 000	7 700	25	27	28	28	31	33
BG	5 500	5 400	5 700	6 000	6 000	6 500	30	28	28	28	27	28
RO	5 300	5 100	5 000	5 100	5 500	5 900	29	26	25	24	24	25
TR	5 100	5 600	5 800	5 600	5 600	5 200	28	29	29	26	25	22
MT	9 900	10 600	11 100	11 700	:	:	54	55	55	55	:	:
CC-13 (¹)	6 400	6 800	7 100	7 300	7 500	7 600	35	35	35	34	33	33
EU-15	18 500	19 400	20 300	21 300	22 600	23 200	100	100	100	100	100	100

NB: For the calculation of per capita GDP, the data for the total population are taken from the national accounts: they may be different from those obtained via demographic statistics.

(¹) Not including Malta in 2000 and 2001.
Source: Eurostat, OECD.

CCs switch from agricultural production to service activities

Table 2.2.7 and Figure 2.2.4 show GVA broken down into the main branches for 1996 and 2001. Production in the CC-13 group as a whole has become slightly less dominated by agriculture (10.9 % in 1996 to 7.3 % in 2001) and more directed towards services. Romania has seen the greatest shift in this direction with agriculture dropping from 20.6 to 14.6 % of GVA and services rocketing from 37.0 to 51.4 %. This pattern of change is also evident in Latvia and Lithuania, though the agriculture branch in these countries was already much smaller, and services larger.

At the same time there are general slight declines for industry and construction in most of the candidate countries.

THE UNION IN THE INTERNATIONAL FRAMEWORK

Table 2.2.6. Main GDP components, (as a % of total GDP)

	Final consumption of households and NPISH 97	99	01	of general government 97	99	01	GFCF 97	99	01	Exports 97	99	01	Imports 97	99	01	External trade balance 97	99	01
BG	73.0	71.3	69.6	12.6	15.2	14.2	11.0	15.1	17.8	58.3	44.6	55.7	53.7	50.3	63.2	4.6	−5.8	−7.5
CY	66.0	:	68.5	18.8	17.7	18.3	18.1	16.1	16.3	47.1	44.6	46.9	52.1	47.6	51.8	−5.0	−3.0	−5.0
CZ	53.6	53.5	53.2	19.8	19.6	19.2	30.6	27.8	28.3	56.5	60.6	71.3	62.5	61.9	74.1	−6.0	−1.3	−2.7
EE	59.3	58.2	56.4	23.0	23.4	20.3	28.1	24.9	26.1	78.4	77.2	90.6	90.0	82.2	94.4	−11.6	−4.9	−3.8
HU	50.3	52.4	52.5	21.9	21.6	22.4	22.2	23.9	23.4	45.5	53.0	60.5	45.5	55.5	62.6	0.0	−2.5	−2.1
LV	66.7	62.9	63.8	19.2	20.6	20.1	18.8	25.2	19.4	51.1	43.9	50.4	59.6	54.2	55.9	−8.5	−10.3	−5.4
LT	65.1	65.5	:	19.0	22.2	:	24.4	22.1	27.3	54.5	39.7	44.9	65.1	50.1	56.2	−10.6	−10.3	−11.3
MT	62.4	62.8	:	20.5	18.7	20.2	25.3	23.4	23.2	85.1	90.7	87.8	93.5	96.3	92.3	−8.4	−5.6	−4.5
PL	63.7	64.4	66.5	16.0	15.5	15.5	23.5	25.5	21.5	25.5	26.1	29.8	29.8	32.5	33.5	−4.3	−6.4	−3.7
RO	74.2	85.4	:	12.3	12.6	:	21.2	17.7	19.0	29.2	28.0	33.5	36.2	32.9	41.6	−7.1	−4.8	−8.1
SK	50.3	52.7	53.6	21.7	19.8	21.3	34.3	30.3	24.9	56.1	61.0	60.1	65.6	65.4	60.5	−9.6	−4.3	−0.4
SI	56.4	55.8	:	20.4	20.2	:	23.4	27.4	:	57.4	52.5	:	58.3	56.9	:	−0.8	−4.4	:
TR	:	:	72.0	12.3	15.2	14.2	26.4	21.9	17.8	24.6	23.2	33.2	30.4	26.9	30.8	−5.8	−3.7	2.4
CC-13	:	:	:	:	:	:	:	:	:	:	:	:	:	:	:	:	:	:
EU-15	57.8	58.3	58.6	20.3	20.0	20.1	19.4	20.2	20.1	31.9	32.4	35.9	29.7	31.2	34.7	2.2	1.1	1.2

Source: Eurostat.

In 2001, Romania had the largest agricultural branch (14.6 %), and Malta the smallest (2.4 %), relative to GDP. Cyprus had the biggest services branch (74.9 %), and Romania the smallest (51.4 %).

Table 2.2.7. Gross value added by branch, (as a % of the total)

	Agriculture, fishing 1996	2001	Industry, including energy 1996	2001	Construction 1996	2001	Service activities 1996	2001
BG (¹)	15.4	14.5	25.9	24.2	4.3	3.6	54.5	57.7
CY (²)	4.8	4.2	14.7	13.3	8.9	7.7	71.6	74.9
CZ	4.8	4.2	36.3	32.9	7.7	7.2	51.1	55.8
EE	8.4	6.3	23.8	22.1	6.3	5.8	61.5	65.8
HU (¹)	6.6	4.3	26.3	28.7	4.3	4.6	62.8	62.4
LV	9.0	4.7	26.4	18.7	4.7	6.2	59.9	70.4
LT	12.2	7.0	25.8	28.4	7.1	6.1	54.9	58.6
MT	2.9	2.4	24.8	24.5	3.1	2.8	69.3	70.4
PL	6.4	3.4	30.1	25.4	7.4	7.5	56.1	63.8
RO	20.6	14.6	35.5	28.5	6.9	5.5	37.0	51.4
SK (¹)	5.6	4.5	31.2	28.9	7.5	5.3	55.8	61.3
SI	4.4	3.1	32.0	31.0	5.6	5.9	58.0	60.1
TR	16.1	12.1	24.0	23.8	5.5	4.8	54.4	59.3
CC-13	10.9	7.3	28.1	26.1	6.3	6.0	54.6	60.6

(¹) 2001 data are not available. 2000 shown instead.
(²) 2001 data are not available. 1999 shown instead.
Source: Eurostat.

Figure 2.2.4. GVA by branch, 2001 (as a % of total GVA)

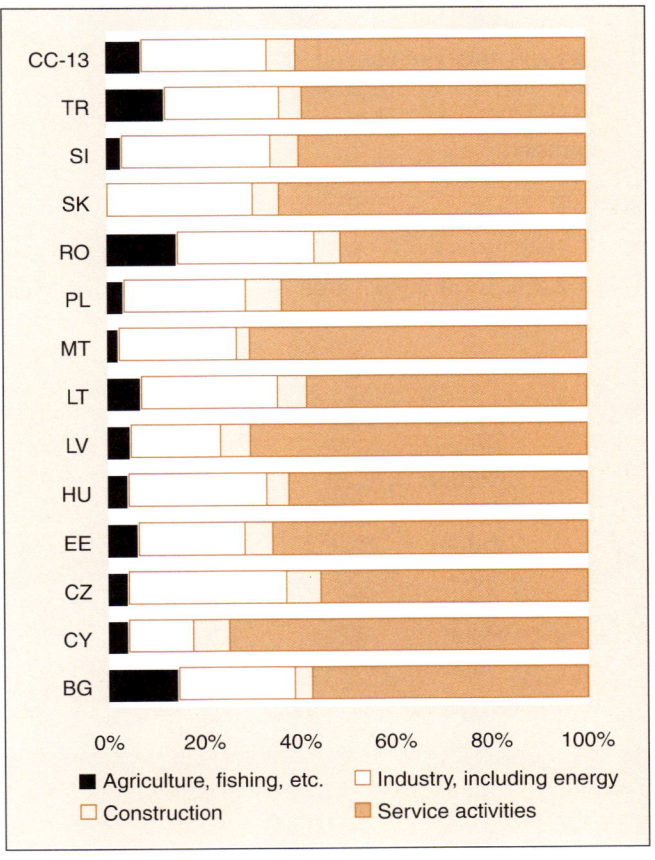

Source: Eurostat.

THE UNION IN THE INTERNATIONAL FRAMEWORK

The candidate countries send data to Eurostat four times each year using the same standardised format as the Member States, though the completeness of the tables varies from country to country. Data for this publication were, in most cases, supplied prior to mid-May 2002, and have been validated by Eurostat.

Data quality

All candidate countries are working towards ESA 95 compliance but this is a long and difficult process. In particular, Turkey currently bases its accounts on SNA 1968 while Malta's data are derived from the national system of 1954, with some elements of SNA 1968.

The CCs have generally made significant progress in improving the coverage and quality of their estimates over the past couple of years. This has been supported by a series of EU-sponsored projects and workshops, which has helped to improve the sources and methods used to compile national accounts and heightened the exhaustiveness and consistency of the different national accounting systems. However, not all the changes have yet been implemented in the accounts for all years and the problem of consistent time series, in particular, remains to be solved in most CCs. Therefore, revisions of both the level and growth rates of GDP should be anticipated in the future.

All data in this publication should therefore still be treated with an appropriate level of caution, as full comparability with EU Member States cannot yet be guaranteed.

Exchange rate regimes

The exchange rate regimes adopted by the candidate countries are as follows:

- managed floating exchange rate; Romania, Slovakia and Slovenia;
- independent floating system: Czech Republic, Poland and Turkey;
- fixed parity (peg): Cyprus, Hungary, Latvia and Malta;
- currency board: Bulgaria, Estonia and Lithuania.

Exchange rates since 1996

An analysis of changes in the rates for the candidate countries' currencies against the euro over the period 1996 to 2001 highlights the contrasts between the countries.

After a period of turbulence during the first half of the 1990s, the Bulgarian lev has been stable since July 1997 following the establishment of the currency board. Since that date, the Bulgarian currency has been tied firstly to the German mark and then, as of 1 January 1999, to the euro. In July 1999, following a new monetary reform, the authorities decided to divide their currency by 1 000 (1 000 old leva are worth one lev).

The Cyprus pound has been extremely stable against the ecu/euro over the whole period under observation. Between 1996 and 2001, it rose 4 % against the ecu/euro, to fluctuate by under 1 % against the euro every year since 1998. Since January 1999, the Cypriot currency has been linked to the euro at the key rate of CYP 0.5853 = EUR 1, fluctuating within a 2.25 % band. This band was widened to +/– 15 % with effect from 1 January 2001, the key rate remaining unchanged.

Table 2.2.8. Exchange rates of candidate countries (period average) 1 EUR/ECU (1) = ...

			1996	1997	1998	1999	2000	2001	January-April 2002
BG	Lev	BGN	0.225	1.902	1.969	1.956	1.953	1.948	1.950
CY	Pound	CYP	0.592	0.583	0.577	0.579	0.574	0.576	0.576
CZ	Koruna	CZK	34.46	35.93	36.32	36.89	35.60	34.07	31.40
EE	Kroon	EEK	15.28	15.72	15.75	15.65	15.65	15.65	15.65
HU	Forint	HUF	193.74	211.65	240.57	252.77	260.05	256.59	243.60
LV	Lat	LVL	0.700	0.659	0.660	0.624	0.559	0.560	0.559
LT	Litus	LTL	5.079	4.536	4.484	4.264	3.695	3.582	3.473
MT	Pound	MTL	0.458	0.437	0.435	0.426	0.404	0.403	0.400
PL	Zloty	PLN	3.422	3.715	3.918	4.227	4.008	3.672	3.613
RO	Leu	ROL	3922	8 112	9 985	16 345	19 922	26 004	28 590
SK	Koruna	SKK	38.92	38.11	39.54	44.12	42.60	43.30	42.10
SI	Tolar	SIT	171.78	181.00	185.96	194.47	206.61	217.98	222.58
TR	Lira	TRL	103 214	171 848	293 736	447 237	574 816	1 102 425	1 188 748

(1) Euro from 1999/ECU until 1998.
Source: Eurostat.

In the Czech Republic, the koruna (CZK) has risen sharply against the ecu/euro since the end of 1997, with the exception of a 2.5 % fall during 1999: the rise was 8 % in 1998, 3 % in 2000 and almost 10 % in 2001. During the first five months of 2002, the CZK has continued to appreciate slightly against the euro.

The Estonian kroon remained stable throughout the reference period, thanks to the fixed exchange rate regime (currency board) adopted by the monetary authorities, firstly against the German mark and then, as from 1999, against the euro.

In Hungary, changes in the forint rate between 1996 and 2001 may be split into three distinct phases. Between 1996 and 1998, the forint lost around 10 % a year against the ecu. This period was followed by a much smaller forint devaluation in 1999 and 2000 and, finally, 2001 saw a rise of around 8 %. During the first five months of 2002, the HUF has continued to rise in value against the euro.

In Latvia, the exchange regime adopted by the monetary authorities is governed by a fixed link with SDRs (special drawing rights). With the exception of 1998, when the lat lost around 2 % against the ecu, the Latvian currency has strengthened steadily since 1996, with a rise of some 13 % in 1999. It rose 2 % against the euro in 2000 and 3.6 % in 2001.

Lithuania, like the other two Baltic countries, also reaped the benefit of a highly stable currency following the setting up of the currency board. The Lithuanian currency was tied to the US dollar at the rate of four litas per dollar between 1994 and January 2002. In 1999, 2000 and 2001, when changes in the euro rate against the USD had a marked effect on the litas, it rose by 16, 8 and 6 % respectively against the euro. Since 2 February 2002, the litas has been fixed against the euro (currency board) at LTL 3.4582 to the euro.

With the exception of 1998, the Maltese pound has risen steadily against the euro since 1996. The sharpest rise occurred in 1999 — almost 6 % — owing largely to changes in the US dollar and sterling rates against the euro. The reference basket comprises the euro (56.8 %), the GBP (21.6 %) and the USD (21.6 %). In 2000 and 2001, the Maltese pound rose by 1.9 % and 2 % respectively against the euro.

In Poland, the zloty lost over 20 % of its value between the end of 1995 and the end of 1999, under a devaluation plan introduced by the monetary authorities (0.3 % a month from March 1999 to 11 April 2000 against a basket comprising 55 % euro and 45 % dollar). Since 12 April 2000, the zloty has been floating freely on the foreign exchange markets, rising by some 8 % in 2000 and 10 % in 2001. During the first four months of 2002, however, the Polish currency lost around 3 % against the euro.

Romania — where inflation remains very high — saw its currency drop from 3 384 lei to the euro at the end of 1995 to 27 817 at the end of 2001. However, although the leu depreciated by over 30 % a year between 1996 and 1999, it fell by only 24 % in 2000 and 12 % in 2001.

Up to August 1998, the Slovak koruna enjoyed the advantages of a relatively stable exchange rate of between 38 and 39 koruny to the ecu. It was then tied to a basket made up of the German mark and the US dollar. On 2 October 1998, the Slovak monetary authorities introduced a managed floating exchange rate, and from that point on the currency's value plummeted, falling 11 % against the ecu over 1998 as a whole. Since then, with the exception of a 3.5 % drop in 2000, the koruna has been more stable, regaining 1.9 % in 1999 and 2.7 % in 2001. The first few months of 2002 would seem to indicate that the rate against the euro is stabilising.

The Slovenian tolar declined steadily against the ecu/euro during the period in question, falling from 177.282 tolars to one euro to 218.836 between the end of 1996 and the end of 2001. With the exception of 1999 and 2001, when the currency fell by only 1 % and 2.4 % respectively, it lost some 5 % of its value every year between 1996 and 2001.

Between the start of 1996 and the end of 2001, Turkey's currency declined by 93.7 % from 80 441 Turkish liras to the ecu/euro to 1 269 500. In 2001 alone, the devaluation rate for the lira against the euro was 51 %, whereas it had fallen by only 13 % in the previous year. However, in the first four months of 2002 the exchange rate recovered a certain amount of stability.

Public deficit and debt

The government deficit/surplus and debt statistics of the candidate countries do not yet fully comply with EU methodological requirements, but may nevertheless be considered fairly reliable measures of the government financial position. Broadly speaking, the deficit /surplus refers here to the national accounts concept of general government net borrowing/net lending of the European system of accounts (ESA 95). General government comprises the subsectors of central government, state (regional) government, local government, and social security funds.

In some cases the public finances of candidate countries compare favourably with those of many EU countries, particularly in terms of the debt position. However, the large structural changes which have taken place in these economies have resulted, for some countries, in sharp swings in the deficit/surplus. Overall, it may be said that no particular trend in government finances has been evident during the years 1997-2001.

On an individual country level, the financial balance of Bulgaria and Estonia has tended to be in surplus or show a small deficit. The outstanding government debt of Estonia is also exceptionally low. Latvia, Lithuania, and Slovenia have also relatively low deficits and debt. Malta and Hungary have recorded sizeable deficits, but the trend was improving until 2001. The double-digit deficit of the Slovak Republic in 2000 was partly caused by writing-off debts of the banking sector. Turkey has recorded persistently high deficits, made worse in 2001 by the financial crisis which broke out towards the end of the previous year, causing also the debt to reach a figure in excess of GDP.

Interest rates

The link between interest rates and inflation has been apparent among the candidate countries: rates have tended to be higher in those countries suffering from relatively high inflation, most notably Romania, Turkey, and (until 1998) Bulgaria. As the general trend in inflation in 1996-2001 has been downwards, so have interest rates fallen. The most spectacular example was in Bulgaria, where inflation fell rapidly following the establishment of a currency board in July 1997.

Interest rates in the Baltic States, Malta and Cyprus have generally been relatively low since 1996, joined by the Czech Republic since 1999. Meanwhile rates in Hungary, Slovenia, and the Slovak Republic have tended to move lower. One exception to the downward trend occurred in 2000, in Poland, where monetary policy was tightened in order to reduce inflationary pressures and the risk of an overheating economy. However, in 2001 Polish rates were eased, the day-to-day money rate falling from around 20 % at the beginning of the year to below 12 % at the end.

Turkish interest rates moved sharply upwards towards the end of 2000, as weaknesses in the stabilisation programme became apparent, causing a financial crisis. The day-to-day money rate reached a peak of 400 % (monthly average) in February 2001, before falling sharply, and ending the year at below 60 %.

Table 2.2.9. Interest rates as a % (day-to-day money market rates, annual average)

	1996	1997	1998	1999	2000	2001
BG	286.4	136.8	2.4	2.6	2.9	3.7
CY	6.9	4.7	4.8	5.2	6.0	4.9
CZ	11.6	19.2	13.6	6.8	5.3	5.0
EE	3.5	6.5	11.7	4.9	4.8	4.5
HU	23.8	20.8	18.0	14.8	11.1	10.9
LV	13.1	3.7	4.4	4.7	3.0	5.2
LT	:	:	6.1	6.3	3.6	3.4
MT	:	5.2	5.5	5.0	4.7	4.7
PL	21.2	22.7	21.1	14.1	18.1	17.1
RO	53.4	86.0	80.9	80.8	44.8	41.0
SK	11.6	24.6	14.5	11.5	8.0	7.3
SI	13.8	9.6	7.4	6.8	6.8	6.7
TR	76.2	70.3	74.6	73.5	56.7	92.0

Source: Eurostat.

Table 2.2.10. General government deficit (–) or surplus (+) (as a % of GDP)

	1997	1998	1999	2000	2001
BG ([1])	– 0.3	1.3	0.2	– 0.6	1.7
CY	:	:	:	:	:
CZ	– 2.7	– 4.5	– 3.2	– 3.3	– 5.5
EE	2.0	– 0.4	4.0	– 0.4	0.2
HU	– 6.8	– 8.0	– 5.3	– 3.0	– 4.1
LV	:	– 0.7	– 5.3	– 2.7	– 1.6
LT ([2])	– 1.1	– 3.1	– 5.6	– 2.7	– 1.9
MT	– 10.7	– 10.8	– 8.3	– 7.0	– 7.0
PL ([3])	– 4.3	– 2.3	– 1.5	– 1.8	– 3.9
RO ([4])	– 4.5	– 3.2	– 4.5	– 4.5	– 3.4
SK	– 5.7	– 4.7	– 6.4	– 12.8	– 5.6
SI	:	– 2.3	– 2.2	– 3.2	– 2.5
TR	– 13.4	– 11.9	– 18.7	– 6.0	– 28.7

([1]) For 2001, sector classification does not appear to be fully in accordance with ESA 95 methodology.
([2]) Data for 1997-2000 are not strictly in accordance with ESA 95 methodology in terms of treatment of accrued expenditure.
([3]) Data for 1999-2001 are subject to verification of sector classification of open pension funds in accordance with ESA 95 methodology.
([4]) Data not fully verified: statistical treatment of financial defeasance does not appear to be in accordance with ESA 95 methodology.
Source: Eurostat.

Table 2.2.11. General government debt (as a % of GDP)

	1997	1998	1999	2000	2001
BG ([1])	107.4	79.6	79.3	73.6	66.3
CY	:	:	:	:	:
CZ	13.0	13.7	14.5	17.0	23.7
EE	6.8	6.0	6.5	5.1	4.8
HU	64.2	61.9	61.0	55.4	53.1
LV	:	10.6	13.7	13.9	16.0
LT ([2])	15.7	17.1	23.0	24.0	23.1
MT	51.5	64.9	59.9	60.7	65.7
PL ([3])	46.9	41.6	42.7	38.7	39.3
RO ([4])	16.5	18.0	24.0	24.0	23.3
SK	29.7	28.9	40.2	45.2	44.1
SI	:	25.1	26.4	27.6	27.5
TR	53.1	50.1	65.9	56.4	102.5

([1]) For 2001, sector classification does not appear to be fully in accordance with ESA 95 methodology.
([2]) Data for 1997- 2000 are not strictly in accordance with ESA 95 methodology in terms of treatment of accrued expenditure.
([3]) Data for 1999-2001 are subject to verification of sector classification of open pension funds in accordance with ESA 95 methodology.
([4]) Data not fully verified: statistical treatment of financial defeasance does not appear to be in accordance with ESA 95 methodology.
Source: Eurostat.

Interest rates tended to ease in the candidate countries in the first three months of 2002, the day-to-day money rate in Hungary, for example, falling below 10 %. Rates fell to particularly low levels (below 2 %) in Bulgaria and Lithuania.

2.3. External trade (¹)

Extra-EU trade

Total extra-EU trade flows

Figure 2.3.1 shows that extra-EU trade increased each year between 1990 and 2001. However, as the figures are measured in nominal terms, it is sometimes difficult to assess the actual size of the increase, especially when there has been high inflation or exchange rate movements.

After a dramatic increase in 2000, the EU deficit fell from EUR 91.4 billion to EUR 44.1 billion in 2001.

Between 1990 and 2001, the average export growth rate has been 8.7 %, due to the combination of sluggish growth during the early 1990s followed by a sharp upturn in EU sales to non-member countries, starting in 1993. In 2001, extra-EU exports recorded a growth rate of 3.7 % over the previous year.

Among the Member States, Germany has always been the main extra-EU exporter, accounting for 29.3 % of the total in 2001. France, the United Kingdom and Italy follow with shares of 14.5 %, 13.2 % and 12.7 % respectively. During the 1990s, the total share of the four leaders has remained almost stable at about 70 %. Ireland, whose export share has more than trebled since 1990, has recorded the most spectacular increase.

The general trend in extra-EU imports has been similar to that for exports. After declining in 1992, EU purchases from non-member countries started rising slightly in 1993 and continued to increase over the years up to 2000. After a sharp increase of about 33 % in 2000, extra-EU imports decreased by 1.2 % in 2001.

Germany was the main outlet for exports from non-member countries to the Union, with 23.8 % of the total in 2001, followed by the United Kingdom (18.2 %), France (12.5 %), Italy (11.1 %) and the Netherlands. The total share of these five countries together was stable during the 1990s, representing over three-quarters of total extra-EU imports.

Between 1991 and 1997 the extra-EU trade balance had improved each year, and a surplus of ECU 48.6 billion was reached in 1997. In 1998 the surplus fell to ECU 22.9 billion and, since 1999, the EU has been recording a trade deficit up to EUR 91.4 billion in 2000. In 2001, the deficit fell to EUR 44.1 billion.

While the total extra-EU trade flows are in deficit, the balances of individual Member States are widely divergent. Germany has usually recorded the greatest surplus among the Member States. During recent years, after absorbing the shock of reunification in the early 1990s, it has again produced the greatest extra-EU surplus, reaching EUR 42.8 billion in 2001. After a strong increase in its trade surplus, Ireland replaced Sweden in second place in 2001 with a surplus of

Table 2.3.1. Extra-EU trade

	1990	1999	2000	2001	1990	1999	2000	2001
	\multicolumn{4}{c}{EU-15 exports (billion EUR)}	\multicolumn{4}{c}{EU-15 imports (billion EUR)}
	390.6	760.2	942.0	977.0	439.4	710.5	779.2	1 025.6
	\multicolumn{4}{c}{Exports as a % of EU-15}	\multicolumn{4}{c}{Imports as a % of EU-15}
B (¹)	5.0	5.2	5.5	4.7	5.8	5.9	5.8	5.4
DK	2.3	2.1	2.0	2.0	1.8	1.7	1.5	1.6
D	28.8	28.5	27.6	29.3	23.2	24.1	23.5	23.8
EL	0.5	0.6	0.7	0.6	1.1	1.2	1.4	1.4
E	3.8	3.7	3.9	3.8	5.7	5.1	5.5	5.5
F	15.5	15.1	14.4	14.5	13.9	12.6	12.3	12.5
IRL	1.0	3.0	3.3	3.5	1.0	2.2	2.0	1.9
I	12.7	12.1	12.3	12.7	12.3	10.2	10.8	11.1
L (¹)	:	0.1	0.2	0.1	:	0.2	0.2	0.3
NL	5.2	5.5	5.7	5.6	8.8	11.1	11.2	10.9
A	2.7	3.0	3.0	3.1	2.6	2.4	2.4	2.6
P	0.6	0.5	0.6	0.6	1.2	1.1	1.0	1.1
FIN	2.0	2.2	2.3	2.3	1.9	1.3	1.4	1.3
S	4.3	4.4	4.4	3.9	3.5	2.7	2.7	2.4
UK	15.6	13.9	14.1	13.2	17.3	18.3	18.2	18.2

(¹) Luxembourg included with Belgium until 1998.
Source: Eurostat, Comext.

(¹) The tables and charts in this chapter on EU trade are compiled by Eurostat using data forwarded by Member States according to harmonised concepts and definitions. Therefore, results may differ from national publications.

Figure 2.3.1. Extra-EU trade flows 1990–2001 (billion EUR)

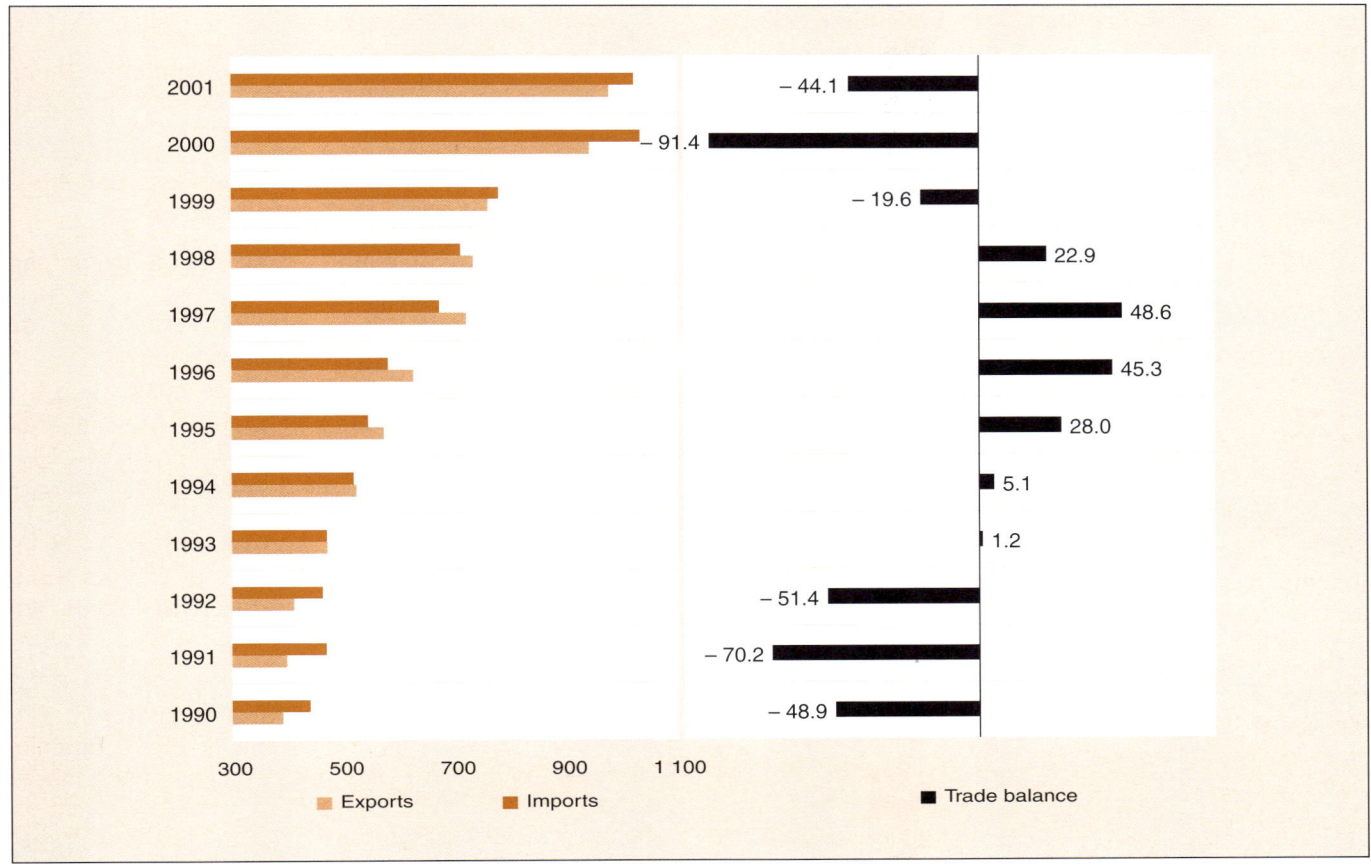

Source: Eurostat, Comext.

EUR 14.7 billion, followed by France (EUR 13.8 billion) and Sweden (EUR 13.7 billion).

Table 2.3.2. Extra-EU trade growth rates (as a %)

	Exports 2001/2000	Exports 2001/1990 (²)	Imports 2001/2000	Imports 2001/1990 (²)
EU-15	3.7	8.7	– 1.2	8.0
B (¹)	– 12.0	8.1	– 8.5	7.3
DK	7.5	7.4	2.6	6.7
D	9.9	8.8	0.0	8.2
EL	– 10.6	10.7	1.0	10.4
E	0.8	8.8	– 0.3	7.7
F	4.3	8.0	0.2	6.9
IRL	11.4	21.8	– 5.8	14.6
I	7.3	8.7	1.0	6.9
L (¹)	– 0.7	:	38.4	:
NL	1.7	9.4	– 3.4	10.1
A	7.3	10.1	8.5	8.0
P	4.3	7.9	2.0	6.9
FIN	1.0	10.0	– 6.4	4.3
S	– 8.5	7.7	– 13.9	4.3
UK	– 2.4	7.1	– 1.1	8.5

(¹) Luxembourg included with Belgium until 1998.
(²) Annual growth rates average.
Source: Eurostat, Comext.

Table 2.3.3. Extra-EU trade balance

	1990	1999	2000	2001	2001/2000
	In billion EUR				Absolute variation
EU-15	– 48.9	– 19.6	– 91.4	– 44.1	47.3
B (¹)	– 6.0	– 6.0	– 8.1	– 9.2	– 1.1
DK	1.0	2.6	2.7	3.7	1.0
D	10.9	28.9	17.1	42.8	25.7
EL	– 3.0	– 4.7	– 7.4	– 8.3	– 0.9
E	– 10.2	– 11.6	– 19.6	– 19.2	0.5
F	– 0.5	16.3	8.2	13.8	5.6
IRL	– 0.3	5.9	9.9	14.7	4.7
I	– 4.6	12.6	4.1	11.4	7.3
L (¹)	:	– 0.8	– 0.7	– 1.5	– 0.8
NL	– 18.4	– 44.7	– 61.6	– 56.8	4.8
A	– 0.7	4.5	3.9	3.9	0.0
P	– 3.0	– 4.3	– 5.6	– 5.6	0.0
FIN	– 0.5	6.3	7.9	9.0	1.1
S	1.5	12.4	13.3	13.7	0.4
UK	– 15.2	– 36.9	– 55.4	– 56.6	– 1.1

(¹) Luxembourg included with Belgium until 1998.
Source: Eurostat, Comext.

By contrast, the Netherlands and the United Kingdom registered, as almost always, the highest deficits totalling EUR 56.8 billion and EUR 56.6 billion respectively in 2001. Nevertheless, the Dutch deficit should be seen in the light of its intra-EU surplus and its transit role in EU trade.

Extra-EU trade by main partner

Exports

In the period under review, the group of industrialised countries made up of the United States, Japan and EFTA represented the main market for the EU as a whole. The United States is the main individual partner for extra-EU exports with a 24.3 % share in 2001. Japan's share of extra-EU exports has fallen from its 1996 peak to 4.6 %, while the share of exports to EFTA has declined slightly to 10.5 %.

The central and east European countries (CEECs) and the Commonwealth of Independent States (CIS) together received 18.0 % of extra-EU exports in 2001, and have steadily increased their share of EU exports over recent years.

African markets dramatically reduced their share, partly due to the fall in primary goods prices.

Latin America's share of extra-EU exports fell to 5.8 % in 2001. In fact, thanks to the economic recovery, the EU export share to these countries began to increase from the beginning of the 1990s.

The export share of the dynamic Asian economies (DAE) reached 8.3 % in 2001, and has begun to recover from the financial crisis in the region.

The relatively low share of extra-EU exports to China in comparison to other partners (3.1 % in 2001) should be noted.

EU exports to Near and Middle Eastern countries have fallen back to below 7 % in recent years.

Oceania's extra-EU export share has remained at around 2 % since 1991.

Imports

The group of industrialised countries constituted by the United States, Japan and EFTA are by far the most important suppliers to the European Union. The United States is also the main individual partner for extra-EU imports, with a share of 19.0 % in 2001. Japan's share has declined, from a peak of 12.2 % in 1992 to 7.4 % in 2001. The share of imports from EFTA has also declined in the last three years, to 10.6 % in 2001.

The CEECs and CIS, which accounted for 9.0 % in 1992, accounted together for 17.0 % of total extra-EU imports in 2001. This trend reflects the economic changes that occurred in these countries during these years. After the crisis that followed the dissolution of Comecon, the CEECs quickly redirected their trade towards the EU markets.

Table 2.3.4. Extra-EU trade, by partner

	1990	1999	2000	2001	1990	1999	2000	2001
	\multicolumn{4}{c}{EU-15 exports (billion EUR)}	\multicolumn{4}{c}{EU-15 imports (billion EUR)}
	390.6	760.2	942.0	977.0	439.4	779.8	1 033.4	1 021.1
	\multicolumn{4}{c}{Exports as a % of EU-15}	\multicolumn{4}{c}{Imports as a % of EU-15}
US	21.2	24.1	24.7	24.3	20.8	20.6	19.3	19.0
JP	6.3	4.7	4.8	4.6	11.7	9.2	8.4	7.4
EFTA	15.3	11.6	10.5	10.5	13.3	10.8	10.5	10.6
CEEC	6.2	13.4	13.3	14.1	5.4	10.2	9.9	11.4
CIS	:	2.8	3.0	3.9	:	4.1	5.3	5.6
Africa	11.9	7.5	7.0	7.1	11.6	7.3	8.1	8.5
Latin America	4.3	6.0	5.8	5.8	6.2	4.8	4.7	4.8
DAE	7.9	8.2	8.7	8.3	8.2	10.9	10.6	9.6
China	1.5	2.5	2.7	3.1	2.6	6.4	6.8	7.4
Near-Middle East	7.9	6.5	6.3	6.6	6.0	4.1	5.1	4.4
Oceania	2.6	2.3	2.1	2.0	1.6	1.3	1.2	1.3
ACP	4.5	4.1	4.1	4.1	4.8	4.2	4.2	4.6
Mediterranean Basin	12.4	11.6	11.6	10.3	10.1	8.1	8.6	8.9
ASEAN	4.4	4.1	4.3	4.3	4.0	7.1	6.9	6.4
OPEC	9.6	5.8	5.7	6.5	10.6	6.2	8.3	7.5
NAFTA	24.9	27.6	28.4	28.1	23.8	22.9	21.7	21.5

Source: Eurostat, Comext and IMF-DOTS.

THE UNION IN THE INTERNATIONAL FRAMEWORK

Table 2.3.5. Extra-EU trade balance, by partner

	1990	1999	2000	2001	1990	1999	2000	2001
	\multicolumn{4}{c}{Billion EUR}	\multicolumn{4}{c}{As a % of total trade (1)}
Extra EU-15	− 48.9	− 19.6	− 91.4	− 44.1	− 5.9	− 1.3	− 4.6	− 2.2
US	− 8.7	22.4	33.4	43.8	− 5.0	6.5	7.8	10.1
JP	− 26.9	− 36.5	− 42.2	− 30.6	− 35.4	− 34.1	− 32.0	− 25.5
EFTA	1.1	3.3	− 9.3	− 5.6	0.9	1.9	− 4.5	− 2.6
CEEC	0.5	21.7	22.3	21.5	1.0	11.9	9.8	8.5
CIS	:	− 11.0	− 27.2	− 19.7	:	− 20.9	− 32.9	− 20.7
Africa	− 4.5	− 0.1	− 17.8	− 17.1	− 4.6	− 0.1	− 11.9	− 11.0
Latin America	− 10.1	8.5	5.7	7.1	− 22.9	10.3	5.5	6.7
DAE	− 5.2	− 23.2	− 27.9	− 16.5	− 7.8	− 15.8	− 14.6	− 9.2
China	− 5.6	− 30.3	− 44.8	− 45.7	− 32.4	− 43.9	− 46.8	− 43.3
Near-Middle East	4.5	17.7	6.9	19.4	7.9	21.8	6.2	17.7
Oceania	2.9	7.3	7.3	6.9	16.9	26.8	23.2	21.2
ACP	− 3.6	− 1.1	− 5.0	− 7.5	− 9.3	− 1.6	− 6.1	− 8.6
Mediterrean Basin	4.3	25.0	20.8	10.0	4.6	16.5	10.5	5.2
ASEAN	− 0.4	− 24.1	− 30.7	− 23.4	− 1.2	− 27.9	− 27.6	− 21.7
OPEC	− 9.1	− 4.4	− 32.2	− 12.7	− 10.8	− 4.8	− 23.0	− 9.1
NAFTA	− 7.1	31.2	42.7	55.2	− 3.5	8.0	8.7	11.2

(1) Imports and exports.
Source: Eurostat, Comext and IMF-DOTS.

Africa, Latin America and Oceania all saw a decrease in their shares during the period under review.

The DAE and China have become very important suppliers to the European Union in recent times. Their shares of total EU imports were 9.6 % and 7.4 % in 2001.

Trade balance

The EU's trade balance with the United States has moved into a significant surplus over recent years, reaching EUR 43.8 billion in 2001.

Both in relative terms (as a percentage of trade with each country), and in value, bilateral trade with China recorded the biggest deficit in 2001 (43.3 % or EUR 45.7 billion), whereas Japan ranked in second place for the same year (25.5 % or EUR 30.6 billion).

The European Union has registered remarkable improvements in its trading position with the CEECs. A surplus of ECU 0.5 billion in 1990 shifted to a surplus of EUR 21.5 billion in 2001.

An increase in the EU exports to the CIS countries led to a significant reduction of the trade deficit in 2001.

The EU balance with Latin America and Near and Middle Eastern countries declined in 2000 (surpluses of EUR 5.7 billion and EUR 6.9 billion respectively) to sharply increase in 2001 (especially with the Near and Middle Eastern countries) reaching surpluses of EUR 7.1 billion and EUR 19.4 billion.

The trade position with the DAE improved in 2001, with a EUR 16.5 billion deficit compared with EUR 27.9 billion in 2000.

The trade deficit recorded with OPEC countries decreased in 2001 due to a combined reduction of prices and volumes of crude oil imports.

Extra-EU trade by main product

The European Union is a traditional exporter of manufactured products; in 2001, the share of manufactured products in total extra-EU exports reached 88.2 %.

Among manufactured products, the biggest share of extra-EU exports was accounted by machinery and transport equipment (47.0 % of total extra-EU exports in 2001). During the period under consideration, the share of chemical products also grew while the group "Other manufactured goods" remained stable at around 27 %.

The corresponding reduction in the share of primary products was mainly due to the declining importance of extra-EU exports of agri-food products (5.2 % in 2001). Meanwhile exports of crude materials were fairly stable at around 2 %.

Table 2.3.6. Extra-EU trade, by product

	1990	1999	2000	2001	1990	1999	2000	2001
	\multicolumn{4}{c	}{Exports (billion EUR)}	\multicolumn{4}{c	}{Imports (billion EUR)}
Total	390.6	760.2	942.0	977.0	439.4	779.8	1033.4	1021.1
	\multicolumn{4}{c	}{Exports as a %}	\multicolumn{4}{c	}{Imports as a %}
Primary products	12.2	9.9	10.5	9.7	33.1	21.6	24.6	24.5
Food, beverages, tobacco	7.4	5.7	5.3	5.2	8.4	6.4	5.3	5.7
Crude material	2.3	2.0	2.0	1.8	7.7	5.2	4.9	4.8
Energy	2.5	2.2	3.2	2.6	17.0	10.0	14.4	14.1
Manufactured goods	81.7	87.4	87.2	88.2	61.0	75.5	72.1	72.3
Chemicals	11.3	14.0	13.8	14.3	6.5	7.6	6.9	7.5
Machinery, transport	39.9	46.3	46.6	47.0	28.3	39.2	38.2	37.0
Other manufactured goods	30.5	27.1	26.9	26.9	26.2	28.7	27.1	27.8
Not classified elsewhere	6.1	2.6	2.2	2.2	5.9	2.8	3.3	3.2

Source: Eurostat, Comext.

The trend in extra-EU imports clearly shows the growing role of manufactured products. Primary products accounted for only 24.5 % in 2001. During the last decade, various factors substantially modified the EU import structure and consequently the share of manufactured imports increased reaching 72.3 % in 2001.

Machinery and transport equipment increased its share and it became the most important group of products imported, reaching 37.0 % in 2001. Chemicals and other manufactured products were more stable, with shares of 7.5 % and 27.8 % in 2001. Over the last four years the rising oil price has led to a dramatic increase in the share of energy in EU imports, from 8.7 % in 1998 to 14.1 % in 2001.

The European Union economy, based on manufacturing industry, has a structural deficit in the primary sector (EUR 155.9 billion in 2001) and a structural surplus in the manufactured goods sector (EUR 123.7 billion in 2001).

The energy deficit stabilised in 2001 (EUR 118.6 billion compared with EUR 118.8 billion in 2000) while the surplus for machinery and transport equipment has strongly increased (EUR 81.5 billion in 2001 compared with EUR 44.5 billion in 2000).

Table 2.3.7. Extra-EU trade balance, by product

	1999	2000	2001	1999	2000	2001
	\multicolumn{3}{c	}{Billion EUR}	\multicolumn{3}{c	}{As a % of total trade ([1])}
Total	– 19.6	– 91.4	– 44.1	– 1.3	– 4.6	– 2.2
Raw material	– 93.1	– 155.3	– 155.9	– 38.1	– 44.0	– 45.2
Food, beverages, tobacco	– 6.5	– 4.9	– 6.6	– 6.9	– 4.7	– 6.1
Crude material	– 24.9	– 31.6	– 30.7	– 44.8	– 45.7	– 45.9
Energy	– 61.7	– 118.8	– 118.6	– 65.0	– 66.3	– 70.3
Manufactured goods	75.6	76.3	123.7	6.0	4.9	7.7
Chemicals	47.7	58.2	63.7	28.8	29.0	29.4
Machinery, transport	45.9	44.5	81.5	7.0	5.3	9.7
Other manufactured goods	– 18.0	– 26.4	– 21.5	– 4.2	– 5.0	– 3.9
Not classified elsewhere	– 2.2	– 12.4	– 12.0	– 5.1	– 22.7	– 22.1

([1]) Imports and exports.
Source: Eurostat, Comext.

Intra-EU trade

The Intrastat system was introduced on 1 January 1993 due to the abolition of customs formalities within the EU. Since that date, data have been collected directly from firms. As the Intrastat system for collecting data is different from the system used in previous years, the change in the figures between 1992 and 1993 should be interpreted with caution.

Share of intra-EU trade in total EU trade flows

Intra-EU trade has always represented more than 50 % of the EU's total trade, and at present it is around 60 %. Since 1970, there have been four periods when intra-EU trade declined as a percentage of total EU trade. During the periods 1973-75, 1979-81 and 1998-2001, the relative importance of intra-EU trade fell sharply due to increases in primary goods prices. The total value of extra-EU imports went up, raising total extra-EU trade figures in comparison with intra-EU trade. In 1993, in spite of implementation of the internal market, another decline in the relative importance of intra-EU trade occurred. At this time the collection of intra-EU data was reorganised. A substantial drop in intra-EU figures, implying a certain degree of underestimation of flows, corresponded with the introduction of Intrastat. In particular, arrivals are underestimated, and dispatches are considered the most reliable figure of intra-EU trade. However, it is difficult to assess to what extent the shift in 1993 is a statistical phenomenon.

The volume of intra-EU trade did in fact increase significantly with the enlargement of the EU in 1995, since the trade of Austria, Sweden and Finland is strongly geared to the EU market. Thus, the intra-EU share of total EU trade before the three new Member States joined the EU was 58 % in 1994. One year later, in 1995,

Figure 2.3.2. Intra-EU trade (as a % of total trade)

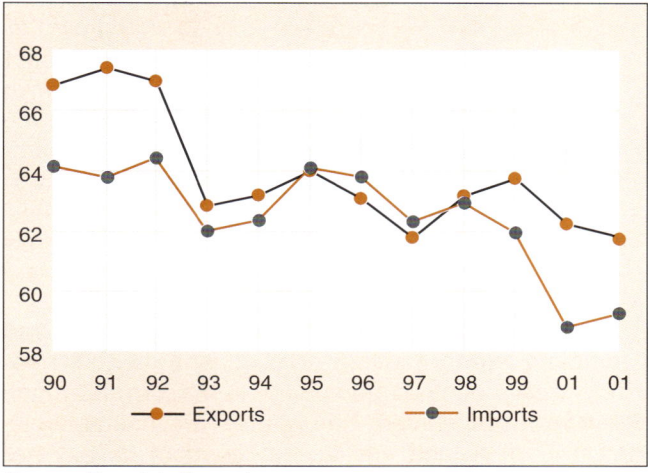

Source: Eurostat, Comext.

Table 2.3.8. Intra-EU dispatches/arrivals

	1990	1999	2000	2001	1990	1999	2000	2001
	\multicolumn{4}{c|}{Dispatches (billion EUR)}	\multicolumn{4}{c}{Arrivals (billion EUR)}
	787.3	1 338.0	1 563.2	1 583.4	786.6	1 270.1	1 484.2	1 488.5
	\multicolumn{4}{c|}{As a % of total exports ([1])}	\multicolumn{4}{c}{As a % of total imports ([2])}
EU-15	66.8	63.8	62.4	61.8	64.2	62.0	59.0	59.3
B ([3])	79.9	76.4	74.4	77.1	74.2	70.4	68.7	70.8
DK	68.4	67.0	66.9	65.8	69.4	69.8	68.3	68.4
D	64.0	57.5	56.5	55.2	62.1	57.8	54.9	55.8
EL	68.0	53.9	43.5	43.9	67.7	66.8	56.0	54.3
E	67.6	71.2	70.3	69.5	62.3	68.7	66.4	64.5
F	65.3	62.4	61.6	60.6	68.1	66.6	65.1	64.9
IRL	78.6	66.0	63.2	62.9	73.9	61.7	62.2	65.2
I	62.8	58.2	55.5	53.8	61.9	61.5	56.7	56.5
L ([3])	:	85.4	84.2	87.2	:	81.7	82.6	78.2
NL	81.4	79.5	78.7	78.6	63.7	55.1	51.1	51.8
A	67.2	62.9	61.4	61.5	70.7	72.3	68.8	68.2
P	81.2	83.2	80.3	79.7	72.0	78.1	75.1	74.1
FIN	62.2	57.7	55.7	53.7	60.5	65.4	61.9	63.5
S	62.3	58.4	55.9	54.7	63.4	67.7	64.2	65.2
UK	57.3	58.6	57.0	57.6	56.5	53.2	49.4	50.0

([1]) Dispatches and exports.
([2]) Arrivals and imports.
([3]) Luxembourg included with Belgium until 1998.
Source: Eurostat, Comext.

THE UNION IN THE INTERNATIONAL FRAMEWORK

when the enlargement took place, the share of intra-EU trade reached around 64 %. The EU time series presented in this publication do not show this shift, because they are calculated as if all 15 Member States had belonged to the EU since the beginning in order to keep the time series stable. Nevertheless, the time series reflects the increasing importance of intra-EU trade within total EU trade. This has become possible because the links among Member States' economies have become stronger over the last few decades.

The share of intra-EU trade varies widely from one Member State to another. As a general rule, for relatively small countries such as Luxembourg, Portugal, Belgium and Denmark, the shares are higher, while Italy, Germany and the United Kingdom have lower ratios. Some countries like France are in an intermediate position.

As mentioned above, dispatches are considered the most reliable figure for analysing intra-EU trade. Manufactured goods registered the highest share of total intra-EU trade with 80.8 % in 2001. As in the case of extra-EU trade, the most dynamic product category in the last 10 years has been machinery and transport equipment, which grew from 36.2 % in 1990 to 41.3 % in 2001, while chemical products increased by two percentage points during the same period.

The intra-EU share for primary products decreased from 17.3 % in 1990 to 15.8 % in 2001. In 2001, intra-EU trade as a percentage of total EU trade in primary products and manufactured products was fairly similar (around 59 % and 61 %), although up to 1992 the ratio for manufactured products was always significantly higher. This reflects the fact that extra-EU trade in manufactured goods is becoming more important. Major differences can be found between product categories. In the case of primary products the intra-EU ratios for food products were conspicuously higher (71.6 % in 2001) than those for fuel products and crude material (42.9 % and 57.1 % respectively), which are more oriented to extra-EU trade. As for manufactured products, the intra-EU ratios for chemicals were higher (66.1 %) than those for machinery and transport equipment and other manufactured goods (both around 60 %).

Figure 2.3.3. Total intra-EU dispatches and arrivals (billion EUR)

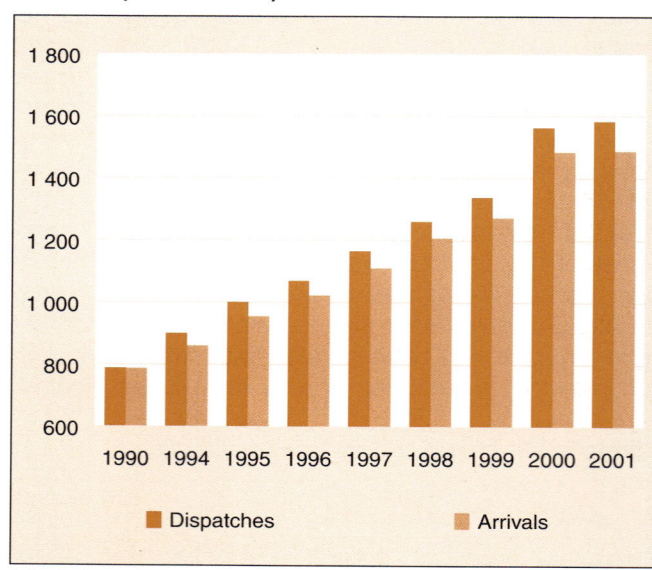

NB: Arrivals have been underestimated since 1993 (introduction of Intrastat).
Source: Eurostat, Comext.

Table 2.3.9. Intra-EU dispatches, by product (as a %)

	1990	1999	2000	2001
Total (billion EUR)	787.3	1 338.0	1 563.9	1 583.4
Shares (as a %)				
Primary products	17.3	15.4	16.1	15.8
Food, beverages, tobacco	9.9	9.5	8.8	8.9
Crude material	4.0	3.0	3.0	2.8
Energy	3.5	2.9	4.3	4.1
Manufactured goods	78.6	82.2	81.8	80.8
Chemicals	10.7	12.6	12.9	13.4
Machinery, transport	36.2	42.0	42.1	41.3
Other manufactured goods	31.7	27.6	26.9	26.0
Not classified elsewhere	4.1	2.4	2.1	3.4

Source: Eurostat, Comext.

Table 2.3.10. Intra-EU share of total trade ([1]) by product (as a %)

	1990	1999	2000	2001
Total	65.5	62.9	60.7	60.6
Raw material	58.4	62.5	58.5	58.7
Food, beverages, tobacco	70.1	72.9	72.1	71.6
Crude material	59.3	58.8	57.8	57.1
Energy	39.0	43.9	42.5	42.9
Manufactured goods	67.5	63.0	61.3	60.7
Chemicals	69.6	67.1	66.7	66.1
Machinery, transport	66.7	62.3	60.4	60.0
Other manufactured goods	67.7	62.3	60.3	59.0
Not classified elsewhere	62.3	61.1	55.5	68.1

([1]) Intra and extra.
Source: Eurostat, Comext.

THE UNION IN THE INTERNATIONAL FRAMEWORK

Intra-EU trade balance

Since 1993 and the introduction of the Intrastat system (see note above), the sums of the intra-EU arrivals and dispatches recorded by the Member States do not tally as they should do theoretically. Before 1993, although divergences existed, they were relatively small, but from 1993 new statistical problems occurred, mainly because of non-response from firms and the threshold system introduced.

As far as the threshold system is concerned, the import (arrival) flow is in principle less concentrated than the export (dispatch) flow and this could partially explain the underestimation of arrivals: with Intrastat, the smaller companies are no longer obliged to make a statistical declaration. Only a few Member States produce "corrected" figures which take account of the threshold effect.

The statistical discrepancies in intra-EU trade flows make it difficult to assess the development of intra-EU trade balances by Member States. This applies particularly to the transition from 1992 to 1993. However, the following can be concluded:

Since 1985, the Netherlands has almost always recorded the largest intra-EU surplus. In 2001, it reached EUR 81.6 billion, followed by Germany (EUR 44.2 billion), Belgium (EUR 21.5 billion) and Ireland (EUR 21.3 billion). Nevertheless, the Netherlands is a special case, as an important part of its trade is "in transit" (i.e. coming from outside the EU and going to another Member State). This is consistent

Table 2.3.11. Intra-EU trade balance (billion EUR)

	1990	1999	2000	2001
B (¹)	4.2	19.5	19.9	21.5
DK	1.4	1.6	3.5	3.3
D	33.9	36.3	42.0	44.2
EL	– 6.3	– 13.5	– 12.9	– 12.3
E	– 10.4	– 17.4	– 24.6	– 17.7
F	– 16.2	– 6.2	– 19.4	– 18.2
IRL	2.6	17.1	18.6	21.3
I	– 4.6	1.4	– 2.2	– 2.2
L (¹)	:	– 2.0	– 2.5	– 0.8
NL	20.7	56.3	77.7	81.6
A	– 5.5	– 9.4	– 8.9	– 8.2
P	– 3.6	– 10.1	– 11.3	– 10.2
FIN	0.2	3.2	4.7	2.8
S	1.2	2.9	2.1	0.4
UK	– 16.9	– 12.5	– 7.8	– 10.6

(¹) Luxembourg included with Belgium until 1998.
Source: Eurostat, Comext.

with its large extra-EU deficit. The growth in the Irish surplus during the 1990s is particularly impressive.

France, Spain, Greece and the United Kingdom recorded the largest intra-EU deficits, totalling EUR 18.2 billion, EUR 17.7 billion, EUR 12.3 billion and EUR 10.6 billion respectively in 2001.

For some countries at different periods, their global deficits (their extra-EU deficits must be added) have shown a dramatic increase in comparison with the size of their economies (e.g. Italy in the early 1980s and Spain in the early 1990s).

Figure 2.3.4. Trade balances of EU Member States in 2001 (billion EUR)

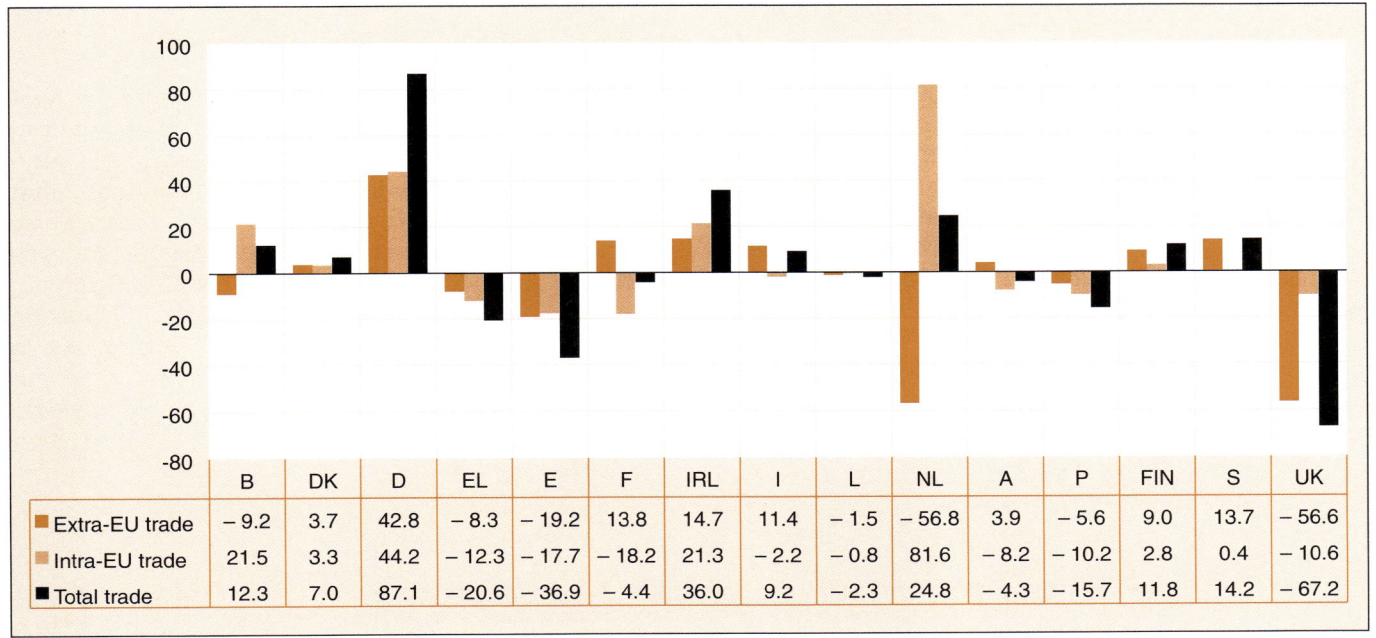

	B	DK	D	EL	E	F	IRL	I	L	NL	A	P	FIN	S	UK
Extra-EU trade	– 9.2	3.7	42.8	– 8.3	– 19.2	13.8	14.7	11.4	– 1.5	– 56.8	3.9	– 5.6	9.0	13.7	– 56.6
Intra-EU trade	21.5	3.3	44.2	– 12.3	– 17.7	– 18.2	21.3	– 2.2	– 0.8	81.6	– 8.2	– 10.2	2.8	0.4	– 10.6
Total trade	12.3	7.0	87.1	– 20.6	– 36.9	– 4.4	36.0	9.2	– 2.3	24.8	– 4.3	– 15.7	11.8	14.2	– 67.2

Source: Eurostat, Comext.

THE UNION IN THE INTERNATIONAL FRAMEWORK

2.4. International trade in services

Balance of payments

A country's external trade in services is registered in its balance of payments (BOP). The balance of payments records all economic transactions undertaken between the residents of a country and the non-residents during a given period of time.

The balance of payments of the European Union is compiled as the sum of harmonised balance of payments accounts of the 15 Member States. The balance of payments of the EU institutions is also added to the European Union aggregate.

The methodological framework is that of the fifth edition of the International Monetary Fund (IMF) balance of payments manual.

In 2000, the EU was the world's largest trader in services. Extra-EU exchanges (exports and imports) of services amounted to EUR 590.8 billion, making for 24 % of total world trade in services. The United States ranked second with EUR 550.9 billion and a share of 22 % whereas Japan's imports and exports of services reached EUR 201.6 billion, leaving an 8 % share in total world exchanges of services.

The extra-EU surplus in services remained stable at EUR 5.6 billion in 2000. Nevertheless, there were disparate trends between the most relevant types of services; hence, the EUR 1.9 billion surplus in other business services ([2]) in 1999 moved into a EUR 3.6 billion deficit in 2000. In contrast, the travel deficit contracted at EUR – 3.0 billion in 2000, EUR 2.0 billion less than in 1999.

Extra-EU trade in services in 2000: almost double 1992 volume

Trade in services has grown markedly since 1992 with EU imports and exports of services rising from ECU 304.5 billion in 1992 to EUR 590.8 billion in 2000. The annual growth rate of trade in services attained in 2000 was the highest since 1992, with both credits and debits growing by 18 %. However, over the same period, debits rose more rapidly than credits, and consequently the surplus diminished from ECU 13.8 billion in 1992 to EUR 5.6 billion in 2000. Since 1997, when the balance of services reached a high of ECU 16.2 billion, the surplus contracted uninterruptedly, although the contraction was much more tempered in 2000 (– 3 % in 2000 against – 43 % in 1999).

Figure 2.4.1. Extra-EU trade in services, 1992-2000 (billion EUR)

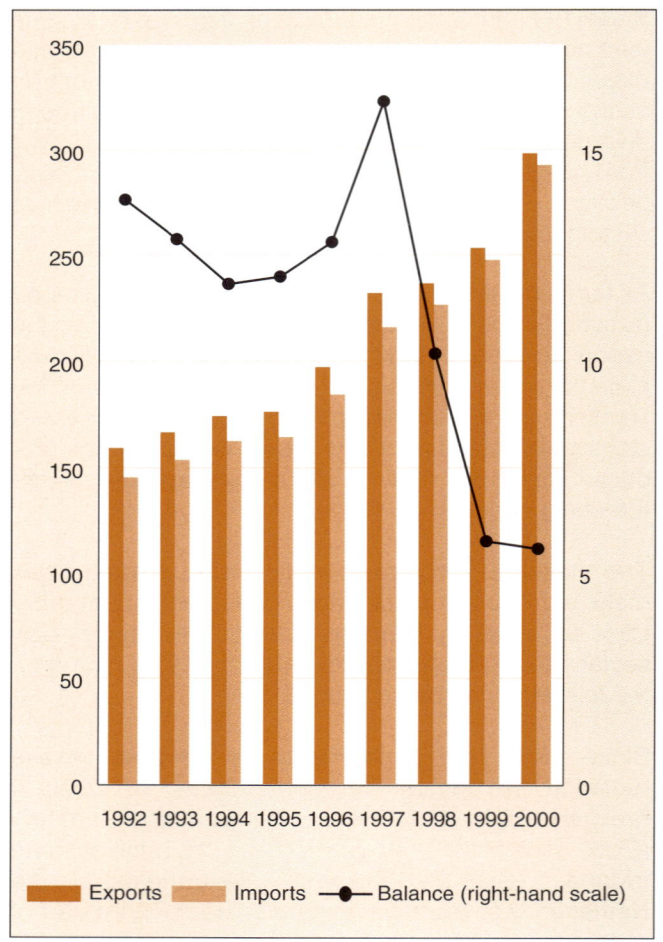

Source: Eurostat.

Composition of extra-EU trade in services remained unchanged in 2000

The share of the main categories of services in relation to the total remained practically unchanged in 2000. Three quarters of the total transactions in services corresponded to transportation, travel and other business services. Royalties and licence fees represented 6 % of total services whilst financial services accounted for 5 % after boosting by 32 % in 2000. Computer and information services and construction services cornered 3 % of EU total transactions in services each. Finally, insurance services, communications services, personal, cultural and recreational services and government services, n.i.e. presented all a share of 2 %.

([2]) The item "other business services" covers merchanting and other trade related services; operational leasing; legal, accounting, management consultancy and public relations services; advertising, market research and public opinion polling services; research and development services; architectural, engineering and other technical services; agricultural, mining and on-site processing; other; services between affiliated enterprises, n.i.e.

Figure 2.4.2. Breakdown of total extra-EU transactions in services in 2000

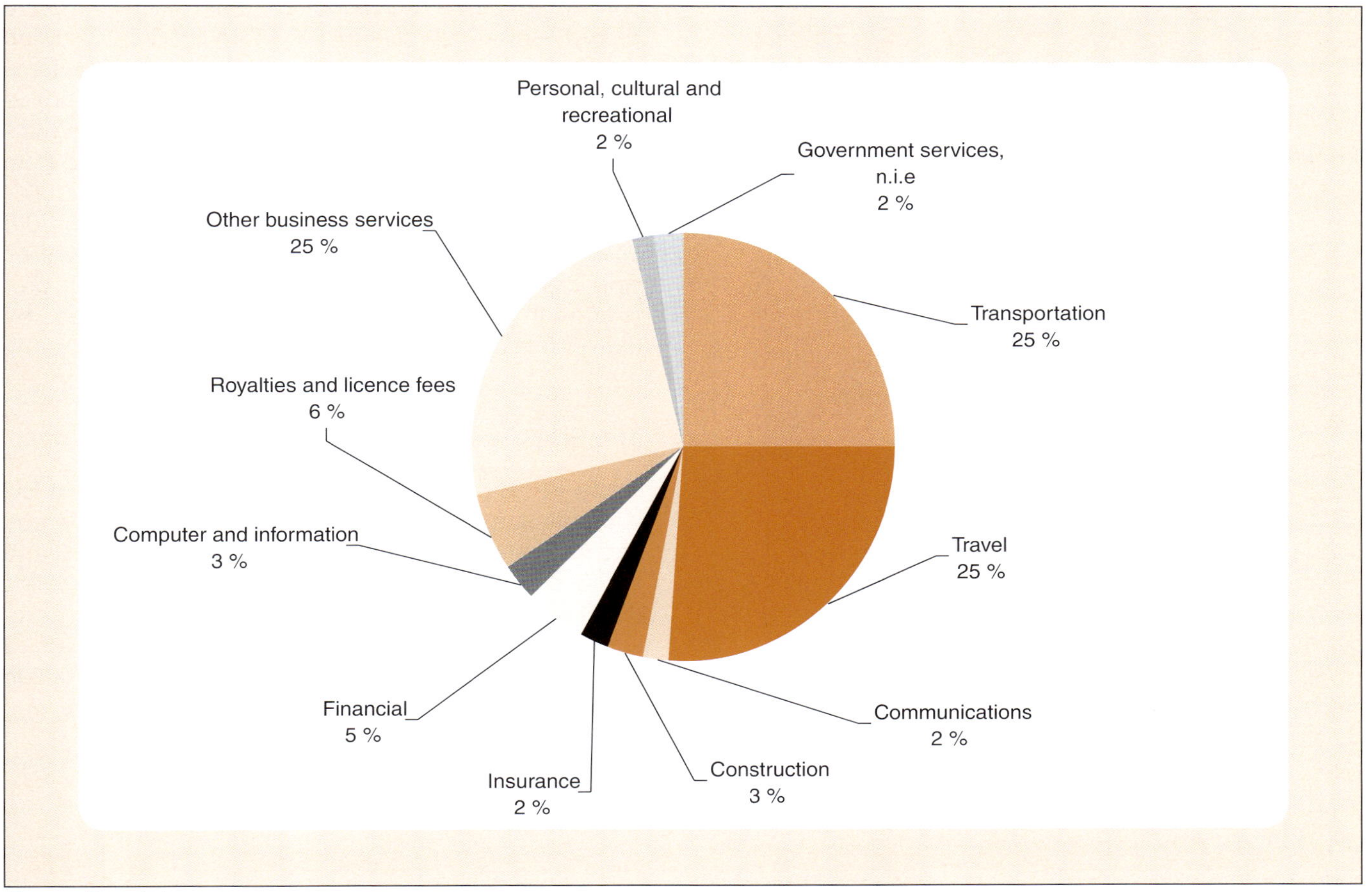

- Personal, cultural and recreational 2 %
- Government services, n.i.e 2 %
- Transportation 25 %
- Travel 25 %
- Communications 2 %
- Construction 3 %
- Insurance 2 %
- Financial 5 %
- Computer and information 3 %
- Royalties and licence fees 6 %
- Other business services 25 %

Source: Eurostat.

EU services in 2000: travel deficit contracted by EUR 2.0 billion and transactions in transportation services boosted by 23 %

Air transport presented a EUR 7.6 billion surplus in 2000, which contrasted with the deficits recorded by sea transport and other transportation, EUR – 3.1 billion and EUR – 1.5 billion, respectively. Moreover, exports and imports of transportation services increased by 23 % and 24 %, respectively, together amounting to EUR 149.7 billion, mainly due to the striking rise of sea transport, which saw a 35 % growth in 2000. Additionally, the deficit in travel contracted notably in 2000, totalling EUR – 3.0 billion. The volume of travel transactions in 2000 was more than double that of 1992.

The customary EU surplus in insurance services rose to EUR 5.3 billion in 2000; however, the main contribution to the EUR 5.6 billion surplus in the balance of services was from financial services, which yielded a EUR 9.3 billion surplus in 2000 (EUR 2.3 billion more than in 1999).

Both exports and imports of financial services rose by 32 % in 2000 in relation to 1999 recording an unprecedented growth rate. Hence, exports amounted to EUR 18.7 billion while imports totalled EUR 9.3 billion. Nevertheless, concerning cumulative growth since 1992, the most stunning rise was recorded in computer and information services; these transactions multiplied more than fourfold during this period, passing from EUR 3.7 billion to EUR 15.7 billion.

The noteworthy deficit recorded in royalties and licence fees (EUR – 7.6 billion), together with the EUR – 3.6 billion deficit in other business services, counterbalanced part of the positive results achieved in other items. Regarding royalties and licence fees, the deficit registered by this item has become a structural phenomenon in the EU, predominantly due to the amount of the deficit accrued with the United States, i.e. EUR – 10.1 billion in 2000. Nevertheless, the deficit narrowed by EUR 0.9 billion in relation to 1999.

THE UNION IN THE INTERNATIONAL FRAMEWORK

Figure 2.4.3. Extra-EU balances by type of services (billion EUR)

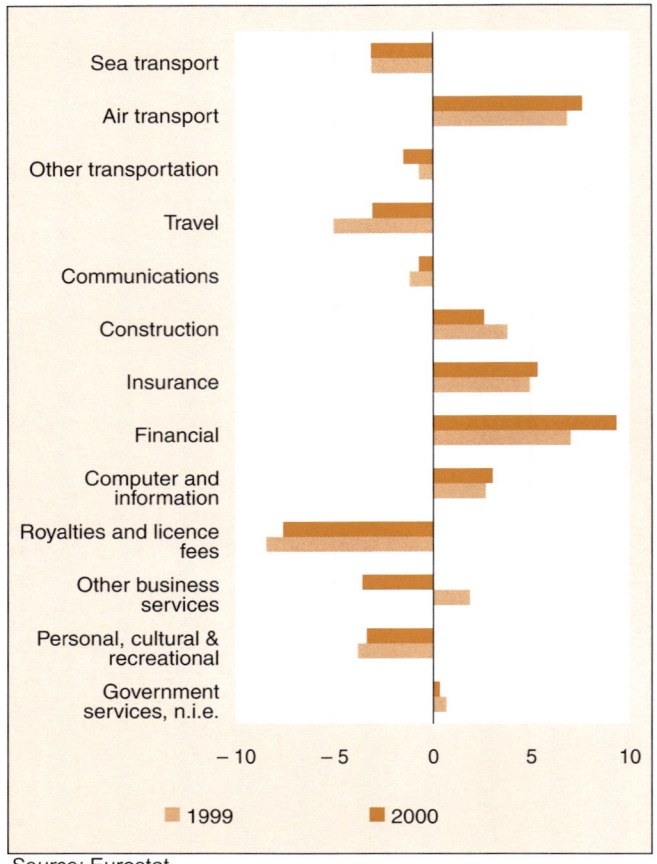

Source: Eurostat.

The most exceptional variation in terms of net flows concerned other business services, passing from a EUR 1.9 billion surplus in 1999 to a EUR – 3.6 billion deficit in 2000. The balances of all its sub-items recorded larger deficits or a less significant surplus than in 1999. Thus, the largest deficit, obtained in merchanting and other trade related services, passed from EUR – 0.2 billion in 1999 to EUR – 3.9 billion in 2000. The deficit in operational leasing stood at EUR – 0.8 billion in 2000 compared to EUR – 0.1 billion in 1999, whereas the surplus in miscellaneous business, professional and technical services decreased by EUR 1.0 billion to EUR 1.2 billion.

The EU partners in trade in services

Trade in services with Japan reported the largest EU bilateral surplus (EUR 8.2 billion) in 2000 whereas exchanges with European countries other than EU and EFTA countries led to the highest bilateral deficit (EUR – 8.1 billion). Exchanges of transportation services with the United States of America left a EUR 7.8 billion surplus whilst the balance of royalties and license fees amounted to EUR – 10.1 billion.

Table 2.4.1. Geographical breakdown of extra-EU trade in services 2000 (billion EUR)

	Extra EU-15	EFTA (1)	Other European countries (2)	Africa	America, excluding USA	United States of America	Asia, excluding Japan	Japan	Oceania and polar regions	Other
Services	5.6	3.5	– 8.1	– 1.3	0.8	2.0	– 0.9	8.2	0.7	0.6
Transportation	3.0	0.6	– 4.2	– 1.7	0.1	7.8	– 2.2	2.3	0.8	– 0.5
Travel	– 3.0	5.0	– 5.8	– 2.9	– 2.6	1.4	– 1.7	4.0	– 0.5	0.1
Other services	5.6	– 2.1	1.9	3.4	3.2	– 7.2	3.0	1.9	0.4	1.0
Communications services	– 0.7	0.0	– 0.4	– 0.1	– 0.2	0.2	– 0.2	– 0.1	0.0	0.0
Construction services	2.6	– 0.1	0.3	1.1	0.4	0.7	0.3	0.0	0.0	0.1
Insurance services	5.3	0.3	0.2	0.2	1.2	2.5	0.6	0.2	0.1	0.0
Financial services	9.3	0.7	1.1	0.5	1.4	3.4	1.0	1.2	0.1	– 0.1
Computer and information services	3.1	1.6	0.5	0.2	0.6	– 0.3	0.2	0.2	0.1	0.0
Royalties and licence fees	– 7.6	– 0.6	0.4	0.3	0.4	– 10.1	1.3	0.2	0.2	0.3
Other business services	– 3.6	– 3.5	0.5	1.5	– 0.1	– 2.1	0.1	0.1	– 0.1	– 0.1
Personal, cultural and recreational services	– 3.3	– 0.4	– 0.2	– 0.1	– 0.2	– 2.6	0.0	0.1	0.0	0.0
Government services, n.i.e.	0.4	– 0.1	– 0.4	– 0.3	– 0.3	1.1	– 0.3	0.0	0.0	0.8
Services not allocated	0.0	0.0	0.0	0.0	0.0	0.0	0.0	0.0	0.0	0.0

(1) European Free Trade Association.
(2) European countries other than EU and EFTA countries.
Source: Eurostat.

2.5. Foreign direct investment

Foreign direct investment (FDI) statistics give information on one of the major aspects of globalisation. For enterprises wanting to sell abroad, FDI is a supplement or an alternative to cross-border trade in goods and services.

Within the balance of payments statistics Eurostat maintains an FDI database that comprises harmonised and thus comparable data with a geographical and activity breakdown of inward and outward FDI flows, positions and earnings for the European Union, its Member States and its major FDI partners.

> **Foreign direct investment (FDI)** is the category of international investment that reflects the objective of obtaining a lasting interest by a resident entity in one economy in an enterprise resident in another economy. The lasting interest implies the existence of a long-term relationship between the direct investor and the enterprise, and a significant degree of influence by the investor on the management of the enterprise. Formally defined, a direct investment enterprise is an unincorporated or incorporated enterprise in which a direct investor owns 10 % or more of the ordinary shares or voting power (for an incorporated enterprise) or the equivalent (for an unincorporated enterprise).

> **FDI flows and positions**
>
> Through direct investment flows, an investor builds up a foreign direct investment position that features on his balance sheet. This FDI position (or FDI stock) differs from the accumulated flows because of revaluation (changes in prices or exchange rates) and other adjustments like rescheduling or cancellation of loans, debt forgiveness or debt-equity swaps.

This section first gives a brief overview of recent trends in FDI activity and presents the latest FDI flows figures (for 2001 and revised data for 2000) for the EU as a whole and for individual EU Member States. Secondly, we look at the detailed geographical breakdown of the EU direct investment outside the EU, using longer and more detailed series that cover flows up to 2000 and end-1999 positions [3].

FDI activity contracted in 2001 after four years of high growth [4]

The acceleration of globalisation in recent years has brought a characteristically strong rise in foreign direct investments (FDI) among the world's main economic actors. For the European Union this trend was especially strong during the second half of the 1990s and in 2000. In 2000, after three years of strong growth, EU outward FDI flows excluding reinvested earnings reached the record level of EUR 323 billion (equivalent to 3.8 % of the EU GDP). By the end of 2000 EU FDI assets had risen to three times their 1995 value and exceeded United States assets abroad. The EU FDI net position was EUR 683 billion, equivalent to 8 % of GDP.

During the same period 1995-2000, the United States reversed their historical role of net investor abroad and became the major world recipient of FDI capital and a net recipient in terms of annual FDI flows. The US net

Figure 2.5.1. EU FDI stocks with extra-EU countries, assets, liabilities and net 1995-2000

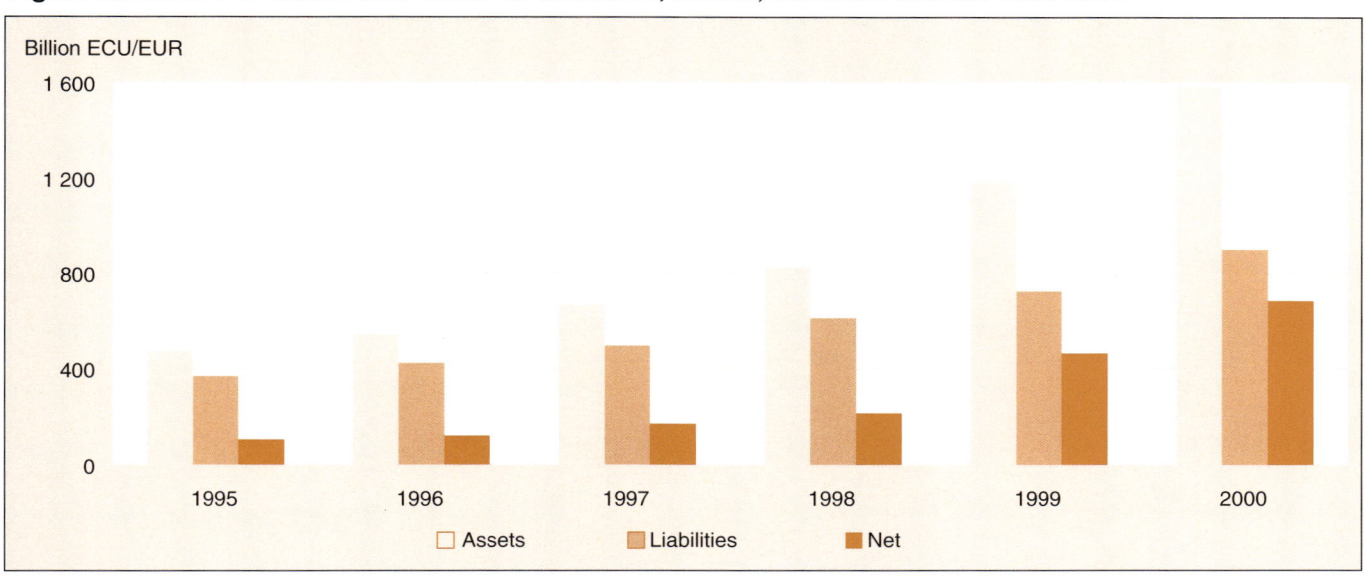

NB: The 2000 figures are estimated by cumulating 2000 flows to end-1999 positions and adjusting assets for exchange rate changes.
Source: Eurostat.

---

[3] See Eurostat EU FDI Yearbook 2001 for a complete presentation of the detailed series, also with respect to its breakdown between industrial activities.

[4] The preliminary figures for 2001 presented here cover equity capital and inter-company loans but exclude reinvested earnings.

THE UNION IN THE INTERNATIONAL FRAMEWORK

Figure 2.5.2. USA FDI stocks with the rest of the world, assets, liabilities and net 1995-2000

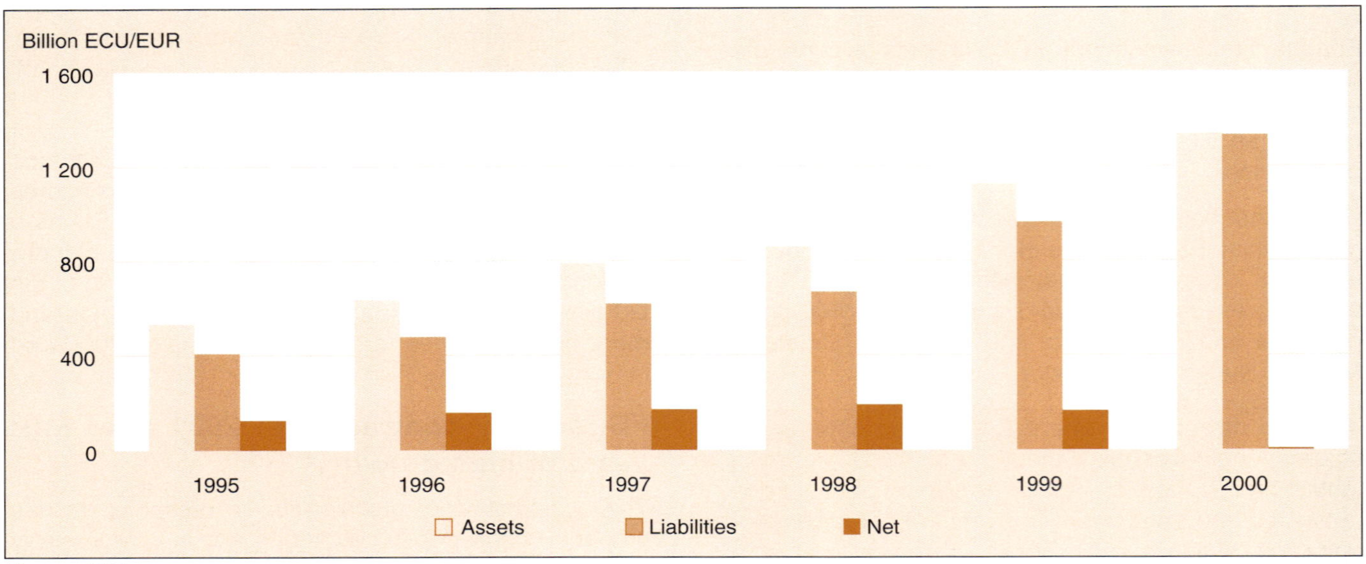

Source: BEA.

FDI position was still positive but close to zero at the end of 2000. A high share of this investment came in fact from the EU itself. At the same time, high growth rates were also recorded for EU inward FDI. In absolute terms, the value of EU inward FDI stocks grew from ECU 367 billion at the end of 1995 to EUR 899 billion at the end of 2000. Comparing the EU with the United States shows that the difference in the value of FDI stocks held invested in the two economies widened most significantly in 1999 and 2000 ([5]).

In 2001, however, EU FDI flows with extra-EU countries saw a reduction by nearly 40 % on 2000, on both the inward (– 39 %) and the outward (– 37 %) side. This reflected a worldwide reduction in international mergers and acquisitions, after seeing all records broken in 2000. The contraction in FDI was generalised and concerned, with comparable intensity, also US investment abroad. On the other hand, the US market appeared to have lost part of its attractiveness for director investors ([6]). The fall in extra-EU outward FDI was in fact largely driven by the reduction by 42 % of EU investment in the United States.

With outflows at EUR 202 billion (2.3 % of EU GDP) and inflows at EUR 97 billion (1.1 % of EU GDP), in 2001 the EU continued to be a net investor abroad.

Figure 2.5.3. Annual rate of growth of EU FDI flows with extra-EU, 1996-2001

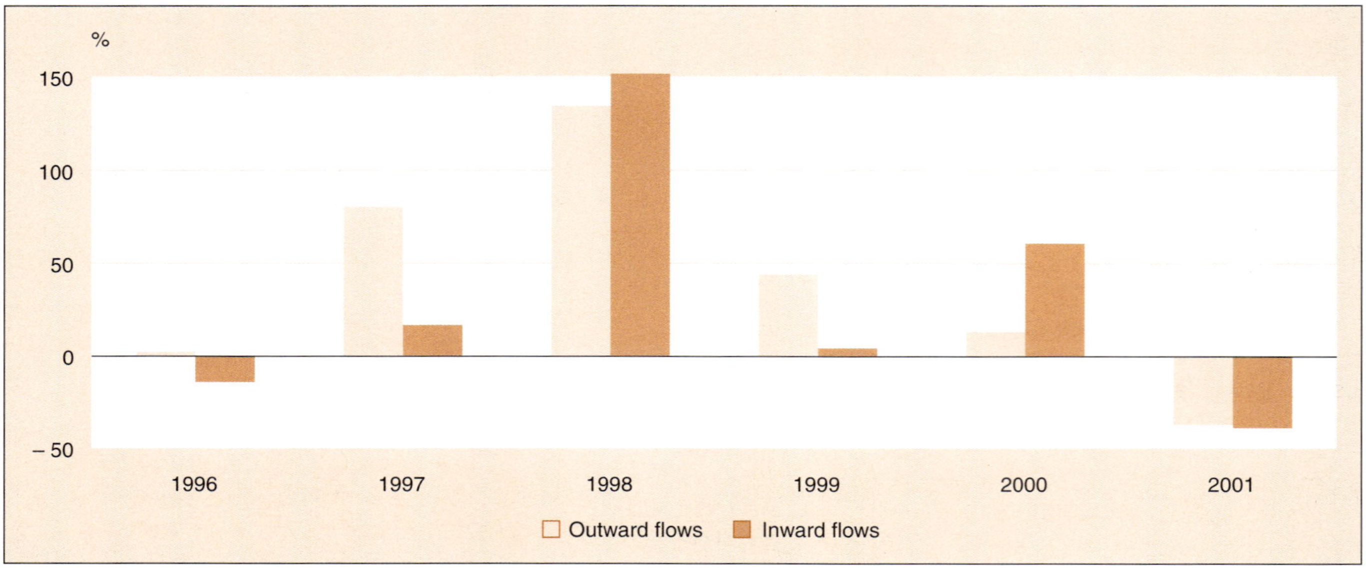

Source: Eurostat.

([5]) It is worth pointing out that the fluctuation in the euro/dollar exchange rate contributed to the growth of US liabilities, measured in euro, as well as to the growth of EU FDI assets abroad, as a large part of them was already located in the United States.

([6]) See data published at http://www.bea.doc.gov/bea/di/.

THE UNION IN THE INTERNATIONAL FRAMEWORK

Figure 2.5.4. EU FDI flows as a percentage of GDP

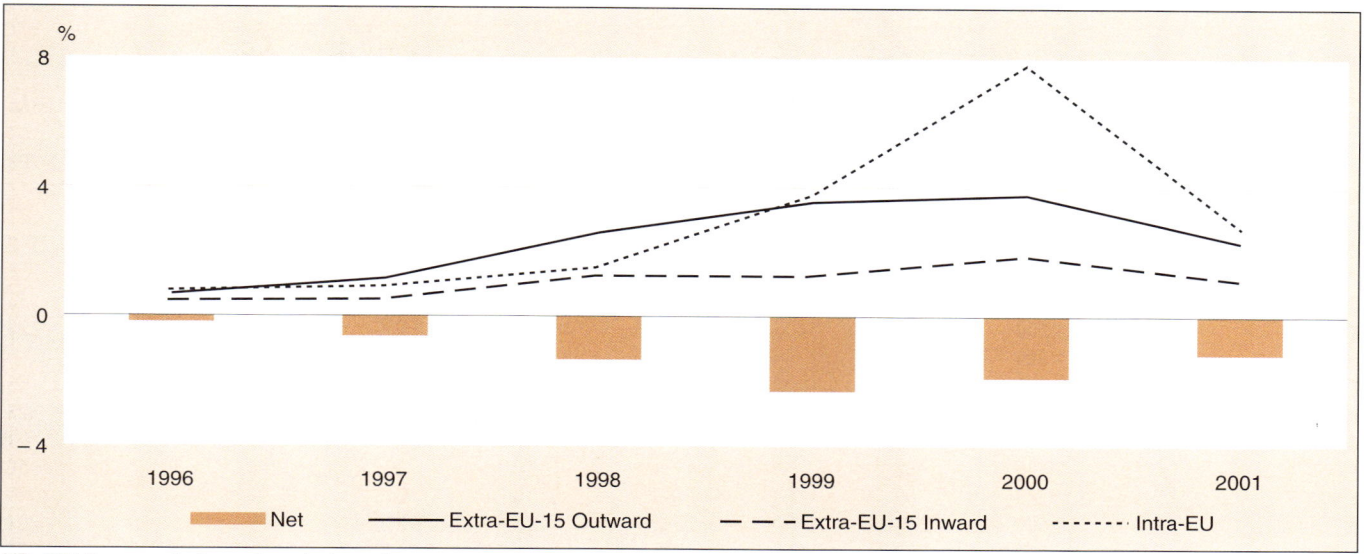

NB: FDI flows excluding reinvested earnings.
Source: Eurostat.

However, the net FDI outflows fell to 1.2 % of GDP as compared to the 1.9 % recorded in 2000. Always considering net investment, Germany was the main contributor to the EU total with a net outflow of EUR 51 billion, followed by France and Spain with EUR 26 and EUR 12 billion, respectively. On the other hand, with inward higher than outward by EUR 18 billion, the United Kingdom was the most important net recipient of FDI capital in 2001. Finland, Sweden and Italy were the only other Member States recording inflows higher than outflows in 2001.

As shown in figure 2.5.4, the fall in 2001 FDI flows was particularly intense for intra-EU investment, but this was also due to the exceptional level they had reached in 2000. After the three-digits growth rates recorded in 1999 and 2000, in 2001 intra-EU FDI flows fell to 2.7 % of the EU GDP, but still remained higher than flows with the extra-EU (inward and outward). In particular, 2001 intra-EU direct investment accounted for two thirds of total FDI inflows received by Member States (78 % in 2000).

The fall in 2001 FDI was widespread among Member States

In 2001, reduced FDI flows were recorded by the vast majority of Member States. The only countries having positive growth rates on both inward and outward investment with the extra-EU were Germany and Greece. For FDI received, also France, the Netherlands and Finland recorded higher inflows than the year before. On the other hand, outflows from Austria, Belgium/Luxembourg and Denmark increased between 2000 and 2001. Ireland recorded a disinvestment in both directions, but the withdrawal of capital from FDI stocks invested in Ireland was particularly high (EUR 12 billion).

With EUR 60 billion and a share of 30 %, Germany was the first contributor to 2001 extra-EU FDI outflows,

Figure 2.5.5a. FDI inflows from extra-EU countries by Member States (as a % of GDP)

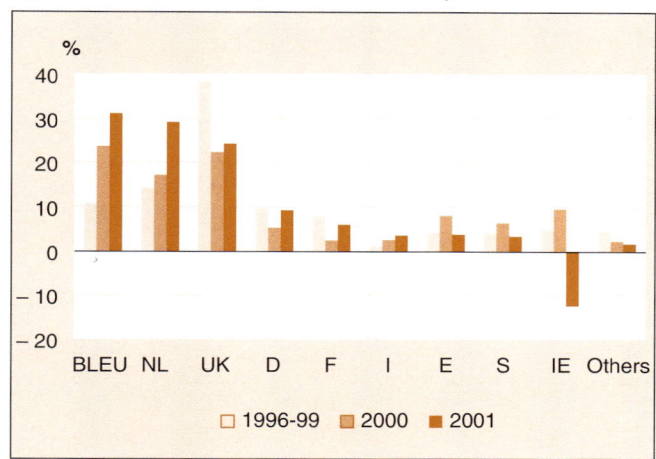

NB: FDI flows excluding reinvested earnings
Source: Eurostat.

Figure 2.5.5b. FDI outflows to extra-EU countries by Member States (as a % of GDP)

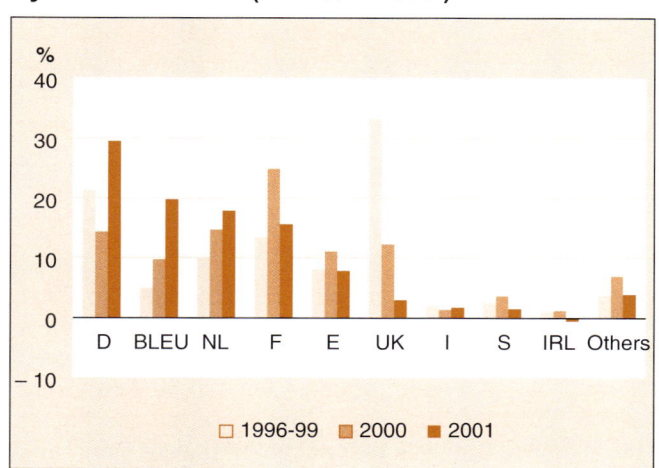

NB: FDI flows excluding reinvested earnings.
Source: Eurostat.

THE UNION IN THE INTERNATIONAL FRAMEWORK

Table 2.5.1. EU FDI flows with extra-EU countries, 2000 and 2001 by source and destination (excluding reinvested earnings, million EUR)

		Outward flows to					Inward flows from				
Year: 2001	Share in total EU %	Extra-EU	USA	Japan	Canada	Share in total EU %	Extra-EU	USA	Japan	Canada
EU-15 [1]	100	202 039	98 249	8 259	18 844	100	96 737	52 752	7 514	5 708
B/L [2]	19.8	39 953	20 248	2 024	− 113	31.2	30 140	15 220	− 26	2 817
DK	1.8	3 556	81	− 40	40	0.5	497	429	54	27
D	29.5	59 566	49 169	362	49	9.2	8 935	5 455	− 454	712
EL	0.2	449	195	0	15	0.1	135	37	0	1
E	7.8	15 820	2 475	291	25	3.8	3 702	1 514	76	13
F	15.6	31 500	14 700	400	300	6.1	5 900	4 200	200	− 20
IRL	− 0.6	− 1 209	:	:	:	− 12.5	−12 088	:	:	:
I	1.7	3 490	889	− 92	100	3.7	3 534	1 770	475	65
NL	17.9	36 140	23 374	− 117	500	29.2	28 199	23 017	394	323
A	1.3	2 681	118	25	6	0.3	285	235	12	1
P	0.9	1 736	82	:	4	0.1	104	171	1	58
FIN	− 0.3	− 585	1 100	50	150	0.7	646	50	0	0
S	1.5	3 009	2 563	157	267	3.4	3 300	273	20	894
UK	2.9	5 934	− 16 162	5 216	16 992	24.2	23 448	9 349	6 067	2 279

		Outward flows to					Inward flows from				
Year: 2000	Share in total EU %	Extra-EU	USA	Japan	Canada	Share in total EU %	Extra-EU	USA	Japan	Canada
EU-15 [1]	100	322 527	168 623	6 372	37 941	100	158 962	73 982	11 734	14 699
B/L [2]	9.7	31 243	15 022	− 1 081	313	23.6	37 507	14 030	− 149	12 167
DK	0.5	1 529	1 798	− 54	174	1.6	2 522	1 650	27	27
D	14.3	46 278	27 571	3 182	195	5.3	8 425	974	860	347
EL	0.1	377	175	5	0	0.1	95	72	− 5	− 2
E	11.1	35 660	7 249	29	0	8.1	12 921	11 252	56	− 10
F	24.9	80 200	32 400	2 500	32 000	2.5	4 000	3 200	100	100
IRL	1.2	3 716	:	:	:	9.6	15 279	:	:	:
I	1.4	4 383	1 870	10	57	2.6	4 171	2 233	83	294
NL	14.7	47 444	34 595	178	1 010	17.1	27 186	17 878	4 997	60
A	0.8	2 629	555	− 2	10	0.4	646	338	28	− 12
P	1.6	5 065	383	0	− 2	0.1	113	− 24	2	32
FIN	3.9	12 733	4 355	78	455	0.2	370	− 89	51	1
S	3.6	11 700	3 713	198	− 96	6.5	10 304	3 046	1 085	31
UK	12.3	39 570	36 925	1 326	3 825	22.3	35 422	18 434	4 597	2 043

[1] EU-15 aggregates with USA, Japan and Canada include estimates for Ireland.
[2] Belgium-Luxembourg Economic Union.
: Not available.
Source: Eurostat.

followed by Belgium/Luxembourg (20 %) and the Netherlands (18 %). The United Kingdom's contribution fell to EUR 6 billion in 2001 (3 % of total EU and − 85 % on 2000). France and Spain followed a similar pattern, with FDI to extra-EU countries falling by 61 % and 56 %, respectively. The decrease was more moderate in the case of Italy (− 20 %), whose share however remained low, at 2 % of the EU total.

Considering inflows from extra-EU countries, in 2001 Belgium/Luxembourg and the Netherlands had a share in the total EU of 31 % and 29 % respectively, followed by the United Kingdom with 24 %. Apart from Ireland, the Member States that recorded the higher falls in FDI inflows with respect to 2000 were Denmark, Spain and Sweden.

EU FDI in major extra-EU areas

80 % of EU FDI went to non-EU OECD countries between 1998 and 2000

Figure 2.5.6 shows the geographical distribution of EU FDI flows by main partners during the period under examination. As said above, the US market was the main target of EU investors. During the whole 1994-2000 period, the proportion of extra-EU FDI flowing to the United States stood at 41 % between 1994 and 1997, and rose to 56 % between 1998 and 2000.

Flows to other OECD countries particularly surged in 2000, aided by the investment of EUR 32 billion made by France in Canada. Another 10 % of 2000 flows was

THE UNION IN THE INTERNATIONAL FRAMEWORK

Figure 2.5.6. Geographical distribution of extra-EU FDI outflows by main partner, 1994-2000

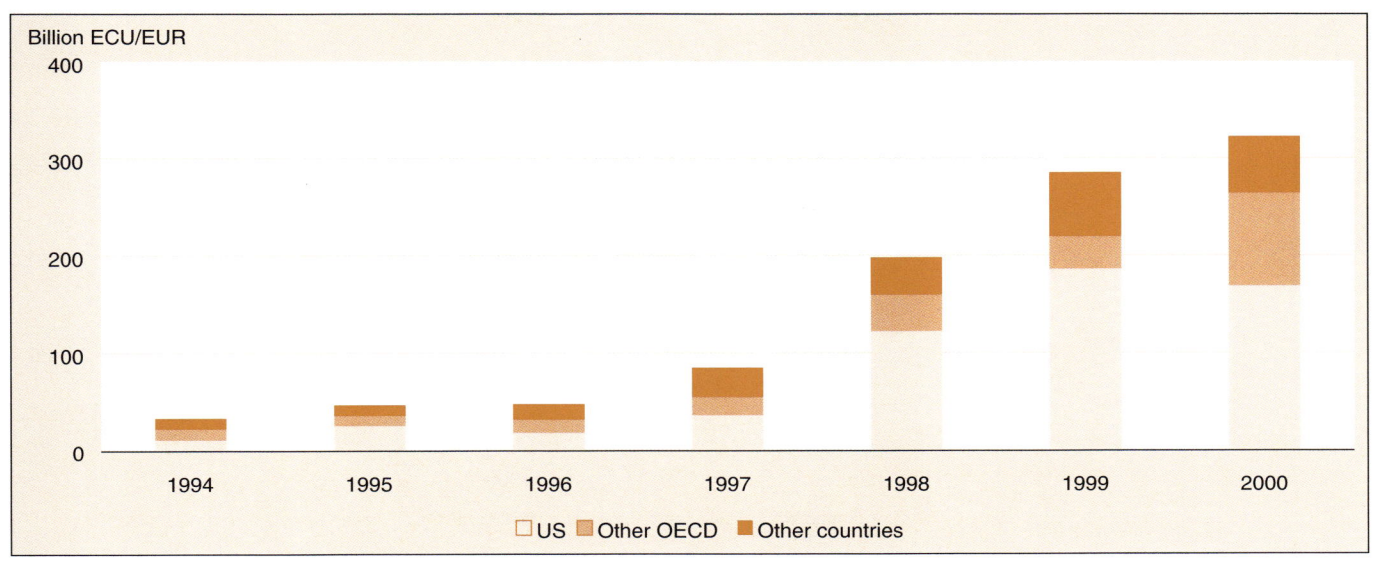

NB: FDI flows excluding reinvested earnings.
Source: Eurostat.

invested in non-EU OECD European countries, primarily Switzerland, Norway and Poland. Traditionally a close country for direct foreign investors, in 1999 Japan became an important destination for EU FDI. From 1999 to 2001, the EU invested in Japan a cumulated amount of EUR 22 billion. This compares with cumulated EUR 4.5 billion invested between 1994 and 1998.

The EU has invested massively in emerging markets

Data on the activity of European enterprises in so-called emerging markets are often the focus of much attention for policy-makers and analysts. These markets are generally characterised by high potential demand and lower labour costs, matched by additional

Table 2.5.2. Geographical distribution of EU-15 FDI assets 1994-1999 (billion ECU/EUR and as a %)

	1994	1995	1996	1997	1998		1999	
Extra-EU-15	444	472	543	667	825	100 %	1 187	100 %
EFTA	49	53	56	64	83	10 %	91	8 %
Other Europe, of which:	15	19	27	43	62	7 %	84	7 %
candidate countries	11	15	20	29	42	5 %	58	5 %
Africa	15	17	18	24	23	3 %	39	3 %
North America, of which:	212	224	252	317	422	51 %	653	55 %
United States	197	207	233	293	398	48 %	622	52 %
Canada	16	17	19	24	24	3 %	30	3 %
Central America	32	32	34	44	37	5 %	45	4 %
South America	33	36	42	56	79	10 %	124	10 %
Asia, of which:	48	52	65	73	79	10 %	110	9 %
Near & Middle East	4	4	4	5	8	1 %	6	0 %
Other Asia, of which:	44	48	61	68	71	9 %	104	9 %
Japan	11	11	12	12	13	2 %	24	2 %
Oceania	24	26	31	34	26	3 %	28	2 %
Memo Items:								
Intra-EU-15	463	508	594	679	786		1 192	
OECD (non-EU)	304	323	377	461	588	50 %	858	72 %
Other OECD (non-US, non-EU)	108	115	144	168	190	16 %	235	20 %
Other countries	140	149	166	206	237	20 %	329	28 %

NB: Differences between totals and sum of components are due to non-allocated assets.
Source: Eurostat.

THE UNION IN THE INTERNATIONAL FRAMEWORK

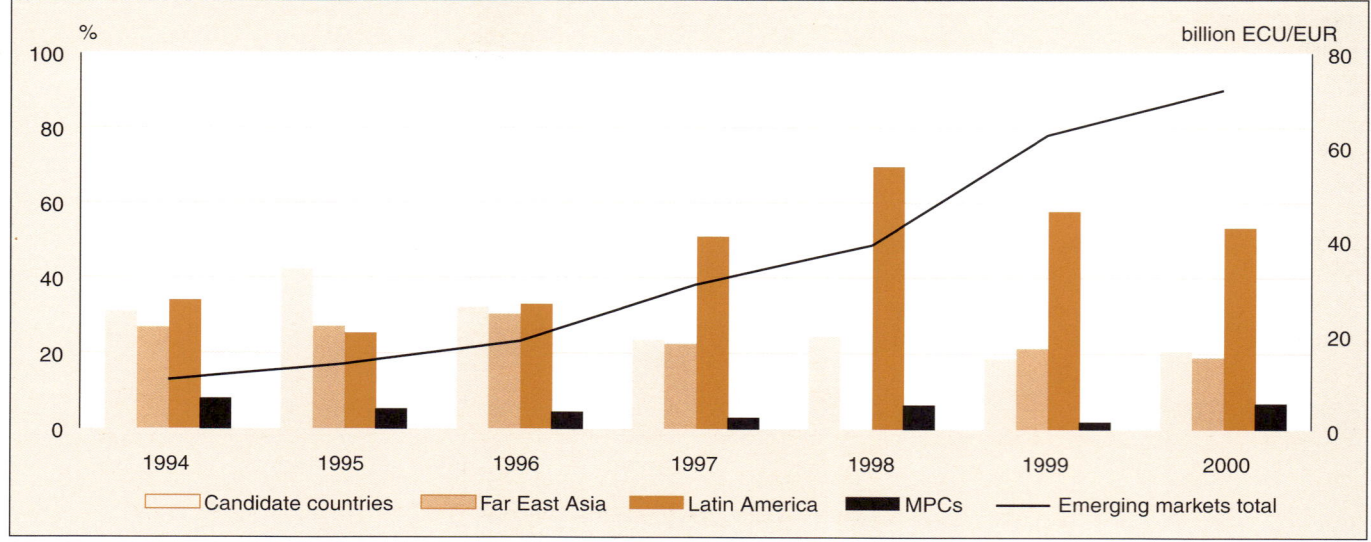

Figure 2.5.7. EU FDI flows towards emerging markets by destination (as a %)

[Chart showing EU FDI flows 1994-2000 with bars for Candidate countries, Far East Asia, Latin America, MPCs, and a line for Emerging markets total. Left axis: %, right axis: billion ECU/EUR]

NB: FDI flows excluding reinvested earnings. MPCs, excluding Cyprus and Malta.
Source: Eurostat.

economic and financial risks. Figure 2.5.7 above shows the evolution of direct investment made by EU investors in four zones having these broad characteristics: candidate countries, Latin America, Far East Asia and Mediterranean partner countries (MPC) [7].

Over the 1994-99 period, EU FDI flows to emerging markets expanded continuously, recording an average annual growth rate of 42.8 %. Flows to Latin America experienced by far the largest rate of growth: from ECU 3.6 billion in 1994, FDI flows soared to EUR 36.1 billion in 1999 (+ 58.8 % average annual growth). Flows to Far East Asia and the grew more modestly, from ECU 2.8 billion in 1994 to EUR 13.4 billion in 1999 (+ 36.6 % average annual growth rate) and from ECU 3.3 billion to EUR 11.7 billion (+ 29.0 %) respectively. Flows to MPC expanded from ECU 0.9 billion in 1994 to EUR 1.3 billion in 1999 (+ 8.8 % average annual growth rate). Except for flows towards Latin America, average annual growth rates over the 1994-99 period were however below those recorded for total extra-EU (+ 54.4 %).

In 2000, EU FDI flows to emerging markets further developed to EUR 72.1 billion (+ 15.4 %). EU FDI flows to the MPC recorded the largest progression (+ 280.4 %, from EUR 1.3 billion in 1999 to EUR 5 billion in 2000), followed by CCs (+ 27.4 %), Latin America (+ 6.6 %) and Far East Asia (+ 2.4 %).

The value of EU FDI assets held in this group of countries reached EUR 370 billion at the end of 2000, as compared with ECU 100 billion in 1995. Figure 2.5.8 details the change between 1995 and 2000 of EU and US FDI assets in the four regions considered here.

FDI into EU Member States

In 2000, inward FDI flows from extra-EU countries (excluding reinvested earnings) accounted for 1.9 % of EU GDP against 1.2 % both in 1999 and 1998. In absolute terms, the 2000 EU FDI flows invested by the rest of the world in the EU jumped by 61 %, the second highest growth rate since 1995. Whilst extra-EU inflows used to fluctuate around EUR 40 billion up to 1997, they more than doubled in 1998 (EUR 95 billion) to reach EUR 159 billion in 2000.

United States companies have traditionally been the main foreign investors in the EU and their commercial presence became even stronger in the second half of the 1990s. With EUR 440 billion, at the end of 1999 the United States owned 61 % of EU FDI liabilities — a progression of 10 percentage points as compared to their 1995 share. In 2000, however, the share of the United States in annual FDI flows dropped to 50 %, while big investments were recorded from other OECD countries, notably Switzerland, Canada and Japan.

---

[7] The exact definitions are as follows: candidate countries includes 13 countries (Bulgaria, the Czech Republic, Cyprus, Estonia, Hungary, Latvia, Lithuania, Malta, Poland, Romania, Slovenia, Slovakia and Turkey). Latin America includes 18 countries (all in South America, except Falkland Islands and Suriname, plus Costa Rica, Cuba, Guatemala, Honduras, Mexico, Nicaragua and Panama). Far East Asia includes 30 countries (Asia, excluding Near and Middle East countries and Japan). Mediterranean partner countries includes 12 countries (Algeria, Cyprus, Egypt, Israel, Jordan, Lebanon, Malta, Morocco, Palestinian Territory, Syria, Tunisia and Turkey).

THE UNION IN THE INTERNATIONAL FRAMEWORK

Figure 2.5.8. FDI assets in emerging markets EU and US, 1995 and 2000

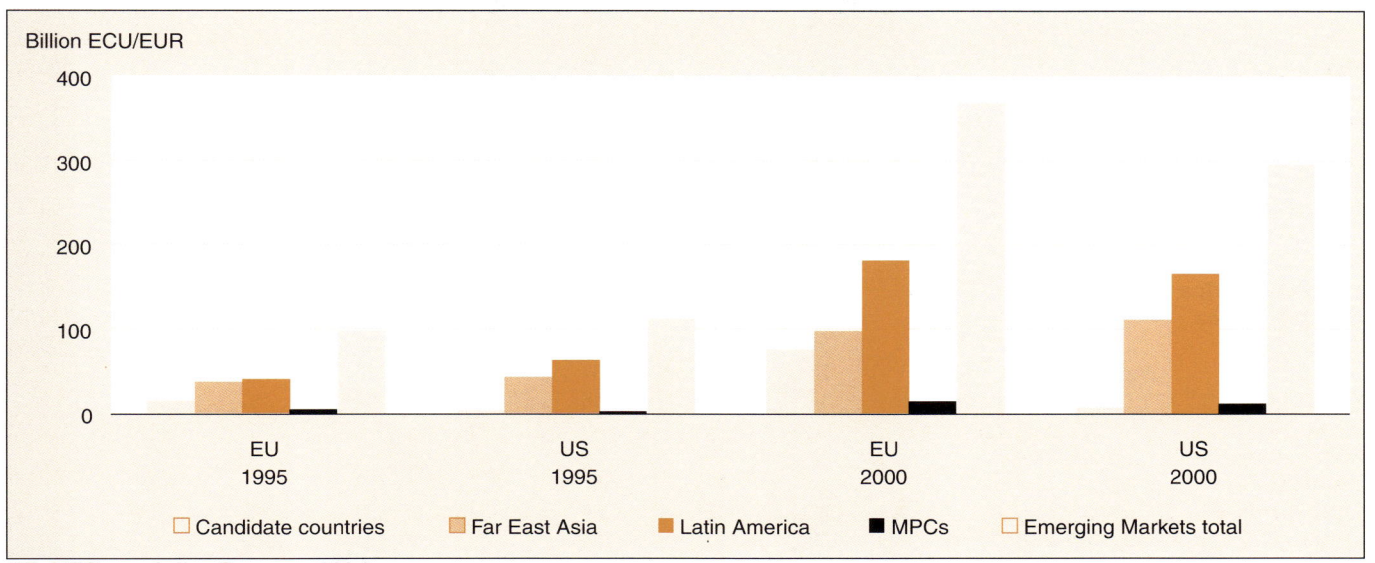

□ Candidate countries ▨ Far East Asia ■ Latin America ■ MPCs □ Emerging Markets total

NB: MPCs, excluding Cyprus and Malta.
Source: Eurostat

Major destinations of FDI in the European Union

As seen above (Figure 2.5.5.a) in recent years the United Kingdom, the Netherlands and Belgium/Luxembourg were the Member States that have received the bulk of extra-EU FDI inflows. Taken together, these four Member States accounted for 63 % of total inflows in 2000. Dividing the period 1994-2000 into two sub-periods (see Figure 2.5.10), one notices that the weight of the United Kingdom has not changed over time, while the role played by the Netherlands and by Belgium/Luxembourg is a more recent phenomenon. Conversely, the share of France and Germany decreased considerably in the most recent past. Ireland (among "others" for the period 1994-97) absorbed 7 % of EU FDI inflows between 1998 and 2000.

Figure 2.5.9. Geographical distribution of extra-EU FDI inflows by main partners, 1994-2000

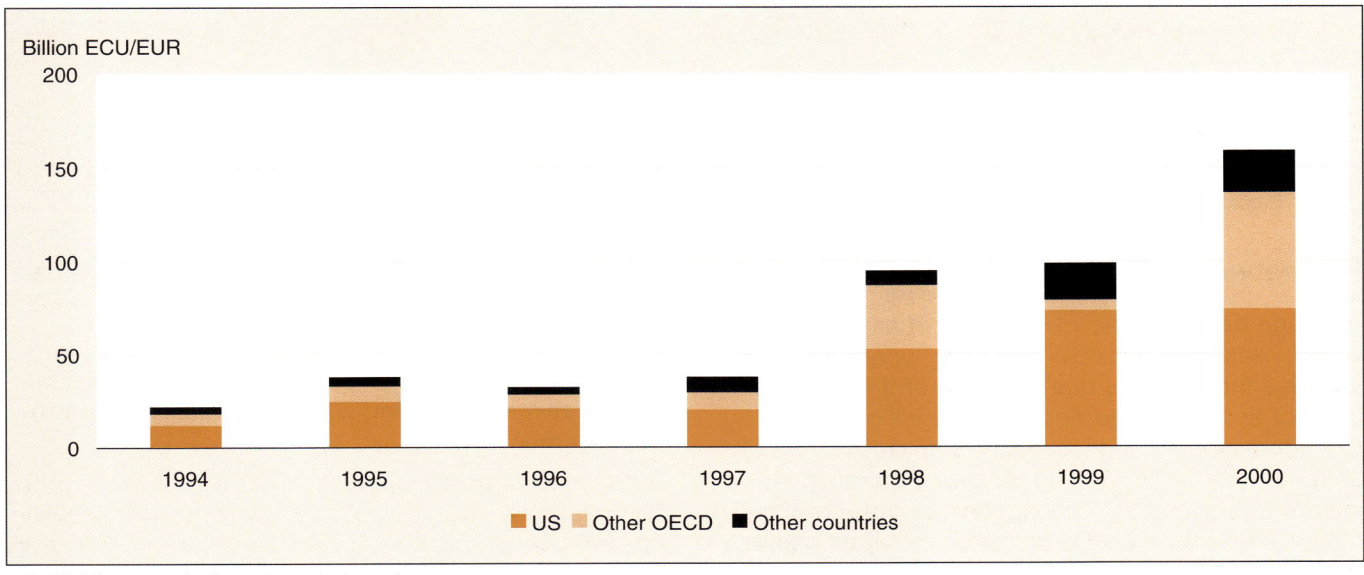

■ US ▨ Other OECD ■ Other countries

NB: FDI flows, excluding reinvested earnings.
Source: Eurostat.

THE UNION IN THE INTERNATIONAL FRAMEWORK

Table 2.5.3. Geographical distribution of EU-15 FDI liabilities, 1994-99 (billion ECU/EUR and as a %)

	1994	1995	1996	1997	1998		1999	
Extra-EU-15	344	367	422	496	611	100 %	723	100 %
EFTA	76	83	99	109	114	19 %	135	19 %
Other Europe	4	5	5	7	12	2 %	20	3 %
Africa	3	3	4	4	5	1 %	5	1 %
North America, of which:	183	199	222	275	388	63 %	458	63 %
United States	171	188	211	263	366	60 %	440	61 %
Canada	12	11	11	12	21	3 %	18	2 %
Central America	15	18	18	25	26	4 %	31	4 %
South America	2	2	2	3	2	0 %	4	0 %
Asia, of which:	39	40	45	50	52	8 %	52	7 %
Japan	28	28	32	35	36	6 %	34	5 %
Oceania	14	12	16	13	12	2 %	13	2 %
Memo Items:								
Intra-EU-15	444	492	552	627	782		1 175	
OECD (non-EU)	300	321	369	432	550	90 %	639	88 %
Other OECD (non-US, non-EU)	129	132	158	169	183	30 %	199	28 %
Other countries	44	46	53	64	61	10 %	84	12 %

NB: Differences between totals and sum of components are due to non-allocated assets.
Source: Eurostat.

Figure 2.5.10. Shares of FDI inflows from extra-EU by recipient, 1994-97 and 1998-2000

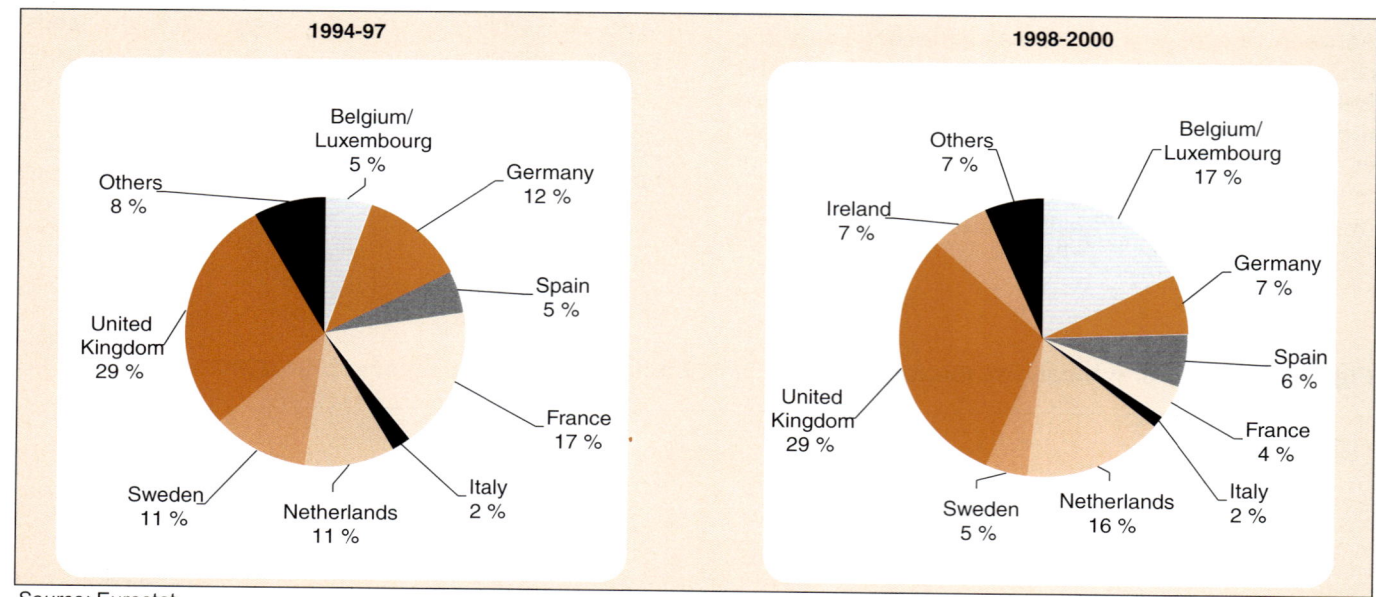

1994-97
- Belgium/Luxembourg 5 %
- Germany 12 %
- Spain 5 %
- France 17 %
- Italy 2 %
- Netherlands 11 %
- Sweden 11 %
- United Kingdom 29 %
- Others 8 %

1998-2000
- Belgium/Luxembourg 17 %
- Germany 7 %
- Spain 6 %
- France 4 %
- Italy 2 %
- Netherlands 16 %
- Sweden 5 %
- United Kingdom 29 %
- Ireland 7 %
- Others 7 %

Source: Eurostat.

FDI between Member States

Although neutral to the EU balance of payments as a whole, data on intra-EU FDI are very interesting because they provide one measure of the extent and pace of economic and financial integration inside the EU. Moreover, they give indications on the regional patterns followed by the process of integration. More specifically, they reflect a long-term dimension of integration that is linked to firms' strategic policies adopted for competing in the single market and internationally.

These policies are mainly carried out through mergers and acquisitions, which in fact constituted a large fraction of intra-EU FDI transactions in recent years.

Intra-EU FDI growth shows impressive acceleration between 1997 and 2000, particularly in northern Member States

After stagnating at about 0.7 % of GDP between 1992 and 1996, in 1997 intra-EU FDI flows started growing faster, reaching 3.7 % of GDP in 1999 and 7.3 % in 2000.

Figure 2.5.11a. Suppliers of intra-EU FDI (shares of 1996-2000 flows)

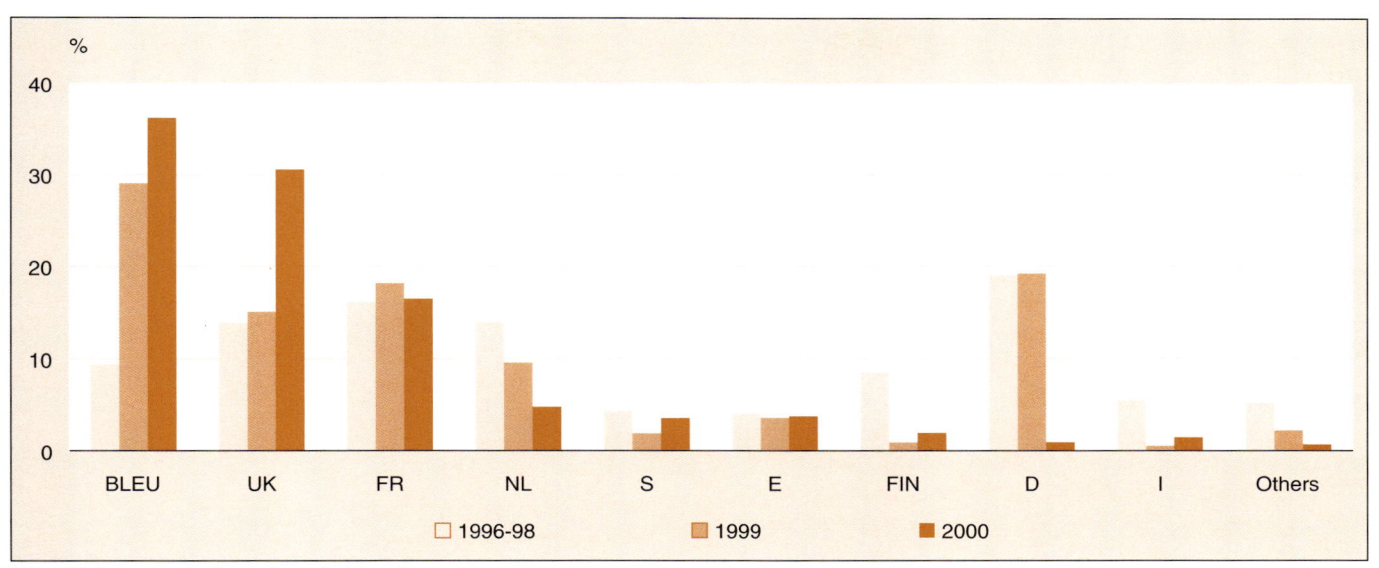

NB: FDI flows, excluding reinvested earnings.
Source: Eurostat.

The 1992-2000 figures also show that FDI relationships between Member States tend to concentrate in northern European countries. Looking at the shares of flows over this period, it emerges that only six Member States (the United Kingdom, Germany, France, Belgium/Luxembourg and the Netherlands) supplied 80 % and received 70 % of cumulated flows. Instead, the shares of countries such as Italy and Spain diminished on both accounts, reaching their lowest values in 1999.

Figure 2.5.11b. Recipients of intra-EU FDI (shares of 1996-2000 flows)

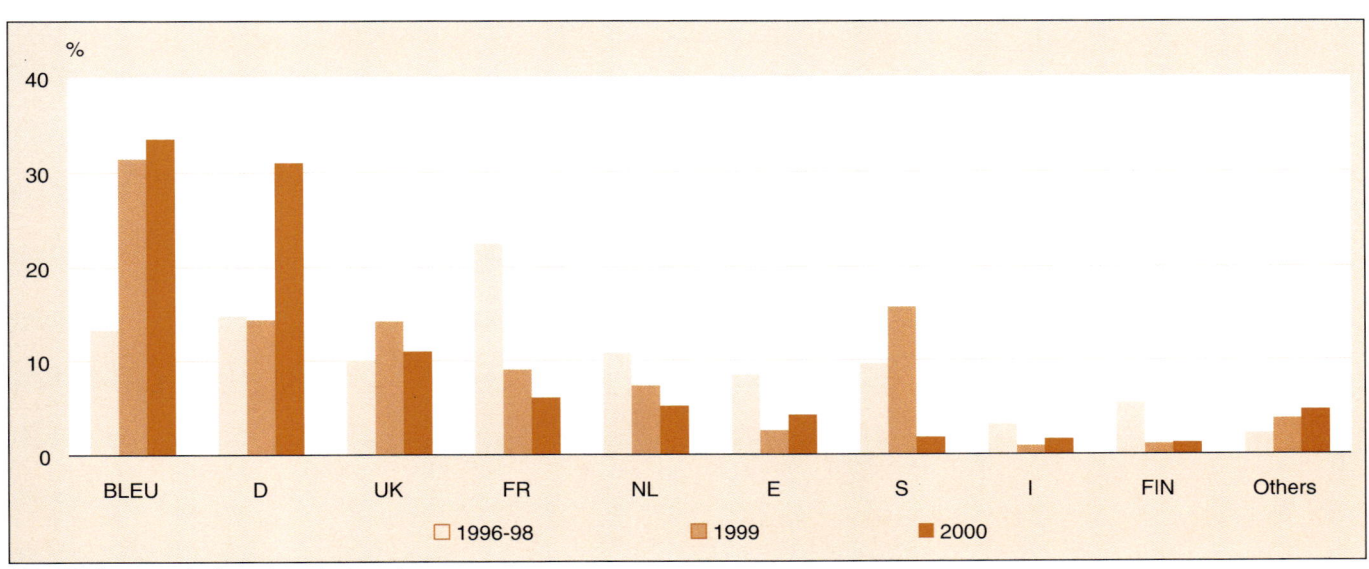

NB: FDI flows, excluding reinvested earnings.
Source: Eurostat

3. Enterprises in the Union

3.1. Structural business developments

The annual structural business statistics (SBS) provide figures on manufacturing, production and distribution of electricity, gas and water, construction, distributive trades and market services (excluding financial services) in each Member State.

Trends

The activities of enterprises in the main economic sectors of the European Union developed steadily between 1995 (taken as the reference year) and 2000.

Table 3.1.1 shows that growth in economic activity (measured by turnover) was stronger in the service sectors (+ 42.3 % in distributive trades between 1995 and 2000 and + 34 % in services between 1996 and 2000) than in industrial sectors. Although the statistical coverage does not allow the effects in terms of value added to be fully analysed, the partial indications suggest growth over the period in excess of 5–10 points in comparison with sectors of industry. This trend is accompanied by gains in productivity significantly lower than in industrial sectors.

> The variables that are analysed to reveal trends are:
>
> 1. **turnover**, comprising amounts invoiced per unit of observation during the reference period, i.e. market sales of goods and services to others;
>
> 2. **value added at factor cost**, meaning the difference between the value of what is produced and intermediate consumption in production, adjusted for production subsidies, costs and taxes;
>
> 3. **apparent labour productivity**, defined as value added per employee; this variable is intended to measure the amount of wealth created in an industry by a given number of workers.
>
> The analysis is based on the first-digit level of the NACE rev.1 classification of economic activities and covers:

> — Section D: manufacturing;
> — Section E: production and distribution of electricity, gas and water;
> — Section F: construction;
> — Section G: wholesale and retail trade;
> — Section H: hotels and restaurants;
> — Section I: transport and communications;
> — Section K: real estate, renting and business services.

Analysis by sector and Member State

Growth was standard in manufacturing, apart from the exceptional figures posted by Ireland: big rises in both activity (+ 228.1 %) and productivity. In contrast, the figures for industry in Germany, Austria and Benelux were middling. Overall, growth in this sector was 3.4 % each year during the reference period, and these figures were achieved with no change in manpower.

With regard to production and distribution of electricity, gas and water, the major contributions came from the United Kingdom and Finland. According to partial figures — some data are still confidential — there were significant gains in productivity in these countries, and in Spain as well. Productivity was down, however, in France and Portugal.

A look at the figures for the building sector shows that the overall performance was especially due to Portugal (+ 238.5 % for turnover between 1995 and 2000), the United Kingdom and Finland. There were no real increases in productivity except in the United Kingdom, however. At the other extreme, the construction industry was fairly sluggish over the period in Germany, France and Austria.

The tertiary sectors (distributive trades and market services) enjoyed regular growth, although the better figures from Italy (distributive trades) and from Finland and France (market services) are worth mentioning. In Portugal, commercial activity was led at the start of the reference period by distributive trades and vehicle repairs. The absence of three big countries (United Kingdom, Germany and Spain) means that general aggregates cannot be compared, but according to the available figures value added grew 5-10 points faster in tertiary sectors than in sectors of industry between 1995 and 1999.

At the same time, increases in productivity were modest (especially for services) while growth in activity had a strong knock-on effect on employment.

Table 3.1.1. Main economic variables by major sector of activity in the EU (1995-2000 for turnover, 1995-99 for value added and productivity; 1995 = 100 except services 1996 = 100)

	Manufacturing	Electricity, gas, water	Construction	Wholesale and retail trade	Market services
Turnover	133.3	119.2	124.2	142.3	134.0
Value added	114.5	111.6	105.1	:	:
Productivity	114.1	116.7	100.9	:	:

Source: Eurostat, SBS database.

ENTERPRISES IN THE UNION

Figure 3.1.1. Main economic variables in manufacturing (Section D of Nace rev.1) (1995-2000 for turnover, 1995-99 for value added and productivity; 1995 = 100)

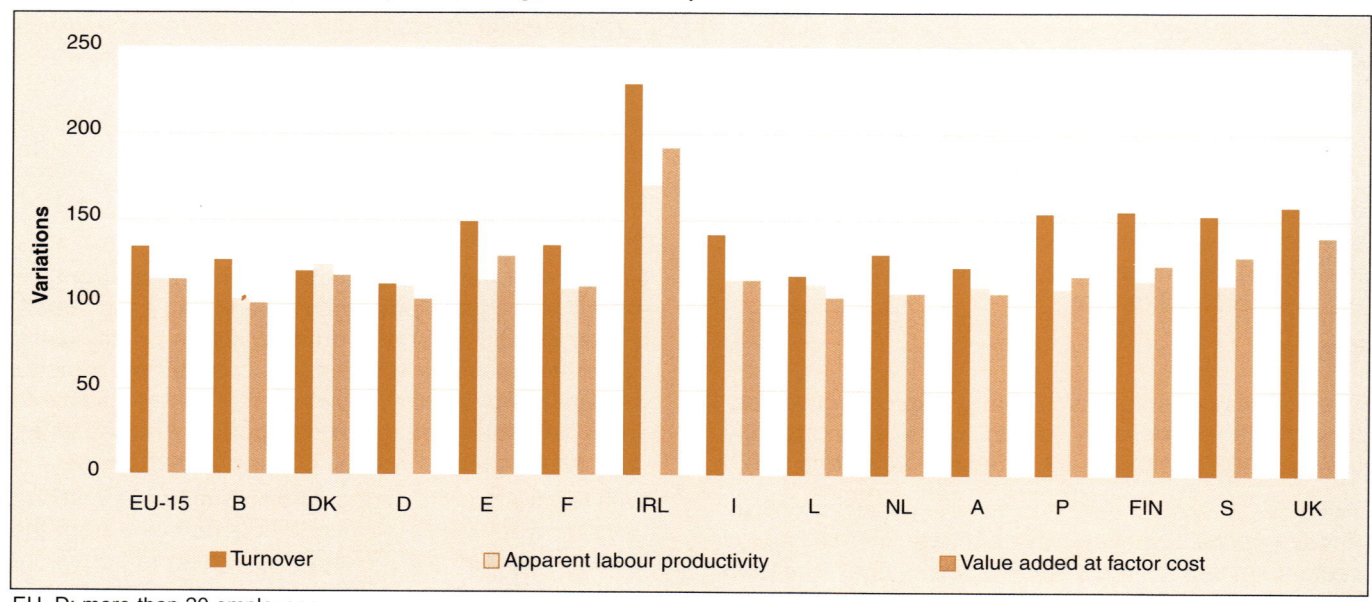

EU, D: more than 20 employees.
EU: productivity estimation for 85 % of the aggregate.
Source: Eurostat, SBS database.

Figure 3.1.2. Main economic variables in production and distribution of electricity, gas and water (Section E of NACE rev.1) (1995-2000 for turnover, 1995-99 for value added and productivity; 1995 = 100)

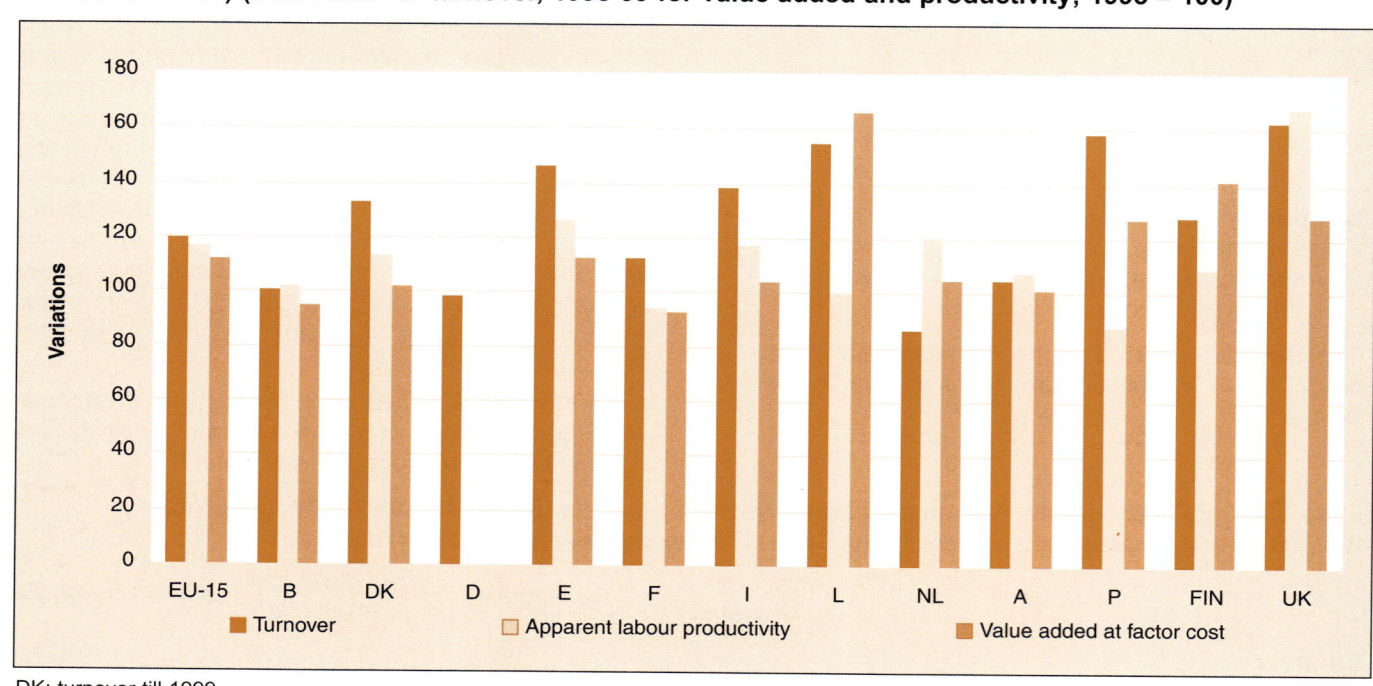

DK: turnover till 1999.
D: VA and productivity till 1998.
EU: VA and productivity estimation for 65 % of the aggregate.
Source: Eurostat, SBS database.

ENTERPRISES IN THE UNION

Figure 3.1.3. Main economic variables in construction (Section F of NACE rev.1) (1995-2000 for turnover, 1995-99 for value added and productivity; 1995 = 100)

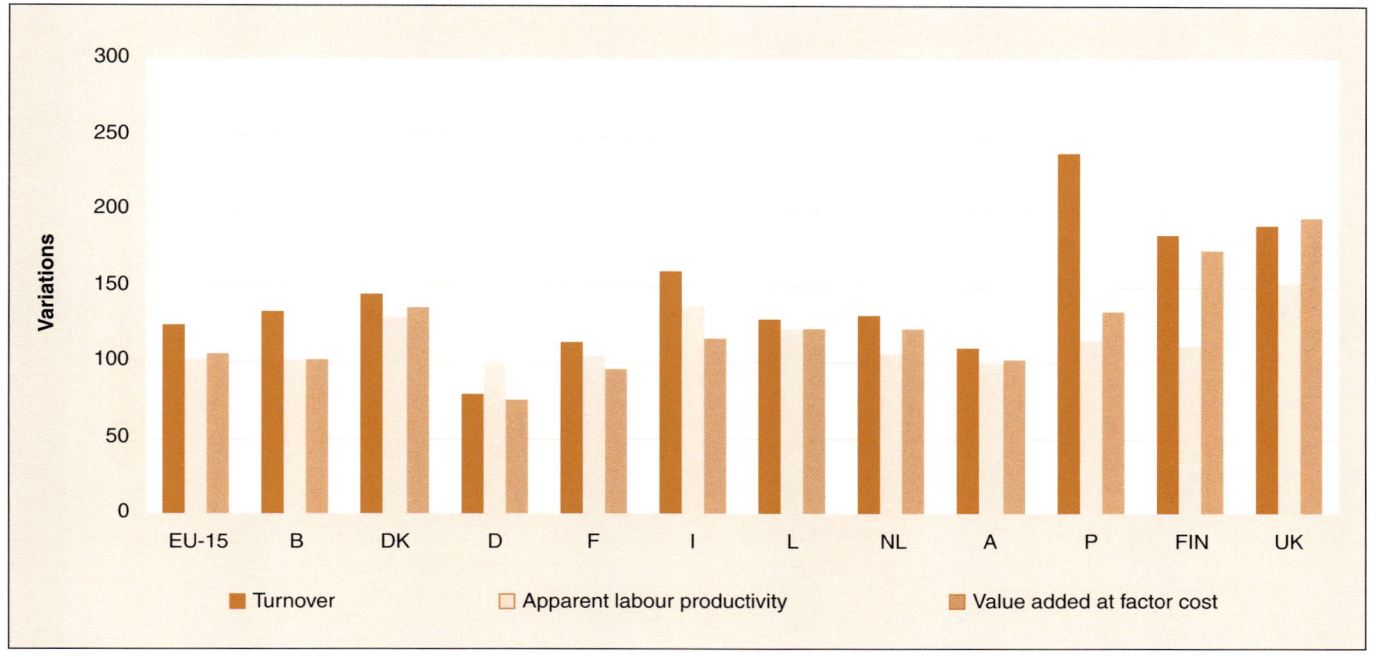

D: more than 20 employees.
P: VA & productivity: from 1996.
EU: estimation for 82 % of the aggregate.
Source: Eurostat, SBS database.

Figure 3.1.4. Main economic variables in wholesale and retail trade (Section G of NACE rev.1) (1995-2000 for turnover, 1995-99 for value added and productivity; 1995 = 100)

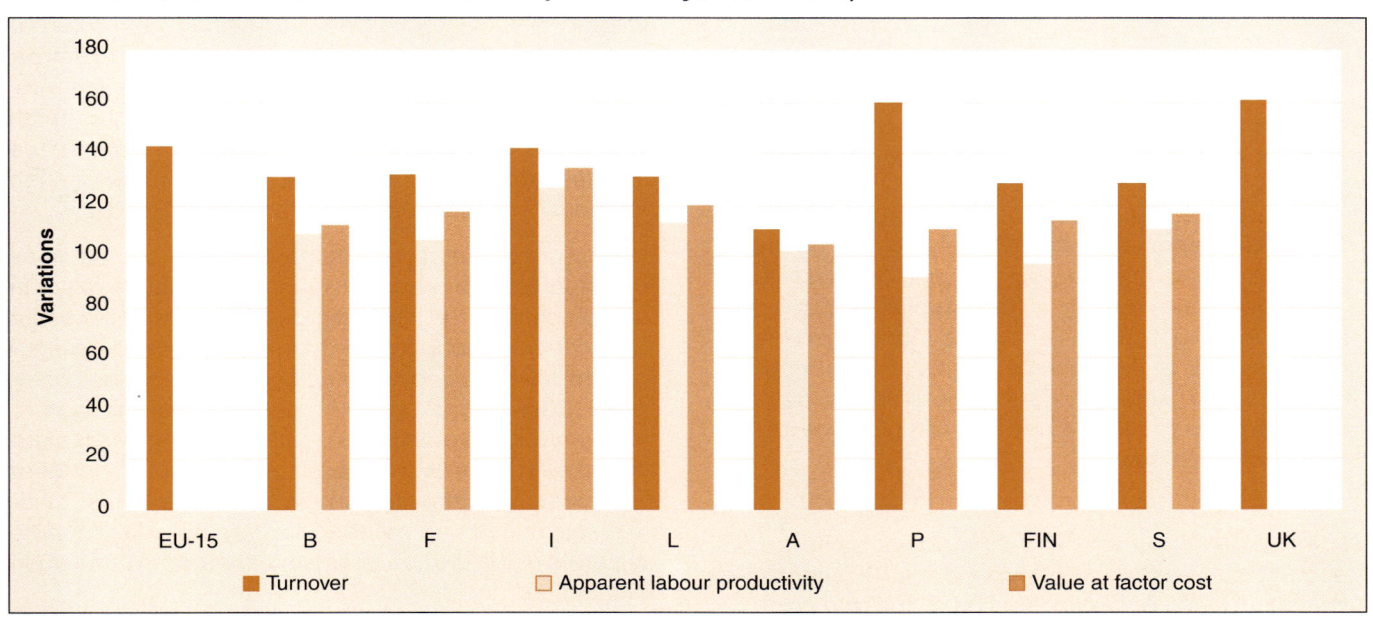

B, FIN, S from 1996.
EU: turnover estimation for 63 % of the aggregate.
Source: Eurostat, SBS database.

ENTERPRISES IN THE UNION

Figure 3.1.5. Main economic variables in market services (excluding trade and financial services) (Sections H, I, K of NACE rev.1) (1996-2000 for turnover, 1996-99 for value added and productivity; 1996 = 100)

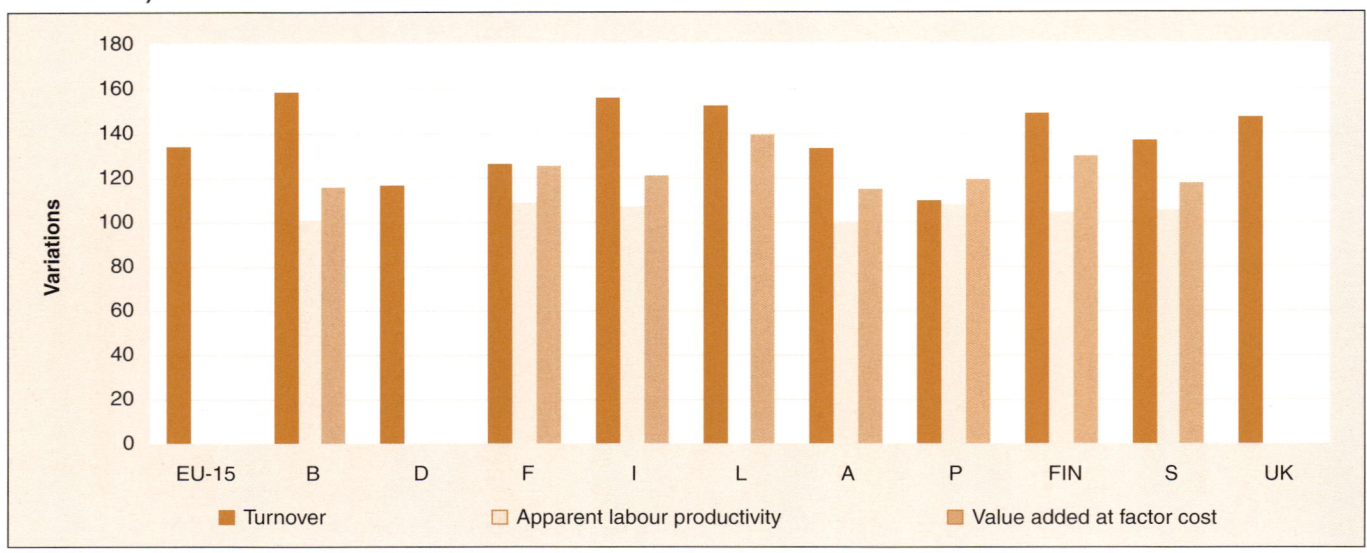

S, A: VA from 1997.
F, D: turnover till 1999.
Source: Eurostat, SBS database.

Performance of enterprises in Europe in 1999 and 2000

The annually compiled structural statistics can be used to draw up detailed tables summarising business activity in the Member States. In some cases — and more and more frequently — it is also possible to estimate the same features at European level. Tables 3.1.2 and 3.1.4 are two examples: one provides a performance indicator (gross operating rate by sector in 1999) and the other indicates the significance of the various economic sectors for employment in Europe (preliminary data for 2000).

The gross operating rate (Table 3.1.2, see box for definition) reached its highest levels in capital-intensive sectors and in countries where capital, compared with the other factors of production, has a more important role in the production process.

> The **gross operating rate** is defined as the ratio between gross operating surplus and turnover. The gross operating surplus is the surplus that results from operating activities after the labour force has been paid. It is the balance available that enables investors and fund providers to be paid, as well as allowing taxes to be paid and providing finance for all or part of investments.

An initial analysis using this rate allows sectors and geographic areas to be compared. But it cannot be used on its own. At the sectoral level, the rate is structurally weaker in distributive trades, where turnover provides a broad definition of activity. It is markedly higher in services and extractive industries, where value added rates (value added on production) are in fact relatively higher. It is also weaker as staff expenditure in value added increases; this generally applies to manufacturing and construction. Table 3.13 supplements the previous one and provides a more detailed analysis.

The same comment can also be made with regard to geographic comparisons. As is revealed by an indicator of production costs (staff/production costs, indicator not calculated in the tables), unit costs for staff in industry are markedly lower in Ireland (1998 data) or even in Italy than in Denmark or Austria, for example. There is a definite impact on the gross operating rate. The United Kingdom combines all these factors (high rate of value added and low share of staff expenditure in value added) and posts rates that are uniformly high for industry, in contrast with France and Germany.

In the light of these explanatory remarks, comparisons between sectors produce some noteworthy results. In manufacturing, the highest gross operating rates occur for economic activities in connection with the manufacture of radio, television and communications equipment (23.1 % in Finland, home of one of the world's telecommunications giants). Other leading sectors are the chemical and the paper industries in northern European countries, printing in the Netherlands, medical appliances and metalworking in Italy, non-metallic minerals in the Iberian peninsula, the textile industry in Finland, etc.

As for the production and distribution of electricity, gas and water, the gross operating rates are uniformly high

Table 3.1.2. Gross operating rates by branch (as a %), 1999

	EU-15	B	DK	D	EL	E	F	IRL	I	L	NL	A	P	FIN	S	UK
Industry																
Food	9.3	7.7	9.4	7.2	14.3	9.8	7.6	16.6	9.5	12.2	8.2	8.3	10.2	8.4	7.6	13.7
Tobacco	8.9	5.8	12.9	6.0	12.5	8.5	:	11.6	2.6	:	26.8	:	22.2	8.6	:	11.7
Textiles	10.0	9.8	9.7	7.4	14.4	11.2	5.7	10.8	12.2	27.7	10.9	8.6	11.0	16.7	8.1	10.7
Clothing	8.2	6.3	9.7	5.4	10.6	8.6	4.1	14.9	10.9	10.0	7.8	5.8	7.2	7.4	-5.1	10.6
Leather and footwear	9.7	9.6	7.9	6.2	11.1	6.5	7.5	10.1	10.8	:	8.1	9.5	6.2	11.7	8.5	18.7
Wood processing and manufacture of articles in wood	9.8	9.7	10.2	6.8	14.9	10.6	7.6	13.4	15.2	18.7	10.0	11.6	8.7	9.0	7.7	13.1
Paper and paperboard	12.5	12.1	12.0	10.2	14.1	14.2	7.0	20.1	11.9	17.0	12.8	14.5	9.7	17.9	16.9	13.3
Publishing, printing, etc	15.2	13.0	11.0	13.4	10.5	15.7	7.2	26.2	13.6	20.6	17.3	14.4	13.8	13.8	8.0	22.8
Nuclear fuels, coking, etc	4.6	3.6	15.4	1.0	16.9	5.9	7.6	:	3.2	:	5.5	:	7.2	4.2	15.7	6.5
Chemicals	12.9	16.1	19.6	8.1	13.6	12.9	10.0	48.7	11.2	13.6	11.7	13.7	13.6	19.0	19.6	14.3
Rubber and plastics	11.4	9.6	14.0	10.4	16.4	12.5	9.1	15.9	12.8	7.9	14.0	12.1	16.3	17.9	11.6	12.6
Non-metallic mineral products	14.3	12.9	15.0	11.3	22.4	17.8	9.9	24.2	16.1	14.9	16.8	14.0	21.3	17.0	11.2	17.0
Metallurgy	7.8	5.9	6.7	6.9	11.5	11.4	4.9	4.4	8.5	5.3	11.2	11.6	11.9	11.2	11.5	6.9
Metalworking	12.0	11.0	12.6	9.4	16.1	12.2	8.4	13.1	16.5	11.6	11.6	10.5	11.5	14.1	8.9	16.5
Machinery and equipment	8.3	9.3	8.8	5.8	11.7	10.2	6.0	17.1	11.7	9.7	9.4	8.5	12.0	7.4	8.9	11.3
Computer and office equipment	7.3	5.8	10.9	9.4	15.0	6.5	3.2	9.4	4.0	12.3	5.8	35.7	6.2	-3.1	8.6	8.7
Electrical appliances	8.2	9.1	6.0	6.1	15.7	11.1	7.6	18.5	9.9	12.4	12.4	10.1	9.1	11.7	8.7	10.3
Radio, etc, equipment	10.5	14.4	11.3	5.9	23.2	6.9	5.2	39.5	8.1	17.9	7.7	8.4	8.3	23.1	7.2	14.6
Medical equipment, etc	10.4	5.2	18.5	7.3	9.8	13.9	6.0	27.2	16.4	17.0	7.7	11.8	11.6	16.2	8.8	15.7
Car industry	4.6	4.7	9.5	2.9	6.3	6.9	4.3	12.0	4.8	4.1	9.3	11.5	10.0	12.6	11.5	4.8
Other transport equipment	10.7	7.3	5.0	7.9	9.8	8.2	5.1	15.0	7.4	8.9	7.3	4.9	-4.5	3.9	9.7	23.4
Furniture, other	10.2	8.7	12.4	7.8	16.8	9.7	7.1	:	11.3	9.3	12.7	11.9	9.7	11.8	4.8	14.8
Recycling	9.0	8.7	11.7	7.0	2.1	7.7	:	20.2	9.1	23.2	12.5	14.4	7.4	4.9	7.0	10.3
Electricity, gas and water																
Productivity and distribution electricity	20.8	16.0	16.3	14.7	:	34.1	24.7	27.8	27.3	20.2	21.8	25.2	27.1	21.7	21.8	19.9
Collection, purification, distribution of water	25.9	18.8	17.0	34.5	:	23.7	2.7	:	11.8	10.5	53.5	39.4	29.1	54.8	40.6	47.8
Construction																
Construction	10.4	9.6	10.8	6.0	20.4	:	6.5	:	14.4	14.4	7.4	9.6	9.3	10.7	12.3	15.8
Wholesale and retail trade																
Car sales and repairs	5.9	3.2	4.0	12.6	:	4.5	3.0	:	5.4	4.5	3.7	5.6	3.6	4.7	3.6	7.5
Wholesale trade	5.3	3.9	4.5	6.8	:	4.8	2.8	:	8.6	6.2	5.7	4.6	5.3	4.8	4.3	7.2
Retail sales and repairs of household goods	6.8	6.7	5.8	8.3	:	9.2	5.5	:	9.4	7.0	8.6	6.0	6.0	6.2	4.1	8.3
Services (excluding financial services)																
Hotels and restaurants	17.5	16.8	15.4	22.4	:	18.2	12.0	16.3	19.8	20.8	18.5	18.3	10.2	10.8	10.4	18.2
Land transport	12.5	15.6	27.5	-5.7	:	27.5	9.3	12.1	15.6	14.2	20.2	21.4	10.3	22.7	8.3	18.3
Water transport	15.4	2.8	13.8	44.4	:	19.3	3.2	:	9.9	:	:	6.4	13.4	13.4	5.6	17.7
Air transport	14.6	0.0	10.8	60.3	:	10.1	3.7	:	-1.3	22.0	:	6.9	4.3	7.2	4.5	15.0
Auxiliary transport services	11.1	7.3	14.6	10.2	:	13.8	12.6	8.8	12.0	7.1	:	5.1	12.3	7.4	4.9	12.0
Post and telecommunications	27.2	23.5	29.9	39.4	:	21.7	20.6	30.7	28.3	52.2	18.4	23.3	35.1	25.2	21.7	24.2
Real estate	:	22.8	50.2	:	:	33.9	22.0	22.9	44.9	32.3	41.4	35.5	16.3	32.9	45.1	:
Leasing without operator	55.0	34.5	29.5	81.0	:	41.2	43.1	27.7	32.4	32.2	40.6	60.9	60.8	33.2	28.1	41.8
Computer activities	22.4	11.2	10.5	45.1	:	12.1	7.9	14.7	19.7	10.2	8.6	15.4	18.1	15.3	8.7	27.8
Research and development	6.9	15.6	-5.9	21.8	:	31.2	4.7	27.8	25.2	5.6	4.4	1.6	-0.9	-5.4	0.4	-2.2
Business services	23.2	12.5	14.4	37.9	:	19.9	5.2	28.0	29.9	12.7	15.9	17.5	16.8	15.6	7.7	24.1

NB: Data is given for ALL enterprises in 1999, except italics.
  EL (Section D : enterprises with more than 20 persons occupied);
  D (Section E), IRL (Sections E to K), and NL (Section K) : data refer to 1998.
  For Ireland, contrary to the general definition, value added contains some taxes connected to turnover.
  Data for EU-15 are Eurostat estimations.
Source: Eurostat, SBS database.

Table 3.1.3. Main ratios by branch and country 1999 (as a %)

	EU	B	DK	D	EL	E	F	IRL	I	L	NL	A	P	FIN	S	UK
Mining and quarrying [1]																
VA/production	56.8	42.6	67.8	65.8	61.2	48.6	33.0	38.5	53.6	50.5	:	49.2	40.2	36.3	33.2	60.2
GOS/turnover	35.1	22.3	63.6	17.6	17.9	15.0	5.7	16.2	40.5	29.4	:	23.1	18.6	18.7	11.1	48.4
Personnel costs/VA	35.8	44.1	6.1	70.6	70.5	70.0	82.2	57.2	27.4	41.9	:	50.1	51.6	47.1	67.9	16.0
Investment/VA [2]	24.0	21.2	13.4	14.8	:	17.1	28.2	65.5	22.3	:	:	30.6	46.6	35.7	57.6	27.6
Manufacturing																
VA/production	30.5	27.8	36.3	33.5	34.0	28.9	24.4	35.9	27.4	32.3	29.0	37.6	28.6	32.3	32.0	35.0
GOS/turnover	9.6	9.5	11.3	6.8	14.6	10.6	6.7	25.7	10.7	11.6	10.7	11.2	11.1	14.1	10.5	13.2
Personnel costs/VA	66.1	62.8	68.0	77.4	55.5	60.2	70.5	25.4	58.5	61.5	59.1	66.9	59.2	54.1	65.2	59.0
Investment/VA [2]	14.7	20.7	15.2	13.3	:	14.6	14.7	13.5	18.1	:	15.2	14.8	28.8	14.8	18.3	12.1
Electricity, gas and water supply [3]																
VA/production	34.1	25.8	26.7	29.9	:	49.4	39.2	42.3	37.6	58.4	33.9	45.7	35.8	52.0	35.3	30.6
GOS/turnover	21.2	16.1	16.3	16.0	:	33.2	20.7	27.8	26.7	19.6	24.7	25.7	27.3	23.4	22.0	22.3
Personnel costs/VA	37.9	38.2	33.3	46.7	:	23.1	49.0	43.1	35.1	36.0	28.7	44.4	26.2	31.0	26.2	27.7
Investment/VA [2]	28.2	21.0	32.3	35.7	:	2.9	26.5	36.3	25.8	:	33.6	31.4	45.3	15.8	50.5	26.0
Construction [4]																
VA/production	35.0	32.7	38.9	40.2	37.7	:	36.6	:	28.3	51.3	32.2	46.2	20.8	32.4	36.9	34.6
GOS/turnover	10.4	9.6	10.8	6.0	20.4	:	6.5	:	14.4	14.4	7.4	9.6	9.3	10.7	12.3	15.8
Personnel costs/VA	70.6	69.9	72.6	85.2	49.4	:	81.8	:	51.3	67.9	77.0	78.4	58.6	67.0	68.9	54.2
Investment/VA [2]	9.7	19.5	11.0	7.5	11.3	:	7.4	:	13.2	:	11.0	8.6	22.6	11.9	11.8	8.6
Wholesale and retail trade; repair of motor vehicles, motorcycles and personal and household goods [5]																
VA/production	50.2	44.2	43.6	62.0	:	58.6	47.3	62.5	32.3	61.2	56.0	50.4	51.2	54.9	53.4	53.5
GOS/turnover	6.4	4.4	4.7	8.1	:	6.0	3.7	:	8.2	:	5.9	5.2	5.1	5.2	4.1	7.6
Personnel costs/VA	56.3	57.8	66.9	54.3	:	55.1	71.4	:	39.5	50.2	55.4	67.3	56.6	60.0	70.5	52.8
Investment/VA [2]	13.2	19.9	12.7	7.7	:	19.4	12.3	:	15.1	:	14.3	12.3	26.7	15.8	16.8	14.3
Market services (Sections H, I and K of the NACE Rev.1) [6]																
VA/production	45.4	41.1	49.8	44.9	:	56.7	45.6	57.6	44.2	58.0	45.9	63.1	36.2	45.8	40.7	40.2
GOS/turnover	17.9	14.4	22.4	19.2	:	22.4	12.0	20.0	23.7	:	18.5	19.6	17.5	17.7	15.2	17.6
Personnel costs/VA	58.4	63.3	52.0	61.0	:	48.1	71.8	51.9	46.6	:	59.4	58.5	50.0	58.6	63.2	54.3
Investment/VA [2]	30.0	34.7	27.0	29.0	:	27.0	29.4	24.8	23.0	:	39.8	37.1	61.9	24.9	37.5	31.5

NB: 1999 except italics   D (Section E: 1998)   IRL (Sections E to K : 1998)   EL (more than 20 persons occupied in 1998)

[1] Mining and quarrying: except NL.
[2] Investment except L, EL.
[3] Electricity, gas and water supply except EL; reference year for D is 1998.
[4] Construction except E, IRL.
[5] Wholesale, retail trade and repair: except EL, IRL.
[6] Market services (partially on 80% of the aggregate): except EL, L; for UK, D, NL data does not include Section K.
Source: Eurostat, SBS database.

Table 3.1.4. Number of persons employed (1 000) by branch, 2000

	EU	B	DK	D	E	F	IRL	I	L	NL	A	P	FIN	S	UK
Industry															
Food	:	99	83	872	363	574	49	466	:	148	77	112	43	:	:
Tobacco	59	3	1	13	7	:	1	9	:	5	:	1	0	:	7
Textiles	1 088	42	9	135	109	121	7	325	1	20	21	109	7	10	:
Clothing	991	12	5	80	134	102	4	346	0	7	12	144	6	4	134
Leather and footwear	478	3	2	28	69	44	1	223	0	3	6	69	3	2	26
Wood processing and manufacture of articles in wood	880	14	16	181	103	88	6	190	1	21	38	59	29	43	88
Paper and paperboard	:	15	9	155	55	91	5	86	:	26	17	16	41	45	103
Publishing, printing, etc	:	39	52	352	142	210	20	177	:	94	27	40	31	57	386
Nuclear fuels, coking, etc	:	5	0	23	8	29	:	26	0	5	:	3	4	3	31
Chemicals	1 702	69	27	494	136	283	23	220	1	71	25	23	19	41	262
Rubber and plastics	1 423	30	23	391	118	232	11	216	4	36	29	24	18	27	257
Non-metallic mineral products	1 281	37	21	294	180	146	11	255	3	34	33	72	17	18	:
Metallurgy	924	41	10	265	73	123	3	156	6	25	32	14	17	35	122
Metalworking	3 197	67	47	836	307	436	14	679	4	107	67	84	38	92	412
Machinery and equipment	3 077	45	70	1 090	180	330	14	595	3	93	75	48	59	104	367
Computer and office equipment	:	1	2	46	8	40	21	27	:	9	1	0	1	5	59
Electrical appliances	1 397	26	21	519	91	172	16	220	0	22	30	35	17	35	192
Radio, etc, equipment	:	19	15	172	30	8	16	101	:	:	31	16	39	48	142
Medical equipment, etc	874	9	14	306	29	140	19	129	2	25	16	7	11	28	139
Car industry	:	54	7	846	165	279	3	186	:	28	29	29	7	85	225
Other transport equipment	:	11	9	137	51	120	5	106	:	29	5	13	12	22	176
Furniture, other	:	29	32	268	165	162	:	313	1	43	50	93	16	35	231
Recycling	:	4	0	13	2	:	0	12	0	2	1	1	0	1	12
Electricity, gas and water	:														
Productivity and distribution electricity	:	20	15	251	43	167	10	139	1	28	33	15	12	25	98
Collection, purification, distribution of water	:	6	3	36	20	31	:	16	0	7	2	13	0	1	29
Construction	:														
Construction	:	252	180	2 152	:	1 231	:	1 488	25	467	238	355	115	236	1 325
Wholesale and retail trade															
Car sales and repairs	2 937	83	65	:	344	436	34	478	6	148	79	117	35	80	614
Wholesale trade	6 477	226	176	:	921	952	56	1 091	13	470	194	237	81	218	:
Retail sales and repairs of household goods	11 319	290	199	:	1 515	1 407	152	1 753	18	713	272	353	115	247	2 974
Services (excluding financial services)															
Hotels and restaurants	:	146	94	:	1 051	995	133	845	12	89	203	205	50	109	1 740
Land transport	:	133	80	979	:	635	24	591	10	203	138	86	68	131	582
Water transport	:	1	10	23	8	15	:	23		14	0	2	8	15	18
Air transport	:	13	12	51	35	66	:	21	3	:	8	11	10	14	96
Auxiliary transport services	1 888	51	32	537	178	268	13	231	2	84	35	32	22	56	347
Post and telecommunications	:	84	62	508	184	:	25	255	4	144	64	39	49	92	518
Real estate	1 688	22	47	400	166	248	9	221	1	64	25	25	19	75	364
Leasing without operator	499	9	8	84	71	65	7	24	1	28	7	9	3	13	171
Computer activities	1 981	47	40	420	135	234	17	271	3	122	33	15	31	105	507
Research and development	:	5	4	131	26	:	0	21	2	35	2	0	1	14	84
Business services	:	379	196	3 394	1 606	1 881	77	1 356	:	987	199	215	113	345	2 825

NB: Figures for L, UK and figures for IRL (Sections E to K) refer to 1999. Figures for Greece are not available.
Data for EU-15 are Eurostat estimations.
Source: Eurostat, SBS database.

for both activities covered by the sector (production and distribution of electricity, gas and heat; collection, treatment and distribution of water). The share of staff expenditure in value added is generally relatively low (except in France, where the gross operating rates for the two sectors differ: 24.7 % and 2.7 % respectively).

Among services, activities relating to "renting without operator" (Germany, Austria, Portugal) and real estate provide the best return according to the indicator. In the latter case, however, the figures for two big countries (Germany and the United Kingdom) are not known.

Table 3.1.4 shows employment measured in terms of the number of people employed. Some data for 2000 are incomplete (United Kingdom, distributive trades in Germany, transport in Spain), but in spite of the gaps in the statistics it can be seen that the biggest contributor to jobs in the European Union is the tertiary sector: non-financial market services with 33.6 million, including 13.6 million solely for business services (K74 in NACE rev.1) and distributive trades with approximately 20.7 million, including 11.3 million in retail trade and repairs. Manufacturing altogether provides jobs for 28.6 million people: mainly metalworking (4.1 million), agri-food industries (3.4 million), electric and electronic equipment (3.3 million), etc. The construction sector employs about 9 million (the exact figure for Spain is not known).

Overall, in the sectors under review the share of the tertiary sector (Sections G-K of NACE rev.1) was close to 59 % for the European Union as a whole. These sectors already account for a majority percentage in the Netherlands (70 %) and the United Kingdom (64 %). At the other extreme, industry is still important — accounting for about 50 % — in Portugal, Italy and Finland.

3.2. Short-term business developments

The indices for total industry ([1]) are based on the components of intermediate goods, capital goods, durable and non-durable consumer goods and energy, also called the main industrial groupings, or MIGs.

The production index measures the volume of output in the industrial sector. Figure 3.2.1 shows that production in total industry has increased by almost 15 % in total since 1995 and its trend is followed closely by the intermediate goods sector. The steady upward trend of the production of capital goods was reversed at the beginning of 2001 and the index has since fallen from almost 135 to 124. The previously mentioned sectors experienced especially rapid growth up until early 2001 but have decreased subsequently. Consumer goods and the energy sector saw more moderate increases; 7.7 % and 8.3 % respectively during the past seven years.

The map indicates the growth of the production index during year 2001 compared to 2000.

Ireland has strongly (10.1 %) increased its production levels for total industry during 2001. Luxembourg expanded production by 3.2 % and Portugal by 2.4 %. Production fell in many Member States for the first time since 1995, most notably in the United Kingdom (– 2.1 %), Spain (– 1.4 %) and Italy (– 1.3 %). Nevertheless, the growth rates of Denmark (1.7 %), France (0.7 %), Germany (0.5 %) and Greece (0.3 %) were somewhat above the European average (– 0.1 %).

Figure 3.2.2 relates the Member States average rate of change in total industrial production during 1996-2001 with the respective weight of the country in the European aggregate. The weights are based in 1995 and calculated on the share of the European total value added at factor cost ([2]) that each Member State demonstrated during 1995. The four largest countries Italy, France, the United Kingdom and Germany account for 75 % and the remaining 11 countries share

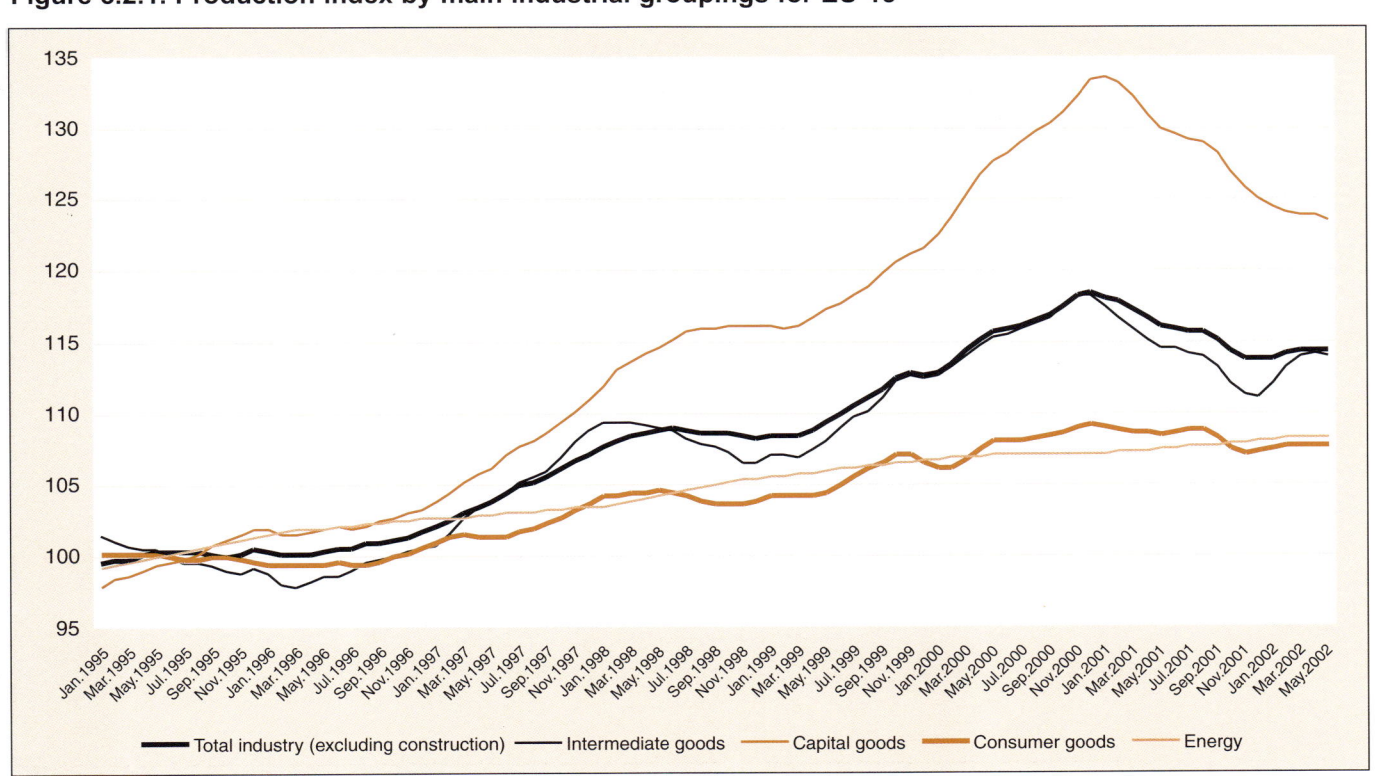

Figure 3.2.1. Production index by main industrial groupings for EU-15

NB: The comparisons are made between the base year value 1995 = 100 and the latest index value available, here May 2002.
Source: Eurostat.

[1] All data in this chapter were extracted from Eurostat's database in July 2001. Data are collected by the Member States and provided to Eurostat. Results and calculations in this text are subject to the availability of data. Total industry does not include construction.
[2] Total value added at factor cost for Sections C, D and E (Industry) of NACE Rev.1

ENTERPRISES IN THE UNION

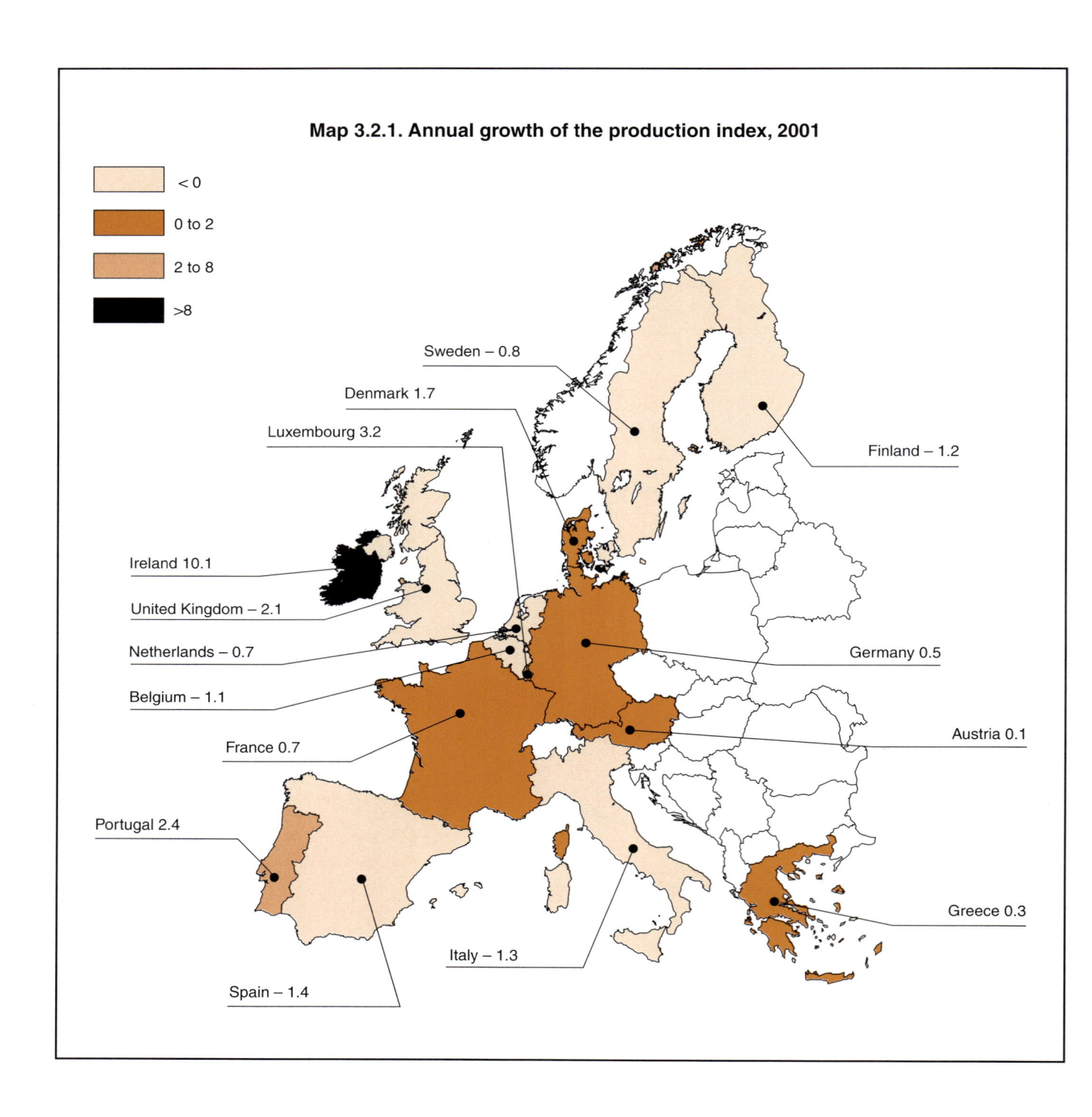

Map 3.2.1. Annual growth of the production index, 2001

< 0
0 to 2
2 to 8
>8

Sweden – 0.8
Denmark 1.7
Luxembourg 3.2
Finland – 1.2
Ireland 10.1
United Kingdom – 2.1
Netherlands – 0.7
Germany 0.5
Belgium – 1.1
Austria 0.1
France 0.7
Portugal 2.4
Greece 0.3
Italy – 1.3
Spain – 1.4

ENTERPRISES IN THE UNION

Figure 3.2.2. Average growth of total industrial production and weight of each country in the European Union's total

	L	EL	IRL	P	FIN	DK	A	S	B	NL	E	I	F	UK	D
Average growth 1996–2001	4.0	3.3	14.3	3.2	6.1	3.1	5.1	3.5	2.3	1.6	2.8	1.1	2.7	0.6	2.8
Weight as a %	0.1	0.6	1.2	1.2	1.6	1.6	2.6	2.9	3.2	3.8	6.2	14.7	15.1	15.6	29.6

Source: Eurostat.

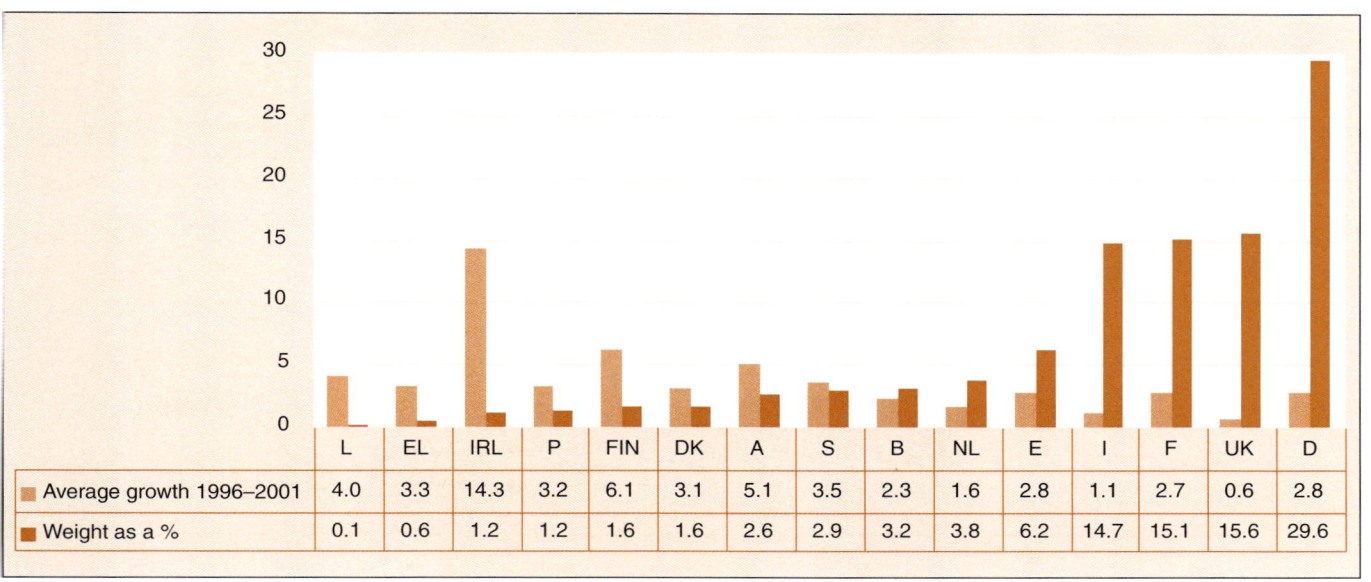

Table 3.2.1. Industries with the lowest/highest production index values in the European Union (1995 = 100)

Industries with the lowest production index values	1996	1997	1998	1999	2000	2001	Average annual growth 1995–2001
Mining of coal and lignite; extraction of peat	94.5	91.4	82.0	78.9	73.2	67.8	– 6.3
Manufacture of wearing apparel; dressing and dyeing of fur	94.9	91.4	89.0	79.8	76.2	75.4	– 4.6
Mining of metal ores	94.1	92.3	91.9	82.6	81.6	79.6	– 3.8
Tanning and dressing of leather; manufacture of luggage, handbags, saddlery, harness and footwear	96.2	97.4	92.5	89.6	87.7	85.9	– 2.5
Manufacture of tobacco products	99.7	99.0	99.2	94.5	92.6	90.2	– 1.7

Industries with the highest production index values	1996	1997	1998	1999	2000	2001	Average annual growth 1995–2001
Manufacture of office machinery and computers	104.3	121.8	143.5	156.7	183.0	178.6	10.1
Recycling	113.6	129.2	135.6	143.3	158.0	163.0	8.5
Manufacture of radio, television and communication equipment and apparatus	106.8	115.2	129.2	141.2	173.9	162.2	8.4
Manufacture of motor vehicles, trailers and semi-trailers	102.9	110.9	123.3	127.6	138.2	140.3	5.8
Manufacture of medical, precision and optical instruments, watches and clocks	103.4	106.0	109.4	111.6	124.3	129.6	4.4

Source: Eurostat.

25 % of the weight in the European aggregate for total industry. Spain has a weight of 6.2 % and the rest of the countries have less than 5 % each.

All countries have recorded positive average annual growth rates, but a general remark is that the smaller countries have increased more rapidly than the larger countries. Most notable is Ireland with an average increase of production of 14.3 % per year. Also the growth rates of Finland (6.1 %) and Austria (5.1 %) deserve attention. The United Kingdom has the lowest average annual growth in production of the Member States, with 0.6 %, accompanied by Italy with 1.1 % per year.

However, there are similar trends in the European Union and in general, the same industrial sectors are increasing production in the different Member States. If we look at the development of the European index values since 1995, we see that it is in particular the manufacture of office machinery and computers and recycling that are increasing rapidly in the EU, with growth

ENTERPRISES IN THE UNION

Figure 3.2.3. Number of persons employed in the European Union by main industrial groupings (¹)

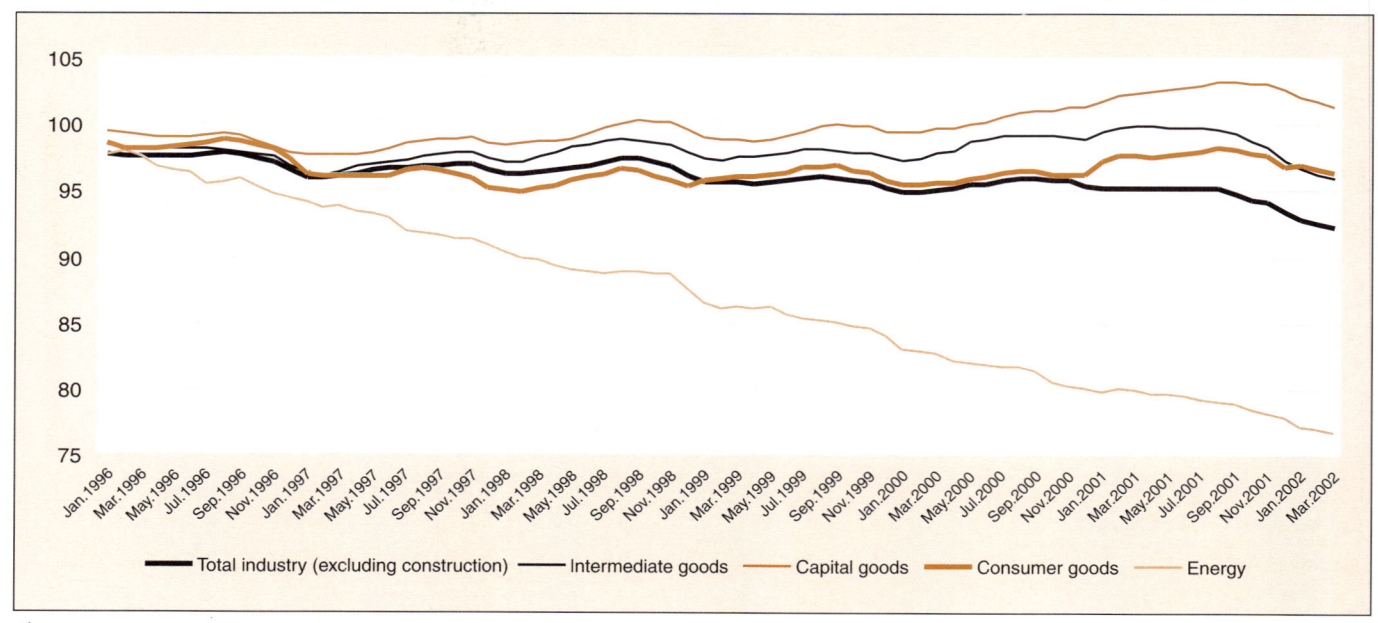

[Line chart showing employment index (1995=100) from Jan.1996 to Mar.2002 for: Total industry (excluding construction), Intermediate goods, Capital goods, Consumer goods, Energy. Values range from about 75 to 105.]

(¹) The employment data come from business statistics in the Member States. The comparisons are made between the base year value 1995 = 100 and the latest index value available, here March 2002.
Source: Eurostat.

Table 3.2.2. Industries with the highest/lowest employment index values in the European Union, 1996-2001 (1995 = 100)

Industries with the highest employment index values	1996	1997	1998	1999	2000	2001	Average annual growth 1995–2001
Recycling	102.5	106.9	110.9	130.2	128.5	133.0	4.9
Manufacture of motor vehicles, trailers and semi-trailers	100.3	101.4	104.0	105.0	107.6	108.5	1.4
Manufacture of medical, precision and optical instruments, watches and clocks	101.3	102.1	102.3	101.3	101.6	105.4	1.0
Manufacture of radio, television and communication equipment and apparatus	100.0	98.1	99.2	100.3	104.7	104.6	0.7
Manufacture of food products and beverages	100.9	99.2	99.6	100.5	101.5	102.3	0.4
Industries with the lowest employment index values	**1996**	**1997**	**1998**	**1999**	**2000**	**2001**	**Average annual growth 1995–2001**
Mining of coal and lignite; extraction of peat	93.2	83.5	73.3	66.5	60.3	53.5	– 9.9
Manufacture of wearing apparel; dressing and dyeing of fur	95.7	91.5	87.3	82.1	76.2	72.3	– 5.3
Electricity, gas, steam and hot water supply	95.5	92.9	90.3	87.2	83.5	80.6	– 3.5
Collection, purification and distribution of water	98.2	96.2	94.2	88.7	84.7	80.6	– 3.5
Manufacture of textiles	96.1	94.3	93.4	90.2	87.4	85.6	– 2.6

Source: Eurostat.

of 78.6 % and 63.0 % respectively. The manufacture of radio, television and communication equipment and apparatus is the third fastest growing sector since 1995 with an average annual increase of 8.4 %.

Mining of coal and lignite; extraction of peat is the industrial sector with the lowest index value year 2001 (67.8). Manufacture of wearing apparel, etc. and the mining of metal ores have on average fallen at European level by 4.6 % and 3.8 % respectively per year since 1995.

The number of persons employed in industry has since 1995 tended to decrease in the main industrial groupings at European level. The most marked fall has occurred in the sector of energy, which has decreased by 23 % since 1995. Employment in capital goods, which is a sector where production has increased remarkably (24 %), has increased only by 1.4 % since 1995.

The sectors of the employment index in industry follow more or less the same pattern as the production index.

ENTERPRISES IN THE UNION

Figure 3.2.4. Number of persons employed in industry, growth rates (as a %)

	P	UK	I	D	A	EU-15	DK	F	B	NL	L	FIN	E
Growth 2001	−3.9	−3.3	−3.0	0.1	0.9	−0.6	−0.9	1.0	−0.1	−0.2	0.6	0.7	3.1
Average annual growth 1995–2001	−2.5	−2.4	−2.3	−1.4	−1.0	−0.9	−0.3	0.0	0.0	0.1	0.7	1.4	3.5

Source: Eurostat.

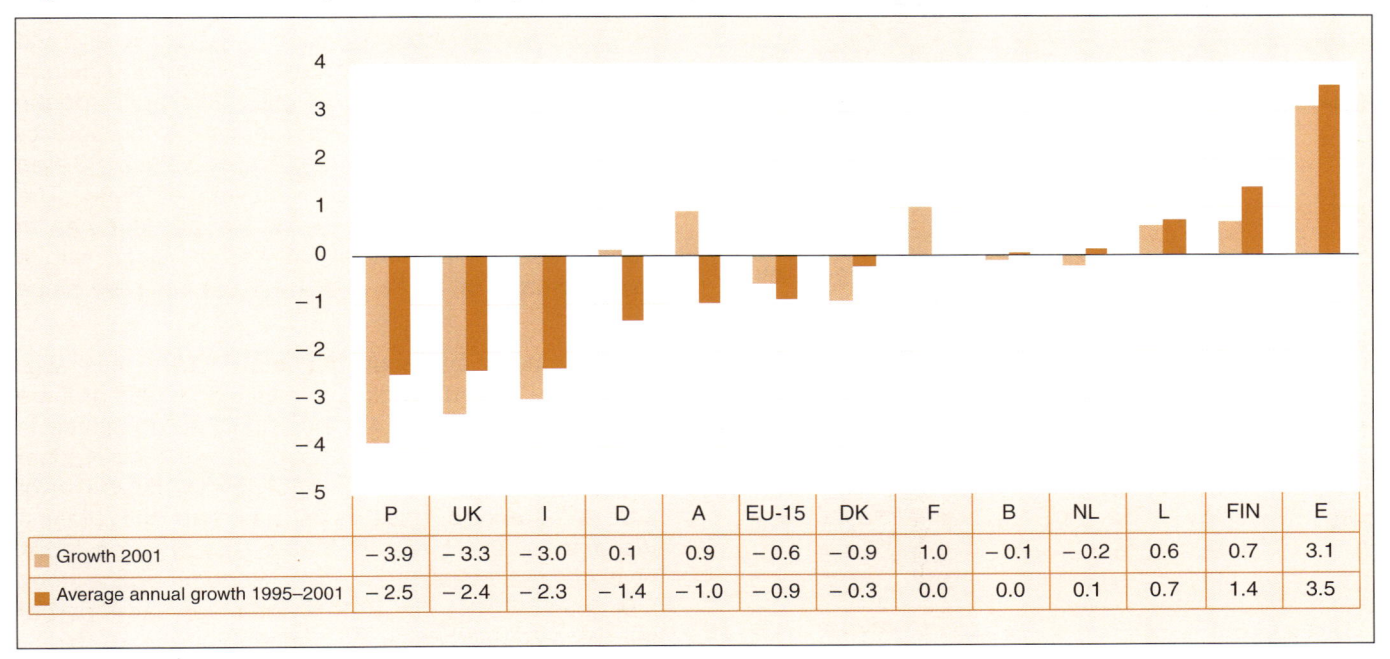

Figure 3.2.5. Index of domestic output prices by main industrial groupings

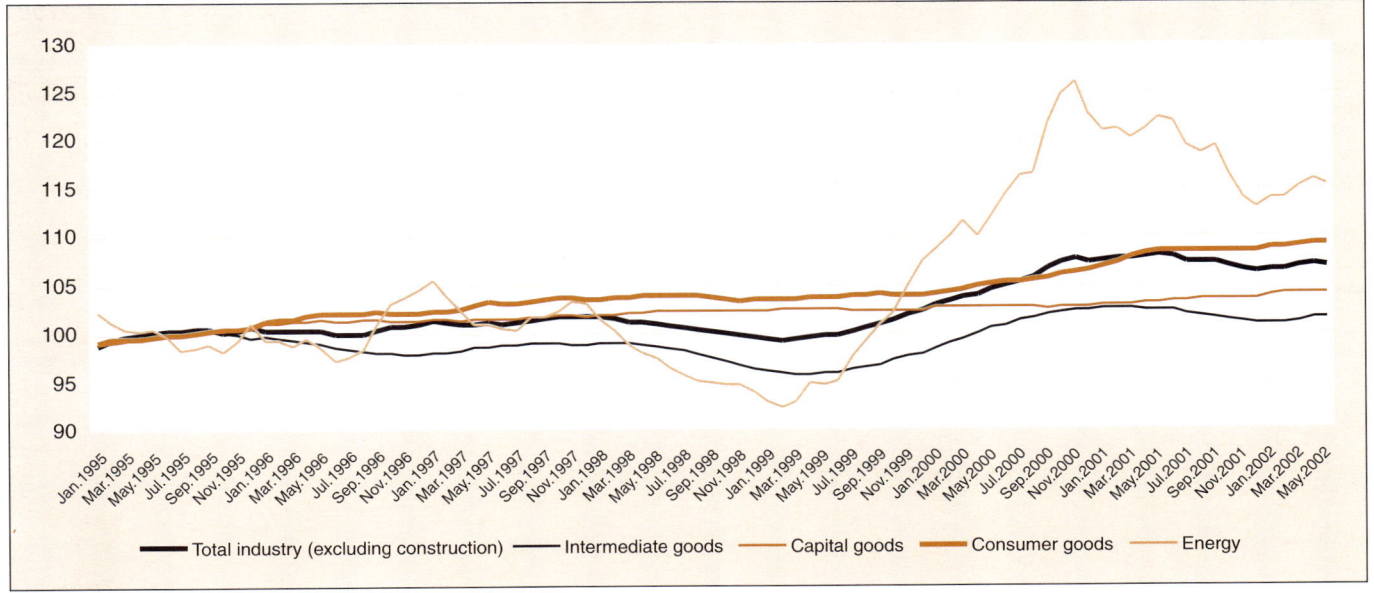

Source: Eurostat.

Recycling is here the sector with the highest growth since 1995, with 33 %, or 4.9 % on average per year. Manufacture of motor vehicles, trailers and semi-trailers had the second highest index value in 2001 (108.5). Similarly, the employment in mining of coal and lignite; extraction of peat has had the most significant decrease of all the sectors, by almost 10 % on average per year.

The employment index for industry had a very varied development in the different Member States between 1995 and 2001. In Portugal, the United Kingdom and Italy, employment fell by around 2.5 % per year. Employment in Germany has decreased by 1.4 % on average during the last seven years; however it increased slightly during 2001, namely 0.1 %. Spain and Finland recorded the highest average growth rates

Table 3.2.3. Index of domestic output prices (1995 = 100)

	1996	1997	1998	1999	2000	2001
EU-15	100.4	101.3	100.7	100.4	105.3	107.3
B	100.6	102.3	101.0	100.6	109.3	110.2
D	98.8	99.9	99.5	98.5	101.8	104.9
DK	101.5	103.3	102.9	104.1	109.2	112.1
EL	106.2	110.4	113.3	117.0	126.0	129.2
E	101.7	102.7	102.0	102.7	108.3	110.2
F	100.2	100.3	98.6	98.4	103.8	105.1
IRL	101.3	101.6	102.6	103.8	109.0	112.7
I	101.9	103.2	103.3	103.1	109.3	111.4
L	95.7	98.5	101.1	99.0	105.1	107.8
NL	101.9	105.2	102.8	102.3	114.3	118.5
A	99.7	99.9	99.3	98.3	102.7	103.5
P	103.8	106.1	102.2	103.6	120.3	121.0
FIN	99.1	100.4	99.0	97.8	105.1	106.7
S	101.2	102.0	100.6	99.4	102.8	107.4
UK	100.5	100.1	100.1	100.4	102.0	102.3

Source: Eurostat.

The level of industrial domestic output prices was kept fairly stable during the years 1995-99, but has since 2000 increased more significantly. This is a trend apparent in all Member States. However the magnitude has varied. Looking at the MIGs at European level, the series for energy has proven to be particularly volatile, varying between index values 92.4 in February 1999 and 126.1 in November 2000. The price index for intermediate goods and for capital goods presents a relatively steady evolution with a total increase of 1.6 % and 4.4 % respectively since 1995.

The European aggregate for total industry has augmented by 7.3 index points in total since 1995 and the largest annual rise, of 4.9 index points, took place in 2000. During the last seven years, the United Kingdom has shown the most stable price levels with a rise of 2.3 %. Greece's price level has had the highest increase of the Member States, reaching an index level of 129.2 in 2001. Moreover, Portugal's price index has risen by 21 % since 1995 and a very large part of this increase was developed during 2000.

Both employment and production in construction faltered slightly in 1996 with a drop of – 1.3 % and – 2.2 % respectively, but have thereafter gradually recuperated. Employment in construction has shown a steady upward trend since 1996, gaining 8.3 % since 1995 and with an average annual increase of 1.3 %. The production level in 2001 was 5.5 % higher than 1995.

(3.5 % and 1.4 % respectively) and Spain's index increased by 3.1 % in 2001.

The index of domestic output prices brings into view the transaction prices for domestic economic activities and is as such an indication of inflationary pressures.

Figure 3.2.6. Growth of employment and production in the construction sector (1995 = 100)

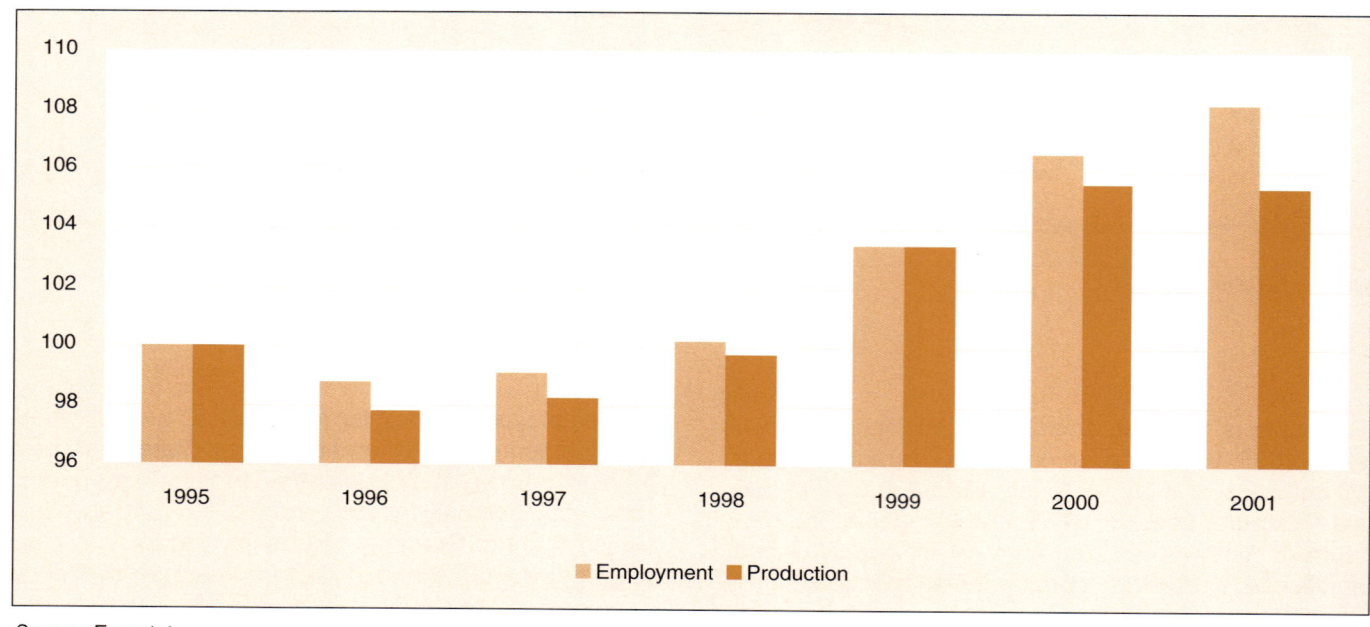

Source: Eurostat.

Figure 3.2.7 displays a comparison between the average annual growth rate of the total retail trade for each Member State, 1996-2001, and the annual growth rate for 2001.

Germany's average annual growth rate in retail trade during the last five years was 0.2 % and 1.0 % for 2001 compared to 2000. Only Italy and Austria registered negative growth for 2001 (− 1.2 % and − 0.4 % respectively). At the other end of the spectrum, Ireland had both the highest average annual growth (7.2 %) and the most rapid expansion for 2001 (7.4 %). Also Portugal showed a high average growth of 4.3 % per year although the index was stable between 2001 and 2000. The United Kingdom and Spain attained both high gains in 2001, with 5.9 % and 4.4 % respectively. The EU average growth reached 2.3 % per year and in 2001 it climbed to 2.4 %.

Figure 3.2.7. Deflated turnover in retail trade (as a %)

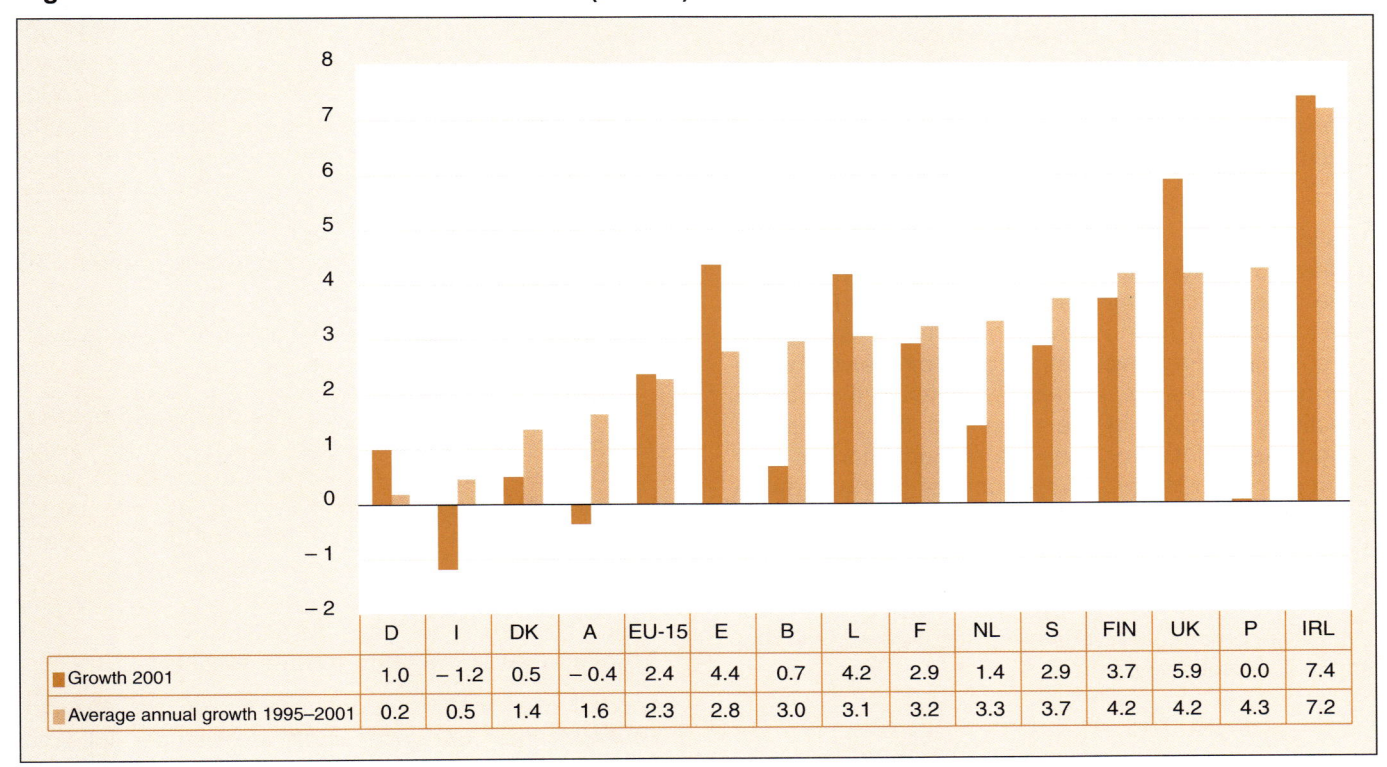

	D	I	DK	A	EU-15	E	B	L	F	NL	S	FIN	UK	P	IRL
Growth 2001	1.0	− 1.2	0.5	− 0.4	2.4	4.4	0.7	4.2	2.9	1.4	2.9	3.7	5.9	0.0	7.4
Average annual growth 1995–2001	0.2	0.5	1.4	1.6	2.3	2.8	3.0	3.1	3.2	3.3	3.7	4.2	4.2	4.3	7.2

Source: Eurostat.

3.3. Developments in agriculture

Introduction

The annual economic accounts for agriculture (EAA), which are satellite accounts in the framework of the European system of accounts (ESA 95), provide a set of three indicators showing income trends in agriculture. The most important of these indicators is Indicator A which measures the change of real agricultural factor income in relation to the change in total agricultural labour input (see box below).

Agriculture as described in the EAA corresponds generally to Division 01 in NACE Rev.1. This means that neither forestry nor fishery are included, which elsewhere in this publication are grouped together with agriculture to form the larger total of NACE Sections AB.

The income indicators in the EAA relate to the income generated by agricultural activities (as well as inseparable non-agricultural, secondary activities) over a given accounting period, even though in certain cases the corresponding revenues will not be received until a later date. It does not, therefore, constitute the income effectively received in the course of the accounting period itself. Moreover, they are not indicators of total income or of the disposable income of farming households; in addition to their purely agricultural income, such households often receive income from other sources (non-agricultural activities, salaries, social benefits, income from property). In other words, agricultural income must not be regarded as the income of agricultural households.

The three agricultural income indicators

Indicator A: Index of the real income of factors in agriculture, per annual work unit

This indicator corresponds to the **real (i.e. deflated) net value added at factor cost of agriculture per total annual work unit.** Net value added at factor cost is calculated by subtracting intermediate consumption, depreciation and other (i.e. non-product-specific) production taxes from the value of agricultural output at basic prices (i.e. including subsidies on products and excluding taxes on products), and adding the value of other (i.e. non-product-specific) production subsidies. Indicator A is obtained by deflating this net value with the implicit price index of gross domestic product at market prices and dividing by the volume of total labour in agriculture.

In order to take account of part-time and seasonal work, agricultural labour input or changes therein are measured in annual work units (AWU). An AWU is equivalent to the time worked by one person employed full time in agriculture on a holding over the whole year. A distinction is drawn between non-salaried and salaried AWU, which together make up the total number of AWU.

Indicator B: Index of real net agricultural entrepreneurial income, per unpaid annual work unit

This indicator presents the changes in net entrepreneurial income over time, per unpaid / non-salaried annual work unit. Net entrepreneurial income is obtained by subtracting the compensation of employees and interest and rent paid from the net value added at factor cost and adding the interest received. This figure, when deflated with the same price index referred to above and divided by the volume of non-salaried labour in agriculture, gives Indicator B.

Indicator C: Real net entrepreneurial income from agriculture

Indicator C defines the change in the real (i.e. deflated) net entrepreneurial income.

For more information see the *Manual on the Economic Accounts for Agriculture and Forestry EAA/EAF97 (Rev. 1.1),* Theme 5, Methods and Nomenclatures, Luxembourg (2000); this manual is available in all 11 official languages of the European Communities.

An overview of the main results for 2001

According to the provisional results of the EAA for 2001, income from agricultural activity per full-time worker equivalent is expected to have increased, in 2001, by 3.3 % when measured by Indicator A, for the European Union as a whole (EU-15) (see Figure 3.3.1 and Table 3.3.1). With this increase, the index of average income from agricultural activity reaches a level of 107.6 in comparison with the average of the three years from 1994 to 1996. For the euro-zone (EUR-12), the index of Indicator A is estimated to have risen by 3.0 % in 2001 thus reaching a level of 112.1 (average from 1994 to 1996 being equal to 100).

Changes in income from agricultural activity usually vary widely across Member States, partly because the various countries started out in different situations, as a result of the developments in previous years, and partly because of the wide variety of structural and economic factors affecting agriculture in the individual Member States of the European Union. This finding is confirmed by the results for 2001. It is however remarkable that all countries, with the exception of Luxembourg, actually recorded increases in the agri-

ENTERPRISES IN THE UNION

Figure 3.3.1. % changes in agricultural income measured by Indicator A for the Member States and the European Union, 2001 (compared to the previous year)

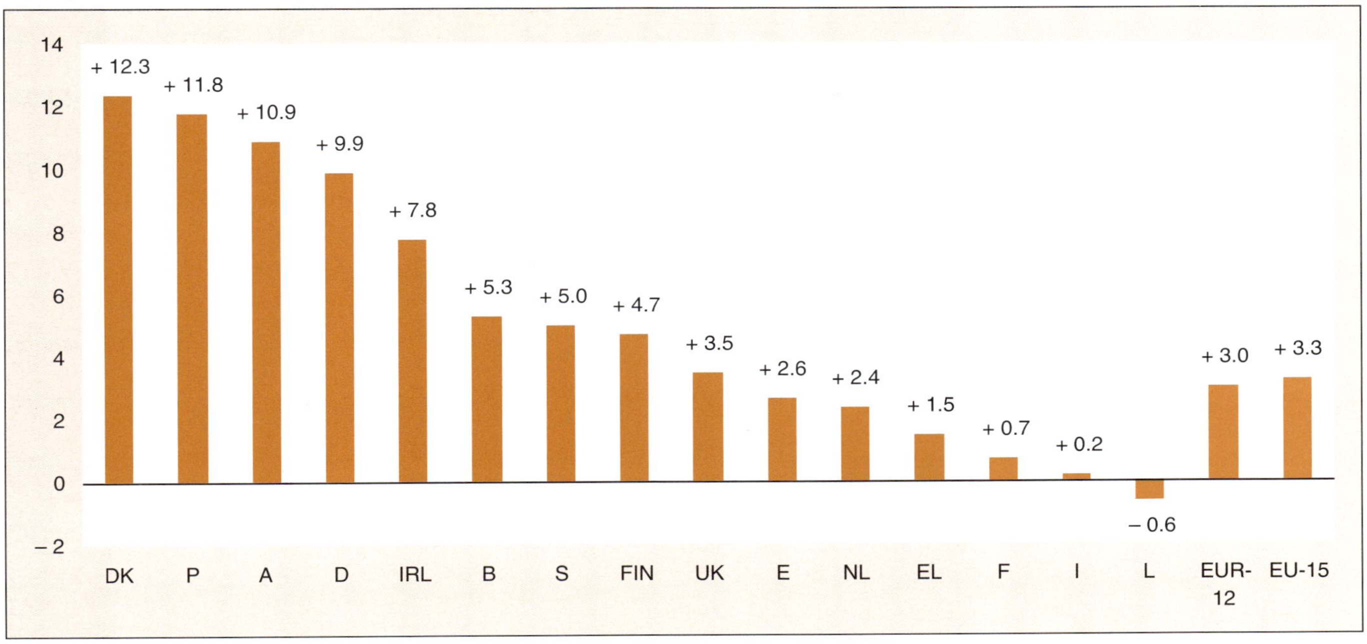

Country	% Change
DK	+ 12.3
P	+ 11.8
A	+ 10.9
D	+ 9.9
IRL	+ 7.8
B	+ 5.3
S	+ 5.0
FIN	+ 4.7
UK	+ 3.5
E	+ 2.6
NL	+ 2.4
EL	+ 1.5
F	+ 0.7
I	+ 0.2
L	− 0.6
EUR-12	+ 3.0
EU-15	+ 3.3

Source: Eurostat.

cultural income Indicator A. The fastest rates of change were measured in Denmark (+ 12.3 %), Portugal (+ 11.8 %), Austria (+ 10.9 %), and in Germany (+ 9.9 %). But also Ireland (+ 7.8 %) recorded a notable income increase. The lowest growth rates were observed in France (+ 0.7 %) and Italy (+ 0.2 %). In Luxembourg, Indicator A fell 0.6 % below the level reached in 2000. Later in this chapter, these estimates for 2001 will be placed in a medium-term perspective.

For EU-15 in 2001, real agricultural factor income (i.e. net value added at factor cost), the basis of Indicator A, was slightly higher than in 2000 (+ 1.2 %). There were increases in 11 Member States with the highest rates measured in Portugal (+ 9.5 %), Austria and Denmark (both + 9.0 %). Real agricultural factor income fell below 2000 levels in four Member States, namely the Netherlands, France, Greece and Luxembourg. However, the ratio of real factor income per annual work unit nevertheless increased in three of these countries as the number of annual work units declined at a faster rate than factor income: in the Netherlands, for example, a decline of 1.1 % in real agricultural factor income, and of 3.4 % in the volume of agricultural labour input resulted in an increase of 2.4 % in Indicator A (Greece: real factor income − 1.4 %, agricultural labour input − 2.9 %, Indicator A + 1.5 %; France: real factor income − 1.1 %, agricultural labour input − 1.8 %, Indicator A + 0.7 %).

Indeed, the volume of agricultural labour input continued to decline in 2001 in all the Member States, with the exception of Italy (+ 0.5 %). For EU-15 as a whole, there was a reduction of 2.0 % in the volume of agricultural labour input, the slowest rate over the last 10 years.

Like Indicator A, real-terms net entrepreneurial income per non-salaried agricultural annual work unit (Indicator B) in agriculture in the European Union is expected to have increased in 2001 (see Table 3.3.1). Figures from EU-15 Member States less Germany ("EU-14", see separate box) suggest that there was an average increase of 4.4 %. This increase is the result of a rise, by 1.4 %, in the real-terms net entrepreneurial income for "EU-14" in 2001 compared to 2000, on the one hand, and of the continued decline in the volume of non-salaried labour input (− 2.9 %), on the other. Indicator C measuring the development in real net entrepreneurial income was 2.2 % higher than in 2000 for the EU-15 as a whole. Ten Member States recorded increases, with rates ranging from + 1.5 % in Italy to + 27.3 % in Denmark. The other Member States recorded declines ranging from − 0.2 % in Spain to − 2.0 % in France.

> **Indicator B** is not calculated for Germany on methodological grounds: in the new *Länder* of eastern Germany there is a number of holdings organised as legal persons, in which, unlike sole proprietorships and partnerships, wages and salaries are paid to all workers, including the members of/partners in the enterprise. Holdings which are legal persons thus produce corporate profits (or losses) with no unpaid labour force. In such a situation, Indicator B, the denominator of which is determined by changes in non-salaried labour input, would be overestimated in relation to an actual individual income.

ENTERPRISES IN THE UNION

Table 3.3.1. % changes in the three indicators of income from agricultural activity in the European Union as a whole and in the Member States, 1999–2001 (compared to the previous year)

	Indicator A			Indicator B			Indicator C		
	1999	2000	2001	1999	2000	2001	1999	2000	2001
EU-15	– 1.0	2.7	3.3	:	:	:	– 5.9	– 2.0	2.2
EUR-12	– 0.7	3.2	3.0	:	:	:	– 6.4	– 2.5	1.5
B	– 14.2	11.6	5.3	– 21.8	19.3	7.8	– 23.7	16.8	4.6
DK	– 3.2	20.8	12.3	– 27.1	95.5	31.2	– 31.4	89.6	27.3
D	– 8.9	19.0	9.9	:	:	:	– 17.2	30.4	14.1
EL	1.7	– 1.5	1.5	2.3	– 1.0	2.9	1.6	– 4.4	– 0.7
E	– 2.9	11.4	2.6	– 2.3	10.8	5.4	– 10.4	– 0.8	– 0.2
F	– 2.2	0.2	0.7	– 3.9	– 0.4	0.8	– 6.5	– 3.0	– 2.0
IRL	– 7.8	5.3	7.8	– 10.7	4.5	9.0	– 18.5	1.6	1.8
I	8.9	– 3.9	0.2	13.8	– 5.3	1.6	5.9	– 9.7	1.5
L	– 9.5	1.8	– 0.6	– 15.2	– 2.3	1.7	– 17.4	– 6.5	– 1.8
NL	– 11.8	– 3.3	2.4	– 20.8	– 6.9	4.6	– 22.4	– 8.1	– 1.2
A	– 3.9	2.6	10.9	– 5.1	1.4	13.2	– 5.9	– 1.5	11.1
P	14.3	– 9.4	11.8	21.0	– 12.4	18.0	12.9	– 12.4	15.5
FIN	9.9	27.6	4.7	13.9	35.1	7.5	5.1	21.9	2.3
S	– 9.2	9.8	5.0	– 19.4	20.3	7.7	– 23.9	15.9	3.8
UK	– 1.9	– 9.4	3.5	– 3.4	– 23.8	10.9	– 6.5	– 26.3	8.9

Source: Eurostat.

It is worth noting that changes in Indicator C, and consequently also in Indicator B, are often more pronounced (in both directions) than changes in Indicator A. This is because the net entrepreneurial income, the basis for both Indicators B and C, is considerably smaller in absolute terms than factor income. The share, in 2000, of factor income in gross value added at basic prices was 79.4 % compared to only 49.6 % for net entrepreneurial income. A given change in any item entering the calculation of factor income, therefore yields a larger change in entrepreneurial income than in factor income.

Key factors driving the income developments in 2001

Which were the key factors at EU-15 level driving the development of real-terms agricultural factor income in 2001? On the whole, the principal aggregates behind factor income changed little, in 2001. On the level of the individual products, however, there were a number of significant changes, which are briefly enumerated in the following.

— **The value at basic prices of the agricultural industry's output was slightly higher in 2001 (+ 0.3 % in real terms)**. Increases in the output values of animals and animal products (+ 2.1 % and + 3.7 % respectively, in real terms) thus outweighed the decline in the value of crop output (– 1.5 % in real terms). The latter decline was mainly the result of lower volumes (– 7.5 %) in cereal production and lower volumes (– 5.7 %) and producer prices (– 3.7 %) in wine production. The increase in the average output value of animals (at basic prices), despite the considerable fall in the output values of cattle (producer prices down by – 13.3 % in real terms), was mainly the result of a further remarkable increase in the producer prices for pigs (+ 16.0 % in real terms). Higher producer prices for milk (+ 3.8 % in real terms) were the main factor behind the rise in the output value of animal products. The overall value of product-specific subsidies (net of taxes) was slightly smaller in 2001 than in 2000 (– 0.4 % in real terms).

— **The cost of intermediate consumption goods and services was slightly higher than in 2000 (+ 0.2 % in real terms)**. Average real-terms prices for intermediate inputs were 0.8 % higher than in 2000, mainly as a result of higher prices for animal feedingstuffs and fertilisers (+ 1.6 % and + 9.7 % respectively, in real terms). The average volume of the input use was reduced by 0.6 % which reflects mostly reductions in the use of fertilisers and of pesticides (down by 6.5 % and 6.3 % respectively).

— **Depreciation was slightly higher (+ 0.2 % in real terms) while the other taxes on production fell below 2000 levels (– 0.4 %). The other subsidies on production increased considerably (+ 9.7 % in real terms)**.

Table 3.3.2. % changes in the main components of the income from agricultural activity in the European Union as a whole and in the Member States, 2001

Values in real terms	EU-15	B	DK	D	EL	E	F	IRL	I	L	NL	A	P	FIN	S	UK
Output of the agricultural industry	+ 0.3	+ 1.8	+ 3.9	+ 1.8	– 1.8	+ 0.6	– 0.1	– 3.8	+ 0.6	– 1.0	– 1.7	+ 2.3	+ 2.9	– 1.9	+ 1.3	– 1.6
Crop output	– 1.5	+ 4.8	– 1.7	– 0.9	– 3.3	– 4.5	– 1.5	+ 0.9	– 1.2	– 9.8	+ 0.3	– 0.2	+ 4.0	– 6.2	– 1.0	– 1.8
Animals	+ 2.1	– 1.2	+ 13.1	+ 3.7	+ 2.8	+ 10.2	+ 2.0	– 9.6	+ 6.3	– 0.2	– 7.1	+ 3.7	+ 3.2	+ 9.9	+ 9.8	– 8.7
Animal products	+ 3.7	+ 1.2	– 1.9	+ 6.9	+ 1.6	+ 8.6	+ 1.4	+ 3.0	– 1.4	+ 6.8	+ 0.2	+ 8.2	– 1.6	– 1.7	– 2.1	+ 13.4
– Intermediate consumption	+ 0.2	+ 1.7	+ 2.0	– 0.1	– 2.3	+ 0.4	+ 0.6	– 0.7	+ 1.1	– 0.1	– 1.2	– 0.4	+ 0.1	– 4.8	+ 2.9	+0.3
= Gross value added at basic prices	+ 0.3	+ 1.9	+ 6.6	+ 4.5	– 1.7	+ 0.8	– 0.9	– 7.4	+ 0.3	– 2.0	– 2.4	+ 5.5	+ 5.9	+ 4.3	– 2.0	– 4.0
– Consumption of fixed capital	+ 0.2	– 1.1	– 2.9	– 1.2	– 1.6	+ 5.8	+ 2.2	– 2.6	+ 0.7	+ 0.0	– 1.4	– 0.4	+ 0.5	– 2.1	– 2.6	– 2.8
– Other taxes on production	– 0.4	– 2.1	+ 21.4	– 0.1	– 2.8	-0.2	– 0.1	+ 58.4	– 1.9	– 2.9	– 1.4	– 2.0	+ 3.1	:	:	– 12.5
+ Other subsidies on production	+ 9.7	– 2.1	+ 1.0	– 14.3	+ 3.9	+ 13.7	+ 12.2	+ 47.5	+ 6.5	+ 0.3	+ 79.0	+ 4.0	+ 22.0	– 2.7	+ 6.5	+ 80.1
= Factor income (1)	+ 1.2	+ 2.7	+ 9.0	+ 5.5	– 1.4	+ 0.8	– 1.1	+ 0.5	+ 0.7	– 2.4	– 1.1	+ 9.0	+ 9.5	+ 1.6	+ 0.8	+1.5
Agricultural labour input (2)	– 2.0	– 2.4	– 3.0	– 4.0	– 2.9	-1.8	– 1.8	– 6.7	+ 0.5	– 1.7	– 3.4	– 1.7	– 2.0	– 3.0	– 4.0	– 1.9
Indicator A (1)/(2)	+ 3.3	+ 5.3	+ 12.3	+ 9.9	+ 1.5	+ 2.6	+ 0.7	+ 7.8	+ 0.2	– 0.6	+ 2.4	+ 10.9	+ 11.8	+ 4.7	+ 5.0	+3.5

Source: Eurostat, SBS database.

In the present context it is important to make a distinction between subsidies on products and other subsidies, on the one hand, and taxes on products and other taxes on production on the other. Capital transfers which represent a further type of grant to agriculture do not enter the calculation of the income indicators. In the EAA, output is valued at basic prices. The basic price is calculated by adding subsidies on products to the producer price, and deducting the taxes on products. Only the other subsidies and the other taxes on production appear therefore as subsidies, respectively taxes, in Table 3.3.2.

Table 3.3.2 shows important increases in the other subsidies on production for Ireland, the Netherlands and for the United Kingdom. In both Ireland and the United Kingdom, this increase was the consequence of a change in the respective support schemes which led to the reclassification of subsidies previously classified as subsidies on products, as subsidies on production. When overall subsidies (subsidies on products, plus subsidies on production), net of any tax, are looked at, there was an increase, in 2001, of only 1.1 % (in real terms) in Ireland, and even a decline of 0.4 % (in real terms) in the United Kingdom. The increase in subsidies in the Netherlands, in 2001, is largely related to payments compensating farmers for losses due to foot-and-mouth disease. In addition, it should be noted that the ratio of overall subsidies, net of taxes, to gross value added at market prices, in the Netherlands, was — despite the most recent increase — still by far the lowest amongst the Member States (6.8 % compared to 31.9 % for EU-15, in 2001).

The results from a medium-term perspective

Figure 3.3.2. puts the changes in agricultural income in 2001 for the various Member States in a medium-term perspective (see also Table 3.3.3). The index of real agricultural factor income per annual work unit (Indicator A) is calculated using a base equal to 100 for the average of the three years from 1994 to 1996. The average of three years has been chosen in order to reduce the impact of strong short-term fluctuations. The graph takes the value of the index in 2000 as the starting point, and shows the change in 2001 as well as the new level of the index for 2001 in each of the Member States.

When interpreting the values of the index shown in Figure 3.3.2, it should be borne in mind that they do not allow a comparison of the income levels between the Member States, but only a comparison of their trends since the mid-1990s.

The Member States can be divided roughly into two main groups. The first covers those countries for whom real-terms average income from agricultural activity in 2001 was above the average level recorded for the years 1994 to 1996. This group comprises in particular Germany, Sweden, Finland, Portugal and Spain, where the income levels attained in 2001 were around 20 % higher than the average of the years 1994 to 1996, and in addition Italy, France, Denmark, Ireland and Belgium. In the case of Denmark, Ireland and Belgium, the income levels in 2000 were still below the average level of 1994 to 1996, and it was therefore the increases recorded in 2001 that brought incomes in these countries above the average level of the years 1994 to 1996.

The second group covers those countries for whom real-terms average income from agricultural activity in 2001 was below the average level recorded for the years 1994 to 1996: Greece, Luxembourg, Austria, the Netherlands and particularly the United Kingdom. In Greece, Luxembourg and Austria, Indicator A in 2001 came (or remained, in the case of Luxembourg) close to the average level of 1994 to 1996. In the Netherlands, Indicator A had reached in 2000 its lowest level (81.9 compared to the average level of 1994 to 1996) since records became available (1987), and the latest modest increase in 2001 did not alter this position by much.

ENTERPRISES IN THE UNION

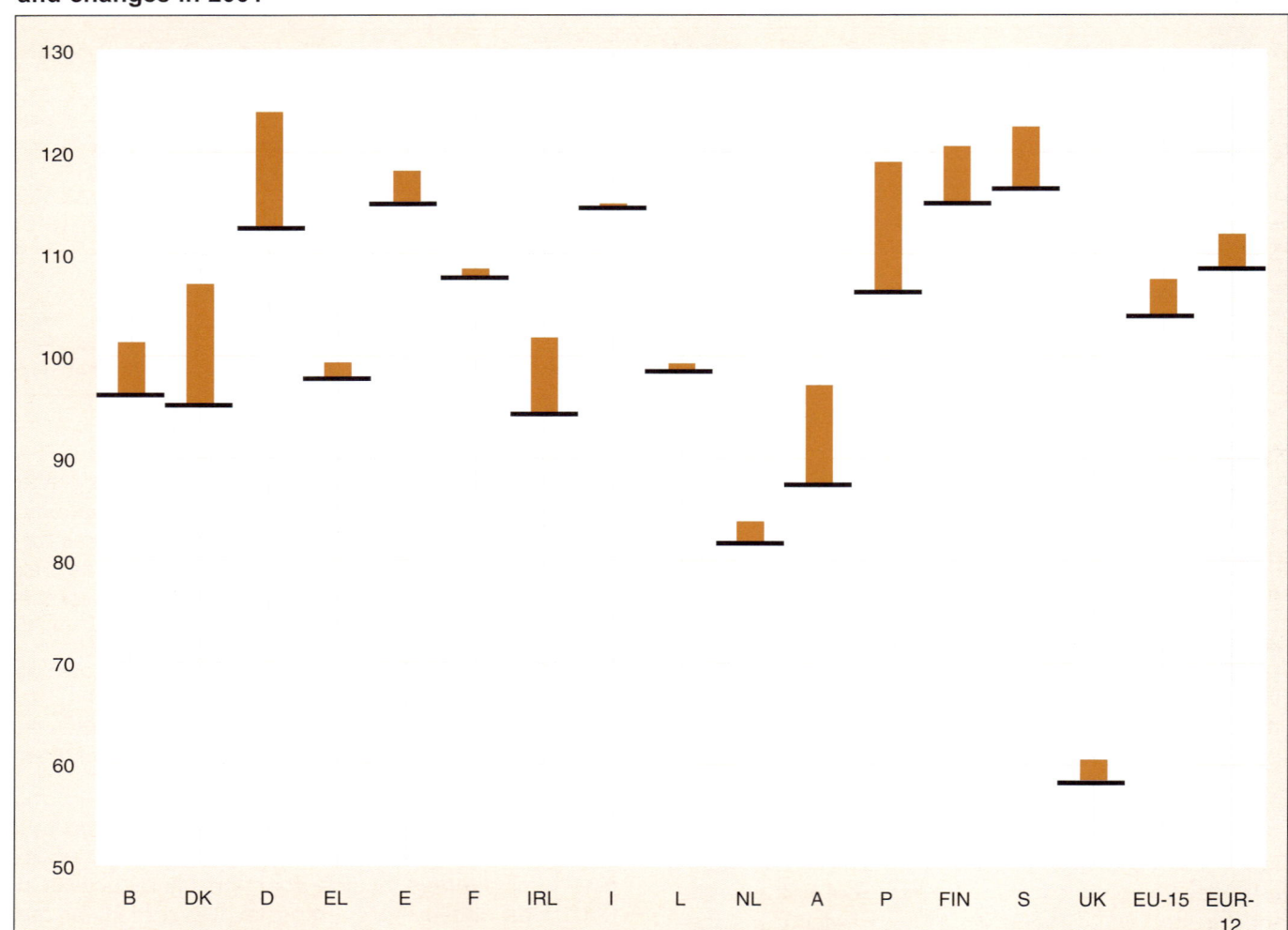

Figure 3.3.2. Indicator A in the Member States, index values 2000 (three-year average 1994 to 1996 = 100) and changes in 2001

[Bar chart showing Indicator A values for B, DK, D, EL, E, F, IRL, I, L, NL, A, P, FIN, S, UK, EU-15, EUR-12, with 2000 (line) and 2001 (bar) values]

Source: Eurostat.

The development in agricultural income in the United Kingdom since the mid-1990s is quite different to that of any other Member State of the European Union. In 1995, Indicator A had reached the highest level over the whole of the period 1973 to 2001. However, sharp declines in the second half of the 1990s and in 2000 (major reasons being the BSE crisis but also the relative strengthening of the value of the pound against the euro) pushed Indicator A to its lowest level since the accession of the United Kingdom to the European Community in 1973. Indicator A remained, in 2001, still about 40 % below the corresponding average level of 1994 to 1996, despite the most recent increase.

According to calculations for EU-15 as a whole, the index of Indicator A in 2001 is expected to reach 107.6 (average 1994 to 1996 being equal to 100), after the increases of 2.7 % in 2000 and of 3.3 % in 2001.

Agricultural income developments in 2001 in the candidate countries

Information available from those eight candidate countries for which data were available reveals annual changes in Indicator A, in 2001, ranging from a fall of 14.4 % (Slovenia) to an increase of 26.8 % (Hungary). There were also income increases in the Czech Republic (+ 20.5 %), Estonia (+ 17.2 %), the Slovak Republic (+ 14.1 %) and in Lithuania (13.6 %). Income from agricultural activity declined a little in Malta (– 1.6 %) and strongly in Poland (– 10.3 %). On average, in these eight countries (CC-8), there was an increase in Indicator A of 2.2 %.

Real agricultural factor income, the basis of Indicator A, developed in most of the candidate countries in a similar way to Indicator A (+ 1.7 % on average in CC-8). The volume of agricultural labour input declined

Table 3.3.3. Indices of Indicator A of the income from agricultural activity in the European Union (three-year average 1994 to 1996 = 100)

	1990	1991	1992	1993	1994	1995	1996	1997	1998	1999	2000	2000 (%)
EU-15	:	88.1	86.4	86.4	94.9	101.0	104.1	104.8	102.1	100.9	104.2	+ 3.3
EUR-12	:	90.0	87.8	86.3	95.1	100.3	104.6	107.6	106.1	105.0	108.8	+ 3.0
B	109.2	109.1	106.1	102.6	104.2	93.4	102.4	106.4	100.5	86.3	96.3	+ 5.3
DK	89.8	86.7	76.7	78.6	88.8	105.8	105.5	102.2	81.5	78.9	95.3	+ 12.3
D	:	90.0	94.1	89.2	92.7	98.3	109.0	114.1	104.0	94.8	112.8	+ 9.9
EL	:	111.7	96.6	86.5	98.9	103.0	98.1	98.4	97.7	99.5	97.9	+ 1.5
E	97.9	96.6	83.7	86.4	96.3	95.9	107.7	108.9	106.4	103.3	115.1	+ 2.6
F	89.4	78.7	85.4	84.9	96.1	101.8	102.0	105.5	110.0	107.6	107.8	+ 0.7
IRL	79.9	80.2	89.2	90.8	92.2	103.6	104.2	101.4	97.3	89.7	94.5	+ 7.8
I	79.0	84.5	83.9	86.2	92.1	101.1	106.8	109.5	109.7	119.4	114.7	+ 0.2
L	97.4	90.6	91.0	94.0	89.9	103.2	106.9	98.7	107.8	97.5	99.3	− 0.6
NL	117.6	114.4	105.6	87.9	98.8	102.1	99.1	107.0	96.1	84.7	81.9	+ 2.4
A	101.7	99.8	92.4	81.4	95.8	107.7	96.5	89.5	88.9	85.4	87.6	+ 10.9
P	94.3	93.6	69.9	67.7	90.9	99.7	109.4	104.3	102.8	117.5	106.5	+ 11.8
FIN	110.8	101.7	89.9	90.4	97.2	111.0	91.8	91.2	82.1	90.2	115.2	+ 4.7
S	114.6	96.7	86.7	92.4	91.7	108.5	99.8	106.4	116.9	106.2	116.6	+ 5.0
UK	71.3	70.1	76.4	90.2	95.6	105.5	98.8	76.7	65.8	64.5	58.5	+ 3.5

Source: Eurostat, Economic Accounts for Agriculture (EAA).

Figure 3.3.3. % changes in agricultural income measured by Indicator A for the candidate countries and the European Union, 2001 (compared to the previous year)

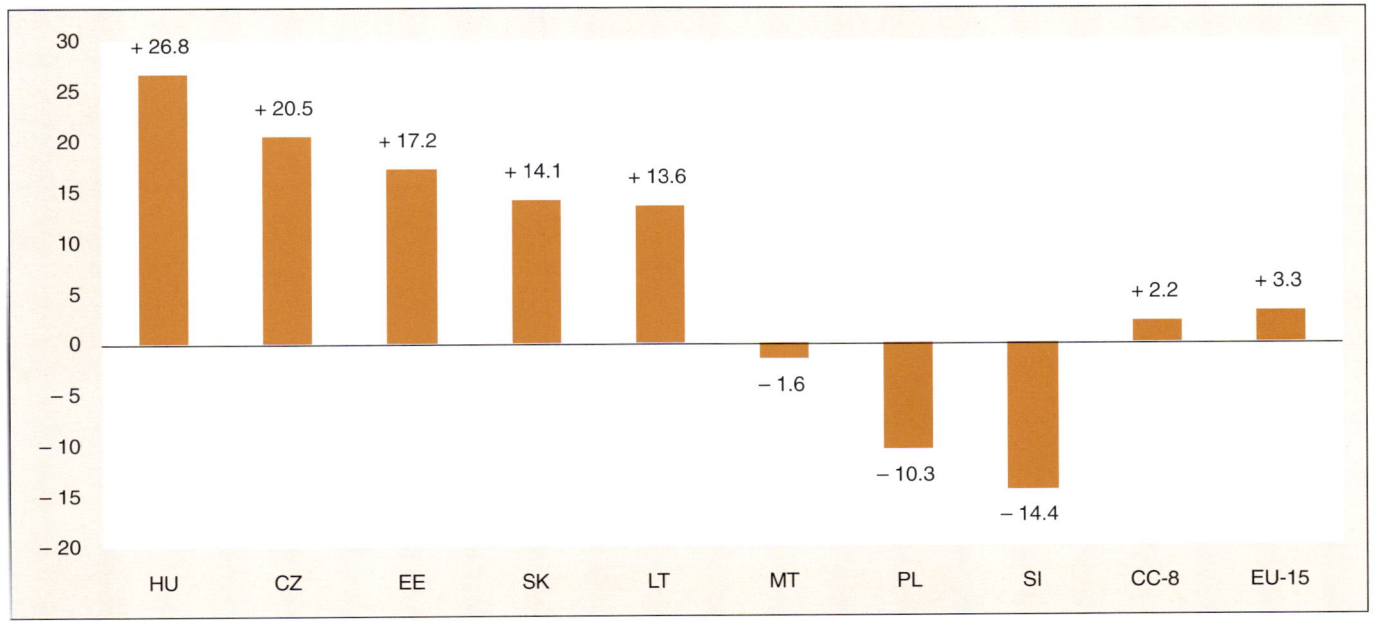

Country	% change
HU	+ 26.8
CZ	+ 20.5
EE	+ 17.2
SK	+ 14.1
LT	+ 13.6
MT	− 1.6
PL	− 10.3
SI	− 14.4
CC-8	+ 2.2
EU-15	+ 3.3

Source: Eurostat.

particularly strongly in Lithuania (− 10.1 %) and the Slovak Republic (− 9.1 %). However, with an increase in agricultural labour input in Poland (which accounts for almost two thirds of the total agricultural labour input of CC-8), the rate of decline was limited to a moderate 0.5 % for the total of the eight candidate countries.

It is obvious from Table 3.3.4 that there are considerable differences in the development of most of the items between the individual countries. For the eight candidate countries as a whole, the key factors driving the development of real-terms agricultural factor income in 2001 can be summarised as follows.

— **Most importantly, there was a rise in the value at basic prices of the agricultural industry's output, in 2001, of 3.1 % (in real terms).** This rise reflects increases in both the output values of crop products and of animals (+ 2.8 % and + 7.2 % respectively, in real terms); for animal products, there was a decline (− 1.3 % in real terms). The increase in animal output was mainly brought about by a strong rise in the real-terms producer price for pigs (+ 15.8 %, very close to the EU-15 price rise; at the same time the output volume was down by 4.4 %). But there was also a considerable growth in the output volume of poultry (+ 10.0 %), combined with higher producer prices (+ 4.2 % in real terms). The increase in the output value of crops was mainly the result of a strong increase in the output volume of cereals (+ 26.5 %) which was only partly offset by a decline in producer prices (− 7.3 % in real terms).

— **The cost of intermediate consumption goods and services was higher than in 2000 (+ 3.6 % in real terms).** This was mainly the result of higher expenditures for animal feedingstuffs (+ 3.3 % in real terms), the most important input item (accounting for nearly half of the value of intermediate consumption in 2001).

— **Depreciation was lower than in 2000 (− 4.2 % in real terms). The other taxes on production increased by 10.0 % (in real terms),** while the other subsidies were reduced by more than 20 % (in real terms). It is worthwhile noting, in this context, that the overall level of all subsidies combined (subsidies on products, plus other subsidies), net of any tax, was reduced, in 2001, by more than one third. The ratio of overall subsidies (net of taxes) to gross value added at market prices consequently diminished to 8.8 % (compared to 31.9 % for EU-15, in 2001).

Table 3.3.4. % changes in the main components of the income from agricultural activity in the candidate countries, in 2001

Values in real terms	CY	CZ	EE	HU	LT	LV	MT	PL	SI	SK	CC-8
Output of the agricultural industry	:	+ 4.5	+ 5.6	+ 12.8	− 1.3	:	+ 0.5	+ 0.2	− 4.5	+ 2.7	+ 3.1
Crop output	:	+ 5.7	− 12.4	+ 11.0	− 10.1	:	− 1.9	− 1.0	− 11.6	+ 39.4	+ 2.8
Animals	:	+ 8.9	+ 35.8	+ 20.6	+ 7.9	:	+ 4.3	+ 5.6	+ 2.3	− 23.2	+ 7.2
Animal products	:	− 3.6	+ 13.1	+ 3.5	+ 13.8	:	− 0.3	− 4.1	+ 1.3	− 4.4	− 1.3
− Intermediate consumption	:	− 0.4	− 0.8	+ 9.4	− 1.3	:	+ 7.3	+ 4.2	+ 1.7	− 4.0	+ 3.6
= Gross value added at basic prices	:	+ 15.6	+ 14.1	+ 18.6	− 1.3	:	− 4.4	− 6.4	− 11.7	+ 23.7	+ 2.1
− Consumption of fixed capital	:	− 8.8	+ 8.1	− 1.2	− 8.3	:	+ 4.7	− 5.4	− 0.6	− 0.3	− 4.2
− Other taxes on production	:	+ 6.6	− 5.1	+ 15.2	− 0.6	:	:	+ 12.8	:	− 11.1	+ 10.0
+ Other subsidies on production	:	− 36.5	+ 26.3	+ 8.1	− 0.6	:	− 2.3	− 24.8	+ 23.9	− 34.7	− 20.4
= **Factor income** (1)	:	+ 18.1	+ 17.2	+ 24.2	+ 2.1	:	− 4.8	− 9.2	− 14.4	+ 3.7	+ 1.7
Agricultural labour input (2)	:	− 2.0	0.0	− 2.0	− 10.1	:	− 3.3	+ 1.2	0.0	− 9.1	− 0.5
Indicator A (1)/(2)	:	+ 20.5	+ 17.2	+ 26.8	+ 13.6	:	− 1.6	− 10.3	− 14.4	+ 14.1	+ 2.2

Source: Eurostat, SBS database.

4. Household consumption expenditure

4.1. Overview

Consumption is certainly an important variable in determining the economic performance of a country. In this respect, it has been presented in Chapter 1. But in addition, consumption also reflects social conditions, in particular related to the welfare of a country.

In 2001 households and non-profit institutions serving households in the EU spent EUR 5 160.7 billion (at current prices) for their consumption. When calculating per capita figures, the average spending of households in the EU in 2001 has been at around 13 600 PPS per head. In 2001 Luxembourg stood out as having the highest per capita private consumption figure; among the bigger Member States, the same is true for the United Kingdom. The lowest figures have been registered in Portugal (24 % below the EU value) and Greece (21 % below the EU average).

These figures have already been presented in Section 1.2. (see Tables 1.2.1 and 1.2.2). But even if consumption, as a total, has a relevant role in the determination of economic results, when splitting household consumption into different items according to purpose, further interesting conclusions become available. This chapter aims at determining consumption patterns, finding differences and similarities between them and pointing out the evolution over time of the spending behaviour of EU households [1].

When considering the structure of consumption in Figure 4.1.1, a first relevant observation is that three items take up the largest part of household consumption, defining clearly the "basic" consumption items in the EU: almost half of the total consumption expenditure is spent on food, housing and transport. Nearly one quarter of household consumption is dedicated to more "recreational" items. The remaining part is spent for minor sub-items of consumption.

Breakdown of consumption by purpose

Household final consumption expenditure is broken down by consumption purpose using the COICOP classification (classification of individual consumption by purpose). The following 2-digit COICOP items will be distinguished here.

— Food and non-alcoholic beverages
— Alcoholic beverages, tobacco and narcotics
— Clothing and footwear
— Housing, water, electricity, gas and other fuels
— Furnishings, household equipment and routine household maintenance
— Health
— Transport
— Communication
— Recreation and culture
— Education
— Restaurants and hotels
— Miscellaneous goods and services

Figure 4.1.1. Structure of consumption expenditure in EU-15, 2000 (as a % of total consumption)

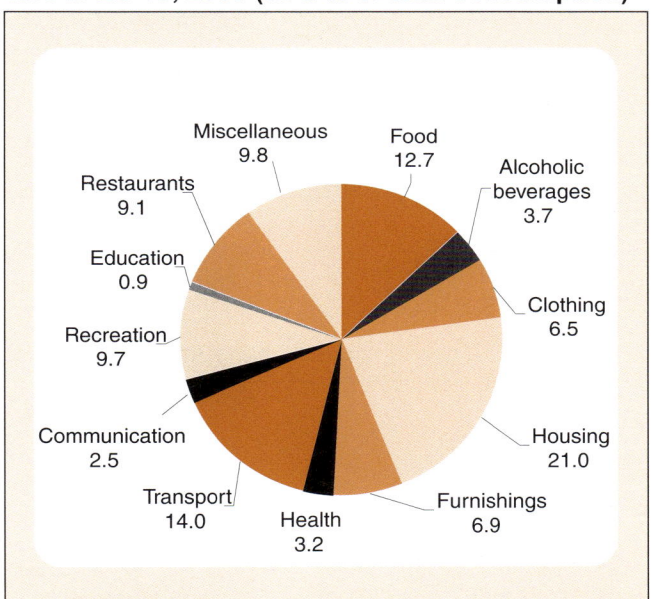

- Miscellaneous 9.8
- Food 12.7
- Alcoholic beverages 3.7
- Restaurants 9.1
- Education 0.9
- Clothing 6.5
- Recreation 9.7
- Housing 21.0
- Communication 2.5
- Transport 14.0
- Health 3.2
- Furnishings 6.9

Source: Eurostat.

---

[1] The latest year for which these breakdowns of household consumption by purpose is available is 2000.

HOUSEHOLD CONSUMPTION EXPENDITURE

Looking at the temporal trend in consumption items in Table 4.1.1, the first evidence is that the share of food consumption in household spending is getting lower over time. This is a natural evolution in developed countries such as the EU Member States. Housing is generally the single most important item in household spending for consumption, followed by expenses for transports.

Moreover, the differences in the structure among EU countries (see Figure 4.1.3) give a quite good indication of the existing models of consumption. The relationship between a country's wealth and the pattern of consumption is confirmed by the fact that Greece and Portugal, which show the smallest GDP per capita figures (used here as an indication of a country's wealth), also show the largest shares of consumption dedicated to food. As well, though somewhat less unambiguous, at least an indication of a certain preference in the pattern of consumption is given by the fact that the largest shares of food consumption are recorded in Mediterranean countries. Households in northern countries, on the other hand, dedicate the largest parts of their consumption to housing. Since consumption expenditure is influenced by a large range of factors that make figures not easily comparable, the figures here should be considered as a simple indication of different models of consumption only.

In terms of growth, expenditure for food and for housing has been rather steady, while spending for transport on average showed higher growth rates. The most dynamic item of consumption in the EU has been expenditure for communication, but these still represent only a minor part of total spending (2.5 % in 2000). Another item of consumption showing particular dynamic growth has been recreation and culture.

Table 4.1.1. Structure of consumption expenditure in the EU-15, 1995-2000 (as a % of total consumption)

	1995	2000
Food and non-alcoholic beverages	14.2	12.7
Alcoholic beverages, tobacco	3.6	3.7
Clothing and footwear	7.0	6.5
Housing, water, electricity, gas	21.4	21.0
Furnishings, household equipment	7.1	6.9
Health	3.3	3.2
Transport	13.5	14.0
Communication	2.0	2.5
Recreation and culture	9.2	9.7
Education	0.9	0.9
Restaurants and hotels	8.6	9.1
Miscellaneous	9.2	9.8

Source: Eurostat.

Figure 4.1.2. Growth rates of consumption expenditure by item in the EU-15, 1997-2000 (as a %)

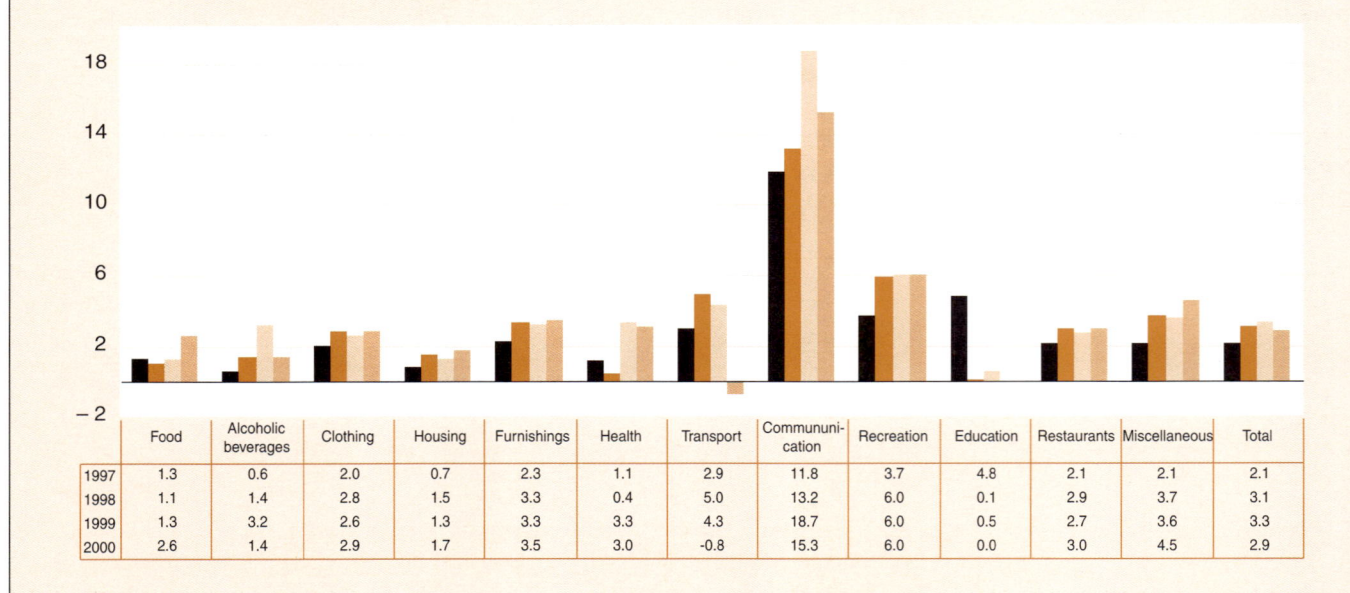

	Food	Alcoholic beverages	Clothing	Housing	Furnishings	Health	Transport	Communication	Recreation	Education	Restaurants	Miscellaneous	Total
1997	1.3	0.6	2.0	0.7	2.3	1.1	2.9	11.8	3.7	4.8	2.1	2.1	2.1
1998	1.1	1.4	2.8	1.5	3.3	0.4	5.0	13.2	6.0	0.1	2.9	3.7	3.1
1999	1.3	3.2	2.6	1.3	3.3	3.3	4.3	18.7	6.0	0.5	2.7	3.6	3.3
2000	2.6	1.4	2.9	1.7	3.5	3.0	-0.8	15.3	6.0	0.0	3.0	4.5	2.9

Source: Eurostat.

HOUSEHOLD CONSUMPTION EXPENDITURE

Figure 4.1.3. Shares of the most important items of consumption expenditure among Member States, 2000 (as a % of total consumption)

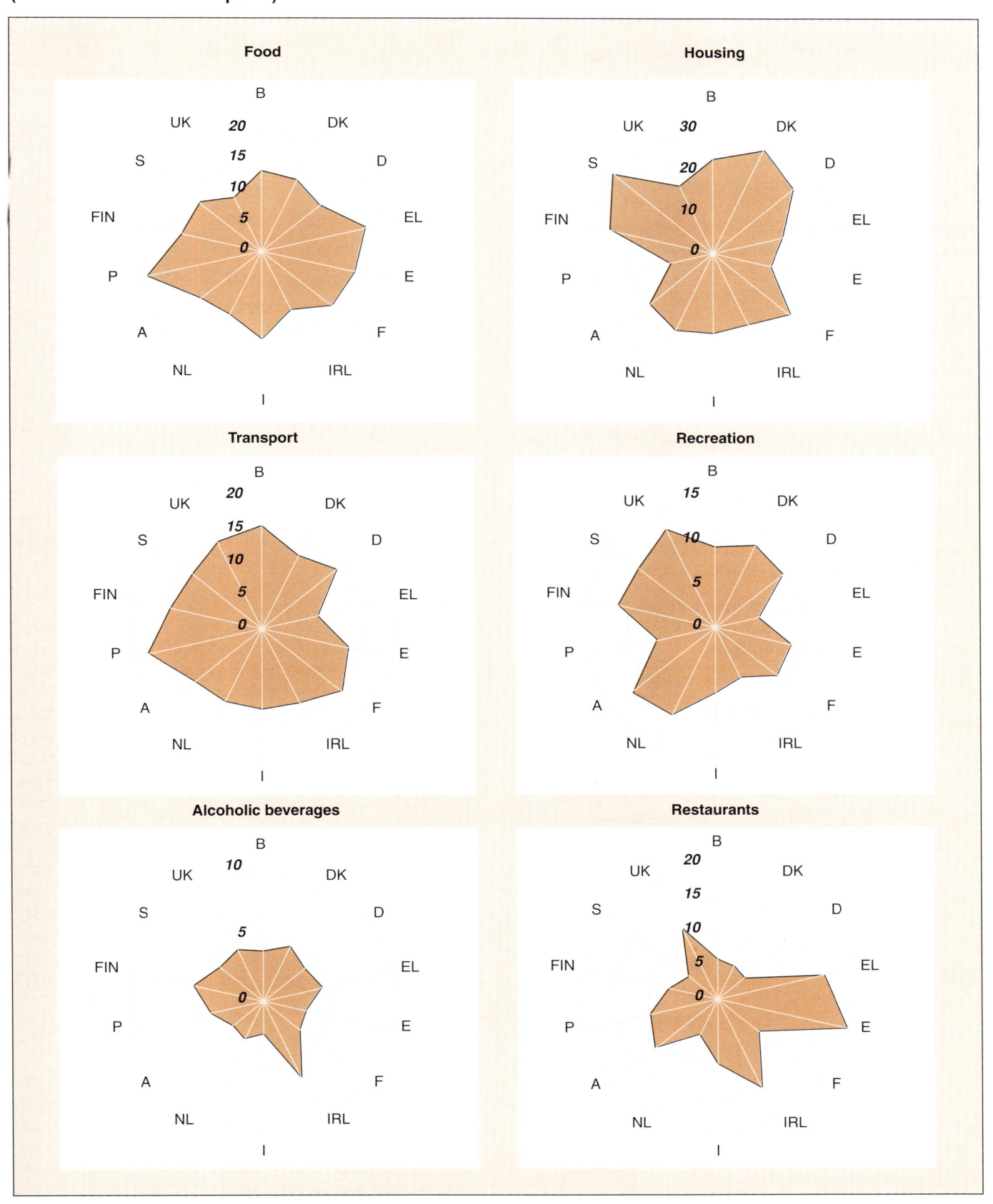

NB: Shares for the Netherlands and Sweden refer to 1999.
Source: Eurostat.

111

4.2. Analysis by purpose

Food and non-alcoholic beverages

In 2000 the highest figures for household expenditure on food were recorded in the Mediterranean countries of the EU. Portugal came first among the Member States, with food and non-alcoholic beverages accounting for 18.5 % of total expenditure. Next came Greece (16.9 %), followed by Spain and Italy (15.2 % and 14.4 %, respectively). Households in the United Kingdom spent least on food: only 9.8 % of total expenditure. The figures in Ireland, Germany and the Netherlands were somewhat higher at around 11 %, and in the other Member States the figures were fairly closely grouped between 12 % and just over 14 %.

When the structure of expenditure in 2000 (the most recent year for which data are available) is compared with the figures for 1995 (the first year for which data compiled according to the ESA 95 are available), it can clearly be seen that expenditure on food is declining as a share of total household spending in all Member States. This is normal in countries where living standards are high and where spending is thus channelled in other directions. The biggest reductions occurred in Ireland, where spending on food as a percentage of total expenditure fell by 5 percentage points, followed by Spain and Italy (down by 2.5 and 2.4 points, respectively).

Table 4.2.1. Consumption expenditure for food and non-alcoholic beverages, 1995-2000 (as a % of total consumption)

	2000	1995
EU-15	12.7	14.2
EUR-12	13.5	14.7
P	18.5	20.5
EL	16.9	18.2
E	15.2	17.7
I	14.4	16.8
IRL	10.7	15.7
F	14.2	15.1
FIN	12.7	14.8
B	13.0	14.5
S	12.6	14.4
DK	12.8	14.0
A	12.4	13.4
NL	11.6	13.0
D	11.8	12.5
UK	9.8	11.2

NB: Shares for the Netherlands and Sweden refer to 1999 instead of 2000.
Source: Eurostat.

Table 4.2.2. Consumption expenditure for food and non-alcoholic beverages, growth index for volume and prices, 2000

(1995 = 100)

	Volume	Price
EU-15	107.1	105.5
EUR-12	106.5	105.7
P	114.0	110.6
EL	113.3	121.5
E	112.0	107.7
UK	111.1	103.8
FIN	110.4	102.0
NL	110.3	105.8
S	110.2	97.7
IRL	108.6	114.2
A	106.9	104.0
D	106.4	101.2
F	104.3	107.2
DK	103.7	108.4
B	103.5	105.4
I	103.2	107.3

Source: Eurostat.

Growth indices were calculated in order to assess the absolute variation (see Table 4.2.2). These indices show how much the volume of consumption expenditure went up between 1995 and 2000, based on 1995 as the reference year. In addition, the growth indices for consumer prices for the consumption item at hand are presented, which may provide a useful background to the interpretation of the consumption volume trends. In 2000 the biggest absolute growth over the past five years was recorded in Portugal, where the volume of spending on food and non-alcoholic beverages was up by 14 % in comparison with the reference year. As a rule, the variations were quite small for a five-year period; in Italy, Belgium and Denmark, volume growth was below 4 %, i.e. below 0.8 % per annum. Overall in the European Union, the 2000 figure for food and non-alcoholic beverages was 7.1 % above the 1995 figure.

Housing

The single biggest share of total household consumption in the European Union is used for housing, water, electricity, gas and other fuels. This heading accounted for just over a fifth (21.0 %) of all household spending in the Union in 2000. The figure was particularly high among the Nordic Members of the EU: 30.6 % in Sweden (1999), 27.9 % in Denmark and 25.5 % in Finland. Corresponding strong deviations from the average show at the other end of the scale, where particularly in Portugal housing, water, electricity, gas and other fuels accounted for only a small percentage of total household expenditure (10.6 %). All in all, there are thus two distinct geographic groups: on the one hand there is the Nordic group (Denmark, Finland and Sweden) where the figures are high; on the other hand, there are three Mediterranean countries — i.e. Portugal, Greece and Spain — and the United Kingdom, where the figures are comparatively low.

When changes in the structure of household consumption are compared over the period from 1995 to 2000, it can be seen that spending as a percentage on housing, water, electricity, gas and other fuels stayed more or less the same. There was a small change in the percentage figure between 1995 and 2000, i.e. a reduction of 0.4 percentage points from 21.4 % to 21.0 %. In virtually every Member State the change was contained over the period under review, the exceptions being Ireland and Sweden. In Ireland, spending on housing increased its share by 3.3 percentage points. In Sweden, the Member State that spends most on housing, water, electricity, gas and other fuels as a percentage of total household consumption, this share fell by 1.9 points from 1995 to 1999.

Table 4.2.3. Consumption expenditure for housing, water, electricity, gas and other fuels, 1995-2000 (as a % of total consumption)

	2000	1995
EU-15	21.0	21.4
EUR-12	21.3	21.4
S	30.6	32.5
DK	27.9	27.4
FIN	25.5	25.3
B	22.7	24.1
F	23.6	23.8
D	24.5	23.4
NL	20.8	21.4
I	19.5	19.4
A	19.4	18.8
UK	17.9	18.4
EL	17.0	17.6
IRL	19.2	15.9
E	14.1	14.7
P	10.6	11.0

NB: Shares for the Netherlands and Sweden refer to 1999 instead of 2000.
Source: Eurostat.

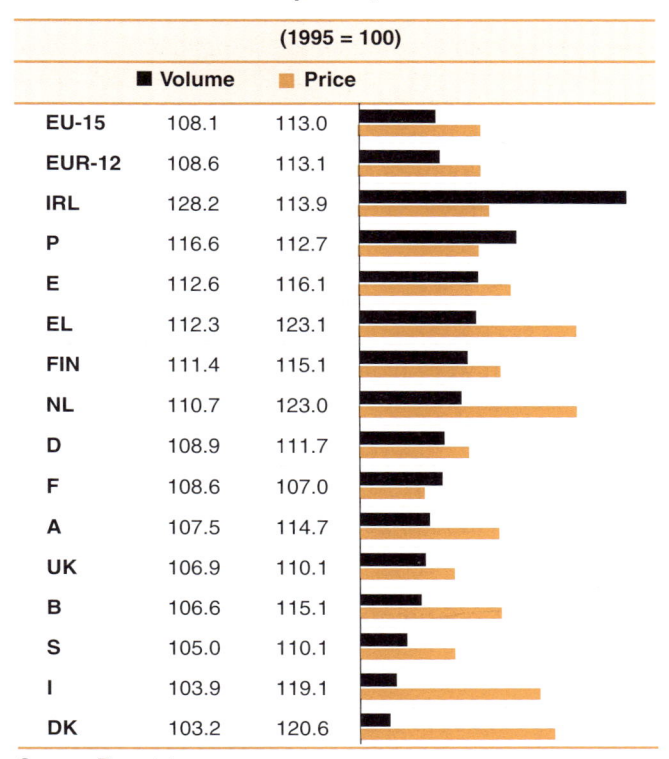

Table 4.2.4. Consumption expenditure for housing, water, electricity, gas and other fuels, growth index for volume and prices, 2000

(1995 = 100)

	Volume	Price
EU-15	108.1	113.0
EUR-12	108.6	113.1
IRL	128.2	113.9
P	116.6	112.7
E	112.6	116.1
EL	112.3	123.1
FIN	111.4	115.1
NL	110.7	123.0
D	108.9	111.7
F	108.6	107.0
A	107.5	114.7
UK	106.9	110.1
B	106.6	115.1
S	105.0	110.1
I	103.9	119.1
DK	103.2	120.6

Source: Eurostat.

Finally, as a way of indicating absolute changes in volumes and prices during the review period, Table 4.2.4 shows the volume and consumer price growth indices. In 2000, expenditure volumes for housing, water, electricity, gas and other fuels were up by 8.1 % compared with the reference year, whereas prices showed a somewhat bigger increase (+ 13.0 %) in comparison to 1995. The strongest increases in the volume of expenditure on housing over the five years from 1995 to 2000 were observed for Ireland (+ 28.2 %) and Portugal (+ 16.5 %), whereas this volume grew only very modestly in Italy (+ 3.9 %) and Denmark (+ 3.2 %).

Transport

Transport is the third biggest consumption item for households in the European Union after housing and food: in 2000, transport accounted for 14.0 % of total consumption in the Union, a share bigger now than that of household spending on food. The highest share of household spending on transport, at 17.4 % in 2000, was recorded in Portugal, with Belgium, France, Germany and the United Kingdom following around two percentage points behind. In Greece (8.6 %), on the other hand, transport is relatively least significant as a consumption item, and its share even declined slightly between 1995 and 2000. This low share of household expenditure on transport in Greece stands apart from the values observed in the other EU countries.

HOUSEHOLD CONSUMPTION EXPENDITURE

Over the period under review, there was only a modest change in the percentage of expenditure devoted to transport in the Union (+ 0.5 percentage points between 1995 and 2000) or in most Member States. Belgium is notable for household expenditure on transport soaring over the period: in 2000 it was 2.4 points higher than in 1995 and the second highest on record in the EU, exceeded only by Portugal, where 17.4 % of total consumption was dedicated to transport. Greece and Denmark are unique, in that the share of spending on transport actually decreased.

The extraordinary growth in spending on transport in some EU countries is all the more visible in view of the growth indices: in 2000, expenditure volumes for transport in Ireland were higher by more than two thirds in comparison to those recorded in 1995 (+ 67.6 %), and spending on transport (at constant prices) grew by 37.2 % in Spain, while Denmark was the only country to record a decline in volume of transport consumption: – 4.7 % from 1995 to 2000.

Table 4.2.5. Consumption expenditure for transport, 1995-2000 (as a % of total consumption)

	2000	1995
EU-15	14.0	13.5
EUR-12	13.9	13.4
P	17.4	16.2
F	15.2	14.6
D	14.5	14.2
UK	14.7	14.2
DK	12.4	13.5
B	15.7	13.3
FIN	13.8	12.8
A	12.9	12.6
I	12.5	12.3
NL	12.4	12.2
S	13.2	12.1
E	13.0	11.6
IRL	12.6	11.4
EL	8.6	8.9

NB: Shares for the Netherlands and Sweden refer to 1999 instead of 2000.
Source: Eurostat.

Table 4.2.6. Consumption expenditure for transport, growth index for volume and prices, 2000

(1995 = 100)

	Volume	Price
EU-15	115.3	113.5
EUR-12	114.8	112.9
IRL	167.6	118.9
E	137.2	116.9
FIN	127.6	114.1
NL	124.9	111.6
S	124.9	109.3
P	123.9	120.4
B	123.2	116.1
EL	120.8	119.5
UK	118.7	117.0
I	116.0	114.0
A	113.6	112.2
F	113.1	110.2
D	105.8	112.7
DK	95.3	114.9

Source: Eurostat.

Recreational items

As has been pointed out, nearly half of all household consumption focuses on the three components of expenditure that have just been described. In the European Union in 2000, households spent 47.7 % of total expenditure on housing, water, electricity, gas and other fuels, transport and food and non-alcoholic beverages.

If we regard these headings as items of "basic" consumption, it is then possible to identify those items that can be better described as "recreational". As a convention, when speaking of recreational consumption expenditure, this covers the items recreation and culture, restaurants and hotels and alcoholic beverages and tobacco. When the figures for these three headings of household consumption are added together, we find that in the EU in 2000 recreational spending accounted for 22.5 % of total expenditure, or well below half of the figure for basic consumption spending.

Table 4.2.7 gives the figures for recreational consumption. A closer look at the European figures reveals that in 2000 households in the European Union spent 9.7 % of their total expenditure on recreation and cul-

HOUSEHOLD CONSUMPTION EXPENDITURE

Table 4.2.7 Consumption expenditure for "recreational" items, 1995–2000, (as a % of total consumption)

	Recreation 1995	Recreation 2000	Restaurants 1995	Restaurants 2000	Alcoholic beverages 1995	Alcoholic beverages 2000	Total "recreational" 1995	Total "recreational" 2000
EU-15	9.2	9.7	8.6	9.1	3.6	3.7	21.5	22.5
EUR-12	8.7	9.0	8.3	8.6	3.5	3.5	20.5	21.1
B	8.9	9.2	5.8	5.8	3.7	3.8	18.5	18.8
DK	10.6	10.6	5.4	5.5	5.0	4.6	21.0	20.7
D	9.4	9.7	5.5	5.0	3.9	3.8	18.9	18.5
EL	4.5	5.1	14.7	15.6	4.2	4.5	23.4	25.1
E	8.5	8.7	18.9	19.0	2.7	3.3	30.1	31.0
F	8.5	8.9	7.3	7.6	3.4	3.4	19.2	19.8
IRL	7.7	6.4	14.6	14.6	6.6	6.5	28.8	27.5
I	7.3	7.6	8.7	9.5	2.5	2.4	18.5	19.6
L	:	:	:	:	:	:	:	:
NL	11.0	11.1	5.8	5.9	3.5	3.2	20.4	20.2
A	11.0	11.9	12.0	11.6	2.7	2.9	25.7	26.3
P	5.9	6.7	9.9	9.8	4.2	4.0	19.9	20.5
FIN	11.0	11.2	7.2	7.1	6.1	5.4	24.2	23.6
S	10.2	11.0	4.6	5.1	4.6	4.1	19.4	20.2
UK	11.5	12.5	11.4	11.5	4.2	4.3	27.1	28.3

NB: Shares for the Netherlands and Sweden refer to 1999 instead of 2000.
Source: Eurostat.

ture, 9.1 % on restaurants and hotels and 3.7 % on alcoholic beverages and tobacco, totalling the 22.5 % just mentioned. It can further be seen that in 2000 households in Spain and the United Kingdom stood out for their high levels of recreational consumption. For Spain, this is primarily due to a high share of consumption expenditure for restaurants and hotels, and for the United Kingdom, both shares for restaurants and hotels and for recreation and culture are relatively high. Germany and Belgium, on the other hand, showed the lowest consumption shares for recreational items, and especially so for restaurants and hotels.

The highest figures for percentage spending on recreation and culture in the EU were recorded in the United Kingdom (12.5 %), followed by Austria, Finland, the Netherlands and Sweden, with figures of around 11 %. Greece was at the other extreme, with a figure of only 5.1 %.

For restaurants and hotels, it is Spain that is well ahead of the other Member States, with Spanish households devoting 19.0 % of their total consumptive expenditure to this heading in 2000. Next come Greece and Ireland, with figures of 15.6 % and 14.6 % respectively. The countries where households spend least on restaurants and hotels are Germany and Sweden, where the figure is about 5 %.

In order to give a general impression, Figure 4.2.1 shows the changes in volume by country for each of the three subheadings, with the countries presented in the order of the magnitude of growth. It can be seen that in the United Kingdom consumption in volume terms for recreation and culture grew by almost 50 % in the review period. In the Union as a whole, the figure showed a rise of 26.9 %, and there were substantial rises in most Member States. The smallest growth observed was that in Germany.

The changes were generally less marked in the case of restaurants and hotels, for which in the EU as a whole the increase over the whole period 1995 to 2000 was 11.9 %. There was a big rise only in Ireland, where the figure for restaurants and hotels posted an increase of 29.0 % in relation to the reference year, followed by Sweden with 24.0 %. In Germany, on the other hand, the 2000 figure was actually slightly down on the 1995 figure (– 2.2 %).

The changes were generally even smaller for alcoholic beverages and tobacco, which recorded a volume increase of only 7.2 % in the EU during the review period. By far the highest growth index was achieved in Ireland, followed by Spain and Austria, but increases were much less marked in the other Member States. Indeed, in France, the 2000 figure was unchanged from 1995, and in Sweden it was 2.5 % lower than in the reference year.

HOUSEHOLD CONSUMPTION EXPENDITURE

Figure 4.2.1. Consumption expenditure for "recreational" items, volume growth index, 2000 (1995 = 100)

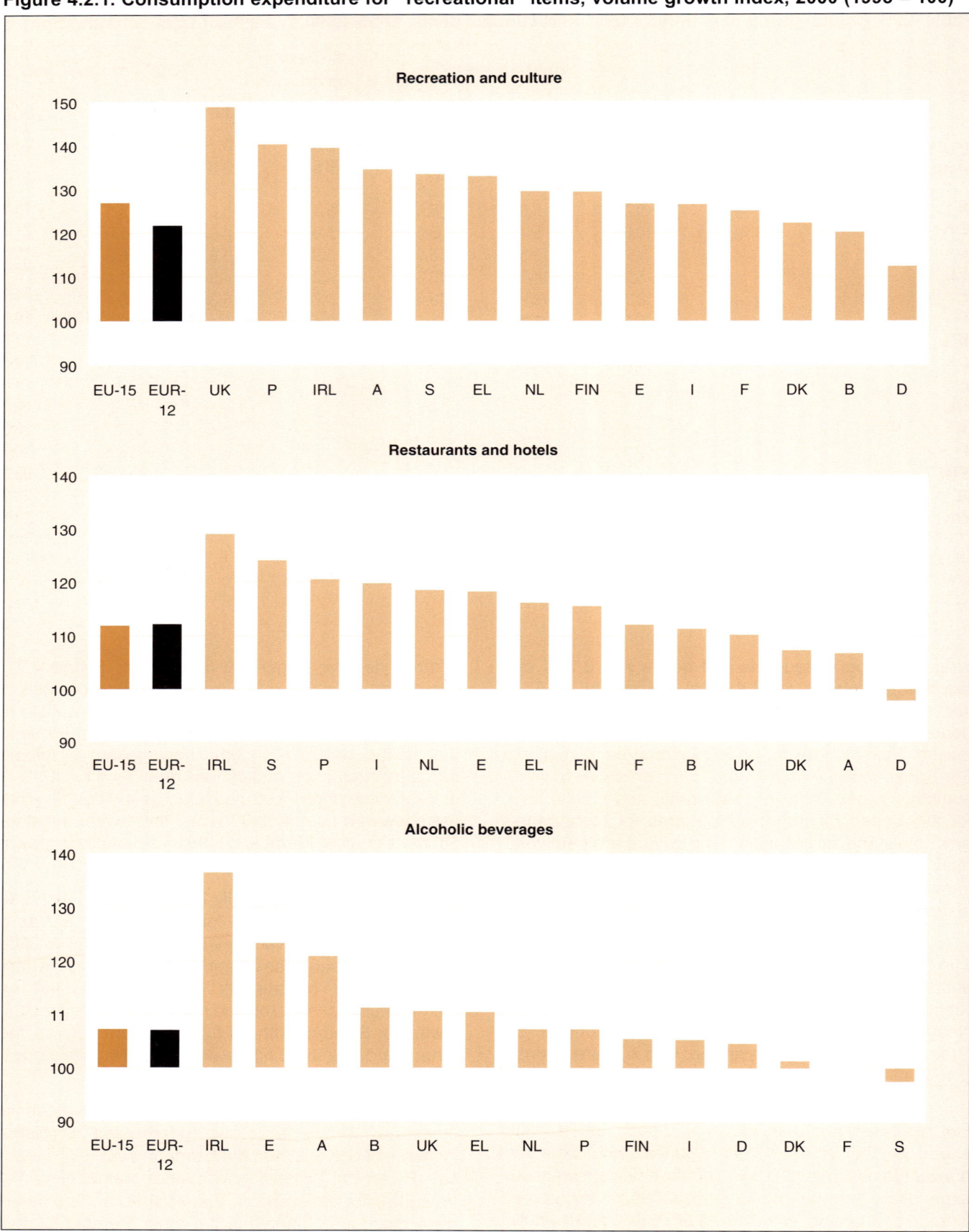

Recreation and culture

Restaurants and hotels

Alcoholic beverages

Source: Eurostat.

Others

In this section we describe the remaining items of consumption. These six items have been grouped together for being of minor importance in total consumption. Altogether, these six items accounted for less than 30 % of total expenditure of households for consumption in the EU. In the following section a short description of the expenses for clothing and footwear (6.5 % of total private consumption expenditure in the EU, 2000), for furnishings, household equipment and routine maintenance of the house (6.9 %) and for communication (2.5 %) will be given. As for the remaining three headings, health (3.2 %), education (0.9 %) and miscellaneous goods and services (9.8 %), no further discussion will be provided. In fact, because of their peculiar characteristics, those three functions are not easily compared among countries and over time.

In 2000 expenditure for clothing and footwear in the European Union was 6.5 % of total consumption. Among Member States, in three southern countries the expenditure for clothing and footwear was proportionally the highest: Greece (11.0 %), Italy (9.3 %) and in Portugal (7.9 %). At the opposite end, households in Finland (4.5 %) and Denmark and France (4.9 % each) spent the smallest shares on this item. Over the period under review all Member States except Greece and Sweden reduced the proportion spent on clothing and footwear (see Table 4.2.8). Considering the absolute growth over the period considered (1995 = 100) in Table 4.2.9, in the EU spending at constant prices for buying clothing and footwear increased by 11.9 %, while the corresponding prices had a smaller variation of 2.5 % only. Among Member States, in Ireland spending on this item showed the most substantial increase, the 2000 figure was more than twice the benchmark value. The next largest variations were recorded in Portugal and the United Kingdom (around + 31 %). It should be noted that in those three countries, concurrent with the large increase in spending volume, prices recorded a contraction.

Spending for furnishings, household equipment and routine maintenance of the house in 2000 took a share of 6.9 % in total consumption — this item thus being slightly ahead of clothing and footwear. Households in Italy (9.4 %) and in Austria (8.2 %) dedicated the largest parts of total spending to this item, while their counterparts in Sweden (4.8 %) and Finland (4.6 %) spent the smallest shares. Over last five years this figure for the EU as a whole fell only marginally. Specifically, among the four biggest economies, in Germany and Italy this item lost importance, whilst in France and the United Kingdom the quota remained virtually unchanged. In no Member State did this item see radical changes, and variations in the quotas were fairly modest, possibly with the exception of Belgium, where the share declined from 6.4 % in 1995 to 5.5 % in 2000 (see Table 4.2.8). When considering the absolute growth of household spending for furnishings, household equipment and routine maintenance of the house the variations are more important: in 2000 spending in Ireland (+ 61.9 %) was much higher than in the reference year 1995, Portugal (+ 33.4 %) and Finland (+ 31.5 %) following somewhat behind. Belgium, on the other hand, saw no increase in volume over the last five years. Prices tended to increase in all Member States, albeit only moderately in most of them.

As a percentage of total consumption, the households in the Union dedicated 2.5 % of their total consumption to communication. Dutch, Italian and Finnish households showed the largest quotas (above 3 %), and in no Member State did this item account for less than 2 % of total consumption. Over the period under consideration (1995/2000) this item expanded its importance in all Member States, and even quite significantly so given the small absolute size of this heading. In particular, the part of consumption dedicated to communication increased strongly in Finland, in the Netherlands, in Italy and in Greece — in those countries the quota increased by roughly one percentage point. Albeit relatively small in absolute terms, communication has been the most dynamic item in household consumption: in the EU in 2000 spending on communication grew by more than 15 % (compared to the

Table 4.2.8. Consumption expenditure for "other" items, 1995-2000, (as a % of total consumption)

	Clothing		Furnishings		Communications	
	1995	2000	1995	2000	1995	2000
EU-15	7.0	6.5	7.1	6.9	2.0	2.5
EUR-12	7.2	6.7	7.4	7.2	1.9	2.5
B	6.6	5.4	6.4	5.5	1.5	2.2
DK	5.2	4.9	5.8	5.8	1.7	2.1
D	7.1	6.4	7.6	7.2	2.0	2.4
EL	10.9	11.0	6.6	6.4	1.5	2.4
E	6.8	6.5	6.2	6.0	1.8	2.3
F	5.5	4.9	6.3	6.3	1.8	2.2
IRL	7.3	7.1	7.0	7.1	1.8	2.2
I	9.6	9.3	9.6	9.4	2.1	3.1
L	:	:	:	:	:	:
NL	6.5	6.2	7.4	7.4	2.1	3.2
A	7.1	6.6	8.9	8.2	2.0	2.8
P	8.1	7.9	7.0	7.5	2.0	2.4
FIN	4.8	4.5	4.4	4.6	1.9	3.1
S	5.4	5.4	4.6	4.8	2.3	3.0
UK	6.3	5.8	5.9	6.0	2.0	2.2

NB: Shares for the Netherlands and Sweden refer to 1999 instead of 2000.
Source: Eurostat.

previous year). Considering absolute growth over the 1995-2000 period, spending in the EU in 2000 was 85.6 % higher than the benchmark figure while prices had dropped. In Ireland, Finland, Greece, the Netherlands, Italy and Austria, consumption volume more than doubled over the reference period. The smallest variation, recorded in Sweden, was still a remarkable + 49.7 % growth in volume. Also considering prices, communication recorded an extraordinary development in EU countries: prices actually tended to fall, with the exception of Belgium (+ 1.9 % in 2000 compared to 1995), the maximum decline in prices was achieved in Ireland, where they were almost 20 % lower in 2000 compared to 1995 (see Table 4.2.9).

Table 4.2.9. Consumption expenditure for "other" items, growth index for volume and prices, 2000

	Clothing (1995 = 100)			Furnishings (1995 = 100)			Communications (1995 = 100)	
	volume	price		volume	price		volume	price
EU-15	111.9	102.5	EU-15	113.5	105.6	EU-15	185.6	90.3
EUR-12	109.0	106.1	EUR-12	111.5	106.2	EUR-12	191.0	90.3
IRL	227.3	82.8	IRL	161.9	113.8	IRL	262.0	80.2
P	131.5	98.1	P	133.4	112.2	FIN	254.4	95.5
UK	130.4	79.6	FIN	131.5	103.2	EL	234.0	94.8
FIN	123.5	99.8	UK	127.1	100.4	NL	214.8	97.8
E	120.4	111.8	NL	124.7	105.8	I	209.8	96.6
EL	119.8	130.6	S	122.5	104.2	A	203.4	93.9
NL	117.7	103.8	E	118.2	113.4	F	191.0	88.5
S	114.4	102.5	EL	116.1	123.7	E	182.2	98.9
A	112.2	97.3	I	112.9	111.5	B	178.0	101.9
DK	111.6	87.9	F	112.2	104.5	D	174.4	84.5
I	109.7	114.0	DK	110.4	107.5	P	171.6	95.5
F	104.4	101.3	A	109.3	102.4	UK	166.2	87.5
D	101.4	102.0	D	105.1	102.0	DK	157.9	90.1
B	95.9	100.9	B	100.0	103.9	S	149.7	97.2

Source: Eurostat.

5. General government in the Union

This section sets out to provide an overview of the size and structure of the public sector in the various Member States (see box entitled "Definition of general government"). After outlining the importance of general government in national economies with the help of the major aggregates of the national accounts, it will first consider the revenue, in particular taxes, and the expenditure of general government and then the difference between the two that amounts to public surplus/deficit.

> **Definition of general government**
>
> According to the "European system of national and regional accounts in the Community" (ESA 95), the general government sector includes "all institutional units which are other non-market producers whose output is intended for individual and collective consumption, and mainly financed by compulsory payments made by units belonging to other sectors, and/or all institutional units principally engaged in the redistribution of national income and wealth". General government is divided into four subsectors: central government, State government, local government and social security funds.

5.1. Major aggregates of general government

In the Union and in the euro-zone, general government output accounts for about one sixth of GDP (see Table 5.1.1). If intermediate consumption — 6.1 % of GDP in the Union, on average — is disregarded, the gross value added of the sector amounted to 11.9 % of GDP in the Union, and 12.4 % in the euro-zone, in 2000. Its span over the Member States ranged from 8.6 to 19.0 %.

Table 5.1.1. Main aggregates of general government, 2000 (as a % of GDP)

	P1 Output	P2 Intermediate consumption	D1 Compensation of employees	P3 Final consumption expenditure	P51 GFCF
EU-15	18.0	6.1	10.2	19.8	2.3
EUR-12	17.1	4.7	10.5	19.8	2.5
B	16.1	3.1	11.4	21.2	1.8
DK	26.8	7.8	16.7	25.1	1.7
D	13.5	3.9	8.1	19.0	1.9
EL	17.0	5.0	11.7	15.5	4.1
E	16.0	4.0	10.4	17.4	3.2
F	21.3	5.3	13.4	23.1	3.0
IRL	13.5	4.9	7.9	13.4	3.8
I	17.4	5.0	10.5	18.0	2.4
L	13.9	3.2	8.0	16.3	4.1
NL	18.8	6.3	10.0	22.7	3.2
A	17.9	5.6	11.4	19.4	1.7
P	20.9	4.2	14.8	20.1	3.8
FIN	24.4	8.8	13.1	20.6	2.5
S	30.5	11.5	16.4	26.2	2.5
UK	20.3	11.4	7.4	18.5	1.2

Source: Eurostat.

General government compensation of employees in the European Union and the euro-zone amounted to 10.2 % and 10.5 % of GDP respectively in 2000, with figures in individual Member States ranging from 7.4 % in the United Kingdom to 16.4 % in Sweden and 16.7 % in Denmark.

Final consumption expenditure of general government in the Member States ranged between 13.4 % (Ireland) and 26.2 % (Sweden) of GDP in 2000, the average being 19.8 % in the Community and euro-zone as well. Gross fixed capital formation amounted to between 1.2 % (United Kingdom) and 4.1 % (Luxembourg and Greece) of GDP in 2000. The average for the Union as a whole was 2.3 %, and for the euro-zone 2.5 %.

GENERAL GOVERNMENT IN THE UNION

5.2. General government revenue and expenditure

On 10 July 2000, the European Commission adopted Regulation (EC) No 1500/2000 implementing Council Regulation (EC) No 2223/96 (the "ESA 95 regulation") with respect to general government expenditure and revenue.

The culmination of the work of a task force that brought together Eurostat, the 15 Member States, the European Central Bank and the Directorate-General for Economic and Financial Affairs, the regulation offers for the first time a common definition of total general government revenue and expenditure. Also, it provides one of the first components of a complete and consistent set of harmonised accounts relating to the public sector in Europe.

It should be noted that according to the regulation, the difference between the total revenue and the total expenditure must be equal to the surplus/deficit of general government (see Section 5.3). Tables 5.2.1, 5.2.2 and 5.3.1 have been updated to match the latest available information on public deficit.

General government revenue

In 2001, total general government revenue (see Table 5.2.1) varied between 34.7 % (Ireland) and 62.3 % (Sweden) of GDP. On average the government revenues accounted for 46.4 % in the European Union; in the euro-zone it was slightly higher (46.7 %). Taxes and social security contributions accounted for nearly 80 % of general government revenue in the Union. Other sources (property income, other current transfers, capital transfers) contributed with a share of about 21 % (see Figure 5.2.1). It is worth noting that the Union's own resources (agricultural levies, customs duties, VAT revenue) appear in the accounts according to the ESA as direct payments to the rest of the world and are therefore not included under either revenue or expenditure of general government.

In 2000 taxes on production and imports and taxes on income and wealth reached 14.4 % and 14.1 % of GDP in the Union (see Table 5.2.2, variables T.P.I. And C.T.I.W.). The figures for the euro-zone were a bit lower with 14.2 % and 12.9 %, respectively. The range for taxes on production and imports (from 12.4 % in Spain to 17.2 % in Denmark) was narrower than for taxes on income and wealth (from 10.4 % in Greece and 10.5 % in Spain to 29.1 % in Denmark).

Social security contributions accounted for a significant percentage of GDP in 2000: 16.6 % on average in the Union and 17.3 % in the euro-zone. Here, too, there were big differences between Member States, since for example actual social contributions as a percentage of GDP (see Table 5.2.2, variable A.S.C.) ranged from 5.3 % in Denmark to 25.8 % in the Netherlands.

Table 5.2.1. Total general government revenue (as a % of GDP)

	1995	1996	1997	1998	1999	2000	2001
EU-15	44.9	46.8	46.9	46.6	47.0	46.8	46.4
EUR-12	46.5	47.3	47.7	47.2	47.7	47.3	46.7
B	48.5	49.0	49.4	49.8	49.7	49.4	49.3
DK	:	58.8	58.3	58.7	59.1	56.5	57.0
D	46.1	46.9	46.6	46.6	47.3	47.0	45.5
EL	40.3	41.8	43.4	45.0	46.0	48.1	46.9
E	38.4	38.8	39.0	39.1	39.7	39.7	39.9
F	49.7	51.4	51.9	51.2	51.8	51.4	51.3
IRL	39.4	39.4	38.6	37.5	37.2	36.5	34.7
I	45.8	46.1	48.4	46.8	47.1	46.3	46.2
L	47.7	47.5	46.6	45.2	45.2	45.4	46.5
NL	47.3	47.8	47.1	46.4	47.6	47.4	46.5
A	52.0	52.8	52.1	51.7	51.7	50.8	52.3
P	40.6	41.8	41.8	41.6	43.0	42.5	42.2
FIN	56.2	56.8	55.3	54.5	54.1	55.7	54.1
S	60.0	62.2	61.6	62.9	61.6	61.4	62.3
UK	38.9	38.6	38.9	40.1	40.3	40.9	41.4

Source: Eurostat.

Figure 5.2.1. Main categories of general government revenue, EU-15, 2000 (as a % of total)

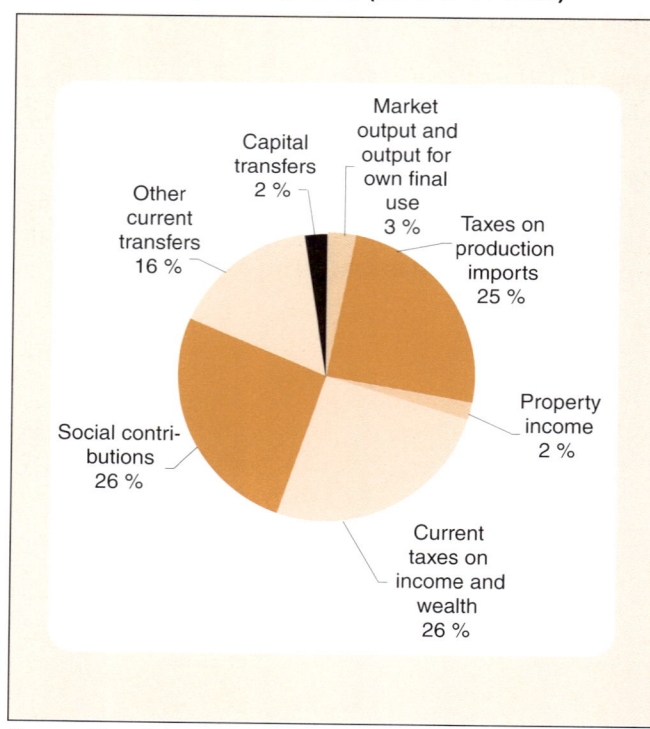

- Market output and output for own final use 3 %
- Taxes on production imports 25 %
- Property income 2 %
- Current taxes on income and wealth 26 %
- Social contributions 26 %
- Other current transfers 16 %
- Capital transfers 2 %

Source: Eurostat.

Table 5.2.2. Main categories of taxes and social contributions 2000 (as a % of GDP)

	D2	D5	D91	D611	D612	Total
	T.P.I	C.T.I.W.	C.T.	A.S.C.	I.S.C.	(¹)
EU-15 (⁴)	14.4	14.1	0.3	16.6	1.6	46.9
EUR-12 (⁴)	14.2	12.9	0.3	17.3	1.7	46.5
B	14.1	17.2	0.5	16.5	3.1	51.4
DK	17.2	29.1	0.2	5.3	1.0	52.8
D	12.7	12.4	0.1	19.3	1.2	45.7
EL	16.0	10.4	0.3	11.4	2.2	40.3
E	12.4	10.5	0.4	13.6	1.6	38.5
F	16.1	12.3	0.6	17.6	2.6	49.2
IRL (²)	:	:	:	:	:	:
I	15.6	14.5	0.1	14.0	1.0	45.2
L (³)	:	:	:	:	:	:
NL	13.1	11.8	0.4	25.8	2.4	53.5
A	15.5	13.4	0.1	15.4	3.2	47.6
P (³)	:	:	:	:	:	:
FIN	14.0	21.1	0.3	13.4	0.0	48.8
S	15.1	22.2	0.1	18.6	0.6	56.6
UK	14.5	16.0	0.2	14.8	1.1	46.6

(¹) The rate of compulsory levies (fiscal burden) cannot be calculated directly from the data in this table as internal consolidation would first be required.
(²) Ireland has a derogation for the transmission of these data.
(³) Luxembourg and Portugal have not transmitted these data.
(⁴) Values for the EU and euro-zone were calculated excluding IRL, L and P.

Source: Eurostat.

General government expenditure

Total general government expenditure in the Union (see Table 5.2.3) accounted on average for 47 % of GDP in 2001; the range of figures was fairly wide, from 33 % in Ireland to more than 57 % in Sweden. Since 1995 the EU and euro-zone average values fell consistently. In 2001 this trend came to a hold when both grew distinctly.

In the European Union, the main component by far of general government expenditure (see Figure 5.2.2) comprised social benefits other than social transfers in kind (nearly 38 % of all expenditure). This was followed by compensation of employees in the public sector (nearly 24 %), intermediate consumption (14 %) and property income (9 %). Gross fixed capital formation accounted for 5 % of general government expenditure of the Member States.

Table 5.2.3. Total general government expenditure (as a % of GDP)

	1995	1996	1997	1998	1999	2000	2001
EU-15	52.1	51.0	49.3	48.3	47.8	46.2	47.2
EUR-12	54.1	51.6	50.3	49.4	49.0	47.2	48.2
B	52.8	52.8	51.3	50.6	50.2	49.3	49.0
DK	:	59.8	58.0	57.6	56.0	54.0	54.2
D	56.1	50.3	49.3	48.8	48.8	45.9	48.3
EL	50.5	49.2	47.4	47.4	47.9	48.9	46.9
E	45.0	43.7	42.2	41.7	40.9	40.3	40.0
F	55.2	55.5	55.0	53.9	53.4	52.8	52.7
IRL	41.5	39.6	37.4	35.2	34.8	32.0	33.0
I	53.4	53.2	51.1	49.9	48.9	46.9	48.4
L	45.1	45.5	43.8	42.1	41.7	39.8	40.4
NL	56.4	49.6	48.2	47.2	46.9	45.3	46.4
A	57.3	56.8	54.1	54.2	54.1	52.5	52.3
P	45.0	45.8	44.8	44.1	45.4	45.4	46.4
FIN	59.9	59.9	56.8	53.2	52.2	48.7	49.1
S	67.6	65.3	63.2	60.8	60.3	57.7	57.4
UK	44.6	43.0	41.1	39.8	39.1	39.3	40.5

Source: Eurostat.

Figure 5.2.2. Main categories of general government expenditure, EU-15, 2000 (as a % of total)

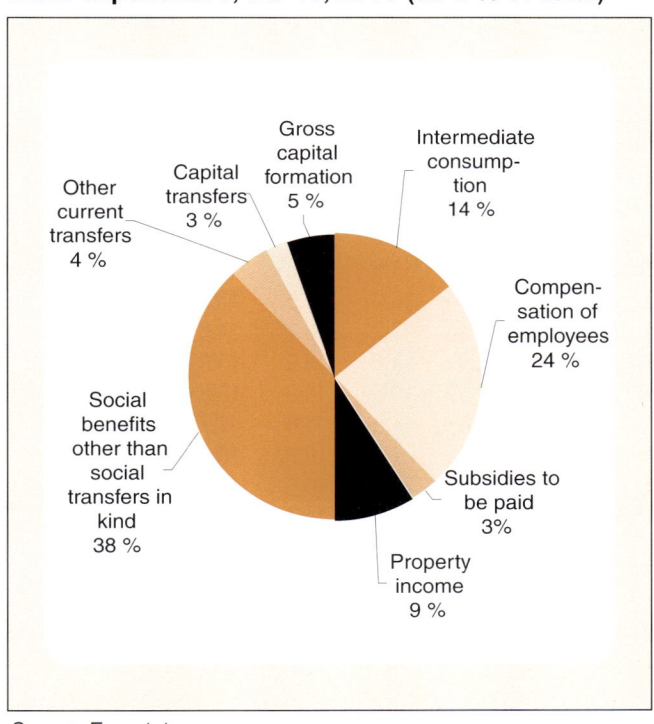

- Intermediate consumption 14 %
- Compensation of employees 24 %
- Subsidies to be paid 3 %
- Property income 9 %
- Social benefits other than social transfers in kind 38 %
- Other current transfers 4 %
- Capital transfers 3 %
- Gross capital formation 5 %

Source: Eurostat.

Some important functions

Among the main items of government expenditure, there are some that merit special attention. Accounting for nearly one sixth of GDP in 2000, social benefits (excluding social transfers in kind) — which include pensions, healthcare, unemployment benefits, etc. — represented the main item of expenditure (see Table 5.2.4). Depending on the Member State, they ranged between 8.2 and 18.8 % of GDP. Topping the table in this category were Germany and Austria followed by Sweden and France. The countries which spent proportionally the least on these benefits were Ireland, the Netherlands and Portugal. Apparently the general trend of these expenditures has been falling since 1996; this can be observed in the Union as well as in the euro-zone and most Member States. In Germany, Italy and Austria the trend is less obvious while in two States, Greece and Portugal, the share of this expenditure has been growing over the years.

Table 5.2.4. Social benefits (other than social transfers in kind) paid by general government (as a % of GDP)

	1995	1996	1997	1998	1999	2000
EU-15	17.2	17.4	17.1	16.6	16.5	16.1
EUR-12	17.3	17.7	17.6	17.1	17.0	16.7
B	16.6	16.6	16.2	16.1	15.7	15.3
DK	20.4	19.8	18.8	18.3	17.7	17.1
D	18.1	19.3	19.3	18.9	19.0	18.8
EL	15.1	15.4	15.6	15.7	16.0	16.3
E	13.9	13.8	13.3	12.8	12.4	12.3
F	18.5	18.7	18.8	18.4	18.3	18.0
IRL	11.8	11.5	10.6	9.9	9.0	8.2
I	16.7	16.9	17.3	17.0	17.2	16.7
L	16.5	16.2	15.4	14.8	14.7	14.1
NL	15.3	14.8	13.9	13.0	12.5	11.9
A	19.5	19.5	18.9	18.6	18.8	18.8
P	11.8	11.8	11.6	11.7	11.9	12.1
FIN	22.2	21.5	19.9	18.4	18.0	16.5
S	21.3	20.3	19.6	19.3	18.8	18.3
UK	15.4	14.8	14.4	13.7	13.4	13.3

Source: Eurostat.

The provision of social benefits to households represents a traditional function of redistribution among the various categories of the population (active population, pensioners, unemployed, sick, etc.). But of course, general government also provides a whole range of other functions for the benefit of the community, e.g. public security, education, national defence, transport, communications, cultural and leisure facilities.

Through the production and consumption activities that these entail, general government has a significant influence on the economy. While compensation of employees and intermediate consumption are the major items of general government expenditure, subsidies paid to businesses and gross fixed capital formation also play a noticeable role.

Production subsidies provided by general government in 2000 amounted to 1.5 % and 1.4 % of GDP in the Union and in the euro-zone respectively (see Table 5.2.5). Apparently a falling trend of these subsidies can be noticed. Governments in Denmark and Austria provided the highest aid payments to the private sector whereas Sweden, which still had the highest share in 1997, has reduced its subsidies in the meantime to the European average. The Member State which subsidised the least was Greece, followed by Spain, Italy and France.

Table 5.2.5. Subsidies paid by general government (as a % of GDP)

	1995	1996	1997	1998	1999	2000
EU-15 [4]	1.8	1.7	1.6	1.6	1.5	1.5
EUR-12 [4]	1.7	1.7	1.5	1.5	1.5	1.4
B	1.5	1.6	1.4	1.5	1.5	1.5
DK	2.5	2.6	2.4	2.3	2.4	2.2
D	2.1	2.0	1.8	1.9	1.8	1.7
EL	0.4	0.5	0.1	0.1	0.2	0.2
E	1.1	1.0	0.9	1.1	1.2	1.1
F	1.5	1.5	1.5	1.4	1.3	1.3
IRL [1]	:	:	:	:	:	:
I	1.5	1.5	1.2	1.3	1.2	1.2
L	1.8	2.1	1.8	1.8	1.5	1.6
NL	1.1	1.2	1.5	1.5	1.6	1.5
A	2.9	2.6	2.6	2.8	2.6	2.6
P [2]	1.3	1.5	1.2	1.5	:	:
FIN	2.8	2.1	1.9	1.7	1.6	1.5
S	3.8	3.3	2.7	2.2	2.1	1.6
UK [3]	:	:	:	:	:	:

[1] Ireland has a derogation for the transmission of these data.
[2] Portugal has not transmitted data for 1999 and 2000.
[3] The United Kingdom has not transmitted data for subsidies paid.
[4] Values for the EU and euro-zone were calculated, excluding the GDP of countries with missing data.

Source: Eurostat.

Table 5.2.6. General government gross fixed capital formation (as a % of GDP)

	1995	1996	1997	1998	1999	2000
EU-15 [3]	2.6	2.4	2.2	2.2	2.2	2.2
EUR-12 [3]	2.7	2.6	2.4	2.5	2.5	2.5
B	1.8	1.6	1.6	1.6	1.8	1.8
DK	1.8	2.0	1.9	1.7	1.7	1.7
D	2.3	2.1	1.9	1.9	1.9	1.9
EL	3.2	3.2	3.4	3.6	4.0	4.1
E	3.7	3.1	3.1	3.3	3.4	3.2
F	3.3	3.2	3.0	2.9	2.9	3.0
IRL [1]	:	:	:	:	:	:
I	2.1	2.2	2.2	2.4	2.5	2.4
L	4.6	4.7	4.2	4.5	4.2	4.1
NL	3.0	3.1	2.9	2.9	3.0	3.2
A	3.1	2.8	2.0	1.9	1.8	1.7
P [2]	3.7	4.2	4.4	3.9	:	:
FIN	2.8	2.9	3.2	2.9	2.9	2.5
S	3.4	3.0	2.7	2.7	2.7	2.5
UK	1.9	1.5	1.2	1.2	1.1	1.2

[1] Ireland has a derogation for the transmission of these data.
[2] Portugal has not transmitted data for 1999 and 2000.
[3] Values for the EU and euro-zone were calculated, excluding the GDP of countries with missing data.
Source: Eurostat.

On average, government investment in fixed capital goods (see Table 5.2.6) amounted in 2000 to 2.2 % of GDP in the Union. The figures differed considerably, ranging from 1.2 % in the United Kingdom to 4.1 % in Greece and Luxembourg. The share of government investment remained rather stable during the examined period in most countries, sometimes with some fluctuations. Only two States show a clear trend: Greece where the percentage has steadily grown since 1996 and Sweden with a slow decrease over time.

5.3. Public deficit and debt

Depending on whether or not a country's revenue covers its expenditure, there will be a surplus or a deficit in its budget. If there is a shortfall in revenue, the government is obliged to borrow. Expressed as a percentage of GDP, a country's annual (deficit) and cumulative (debt) financing requirements are significant indicators of the burden that government borrowing places on the national economy. These are in fact two of the criteria used to assess the government finances of the Member States that are referred to in the Maastricht Treaty in connection with qualifying for the single currency (see box).

> **Budgetary discipline and notification of public debt and deficit**
>
> The Maastricht Treaty states that the Member States are required to avoid excessive public deficits. To this end, they must fulfil two conditions. Firstly, the ratio of government deficit to GDP must not exceed a reference value (3 %), unless the ratio has declined substantially and continuously and reached a level close to the reference value, or that the reference value has been exceeded only exceptionally and temporarily and the ratio is close to the reference value. Secondly, the ratio of government debt to GDP must not exceed a reference value (60 %), unless the ratio is diminishing sufficiently and approaching the reference value at a satisfactory pace.
>
> At the Madrid Summit in December 1995, the European Council stressed the need for budgetary discipline both before the introduction of monetary union and after the start of stage 3 on 1 January 1999. This determination was reflected in the Growth and Stability Pact, which is intended to prevent any country, no longer able to rely on exchange rates and interest rates, to resort to budgetary policy to revive its economy, since such a solution could very quickly have a negative effect on its public deficit, thereby prompting a rise in interest rates which would be detrimental to all the participants in EMU.

Public deficit (see Table 5.3.1) is defined in the Maastricht Treaty as general government's net borrowing according to the European system of accounts (see box).

The average values for the European Union and the euro-zone suggest that the year 2001 saw a certain drawback for the efforts to balance government budgets in the Community. However, in 2001, 11 Member States achieved a balanced budget or a surplus. Only five had to borrow in order to finance their budget. With the exception of Portugal their deficits stayed below the reference value.

Nevertheless it cannot be neglected that namely Italy and Germany who had managed since 1996 to constantly enhance their budgetary situation faced a trend reversal in 2001. In Portugal this reversal occurred already in 2000 and the deficit increased in 2001. France could not further reduce its public deficit but kept the same value as in the preceding year. For Italy and Portugal the growing deficit was caused by a rise in State expenditure. In Germany decreasing revenues aggravated the same development.

The euro-zone showed a similar development. While the deficit was reduced steadily since 1995 and had disappeared in 2000 it grew in 2001 for the first time in the period examined. The reason was a noticeable growth in the share of public expenditure whereas revenue percentage fell slightly.

Public debt (see Table 5.3.2) is defined in the Maastricht Treaty as total general government gross, nominal and consolidated debt outstanding at the end of the year.

In the past years, endeavours to reduce general government debts were again fruitful. At the end of 2001, 11 States of the Union had a level of public debt below the 60 % threshold, with Austria only slightly above this percentage. Two Member States — Italy and Belgium — were still above 100 %, while Greece reached for the first time a two-digit percentage.

Table 5.3.1. General government deficit (as a % of GDP)

	1996	1997	1998	1999	2000	2001
EU-15	-4.2	-2.4	-1.7	-0.8	0.6	-0.8
EUR-12	-4.3	-2.6	-2.3	-1.3	0.1	-1.5
B	-3.8	-1.9	-0.8	-0.5	0.1	0.3
DK	-1.0	0.3	1.1	3.1	2.5	2.8
D	-3.4	-2.7	-2.2	-1.5	1.1	-2.8
EL	-7.4	-4.0	-2.4	-1.9	-0.8	0.0
E	-4.9	-3.2	-2.6	-1.2	-0.6	-0.1
F	-4.1	-3.1	-2.7	-1.6	-1.4	-1.4
IRL	-0.2	1.2	2.3	2.4	4.5	1.7
I	-7.1	-2.7	-3.1	-1.8	-0.6	-2.2
L	2.0	2.8	3.1	3.5	5.6	6.1
NL	-1.8	-1.1	-0.8	0.7	2.1	0.1
A	-4.0	-2.0	-2.5	-2.4	-1.7	0.0
P	-4.0	-3.0	-2.5	-2.4	-2.9	-4.2
FIN	-3.1	-1.5	1.3	1.9	7.0	5.0
S	-3.1	-1.6	2.1	1.3	3.7	4.9
UK	-4.4	-2.2	0.3	1.2	1.6	0.9

Source: Eurostat.

GENERAL GOVERNMENT IN THE UNION

Figure 5.3.1. Variation of general government net lending/net borrowing in the euro-zone (as a % of GDP)

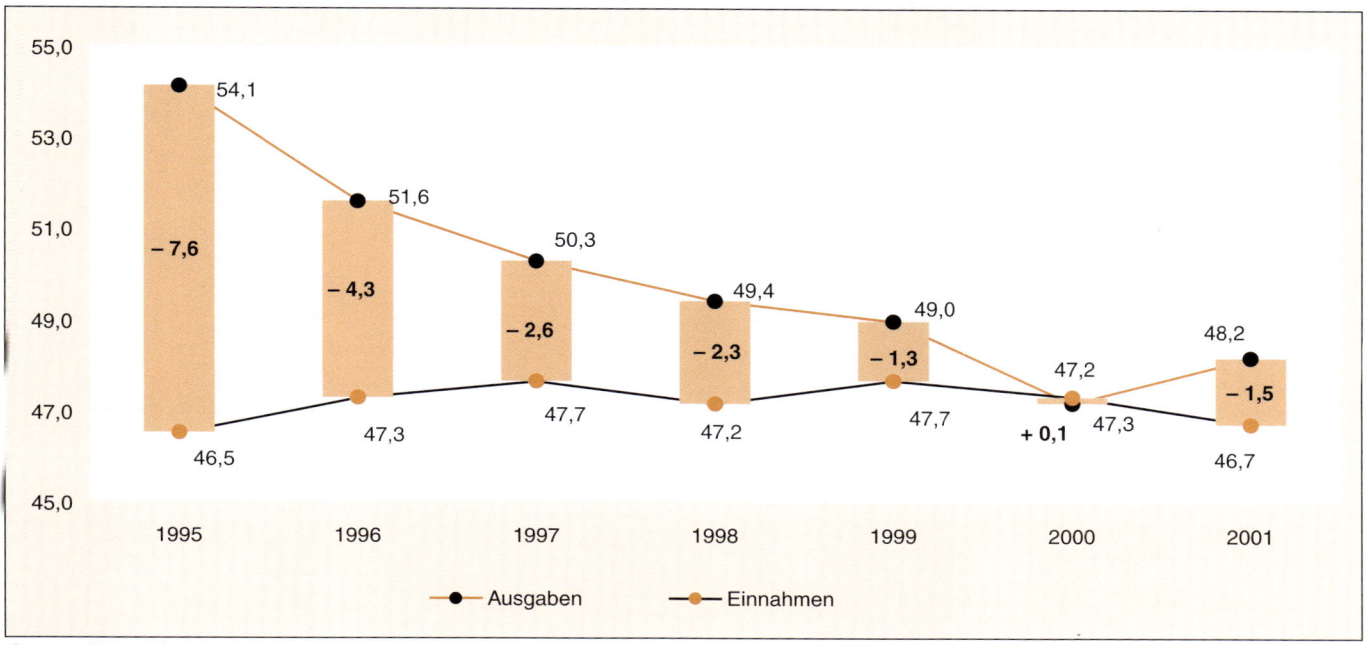

Year	Ausgaben	Einnahmen	Net
1995	54,1	46,5	−7,6
1996	51,6	47,3	−4,3
1997	50,3	47,7	−2,6
1998	49,4	47,2	−2,3
1999	49,0	47,7	−1,3
2000	47,2	47,3	+0,1
2001	48,2	46,7	−1,5

Source: Eurostat.

Table 5.3.2. General government debt (as a % of GDP)

	1996	1997	1998	1999	2000	2001
EU-15	72.5	71.1	68.8	67.8	63.9	63.0
EUR-12	75.1	74.9	74.1	72.5	70.1	69.1
B	130.1	125.3	119.3	115.0	109.3	107.5
DK	65.1	61.2	56.2	52.7	46.8	44.5
D	59.8	61.0	60.9	61.3	60.3	59.8
EL	111.3	108.2	105.0	103.8	102.8	99.7
E	68.1	66.7	64.6	63.1	60.4	57.2
F	57.1	59.3	59.5	58.5	57.4	57.2
IRL	74.3	65.1	55.1	49.6	39.0	36.6
I	122.1	120.2	116.4	114.5	110.6	109.4
L	6.2	6.1	6.3	6.0	5.6	5.5
NL	75.2	69.9	66.8	63.1	56.0	53.2
A	69.1	64.7	63.9	64.9	63.6	61.7
P	62.7	58.9	54.8	54.2	53.4	55.6
FIN	57.1	54.1	48.8	46.8	44.0	43.6
S	76.0	73.1	70.5	65.0	55.3	56.0
UK	52.3	51.1	47.6	45.2	42.4	39.0

Source: Eurostat.

In 2001 the average debt ratio for the 15 Member States of the Union was reduced by almost one percentage point to 63.0 %. As in the year before the average for the countries in the euro-zone followed at a distance of about 6 percentage points (69.1 %).

6. Population, labour market and social protection in the Union

6.1. Population

The EU, the world's third most populous economic area

Having 379 million inhabitants in mid-2001, the European Union is the third most populous economic area after China (1 273 million) and India (1 030 million), which reached its first billion well before the millennium change. Indeed, after these two giants, its population is almost as large as those of the United States (278 million) and Japan (127 million) together.

The European Union currently covers 70 % of the population of the whole of Europe (excluding most of the former Soviet Union and parts of the former Republic of Yugoslavia). The 10 central European countries plus Cyprus, Malta and Turkey, which are potential future Member States of the Union have a total population of about 176 million people. Turkey is the largest of those countries with a population of 68 million, Poland is the second largest with 38.6 million. Romania (22.4 million), the Czech Republic and Hungary (both 10 million) rank in the medium-size group of countries and the remainder have less than 10 million inhabitants.

The six largest EU countries by area (France, Spain, Sweden, Germany, Finland and Italy) occupy nearly 80 % of the total EU territory. The five countries with the highest populations i.e. Germany, the United Kingdom, France, Italy and Spain, represent 80 % of the whole population of the Union. Population density ranges from just 15 per km² in Finland to nearly 400 per km2 in the Netherlands. The population is most dense in a belt running from northern Italy through south and west Germany and the Benelux countries to southern England. Border regions in all directions tend to be less densely populated. In 1991, more than half of the population of the EU countries lived in urban settlements (defined as compact areas with a population density of at least 500 persons per km²). This percentage ranges however from a low of 21 % in Sweden to a high of 77 % in the United Kingdom.

Slow population growth as compared with the United States

Population growth in the EU slowed in the 1970s and 1980s but accelerated in the early 1990s. This was due to a temporary increase in immigration. The long-term trend points to a decline in the growth rate. The United States' population has grown steadily since the 1970s until recently. In Japan, population growth diminished substantially during the same period.

Table 6.1.1 shows the recent development of the components of the population change in 1997-2001. The population of the EU increased in 2001 by 0.41 %, a rate clearly higher than that of Japan (+ 0.17 %), but much lower than that of the United States (+ 0.90 %). Net migration is still the most important source of population growth in the Union. Its share of total population increase was 75 %. In the United States, net migration is also important but the natural increase is the major driving force of the relatively strong population growth. Japan faces a situation of near zero net migration, thus migration having no role in the population growth.

Table 6.1.1. Components of population change, 1997-2001 (as a %)

	Natural increase +	Net migration =	Population change
EU-15			
2001	0.11	0.31	0.41
2000	0.10	0.31	0.41
1999	0.07	0.25	0.32
1998	0.08	0.17	0.25
1997	0.10	0.13	0.23
EUR-11			
2001	0.11	0.32	0.43
2000	0.10	0.31	0.41
1999	0.07	0.24	0.36
1998	0.07	0.13	0.19
1997	0.09	0.13	0.22
US			
2001	0.55	0.35	0.90
2000	0.55	0.34	0.89
1999	0.56	0.35	0.91
1998	0.59	0.36	0.95
1997	0.59	0.32	0.91
JP			
2001	0.17	0.00	0.17
2000	0.18	0.00	0.18
1999	0.19	0.00	0.19
1998	0.20	− 0.04	0.20
1997	0.23	− 0.04	0.19

Source: Eurostat.

Increasing share of non-EU nationals

The European Union has witnessed a slow but steady growth in the share of the non-national population during recent decades. The total number of non-nationals has increased from 13.6 million in 1985 to 19.4 million in 2000. In 2000 the share of the non-nationals from other EU countries was 29 % of total number of non-nationals, and the share of those from outside the Union was 71 %.

Non-EU nationals account for a greater share of the total population in Austria (estimated at about 8 %) and Germany (6.7 %) than in any of the other Member States where the equivalent figures range from 1 % and 4 %. As a proportion of the total population, EU nationals of other Member States are most significant in Luxembourg (32 %) and Belgium (5.5 %), the figures in other countries of the Union varying between 0.5 % and 2.5 %.

The share of the non-EU nationals of the EU total population has been growing slowly but steadily from 3.8 % in 1985 to 5.1 % in 2000. This is due to the fact that net migration of the whole EU has exceeded natural increase since 1989. Also the compositions of inflows (immigration) and outflows (emigration) have favoured non-EU nationals being on average 55 to 45 in immigration and even 50 to 50 in emigration during the whole period. In 1999, 41 % of immigrants to EU countries were citizens of some EU country. They were either returning to their own country or moving to another EU country. The rest, some 59 %, were nationals of non-EU countries.

Ageing population and labour force

Figure 6.1.1 shows the age and sex structure of the European Union in 2001 in the form of a population pyramid. The pyramid has a broad waist and narrow shoulders. But things will change. The waist will rise upwards and the shoulders will broaden in the coming years. This is because the low fertility continues to decrease the younger age classes and expanding life expectancy tends further to increase the share of the older age classes.

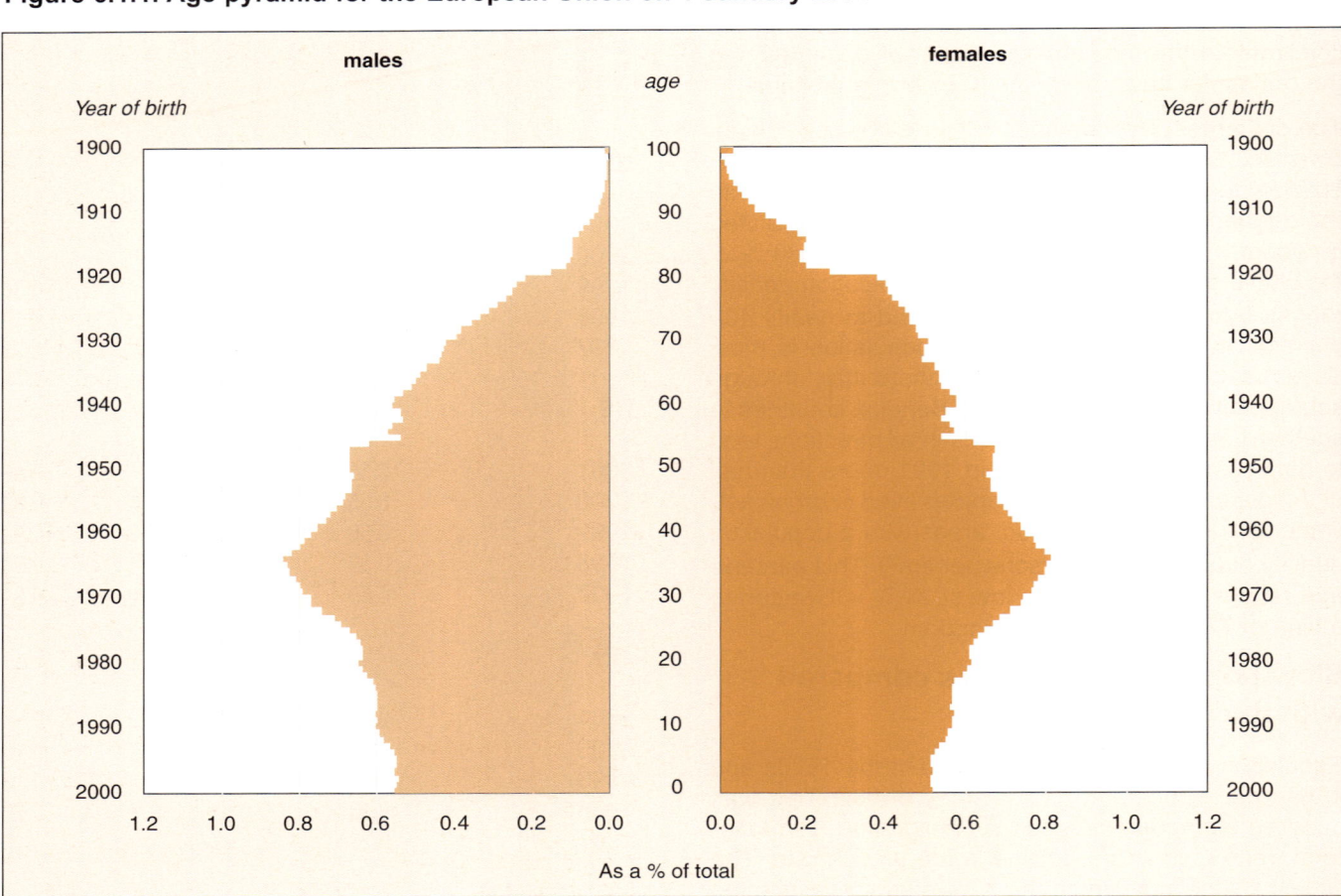

Figure 6.1.1. Age pyramid for the European Union on 1 January 2001

Source: Eurostat.

Long-term changes in fertility of the EU and Japan have been remarkably similar. In 1970, both had total fertility higher than 2 (EU 2.38 and Japan 2.09). After a rapid decrease in the 1970s there was a steady downward slope to the bottom levels 1.42 for EU in 1995 and 1.39 for Japan in 1997, which are well below the level of reproduction. Now, the direction seems to be upwards, although the total fertility rate of the EU declined slightly from 1.48 in 2000 to 1.47 in 2001. A slight rise was also seen in Japan from 1.40 to 1.41. The United States, on the other hand, had the highest level in 1970 (2.48) dropping to nearly 1.7 in the mid-1970s, but turning up again and staying just over 2 in the whole 1990s (2.06 in 2001).

Since 1945, life expectancy at birth in the EU has increased almost continuously. Following an interruption in 1995, the upward trend resumed in 1996. For the Union as a whole, and based on mortality rates measured in 2000, it is estimated that life expectancy is now at an all-time high: at birth, girls can now expect to live an average of 81.4 years and boys 75.1 years, well over 10 years more than in 1945.

The corresponding figures for the United States were 74.2 for men and 79.7 for women and for Japan 77.5 and 84.0. In most other developed countries, average life spans are shorter than in the EU: the most extreme case appears to be the Russian Federation, where the average man now lives 15 years less than his EU counterpart.

In Table 6.1.2. the population is split into several age groups for 1970, 1995 and 1998-2001. In all three areas the proportion of young persons (0-14) has declined in the last 25 years. However, in the United States the share of this group remains much higher than in the Union or Japan. Within the European Union, the southern Member States, Spain, Italy and Portugal have experienced the greatest fall in share of young people and this trend is expected to continue. In all three economic areas and especially in Japan, the proportion of elderly people (65 +) increased considerably.

The population of 15 to 64 year-olds is a good indicator of the actual and potential labour force. In the European Union and the United States, this age group accounted for a substantially higher percentage of the population in 2001 than in 1970. In Japan, although there was virtually no change over the same period, the 15-64 cohort remained a larger component of the Japanese population than that in the EU or the United States. In recent years (1998-2001), the share of this age group has been almost constant in all three countries. However, the internal structure has been changing in all three countries during the 1990s. The share of the older part of the potential labour force (40 to 64 years) increased from 1990 to 2001 in the EU from 44.1 to 46.5 %, in Japan from 49 to 50.4 % and in the United States from 38.9 to 45.3 %. This indicates ageing of the labour force, which will also continue in the coming years.

The old-age dependency ratio (65 +/15-64) increased from 1970 in all three areas more than doubling (to 26.0 %) in Japan which reached the level of the EU as compared with 19.0 % in the United States.

The total age dependency ratio (the number of people aged 0-14 and 65 and over related to the number of people aged 15-64) has dropped substantially since 1970 in the EU and in the United States with the EU being most affected. In Japan, a fall in the proportion of young people was counterbalanced by a rise in that of the elderly. However, during recent years (1998-2001) the ratio has been almost constant in all three economic areas.

Demographic consequences of a possible enlargement of the Union

The candidate countries have clearly a younger age structure (more young people and less old ones) than the present Member States. However, because of low fertility and life expectancy, most of the candidate countries have a declining population. So, enlargement of the EU, especially, by the present candidate countries would slightly postpone the ageing trend but hasten the start of the population decline of the Union by a few years.

What concerns the development of the working population, the trends in the candidate countries considered are somewhat different than in the present EU. Nearly all the candidate countries have a total age dependency ratio that is not only lower than the EU-15 average but also declining faster. Only when the small birth cohorts from the 1990's enter the working age will there be a rapid increase in the total dependency ratio.

Therefore, although enlargement of the European Union would, in the medium-term lighten the demographic burden on the working population of the Union, it would hardly alter the longer-term decline in this age group.

POPULATION, LABOUR MARKET AND SOCIAL PROTECTION IN THE UNION

Table 6.1.2. Population shares in major age groups and age dependency ratios 1970, 1995, 1998-2001 (as a %)

	Population shares			Age dependency ratios	
	0-14	15-64	65+	65+/15-64	(0-14 and 65+)/15-64
EU-15					
2001	16.9	66.9	16.2	24.2	49.5
2000	16.8	66.9	16.3	24.4	49.5
1999	17.0	66.9	16.1	24.1	49.5
1998	17.1	66.9	16.0	23.9	49.5
1995	17.6	67.0	15.4	23.0	49.3
1970	24.7	63.1	12.2	19.3	58.5
US					
2001	21.1	66.3	12.6	19.0	50.9
2000	21.2	66.1	12.7	19.2	51.3
1999	21.4	65.9	12.7	19.3	51.7
1998	21.5	65.8	12.7	19.3	52.0
1995	21.8	65.4	12.8	19.6	52.9
1970	28.3	61.9	9.8	15.8	61.6
JP					
2001	14.6	67.8	17.6	26.0	47.5
2000	14.8	68.1	17.1	25.1	46.8
1999	15.0	68.5	16.5	24.1	46.0
1998	15.2	68.8	16.0	23.3	45.3
1995	16.2	69.6	14.2	20.4	43.7
1970	24.0	69.0	7.0	10.1	44.9

Source: Eurostat.

6.2. Employment

Increase of employment by 1.2 % in 2001

Employment increased by 1.2 % in 2001 although the growth did not reach the 1.8 % rate of 2000 (the largest increase since 1995). Spain, France, Ireland, Italy, Luxembourg, the Netherlands, Portugal and Sweden were still above the EU average. The most important breaks between 2000 and 2001 were for Germany (from 1.6 to 0.2 %) and Ireland (from 4.7 to 2.9 %). Employment growth remained high in Luxembourg (5.6 %).

63.9 % of the population aged 15-64 is employed

At the Lisbon European Council of March 2000 a target was set whereby by 2010 the overall employment rate should stand at 70 % with 60 % for women. Later, in March 2001, the Stockholm European Council set an intermediate target of 67 % for the overall employment rate and 57 % for the female employment rate in 2005.

In 2001, the EU employment rate (% of employed persons in the population aged 15-64) was 63.9 %, against 63.2 % in 2000. This rate was 2 points more than the employment rate for the euro-zone. Denmark, the Netherlands, Sweden and the United Kingdom have already reached an employment rate of 70 %. Austria, Portugal and Finland have attained the intermediate target of 67 %. As for the female employment rate, eight countries have reached the 2005 objective: Denmark, Germany, the Netherlands, Austria, Portugal, Finland, Sweden and the United Kingdom.

Compared with 2000, the overall 2001 employment rate increased by 0.7 points in the EU but significantly more in Spain, France, Italy and the Netherlands (between 1.1 and 1.4 points). It slightly decreased or remained stable in Belgium, Greece and Austria. The

Table 6.2.2. Employment rates (15-64 years) by sex, 2001 (as a % of the total population of the same age)

	Total	Male	Female
EU-15	63.9	73.0	54.9
EUR-12	62.0	71.8	52.3
B	59.9	69.1	50.5
DK	76.2	80.2	72.0
D	65.8	72.6	58.8
EL	55.4	70.8	40.9
E	56.3	70.9	41.9
F	63.1	70.3	56.1
IRL	65.7	76.4	55.0
I	54.8	68.5	41.1
L	62.9	74.8	50.9
NL	74.1	82.8	65.2
A	68.4	76.7	60.1
P	68.9	76.9	61.1
FIN	68.1	70.9	65.4
S	70.9	72.3	69.4
UK	71.7	78.3	65.1

Source: Comparable estimates based on the labour force survey (QLFD).

Table 6.2.1. Employment and annual employment growth

	x 1 000			% growth	
	1999	2000	2001	2000/1999	2001/2000
EU-15	162 578	165 537	167 599	1.8	1.2
EUR-12	128 056	130 616	132 343	2.0	1.3
B	3 856	3 918	3 965	1.6	1.2
DK	2 745	2 765	2 771	0.7	0.2
D	38 081	38 706	38 773	1.6	0.2
EL	3 910	3 898	3 894	-0.3	-0.1
E	15 161	15 633	16 026	3.1	2.5
F	23 484	24 037	24 535	2.4	2.1
IRL	1 617	1 693	1 743	4.7	2.9
I	22 701	23 129	23 505	1.9	1.6
L	248	262	277	5.6	5.6
NL	7 938	8 122	8 291	2.3	2.1
A	3 999	4 019	4 028	0.5	0.2
P	4 818	4 914	4 994	2.0	1.6
FIN	2 243	2 285	2 313	1.9	1.2
S	4 161	4 247	4 326	2.1	1.9
UK	27 616	27 910	28 160	1.1	0.9

Source: Comparable estimates based on the labour force survey (QLFD).

situation was more favourable for women: at EU level, the female employment rate increased by 0.5 points more with respect to males. The difference reached even 1 point or more in Germany, the Netherlands and Austria.

However, in 2001, the EU female employment rate was still 18 points less than the male rate. The gender gap narrowed slightly from 18.6 to 18 points between 2000 and 2001. In Greece, Ireland, Spain, Luxembourg and Italy, this gap was still wide (between 20 and 30 points), the low female employment rate being often related to a low part-time employment rate. On the other hand, the gender gap was still much smaller in Denmark, Finland and Sweden (less than 9 points).

33.5 % of women in part-time employment against 5.7 % for men

The gender gap is also obvious in part-time work. Female part-time work represents 33.5 % of female employment in the EU while it represents 5.7 % for males. In the Netherlands, female part-time employment is particularly high, with two in three women working part-time. Other Member States with a high female part-time employment are Belgium, Germany, Sweden and the United Kingdom (more than 35 % in 2001).

Compared to 2000, the share of part-time employment remained stable in 2001 in the EU and most Member States (17.7 % of total employment) except in Belgium and Denmark (by + 2 points), and Germany and the Netherlands (by – 1 points). By gender, the differences were slightly more significant for women, especially in Belgium and Denmark (+ 3 points or more) and Germany (– 1.3 points).

About 15 % of employed people in the EU were working part-time in 2001 because they could not find a full-time job. However, involuntary part-time employment continued to decrease (compared with 15.8 % in 2000 and 17.3 % in 1999). In Denmark, the Netherlands and the United Kingdom, where part-time employment is prevalent, as well as in Germany and Austria, involuntary part-time employment was below the EU average. The situation is clearly different for men and women. In general, relatively more men work part-time because they could not find a full-time job. In Denmark, Portugal, Finland and Sweden relatively more women were involuntary part-time workers.

Table 6.2.3. Share of part time employment by sex, spring 2001 (as a % of the population in employment of the same sex)

	Total	Male	Female
EU-15	17.7	5.7	33.5
EUR-12	16.1	5.2	31.1
B	18.2	4.8	36.6
DK	19.6	9.6	31.2
D	19.9	4.7	39.0
EL	3.8	2.0	6.8
E	8.1	2.7	17.2
F	16.3	4.9	30.3
IRL	16.3	6.0	30.9
I	8.9	3.6	17.7
L	11.3	1.7	25.7
NL	41.9	19.3	71.3
A	16.9	3.9	33.3
P	8.1	3.6	13.6
FIN	11.6	7.0	16.6
S	21.8	9.1	35.7
UK	24.1	7.9	43.9

Source: Labour force survey.

Table 6.2.4. Involuntary part-time by sex, spring 2001 (as a % of part-time employment of the same sex)

	Total	Male	Female
EU-15	14.8	20.2	13.4
EUR-12	16.4	21.3	15.2
B	20.4	31.7	18.3
DK	13.6	10.5	14.8
D	11.9	15.8	11.2
EL	46.5	51.7	43.9
E	20.9	20.8	20.9
F	25.0	36.2	22.7
IRL	14.2	28.5	9.9
I	33.8	43.0	30.4
L	8.3	18.8	7.2
NL	2.5	3.9	2.0
A	10.8	17.6	9.7
P	15.9	7.9	19.7
FIN	32.8	26.6	35.9
S	23.2	22.0	23.5
UK	9.0	17.6	6.8

Source: Labour force survey.

POPULATION, LABOUR MARKET AND SOCIAL PROTECTION IN THE UNION

6.3. Unemployment

In 2001, the total number of unemployed in the EU averaged 12.9 million or 7.4 % of the labour force. The EU unemployment rate has been continuously decreasing since 1992. Compared to 2000, the decline was the largest in Italy (1 point), Spain, France and Finland (0.7 points) while the rate remained stable in Germany and Portugal. In six Member States, the unemployment rate was below 5 %, close to 2 % in Luxembourg and the Netherlands.

Table 6.3.1. Unemployment rate ([1]), yearly average (as a %)

	2000	2001
EU-15	7.9	7.4
EUR-12	8.5	8.1
B	6.9	6.6
DK	4.4	4.3
D	7.9	7.9
EL	11.1	10.5
E	11.3	10.6
F	9.3	8.6
IRL	4.2	3.8
I	10.4	9.4
L	2.3	2.0
NL	2.8	2.4
A	3.7	3.6
P	4.1	4.1
FIN	9.8	9.1
S	5.9	5.1
UK	5.4	5.0

[1] Harmonised unemployment rate.
Source: Eurostat.

Definition of unemployment

Harmonised unemployment rate

Eurostat harmonised unemployment rates are based on definitions recommended by the International Labour Organisation. As from 2001, unemployment is defined as follows in the Commission Regulation (EC) No 1897/2000 of 7 September 2000 (the main new elements of the definition are set in bold):

Unemployed persons comprise persons **aged 15 to 74** who were:
— without work during the reference week, i.e. neither had a job nor were at work (for one hour or more) in paid employment or self-employment;
— currently available for work, i.e. were available for paid employment or self-employment before the end of the two weeks following the reference week;
— actively seeking work, i.e. had taken specific steps in the four-week period ending with the reference week to seek paid employment or self-employment or who found a job to start later, i.e. **within a period of at most three months.**

Adjustments on data prior to 2001 have been performed to take account of this new definition and ensure comparability. Counts of the number of persons registered at public employment offices are not suitable for international comparison because of effects of changes in national administrative rules and procedures.

Higher unemployment among women and young people

In 2000, the female unemployment rate in the EU was below 10 % for the first time since 1992. It went on decreasing in 2001 (8.7 %). The gap with men was getting narrower but still reached 2.3 points in 2001 (against 2.7 points in 2000, and 2.9 points in 1999). This less favourable situation for women occurred in all Member States except Ireland, Sweden and the United Kingdom (less than 1 point of difference). The situation was still unfavourable to women in Greece and Spain, where the female unemployment rate was twice the male unemployment rate.

Table 6.3.2. Unemployment rate by sex ([1]), yearly average 2001 (as a %)

	Males	Females
EU-15	6.4	8.7
EUR-12	6.7	9.8
B	6.0	7.4
DK	3.8	4.9
D	7.7	8.1
EL	7.0	15.6
E	7.5	15.5
F	7.1	10.5
IRL	3.9	3.7
I	7.3	12.9
L	1.7	2.4
NL	1.9	3.0
A	3.0	4.3
P	3.2	5.1
FIN	8.6	9.7
S	5.2	4.9
UK	5.5	4.4

[1] Harmonised unemployment rate.
Source: Eurostat.

When the unemployment rates are compared by age, the 2001 youth unemployment rate in the EU and in most Member States was still twice or more the rate of those aged 25 and over, except in Germany. In Belgium, Greece, Italy, Luxembourg and the United Kingdom, the youth unemployment rate was more than three times the rate of those aged 25 and over. The large difference between the youth unemployment rate and the rate of those aged 25 and over is partly due to a low labour participation.

Table 6.3.3. Unemployment rate by age ([1]), yearly average 2001
(as a % of the labour force of the same age)

	Less than 25 years	25 years and over
EU-15	14.9	6.3
EUR-12	16.0	7.0
B	17.6	5.4
DK	8.5	3.6
D	9.4	7.7
EL	28.1	8.3
E	21.5	8.9
F	19.5	7.4
IRL	6.6	3.2
I	28.1	7.4
L	7.5	1.4
NL	5.5	1.8
A	5.8	3.2
P	9.3	3.2
FIN	19.7	7.6
S	11.1	4.3
UK	11.9	3.8

([1]) Harmonised unemployment rate.
Source: Eurostat.

The youth unemployment population ratio, on the other hand, does not depend on the participation rate because the basis is the total youth population instead of the labour force. In the EU, the 2001 youth unemployment population ratio was 7.1 %, a decrease of 0.7 points compared with 2000, 1.5 points compared with 1999. The youth unemployment population ratio decreased mainly in Spain and Greece, Italy and Finland, countries with the highest rates in the EU (still more than 9 %).

Higher unemployment among those with a lower level of education

The risk of unemployment is still higher among those aged 25-64 with an educational level below upper secondary education. It shows the importance of further education and training in a period of employment growth, job vacancies and decreasing unemployment. In Belgium, Germany, Ireland, Austria and the United Kingdom, the 2001 unemployment rate for people with third level education was less than one third of those with at most lower secondary education. The difference was also significant between upper and lower secondary education for the same countries except Germany.

Table 6.3.4. Youth unemployment population ([1]) ratio (15-24 years), yearly average 2001 (as a % of the total population of the same age)

EU-15	7.1
EUR-12	7.1
B	6.1
DK	5.9
D	4.8
EL	10.2
E	9.1
F	7.1
IRL	3.3
I	10.2
L	2.7
NL	4.1
A	3.2
P	4.5
FIN	10.3
S	5.2
UK	7.7

([1]) Harmonised unemployment.
Source: Eurostat.

Table 6.3.5. Adult unemployment rates (25-64 years) by educational attainment, spring 2001 (as a % of the labour force of the same age and level of education)

	Third level	Upper secondary	Less than upper secondary
EU-15	4.1	6.2	9.6
EUR-12	4.7	7.0	9.8
B	2.7	4.3	9.1
DK	3.2	3.3	5.0
D	4.2	8.2	12.9
EL	6.6	9.8	7.6
E	8.4	10.4	12.7
F	4.6	6.6	11.5
IRL	1.5	2.4	5.6
I	5.3	6.6	9.2
L	1.2	1.1	1.9
NL	1.5	1.5	2.1
A	1.9	3.4	6.7
P	2.2	3.0	3.6
FIN	4.1	8.5	11.1
S	3.0	5.2	8.0
UK	2.0	3.7	7.3

Source: Labour force survey.

Long-term unemployment

In the coordinated European employment strategy which was launched by the extraordinary Summit of Luxembourg in November 1997, the prevention of long-term unemployment was strongly emphasised. Since 1997, there has been a steady decline and the long-term unemployment rate (unemployed persons looking for a job for one year or longer) reached 3.3 % in 2001 (against 3.7 % in 2000). The largest decline compared to 2000 was for Belgium, Spain, France (by 0.8 points), Greece and Italy (by around 0.6 points) although the rate remained above 5 % in Greece, Spain and Italy.

Table 6.3.6. Long-term unemployment rate [1], yearly average (as a % of the labour force)

	2000	2001
EU-15	3.7	3.3
EUR-12	4.3	3.8
B	3.8	3.0
DK	1.0	0.9
D	4.0	3.9
EL	6.1	5.4
E	5.9	5.1
F	3.7	2.9
IRL	1.6	1.3
I	6.4	5.9
L	0.5	0.5
NL	1.1	0.8
A	1.0	0.9
P	1.6	1.5
FIN	2.8	2.5
S	1.8	1.8
UK	1.5	1.3

[1] Harmonised unemployment rate — 12 months and more.
Source: Eurostat.

The female long-term unemployment rate was still 1 point higher in 2001 compared to males. The gaps were still wide in Greece and Spain (more than 5 points) and Italy (3.5 points) but decreased significantly by 1 point with respect to 2000. In Ireland, Finland, Sweden and the United Kingdom, the long-term unemployment rate is slightly higher for males than for females.

Table 6.3.7. Long-term unemployment rate by sex [1], yearly average 2001 (as a % of the labour force)

	Males	Females
EU-15	2.8	3.9
EUR-12	3.1	4.7
B	2.8	3.4
DK	0.8	1.0
D	3.7	4.1
EL	3.2	8.7
E	3.1	8.1
F	2.4	3.5
IRL	1.6	0.8
I	4.5	8.0
L	0.5	0.5
NL	0.7	1.0
A	0.9	1.0
P	1.2	1.9
FIN	2.7	2.3
S	2.1	1.5
UK	1.7	0.8

[1] Harmonised unemployment rate — 12 months and more.
Source: Eurostat.

6.4. Social protection and pensions

The data on expenditure and receipts of social protection schemes presented here are drawn up according to the "Esspros Manual 1996". Esspros stands for European system of integrated social protection statistics, a harmonised system providing a means of analysing and comparing social protection financial flows.

In this manual, social protection is defined as follows: "Social protection encompasses all interventions from public or private bodies intended to relieve households and individuals of the burden of a defined set of risks or needs, provided that there is neither a simultaneous reciprocal nor an individual arrangement involved.

The list of risks or needs that may give rise to social protection is fixed by convention as follows:

— sickness/healthcare;
— disability;
— old age;
— survivors;
— family/children;
— unemployment;
— housing;
— social exclusion not elsewhere classified."

Social benefits are recorded without any deduction of taxes or other compulsory levies payable on them by beneficiaries.

"Tax benefits" (tax reductions granted to households for social protection purposes) are generally excluded.

6.4.1. Social Protection

Expenditure on social protection

In 1999, social-protection expenditure as a percentage of GDP in EU-15 remained stable at the 1998 level of 27.6 %. The trend in this ratio was, however, irregular in the period 1990-99.

Substantial growth was registered between 1990 and 1993, the ratio increasing by 3.3 percentage points to a peak of 28.8 % in 1993 (EU-15), primarily as a result of a slowdown in the growth of GDP and a rise in unemployment benefits. This growth was particularly marked in Finland (from 25.1 % of GDP in 1990 to 34.6 % in 1993), since the country was in recession during the period concerned.

Between 1993 and 1996, expenditure on social protection as a percentage of GDP showed a slight downward trend, due partly to an upturn in GDP and partly to a slowdown in the growth of social-protection expenditure (largely a result of a drop in unemployment benefits).

These trends continued during the period 1996-99, when the expenditure/GDP ratio in EU-15 fell by 0.9 points. Expenditure began to increase again in 1999, however.

The fall in the share of expenditure in GDP between 1996 and 1999 was most obvious in Finland (– 4.9 points) and Ireland (– 3.1 points). In Ireland, the strong growth in GDP in recent years largely explains the fall in the ratio. Denmark also registered a sharp drop (– 2.0 points).

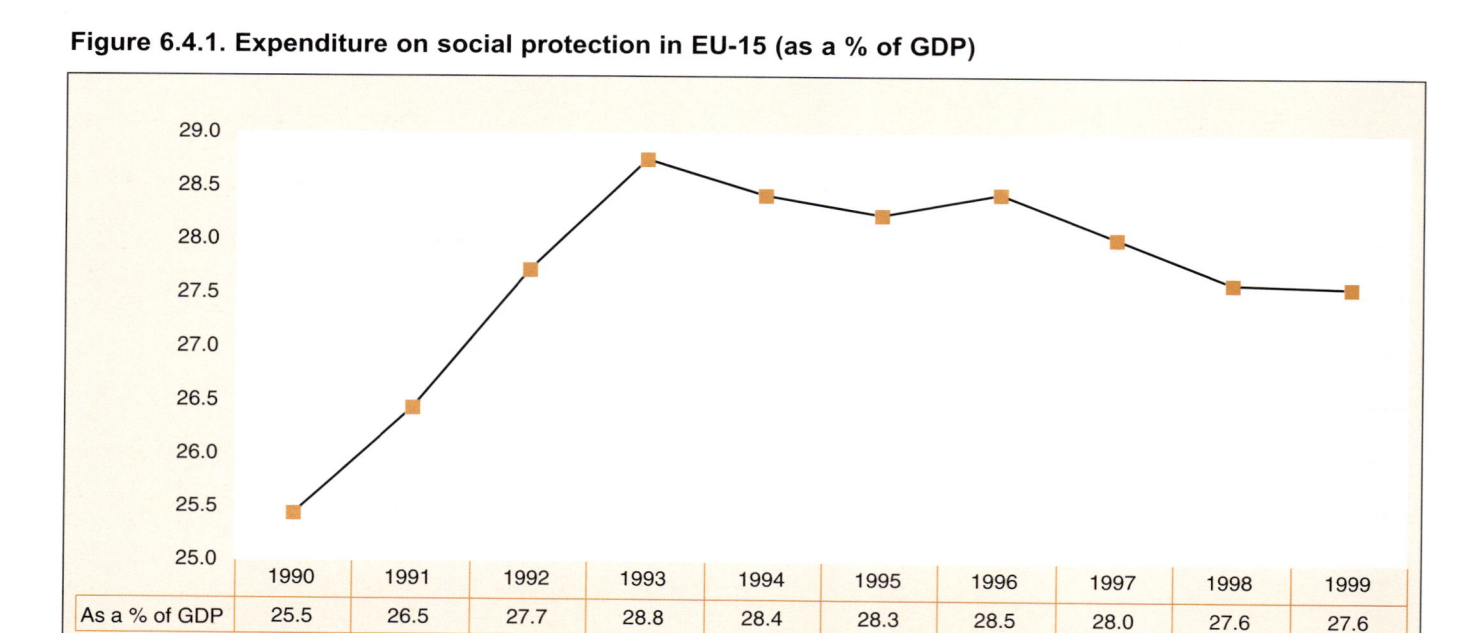

Figure 6.4.1. Expenditure on social protection in EU-15 (as a % of GDP)

	1990	1991	1992	1993	1994	1995	1996	1997	1998	1999
As a % of GDP	25.5	26.5	27.7	28.8	28.4	28.3	28.5	28.0	27.6	27.6

Source: Eurostat, Esspros.

Table 6.4.1. Expenditure on social protection (as a % of GDP)

	1990	1993	1996	1997	1998	1999
EU-15	25.5	28.8	28.5	28.0	27.6	27.6
EUR-12	25.5	28.3	28.2	27.8	27.5	27.5
B	26.4	29.5	28.7	28.1	28.2	28.2
DK	28.7	31.9	31.4	30.4	29.9	29.4
D	25.4	28.4	30.0	29.5	29.3	29.6
EL	22.9	22.0	22.9	23.3	24.3	25.5
E	19.9	24.0	21.8	21.1	20.6	20.0
F	27.9	30.7	31.0	30.8	30.5	30.3
IRL	18.4	20.2	17.8	16.7	15.5	14.7
I	24.7	26.4	24.8	25.5	25.0	25.3
L	22.1	23.9	24.0	22.9	22.4	21.9
NL	32.5	33.6	30.1	29.4	28.5	28.1
A	26.7	28.9	29.6	28.8	28.3	28.6
P	15.2	20.7	21.3	21.6	22.4	22.9
FIN	25.1	34.6	31.6	29.3	27.3	26.7
S	33.1	38.6	34.5	33.6	33.2	32.9
UK	23.0	29.1	28.3	27.7	27.2	26.9
IS	16.9	18.8	18.8	18.5	18.6	19.1
NO	26.3	28.4	26.2	25.6	27.5	27.9
EEA	25.5	28.8	28.4	28.0	27.6	27.6
CH	19.9	24.8	26.9	28.0	28.0	28.3
SK	:	:	21.7	21.4	21.5	21.2
SI	:	:	26.0	26.5	26.5	26.5

Source: Eurostat, Esspros.

Table 6.4.2. Expenditure on social protection per capita at constant prices (index 1990 = 100)

	1993	1996	1997	1998	1999
EU-15	113	118	119	121	124
EUR-12	111	116	117	119	122
B	115	117	118	122	125
DK	113	122	121	122	123
D	104	114	112	114	117
EL	96	104	111	120	130
E	124	122	123	125	127
F	110	114	115	118	120
IRL	119	130	137	142	150
I	108	108	113	113	116
L	120	135	138	141	149
NL	104	102	103	103	105
A	110	118	118	120	125
P	144	163	174	189	201
FIN	116	122	120	120	120
S	108	106	106	110	113
UK	129	136	136	136	139
IS	104	113	118	127	135
NO	112	119	122	130	137
EEA	113	118	119	121	124
CH	117	125	131	135	136
SK	:	:	:	:	:
SI	:	:	:	:	:

Source: Eurostat, Esspros.

Although the fall-off in the ratio was fairly general, some countries recorded increases in the recent period. One group of countries included those spending relatively little of their GDP on social protection, such as Greece and Portugal (+ 2.6 points and + 1.6 points respectively). At the other end of the scale, although the ratio in Norway and Switzerland was already high, it increased again between 1996 and 1999 to a level above the European average.

Growth in per capita expenditure in real terms accelerates in 1999

Per capita expenditure on social protection in EU-15 increased in the period 1990-93 by approximately 4.1 % per year. The growth was particularly marked in Portugal (12.8 % per year) and the United Kingdom (8.9 % per year). Greece is the only country in which per capita expenditure fell in real terms during the period.

During the period 1993-96, however, average growth was only 1.6 % per year at EU-15 level. In Portugal and the United Kingdom, the real rate of growth thus fell sharply from the level of the previous period (by 4.3 % and 1.6 % respectively per year between 1993 and 1996). This was due mainly to a reduction in benefits linked to sickness and unemployment. In Spain, Sweden and the Netherlands, per capita expenditure actually fell in real terms. Only Germany, Greece and Iceland saw a strong upturn in the real rate of growth.

The rate of growth in EU-15 between 1996 and 1999 was similar, at 1.5 % per year. Rates increased in all countries except Finland, where expenditure fell in real terms. Greece and Portugal recorded strong increases, however.

In 1999, expenditure resumed its growth in all countries (the rate of increase in per capita expenditure in real terms was 2.4 % in 1999 in EU-15) except Finland, where per capita spending remained stable in real terms. In Austria, for example, the increase (+ 4.3 %) was due in part to an extension of eligibility for unemployment benefits and a rise in the level of family benefits.

Expenditure on social protection: major differences between countries

The average figure for expenditure on social protection in EU-15 as a percentage of GDP (27.6 % in 1999) conceals wide disparities between Member States. Sweden (32.9 %), France (30.3 %) and Germany (29.6 %) have the highest ratios and Ireland the lowest (14.7 %). Outside EU-15, Iceland (19.1 %) and Norway (27.9 %) are at the two ends of the spectrum.

When this expenditure is expressed in per capita PPS

POPULATION, LABOUR MARKET AND SOCIAL PROTECTION IN THE UNION

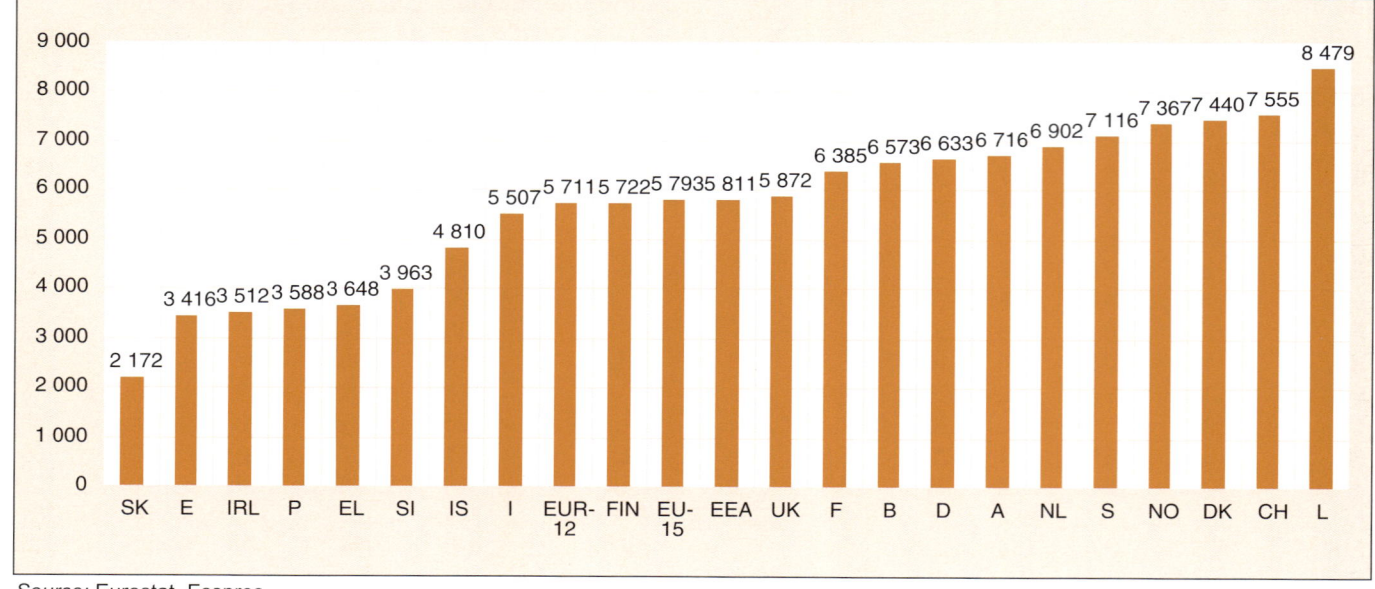

Figure 6.4.2. Expenditure on social protection in PPS per capita, 1999

SK	E	IRL	P	EL	SI	IS	I	EUR-12	FIN	EU-15	EEA	UK	F	B	D	A	NL	S	NO	DK	CH	L
2 172	3 416	3 512	3 588	3 648	3 963	4 810	5 507	5 711	5 722	5 793	5 811	5 872	6 385	6 573	6 633	6 716	6 902	7 116	7 367	7 440	7 555	8 479

Source: Eurostat, Esspros.

(purchasing-power standards), the differences between countries are wider still and the rank order changes.

In EU-15, Luxembourg spends most (8 479 PPS per capita), followed by Denmark (7 440 PPS per capita). Spain, Greece, Ireland and Portugal record a low level of social redistribution, at less than 4 000 PPS per capita. The ratio between the countries that spend most and least within EU-15 was thus 2.5 in 1999 (compared with 3.6 in 1990).

The gaps between countries are generally related to disparate levels of wealth and reflect differences in social-protection systems, demographic change, the unemployment rate and other social, institutional and economic factors.

Social benefits

Total benefits dominated by the "old age" and "survivors" functions

In most Member States, the highest proportions of social-protection benefits in 1999 were linked to the old age and survivors functions, which accounted for 46.0 % of total benefits in EU-15, or 12.2 % of GDP.

This feature is particularly marked in Italy, where more than 60 % of total benefits were devoted to these functions. The contributory factors include the high percentage of the population aged 65 or over (17.7 %, as against an average of 16.1 % in EU-15). In Ireland, however, less than 30 % of benefits come under the "old age" and "survivors" headings. The population of Ireland is the "youngest" in Europe: 31.4 % of the population was aged under 20 in 1999 (against an EU-15 average of 23.1 %), and only 11.3 % were aged over 65.

Figure 6.4.3. Social benefits by group of functions in EU-15, 1999 (as a % of total benefits and as % of GDP)

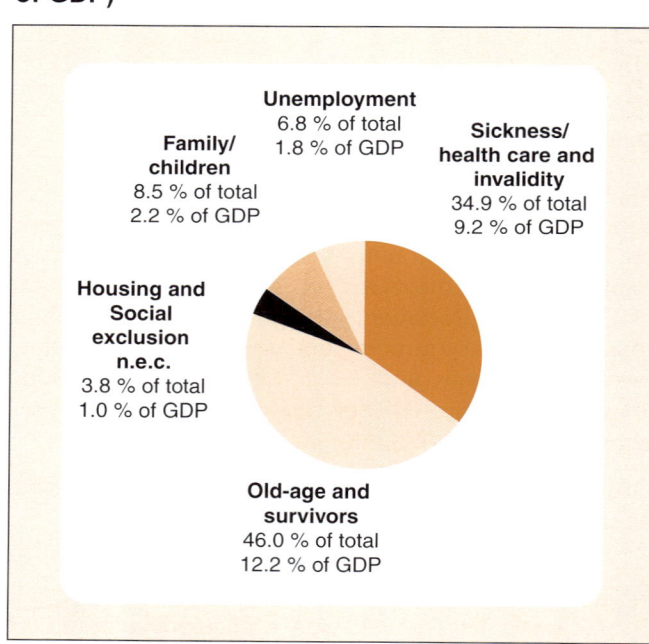

- Unemployment: 6.8 % of total, 1.8 % of GDP
- Family/children: 8.5 % of total, 2.2 % of GDP
- Sickness/health care and invalidity: 34.9 % of total, 9.2 % of GDP
- Housing and Social exclusion n.e.c.: 3.8 % of total, 1.0 % of GDP
- Old-age and survivors: 46.0 % of total, 12.2 % of GDP

Source: Eurostat, Esspros.

The sickness/healthcare and invalidity functions account for nearly 35 % of all benefits, exceeding expenditure on the old age and survivors functions in Portugal, Ireland and Finland. Outside EU-15, Iceland, Norway and Slovakia are in a similar position.

The family/children function accounts for 8.5 % of total benefits in EU-15, or for 2.2 % of GDP. At least 13 % of all benefits in Luxembourg, Denmark and Ireland, and also in Norway, come under this heading. In

Table 6.4.3. Social benefits by group of functions, 1999 (as a % of total social benefits)

	Old-age and survivors	Sickness/ health care and disability	Family/children	Unemployment	Housing and Social exclusion n.e.c.
EU-15	46.0	34.9	8.5	6.8	3.8
EUR-12	46.5	34.9	8.2	7.4	2.9
B	43.0	33.6	9.1	12.1	2.2
DK	38.0	31.7	13.0	11.2	6.1
D	42.1	36.0	10.5	8.8	2.6
EL	50.7	31.0	7.6	5.7	5.0
E	46.2	37.0	2.1	12.9	1.9
F	44.2	34.0	9.8	7.4	4.6
IRL	25.2	45.3	13.0	11.1	5.4
I	64.0	30.0	3.7	2.2	0.2
L	41.4	39.5	15.5	2.5	1.1
NL	41.5	40.7	4.3	6.2	7.4
A	47.4	35.4	10.3	5.4	1.6
P	43.7	45.6	5.2	3.7	1.8
FIN	35.1	37.2	12.8	11.3	3.7
S	39.5	36.9	10.5	8.1	4.9
UK	46.1	34.8	8.8	3.2	7.0
IS	31.2	51.8	12.1	1.8	3.0
NO	31.2	49.7	13.2	2.5	3.3
EEA	45.8	35.2	8.6	6.8	3.7
CH	50.7	36.4	5.2	4.0	3.7
SK	36.5	40.6	11.1	5.7	6.1
SI	45.4	39.6	8.7	4.7	1.6

Source: Eurostat, Esspros.

Spain, Italy and the Netherlands, however, expenditure on this function accounts for less than 5 % of all social benefits paid.

There are wide gaps between Member States in the weight of benefits linked to unemployment: compared with an average of 6.8 % in EU-15, more than 11 % of all benefits in Spain and Finland are linked to this function, but less than 3 % in Italy, Luxembourg, Iceland and Norway.

The amount of benefit paid under the "unemployment" heading is not always related to the level of unemployment in the country concerned: there are substantial differences in the coverage and amount of unemployment benefit.

The structure of social benefits changes over time

Between 1990 and 1999, the structure of social benefits changed in line with the different growth rates in the various functions. The variations observed arise both from changing needs and from amendments to social protection legislation.

Per capita expenditure under the old age and survivors functions rose by 25 % in real terms between 1990 and 1999 in EU-15. The increase was regular over the period and was reflected in a slight increase in the weight of these functions in total expenditure.

In Italy, the weight of this expenditure in total benefits increased by some 6 points between 1990 and 1999. In parallel, per capita expenditure on these functions in real terms was up by some 3.0 % per year during the period, against an EU-15 average of 2.5 % per year. In Portugal, a higher growth rate (8.5 % per year) was accompanied by an increase of only 1.8 points in the share of total benefits.

Faced with the ageing of their populations (the percentage of the population aged 65 or over rose from 14.5 % in 1990 to 16.1 % in 1999), several countries are overhauling their retirement systems; the effects of these reforms will make themselves felt in due course.

The sickness/healthcare and disability functions together showed a more moderate growth rate than the average increase of 24 % in total per capita benefits in real terms, so that the weight of these functions fell by 1.2 points in EU-15 between 1990 and 1999. This reflects, *inter alia*, the efforts made by Member States to cope with the costs incurred in these domains. Per capita expenditure in real terms on these functions diminished in the Netherlands and remained stable in Italy.

POPULATION, LABOUR MARKET AND SOCIAL PROTECTION IN THE UNION

Table 6.4.4. Social benefits per capita at constant prices in EU-15 (index 1990 = 100)

	1993	1996	1997	1998	1999
Old-age and survivors	109	118	120	122	125
Sickness/health care and disability	111	115	114	117	120
Family/children	111	126	129	130	135
Unemployment	148	130	123	119	119
Housing and social exclusion n.e.c.	121	144	142	146	146
Total benefits	113	119	120	121	124

Source: Eurostat, Esspros.

Table 6.4.5. Social benefits by group of functions in EU-15 (as a % of total social benefits)

	1990	1993	1996	1997	1998	1999
Old-age and survivors	45.9	43.9	45.0	45.9	45.8	46.0
Sickness/health care and disability	36.1	35.3	34.8	34.4	34.9	34.9
Family/children	7.7	7.7	8.3	8.4	8.4	8.5
Unemployment	7.3	9.7	8.1	7.5	7.1	6.8
Housing and social exclusion n.e.c.	3.0	3.4	3.8	3.8	3.8	3.8

Source: Eurostat, Esspros.

Expenditure on the family/children function as a percentage of total benefits in EU-15 rose from 7.7 % in 1990 to 8.5 % in 1999, however. This growth (+ 35 % in real terms between 1990 and 1999) was more marked in 1996, when Germany introduced reforms and extended the family benefit system. Luxembourg and Ireland recorded a growth rate which was well above average during the period, as did Norway. Only the Netherlands and Italy saw their per capita expenditure linked to the family fall in real terms.

Expenditure on the unemployment function rose by 19 % in real terms in EU-15 between 1990 and 1999. The increase was particularly obvious in Finland (a growth rate of some 9 % per year in real terms), where unemployment rose more sharply than elsewhere. In Switzerland these benefits also saw a substantial upturn between 1990 and 1999.

In EU-15, however, the trend was irregular during the period, since the total level of these benefits generally depends on the trend in unemployment. Between 1990 and 1993 these benefits rose very rapidly in EU-15, and their share of total social benefits increased from 7.3 % in 1990 to 9.7 % in 1993.

Per capita benefits at constant prices linked to unemployment fell from 1993, and their share of total benefits declined in EU-15 (from 9.7 % in 1993 to 6.8 % in 1999). This fall-off was determined in part by a gradual improvement in the economic situation and in part by reforms in the compensation system in some countries, limiting the duration of payment of benefits and changing the conditions of eligibility for such benefits. The fall was most marked in Spain, Denmark, Ireland and Norway. Greece, where the share of these benefits rose during the period, was an exception.

The financing of social protection

Systems for funding social protection differ widely between countries

Figure 6.4.4. Receipts of social protection by type in EU-15, 1999 (as a % of total receipts)

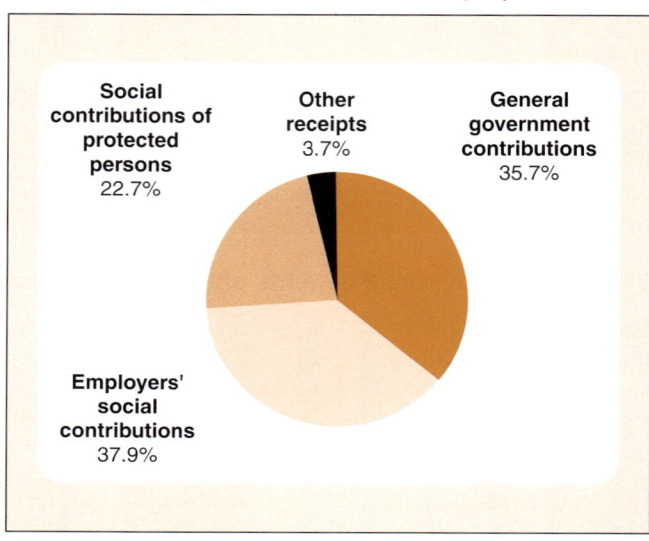

- Social contributions of protected persons 22.7%
- Other receipts 3.7%
- General government contributions 35.7%
- Employers' social contributions 37.9%

Source: Eurostat, Esspros.

In 1999 the main sources of funding of social protection at EU-15 level were social contributions (paid by protected persons and employers), representing 60.6 % of all receipts, and general government contributions derived from taxes (35.7 %). Social contributions can be broken down into contributions by protected persons (employees, self-employed persons, retired persons and others) and employers' contributions.

The European average irons out substantial differences between countries in the structure of social-protection financing. The share of funding derived from social contributions is highest in Belgium, Spain, France, the Netherlands and Germany, where this mode of financing accounts for 65 % of all receipts. This is also true of Slovenia.

Conversely, Denmark and Ireland (and also Norway) finance their social-protection systems largely from taxes, whose relative weight in total receipts is over 59 %. The United Kingdom, Luxembourg and Sweden (and Iceland) also rely heavily on general government contributions.

This divergence is the fruit of history and the institutional reasoning behind social-protection systems. As financing from taxes gains ground in countries where it used to be less important, the gaps are gradually narrowing.

General government contributions are taking over from social contributions

During the economic slowdown of 1990 to 1993, per capita general government contributions increased in real terms in EU-15 more rapidly (+ 24 %) than other sources of finance (+ 13 % for total receipts and + 4 % for social contributions).

Between 1993 and 1996, a period of economic revival and constraints on public expenditure, the increase in general government contributions slowed down to 1.5 % per year on average, while the rise in social contributions by protected persons accelerated (to 3.1 % per year on average).

Between 1996 and 1999, social contributions paid by protected persons fell by 1.2 % per year on average. This downturn was due *inter alia* to measures for combating unemployment introduced by several countries, which also explained the slowdown in employers' contributions (exemption from contributions as an incentive to recruit staff, for example).

This downturn was counterbalanced by a sharp rise in general government contributions (4.1 % per year on average in EU-15), affecting France and Italy in particular. The steep increase in this source of funds in France came as a result of the expansion in 1997 and 1998 of the *contribution sociale generalisée* or generalised social contribution, classed as tax revenue. This tax largely replaced the sickness insurance contributions paid by protected persons.

Between 1990 and 1999, the overall share of general government contributions in total receipts increased in EU-15 by 6.9 points.

Although general government contributions increased faster in France and Italy than in Europe on average, their share of total receipts fell sharply in Denmark and the Netherlands as a result of the growth in social contributions. It dropped considerably in Iceland for the same reasons.

The share of employers' social contributions fell in EU-15 by 4.6 points between 1990 and 1999. It fell in all countries except the Netherlands, Belgium and Denmark, even though Denmark remained the country in which these contributions are least significant. The decline was particularly steep in Italy, Portugal and Finland.

The share of social contributions paid by protected persons also fell between 1990 and 1999, from 24.6 to 22.7 % for EU-15. Although most countries experienced this downturn, the weight of these contributions rose in Denmark by over 10 points. A new contribution known as the "labour market contribution" was introduced there in 1994 in order to finance sickness and unemployment insurance and vocational training.

6.4.2. Expenditure on pensions

The Esspros methodology distinguishes between cash benefits and benefits in kind. Cash benefits can be periodic or lump sum. The "pensions" aggregate only includes some periodic cash benefits in the disability, old age, survivors' and unemployment functions. More specifically, the "pensions" aggregate is defined in this publication as the sum of the following social benefits (with the function to which the category of benefit belongs in brackets):

Table 6.4.6. Receipts of social protection per capita at constant prices in EU-15 (index 1990 = 100)

	1993	1996	1997	1998	1999
General government contributions	124	130	131	143	149
Social contributions	104	110	112	110	112
– by employers	103	106	107	108	111
– by protected persons [1]	107	118	119	112	114
Other receipts	103	107	106	106	110
Total receipts	113	119	120	121	124

[1] Employees, self-employed, pensioners and others.
Source: Eurostat, Esspros.

POPULATION, LABOUR MARKET AND SOCIAL PROTECTION IN THE UNION

Table 6.4.7. Receipts of social protection by type (as a % of total receipts)

| | General government contributions || Social contributions ||||| Other receipts ||
| | ^^ | ^^ | Total || Employers || Protected persons (1) || ^^ | ^^ |
	1990	1999	1990	1999	1990	1999	1990	1999	1990	1999
EU-15	28.8	35.7	67.1	60.6	42.5	37.9	24.6	22.7	4.1	3.7
EUR-12	24.8	31.9	70.9	64.0	46.1	40.9	24.8	23.1	4.3	4.2
B	23.8	25.7	67.0	71.8	41.5	49.4	25.5	22.4	9.2	2.5
DK	80.1	65.2	13.1	28.5	7.8	9.2	5.3	19.2	6.8	6.4
D	25.2	32.8	72.1	65.0	43.7	36.9	28.4	28.1	2.7	2.3
EL	33.0	28.6	59.0	61.1	39.4	37.7	19.6	23.4	8.0	10.3
E	26.2	26.8	71.3	69.2	54.4	52.2	16.9	17.0	2.5	4.0
F	17.0	30.4	79.5	66.8	51.0	46.5	28.5	20.3	3.5	2.8
IRL	58.9	59.8	40.0	39.0	24.5	24.2	15.6	14.8	1.0	1.2
I	27.2	38.9	70.3	58.0	54.9	43.6	15.5	14.4	2.5	3.1
L	41.5	46.9	50.5	49.1	29.5	24.7	21.0	24.4	8.1	4.0
NL	25.0	15.3	59.0	65.8	20.0	28.4	39.1	37.4	15.9	18.9
A	35.9	35.0	63.1	64.3	38.1	37.4	25.1	26.9	0.9	0.7
P	33.8	40.9	57.0	44.4	36.9	27.6	20.1	16.8	9.2	14.7
FIN	40.6	43.4	52.1	50.0	44.1	37.2	8.0	12.8	7.3	6.6
S	:	48.9	:	45.9	:	36.3	:	9.6	:	5.2
UK	42.6	47.3	55.0	51.8	28.1	27.7	26.9	24.0	2.4	0.9
IS	67.8	50.2	32.2	49.8	24.9	41.3	7.3	8.5	0.0	0.0
NO	63.1	59.8	36.4	38.8	24.0	24.6	12.5	14.2	0.5	1.4
EEA	29.4	36.1	66.6	60.2	42.2	37.6	24.4	22.5	4.0	3.7
CH	19.3	21.0	64.1	58.7	32.6	28.4	31.6	30.3	16.5	20.3
SK	:	30.1	:	64.5	:	46.7	:	17.8	:	5.4
SI	:	32.3	:	66.8	:	28.4	:	38.4	:	0.9

(1) Employees, self-employed, pensioners and others.
Source: Eurostat, Esspros.

— disability pensions (disability function);
— early retirement benefits due to reduced capacity to work (disability function);
— old age pensions (old age function);
— anticipated old age pensions (old age function);
— partial pensions (old age function);
— survivors' pensions (survivors' function);
— early retirement benefits for labour market reasons (unemployment function).

These benefits are divided into means-tested and non-means-tested benefits. The value of the "pensions" aggregate was calculated for all countries in accordance with the above definition, regardless of national differences in the institutional organisation of social protection systems. Some of the benefits which make up the "pensions" aggregate (for example disability pensions) are paid to people who have not reached the standard retirement age.

The definitions of the different categories of social benefits can be found in the Esspros manual 1996. In accordance with Esspros, pensions are recorded without any deduction of taxes or other compulsory levies payable on them by beneficiaries. On the other hand, the values of pensions do not include the social contributions which pension schemes pay on behalf of their pensioners to other social protection schemes (e.g. health schemes). Esspros records these payments under the heading "re-routed social contributions".

In 1999, expenditure on pensions in EU-15 was equivalent to 12.7 % of GDP. In Italy, it amounted to more than 15 % of GDP, followed by Austria, France and the Netherlands, at over 13 %. The ratios of social expenditure to GDP for these three countries are also among the highest (over 26 %).

Conversely, Ireland had the lowest rate of social expenditure to GDP (14.1 %) and allocated only 3.8 % of its GDP to expenditure on pensions (1). In Iceland and Slovakia, the percentage was also low (less than 8 % of GDP).

(1) For Ireland no data are available on occupational pension schemes for private-sector employees with constituted reserves.

Figure 6.4.5. Expenditure on pensions and on total benefits, 1999 (as a % of GDP)

Source: Eurostat, Esspros.

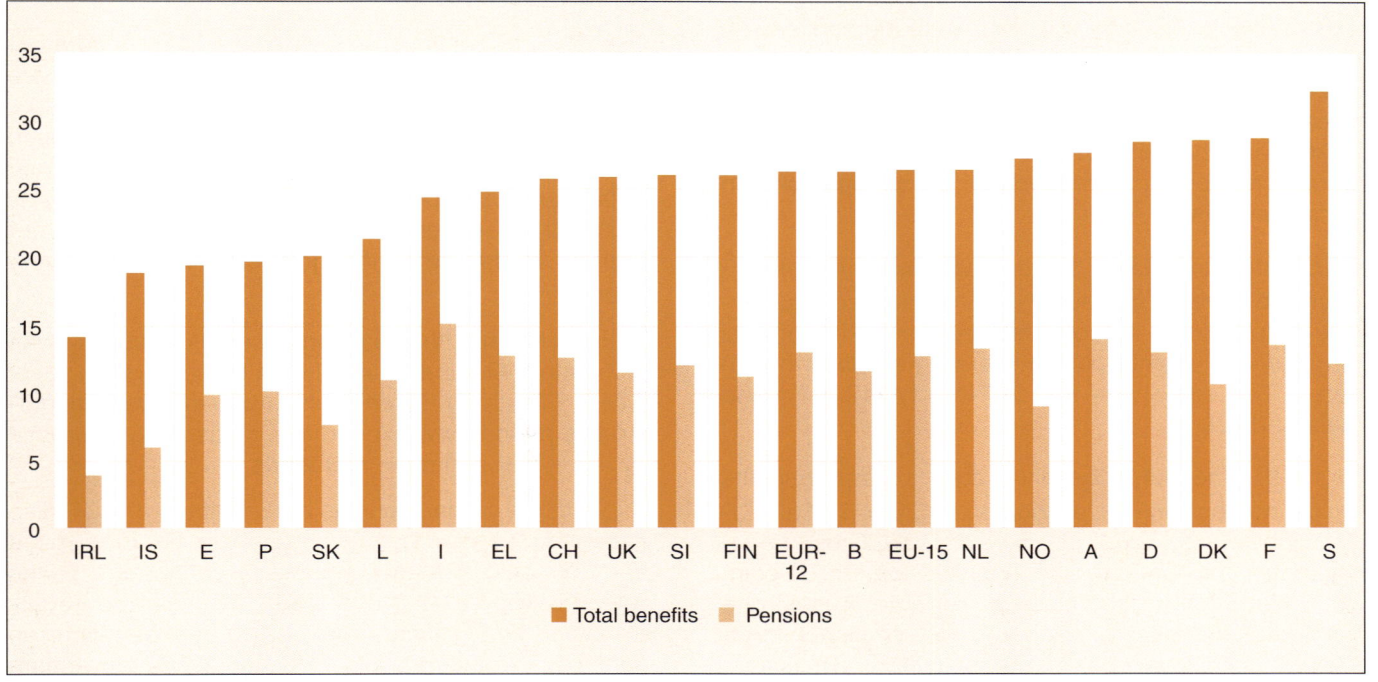

Table 6.4.8. Social benefits, 1999

	Pensions % of GDP	Pensions % of total	Benefits in kind % of GDP	Benefits in kind % of total	Other cash benefits % of GDP	Other cash benefits % of total	Total benefits % of GDP
EU-15	12.7	47.9	8.3	31.5	5.5	20.6	26.4
EUR-12	13.0	49.3	7.9	29.9	5.5	20.7	26.3
B	11.6	44.1	6.8	25.9	7.9	30.0	26.3
DK	10.7	37.3	11.0	38.6	6.9	24.0	28.6
D	13.0	45.5	8.7	30.3	6.9	24.2	28.6
EL	12.7	51.4	8.5	34.5	3.5	14.1	24.7
E	9.9	50.8	5.7	29.5	3.8	19.6	19.4
F	13.5	47.0	9.7	33.6	5.6	19.4	28.8
IRL	3.8	27.1	6.2	44.5	4.0	28.4	14.1
I	15.1	62.0	5.6	23.0	3.6	15.0	24.4
L	10.9	51.2	6.1	28.9	4.2	19.8	21.2
NL	13.3	50.1	7.8	29.6	5.4	20.3	26.5
A	14.0	50.3	8.3	30.0	5.5	19.7	27.7
P	10.1	51.3	7.3	36.8	2.4	11.9	19.7
FIN	11.2	43.0	8.7	33.3	6.1	23.6	26.0
S	12.2	37.9	13.4	41.8	6.5	20.3	32.2
UK	11.5	44.6	9.2	35.6	5.1	19.8	25.8
IS	6.0	31.7	9.8	52.1	3.0	16.2	18.8
NO	9.0	32.9	11.6	42.3	6.8	24.8	27.3
CH	12.6	49.1	6.9	26.7	6.2	24.2	25.7
SK	7.6	37.8	6.4	32.2	6.0	30.0	20.0
SI	12.1	46.5	7.9	30.5	6.0	23.0	25.9

Source: Eurostat, Esspros.

In almost all Member States, pensions were the main component of social protection expenditure in 1999, accounting for 47.9 % of EU-15 total expenditure on social benefits. The situation in Italy was particularly marked, with over 60 % of all social benefits being pensions. In Greece, Portugal, Luxembourg, Spain, Austria and the Netherlands, expenditure on pensions also accounted for more than half of total spending on social benefits.

By contrast, in Ireland, Sweden and Denmark, expenditure on benefits in kind [2] was higher than expenditure on pensions. It accounted for almost half of total benefits and mainly concerned sickness and health care. The same was true of Norway (42.3 %) and Iceland (52.1 %).

In 1999, other cash benefits, that is, cash benefits excluding pensions [3], accounted for 20.6 % of all EU-15 benefits, equivalent to 5.5 % of GDP. These benefits made up more than 28 % of the total in Belgium and Ireland (as well as in Slovakia), with at least one third allocated to expenditure on family/children (Ireland and Slovakia) or to unemployment (Belgium).

The growth in expenditure on pensions in real terms is stabilising

The trend in pensions expenditure in EU-15 throughout the period 1990-99 was noticeably different. There was a substantial upturn between 1990 and 1993, when expenditure as a percentage of GDP increased by one percentage point to reach 12.9 %. This was due in part to GDP growing more slowly than the average increase in expenditure on pensions (4.7 % per annum) in real terms, though this is not true of every country [4].

Thus, in Finland, this ratio increased more quickly than in the other Member States (+ 3.4 percentage points of GDP). Effectively Finland, which was in recession during this period, saw expenditure on pensions increase by 4.5 % per annum in real terms.

Expenditure on pensions as a percentage of GDP also increased at an above-average rate in the United Kingdom and Portugal (almost 2 percentage points higher between 1990 and 1993). This can be largely explained by significant real growth in expenditure on pensions (an average of 7.2 % and 9.7 % per annum

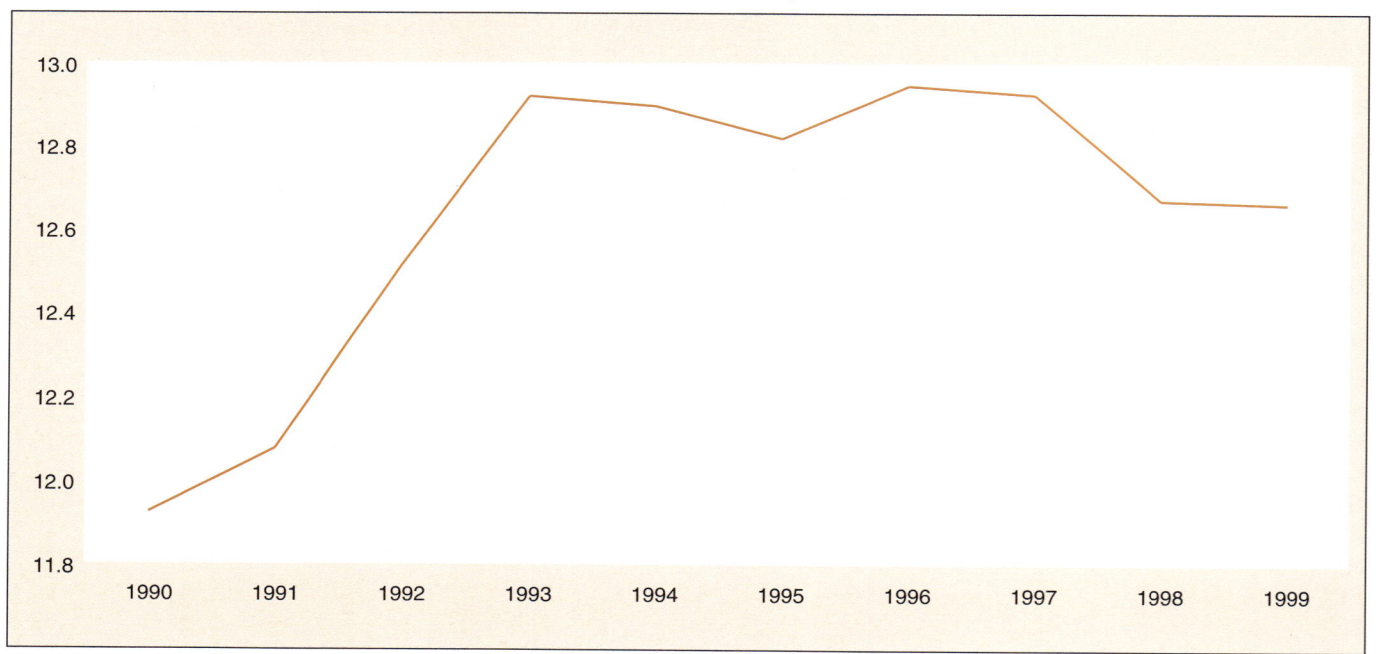

Figure 6.4.6. Expenditure on pensions, EU-15 (as a % of GDP)

Source: Eurostat, Esspros.

[2] Benefits in kind: for example hospital and outpatient care, accommodation for old or disabled people, child day care, etc.
[3] Other cash benefits: family allowances, birth grants, death grants, unemployment benefit, vocational training allowance, paid sick leave, parental leave benefit, etc.
[4] Due to integration of the new Länder in Germany in 1991, the growth in total expenditure in EU-15 was 3 points higher in 1991 than it would have been if the geographical situation had been unchanged. The spread is of the same order for the old age and disability pensions; it is more significant for the other categories of pensions (10 points) and negligible for the survivors' pension.

Table 6.4.9. Expenditure on pensions (as a % of GDP)

	1990	1993	1996	1997	1998	1999
EU-15	11.9	12.9	12.9	12.9	12.7	12.7
EUR-12	12.2	13.1	13.1	13.2	13.0	13.0
B	11.8	13.1	12.2	11.9	11.7	11.6
DK	9.6	10.1	11.5	11.2	10.9	10.7
D	12.0	12.5	12.9	13.0	12.9	13.0
EL	11.9	11.3	11.6	11.7	12.4	12.7
E	9.4	10.3	10.5	10.3	10.2	9.9
F	12.5	13.4	13.7	13.7	13.5	13.5
IRL	5.6	5.6	4.7	4.4	4.1	3.8
I	13.4	14.9	14.8	15.3	14.8	15.1
L	12.1	13.0	12.5	12.0	11.5	10.9
NL	15.4	15.6	14.0	13.7	13.2	13.3
A	13.7	14.2	14.6	14.3	14.0	14.0
P	7.5	9.3	10.0	9.9	10.1	10.1
FIN	10.4	13.8	12.8	12.0	11.3	11.2
S	:	13.7	12.9	12.7	12.5	12.2
UK	10.2	12.2	12.0	12.1	11.6	11.5
IS	4.5	5.5	5.7	5.7	5.8	6.0
NO	8.6	8.9	8.3	8.1	8.8	9.0
CH	9.1	10.7	11.7	12.1	12.4	12.6
SK	:	:	7.5	7.4	7.6	7.6
SI	:	11.8	12.1	12.1	12.0	12.1

Source: Eurostat, Esspros.

respectively). Contrarily, in Greece, the only country to experience a negative real growth rate during this period (– 1.3 %), expenditure on pensions as a percentage of GDP actually decreased from 1990 to 1993.

Between 1993 and 1996, expenditure on pensions in EU-15 as a percentage of GDP stabilised at around 12.9 %. This was a result of both faster GDP growth and a slowing of expenditure on pensions. In most Member States, the rate of increase of this expenditure decreased in real terms, with the exception of Denmark (+ 8.0 %), Greece (+ 3.1 %) and, outside EU-15, Norway (+ 3.0 %). In Belgium, expenditure on pensions actually decreased in real terms.

Between 1996 and 1999, expenditure on pensions as a percentage of GDP in EU-15 dropped slightly from 12.9 % to 12.7 %. This is true for most of the Member States. The exceptions are Greece, where expenditure on pensions grew significantly in real terms (an average of + 7.0 % per annum), and, outside EU-15, Iceland, Norway and Switzerland.

The drop in the ratio was particularly marked in Finland (– 1.6 percentage points of GDP), where the economy grew strongly and the increase in expenditure on pensions was more restrained than in the other countries (+ 1.1 % per annum as compared to an EU-15 average of + 2.1 %).

However, in 1999, the real rate of growth of this expenditure picked up again in almost all of the countries, (+ 2.7 % in EU-15 in 1999), with Greece, Ireland and Spain being the exceptions.

Figure 6.4.7. Expenditure on pensions in real terms (index 1990 = 100), annual growth rates (as a %)

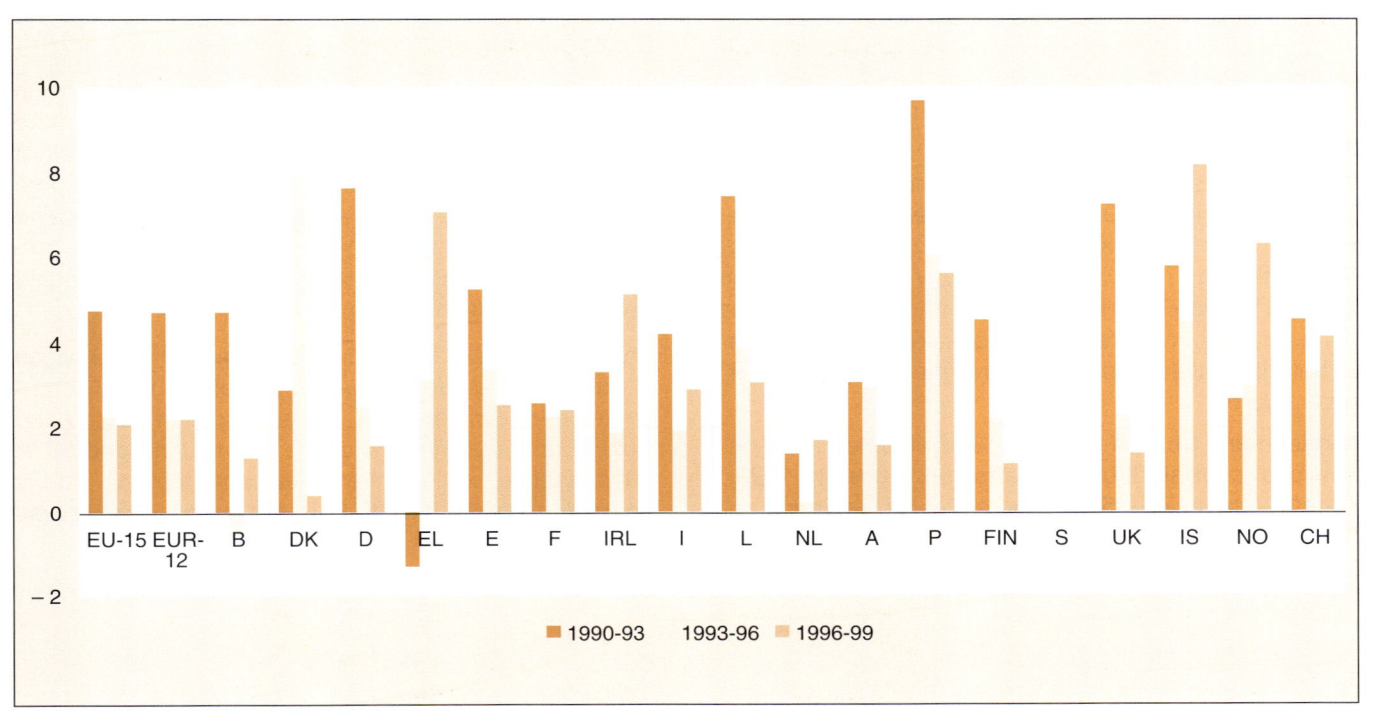

Source: Eurostat, Esspros.

Old age pensions dominate pension expenditure

In 1999, expenditure on old-age pensions (5) was the main component of pension expenditure in every country, accounting for 75.3 % of the total, or 9.5 % of EU-15 GDP. This is particularly true in the United Kingdom, Germany and France (and in Slovakia) where approximately 80 % of pensions are of this kind. Ireland recorded the lowest value, at 46.2 %.

Figure 6.4.8. Breakdown of pension expenditure between categories, EU-15, 1999 (as a % of total pensions and of GDP)

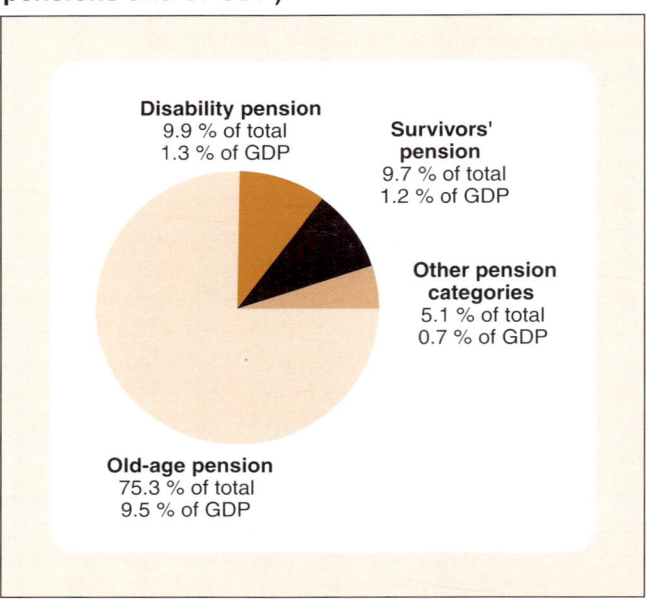

Disability pension
9.9 % of total
1.3 % of GDP

Survivors' pension
9.7 % of total
1.2 % of GDP

Other pension categories
5.1 % of total
0.7 % of GDP

Old-age pension
75.3 % of total
9.5 % of GDP

Source: Eurostat, Esspros.

Table 6.4.10. Breakdown of pension expenditure between categories, EU-15, 1999 (as a % of total)

	Old-age pension	Disability pension	Survivors' pension	Other pension categories
EU-15	75.3	9.9	9.7	5.1
EUR-12	74.7	9.1	10.5	5.8
B	64.0	10.9	20.5	4.6
DK	62.3	14.7	0.0	23.0
D	79.2	8.4	3.0	9.4
EL	66.8	6.3	6.4	20.5
E	74.7	12.4	8.1	4.8
F	79.1	6.2	11.9	2.8
IRL	46.2	15.3	21.8	16.7
I	74.8	6.5	18.0	0.7
L	72.2	19.2	6.0	2.6
NL	60.7	22.0	10.6	6.7
A	58.4	8.7	19.6	13.4
P	65.4	20.4	12.7	1.5
FIN	59.2	19.4	9.0	12.4
S	75.4	17.8	5.9	0.8
UK	80.1	12.2	7.7	0.0
IS	65.4	25.4	9.2	0.0
NO	65.4	30.5	3.7	0.4
CH	74.0	16.7	9.2	0.0
SK	82.3	12.0	5.0	0.8
SI	64.6	10.2	3.2	22.0

Source: Eurostat, Esspros.

The proportion of the population aged 65 or over partly explains the differences between countries. For example, in Ireland the over-65 age group makes up only 11.3 % of the population, compared to an EU-15 average of 16.1 %.

Disability pensions accounted for almost 10 % of the EU-15 total in 1999. They are very high in the Netherlands, Portugal and Finland (approximately 20 % of the total), as well as in Norway and Iceland. By contrast, France, Italy and Greece spend less than 7 % of the total expenditure on pensions. The various rules on benefits linked to disability are one explanation for these figures.

In Ireland and Belgium, over 20 % of all expenditure on pensions consisted of survivors' pensions in 1999, compared to an EU-15 average of 9.7 %. Denmark, on the other hand, spends practically nothing on this.

There are considerable differences between Member States with regard to the other categories of pensions (6).

In comparison with an EU-15 average of 5.1 % in 1999, countries such as Denmark, Greece (and Slovenia) spend over 20 % of the total, almost all of which consists of anticipated old-age pensions. Some other countries (Ireland, Austria and Finland) spend over 12 %. In contrast, the United Kingdom and, outside EU-15, Iceland and Switzerland do not allocate any funds to this benefit.

The proportion of the population aged 50 to 59 which is not economically active partly explains the discrepancies between countries. For example, in Ireland and Austria, more than 40 % of the population aged 50 to 59 is inactive, while in the United Kingdom this rate is approximately 26 %. The EU-15 average in 1999 was 35.9 %.

---

(5) Old-age pensions are paid to protected persons having reached the statutory retirement age fixed by the reference scheme.

(6) This includes anticipated old-age pensions, partial pensions, early-retirement benefit due to reduced capacity to work and early-retirement benefit for labour market reasons.

Figure 6.4.9. Trend of the expenditure on pensions by categories at constant prices, EU-15 (index 1990 = 100)

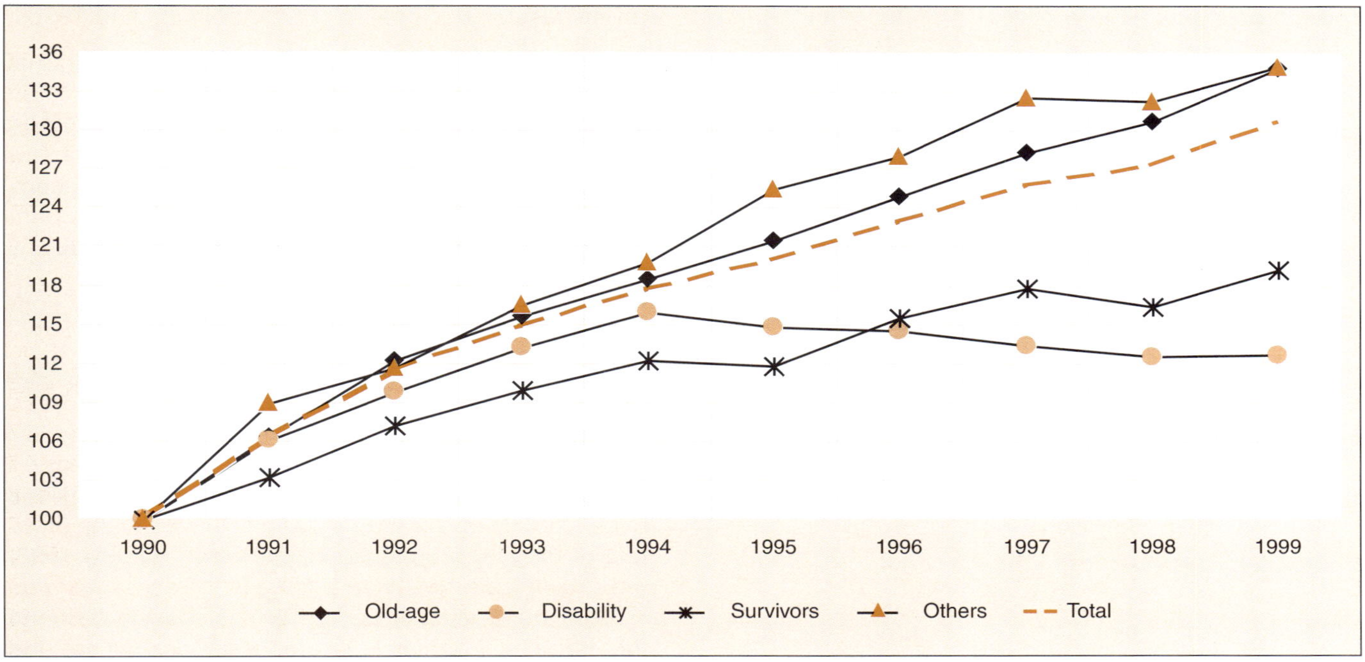

Source: Eurostat, Esspros.

The regular real growth in expenditure on old age pensions leads to an increase in its proportion of total pension expenditure

From 1990 to 1999, the various components of pension expenditure grew at different rates, reflecting the reforms undertaken over the last few years by the Member States and the demographic evolution. These variations affect the structure of the pensions.

In real terms, expenditure on old-age pensions in EU-15 increased by 35 % between 1990 and 1999. This growth led to an increase in its proportion of total pension expenditure (+ 2.5 %), which reached 75.3 % of the EU-15 total in 1999.

In Portugal and Luxembourg, these pensions rose considerably faster than the average EU rate for 1990 to 1999, namely + 8.4 % and 5.3 % per annum in real terms, compared to the EU-15 average of + 3.4 %. In these countries, over that period, the proportion of old-age pensions in total pensions nonetheless remained below the European average, even though it came closer to the average. Luxembourg's situation is unusual, in that an increasing percentage of pensions are being paid to non-residents, which complicates the interpretation of rates of growth.

In Spain, Greece and Italy, the rate of growth in real terms was also higher than the EU-15 average. In contrast, expenditure rose more slowly in Ireland and the Netherlands (1.4 % and 2.1 % respectively).

However, if real expenditure on old-age pensions is looked at on a per capita basis for the over-65s (excluding the demographic factor), the highest rate is still to be found in Portugal (+ 6.7 % per annum between 1990 and 1999), though Denmark and the United Kingdom are close behind.

In contrast, in Greece and Italy, the rate of growth in real terms on a per capita basis for the over-65s is below the European average. This is in part due to rapid growth in the population over 65 between 1990 and 1999 (over 2.0 % per annum, compared to the EU-15 average of 1.4 %, excluding the effect of the integration of the new *Länder* in Germany).

The trend in pensions expenditure in EU-15 on a per capita basis for the over-65s was irregular throughout the period in question. The changes depend on the previous careers of the new pensioners, the reforms undertaken in their countries, and their policies on pension adjustments.

Thus, in real terms, this expenditure grew by 1.6 % per annum between 1990 and 1993 despite the decrease of the average pensions in Germany in 1991 due to the integration of the new *Länder*. In contrast, the average increase in pension expenditure per capita from 1993 to 1998 was just 1.3 % per annum in EU-15. Lastly, in 1999, growth in expenditure on old-age pensions picked up again (+ 1.8 % per annum in EU-15).

Table 6.4.11. Expenditure on old-age pensions at 1995 constant prices (index 1990 = 100) per head (population over 65)

	1993	1996	1997	1998	1999
EU-15	105	109	110	112	114
EUR-12	103	106	106	108	110
B	114	108	108	109	111
DK	109	137	137	138	140
D	96	100	99	100	102
EL	91	95	99	107	111
E	110	114	115	115	116
F	102	108	105	110	111
IRL	103	96	99	105	108
I	107	106	111	110	113
L	119	125	129	128	132
NL	100	98	100	103	108
A	108	112	111	111	114
P	128	155	156	166	179
FIN	108	112	112	112	114
S	:	:	:	:	:
UK	118	126	131	130	134
IS	105	111	117	128	135
NO	108	119	123	133	139
CH	110	115	118	122	124

Source: Eurostat, Esspros.

The average increase in total expenditure on pensions from 1990 to 1999 was 31 % in real terms. The type of pension for which expenditure increased least was disability pensions, at 13 % in real terms. As a percentage of total pension expenditure, these account for steadily less over the period (11.5 % in 1990 compared to 9.9 % in 1999).

In the face of increasing expenditure and numbers of beneficiaries during the 1980s, many attempts were made to limit entitlement to this benefit to those individuals who really were unable to work because of their disability. This was particularly the case in the Netherlands, where the conditions to qualify for a disability pension became much stricter in the mid-1990s.

In Ireland, at the other end of the scale, growth in real terms was high: 6.9 % per annum as compared to an EU-15 average of 1.3 % per annum from 1990 to 1999. This is partly due to the increase over the last few years in disability pensions granted to persons receiving care in an institution and to an increase in the benefit paid to couples where both parties are disabled.

In spite of the ageing population throughout the EU, one of the main trends in the structure of pension expenditure from 1990 to 1999 was the growth in expenditure on other pensions categories, which was equal to that on old-age pensions.

Part of this increase can be attributed to the recession in the early 1990s, when early retirement pensions were seen as one of the possible solutions to the problem of long-term unemployment. From 1990 to 1993, the growth rate for these pensions in real terms was + 5.2 % per annum in EU-15. This is especially due to the trend in Germany for this category, where the growth was + 5.4 % per annum. This category covers mainly expenditure on early retirement benefits for labour market reasons, largely due to the integration of the new *Länder*.

In the years that followed, the conditions for obtaining early retirement pensions were made stricter, which slowed down the growth in expenditure in this area in EU-15. In real terms, its growth rate decreased from 1993 to 1999 (+ 2.5 % per annum), as did its share of total pension expenditure. In Italy, Portugal and Belgium, the expenditure actually decreased, particularly from 1996 onwards.

Lastly, expenditure on survivors' pensions increased in real terms at a rather weak 2.0 % per year in EU-15 from 1990 to 1999 and their share of total pension expenditure decreased.

Table 6.4.12. Breakdown of pension expenditure between categories, EU-15 (as a % of total)

	1990	1993	1996	1997	1998	1999
Old-age pension	72.8	73.4	74.0	74.4	75.0	75.3
Disability pension	11.5	11.2	10.6	10.3	10.1	9.9
Survivors' pension	10.8	10.2	10.0	10.0	9.7	9.7
Other pension categories	4.9	5.1	5.3	5.2	5.1	5.1
Total pensions	100.0	100.0	100.0	100.0	100.0	100.0

Source: Eurostat, Esspros.

7. Money, interest rates and prices in the Union

7.1. Exchange rates, the euro and EMU

The third stage of economic and monetary union (EMU) began with the introduction of the single currency, the euro, on 1 January 1999. In May 1998 the European Council announced the 11 countries that would be part of economic and monetary union from the outset: Austria, Belgium, Finland, France, Germany, Ireland, Italy, Luxembourg, Netherlands, Portugal and Spain. On 1 January 1999 the currencies of these countries were fixed against the euro at an irrevocable conversion rate (see Table 7.1.1) and they thus became non-decimal subdivisions of the euro. On that date the euro also replaced the ecu at a rate of 1 to 1. Rounding rules apply for the conversion of currencies (see box).

> **Rounding rules (summary)**
>
> *Conversion from national currency to euro*
>
> The official euro conversion rates are always to six figures. In order to ensure accuracy, these rates must not be shortened or rounded off during conversion. To convert a national currency amount into euro, the amount must be multiplied by the appropriate conversion rate. An amount in euro can be converted to national currency by dividing by the conversion rate.
>
> *Conversion of two euro-zone currencies*
>
> Conversion must always be via the euro, using the conversion rates.
>
> *Conversion of euro-zone currency and third currency*
>
> Conversion must also be via the euro, but using the third currency's current exchange rate against the euro.

> **Milestones in EMU**
>
> **1 January 1999**
>
> — Introduction of the euro and its use in non-cash form
> — Entry into force of the legislation (principle of "neither obligation nor prohibition", the rounding rules)
> — Definition and implementation of monetary policy by the ECB and the ESCB
> — Exchange transactions in euro
> — Public debt issuance in euro
> — Introduction of TARGET settlement system
>
> **1 January 2002**
>
> — Introduction of euro notes and coins
> — All accounting in euro
> — Gradual withdrawal of national currency notes and coins
>
> **28 February 2002 (D: 31/12/2001, NL: 28/01/2002, IRL: 09/02/2002, F: 17/02/2002)**
>
> — National currencies no longer legal tender

In June 2000 the European Council agreed that Greece would join the list of euro-zone countries with effect from 1 January 2001. Euro notes and coins were introduced in cash form throughout the 12 countries of the euro-zone in January 2002, and by the end of February 2002 national currency denominations lost their legal tender status.

ERM and ERM II

Between March 1979 and the end of 1998 the exchange rate mechanism (ERM) linked the currencies that were part of the European Monetary System (EMS). From August 1993 their exchange rates were obliged to remain within fluctuation bands of 15 % around the bilateral central rates. In March 1998, when the Greek drachma joined the ERM, the central rates were adjusted for the last time, with the Irish pound being revalued by 3 %. For the last 10 months of its existence the ERM included 13 Member State currencies: only the pound sterling and the Swedish krona (a "notional" central rate applied to the former) were not part of the system.

ERM II came into existence on 1 January 1999, linking to the euro the Greek drachma and the Danish krone, the currencies of two Member States that did not join the euro-zone from the outset. (The other two currencies, the pound sterling and the Swedish krona, did not join ERM II). The aim of ERM II is to prepare the second-wave countries for eventual participation in the euro-zone, while helping to ensure exchange rate stability within the EU. The two currencies had a central rate against the euro of 340.750 in the case of the GRD and 7.46038 for the DKK. Their fluctuation bands were ± 15 % for the GRD and ± 2.25 % for the DKK. The fluctuation band is supported at the margins by unlimited intervention, with short-term financing available. However, the European Central Bank (ECB), as well as the national central banks not participating in the euro-zone, can suspend intervention if the main purpose — maintaining price stability — can no longer be guaranteed.

Greece entered the euro-zone in January 2001 at a conversion rate against the euro identical to its central rate in ERM II. Therefore, from 1 January 2001 only the DKK remains a member of ERM II.

MONEY, INTEREST RATES AND PRICES IN THE UNION

Exchange rates

The official exchange rates for the ecu, as it existed until 31 December 1998, against its constituent currencies and other currencies were calculated every day by the European Commission on the basis of the composition of the ecu basket.

From 1 January 1999 (1 January 2001 for Greece), the exchange rates of the countries which formed the euro-zone were fixed to the euro, before being replaced by the euro in 2002. Every day the European Central Bank provides the official reference rates for the main international currencies against the euro.

Table 7.1.1 shows the exchange rates of the ecu (until 1998) and euro (from 1999) against the national currencies of the EU Member States, the USD and JPY since 1990. The figures indicate the value of an ecu or euro in national currency. For the countries belonging to the euro-zone from 1 January 1999, the exchange rates shown from 1999 to 2001 are the fixed conversion rates to the euro.

Table 7.1.2 shows the nominal effective exchange rate indices of EU currencies, the base year being 1995. Nominal effective series measure changes in the value of a currency against a trade-weighted basket of currencies. A rise in the index means a strengthening of the currency. The trade-weighted basket contains 24 industrial countries, using double export weights. The EU-15 and euro-zone aggregates are calculated by taking as weights each country's share of extra-EU or extra-EMU trade. The effective exchange rates for individual euro-zone countries will continue to vary even in a monetary union because of differing trade patterns and cost or price trends.

In 2001, between 1 January and 31 December, the following fluctuations against the euro took place:

— ERM II member currencies: the Danish krone (DKK) appreciated by 0.36 % ;
— the pound sterling (GBP) gained 2.56 % and the Swedish krona (SEK) lost 5.05 %;
— the US dollar (USD) appreciated by 5.58 % and Japanese yen (JPY) depreciated by 7.29 %.

In the first five months of 2002 these currencies fluctuated against the euro as follows:

— the Danish krone (DKK), which is for the moment the only member of ERM II, appreciated by 0.06 %;
— the pound sterling (GBP) depreciated by 5.0 % and the Swedish krona (SEK) appreciated by 2.13 %;
— the US dollar (USD) and the Japanese yen (JYP) lost 6.11 % and 0.91 % of their value respectively.

Table 7.1.1. Ecu/eur exchange rates, annual average

		1996	1997	1998	1999 [1]	2000 [1]	2001 [1]	January to May 2002
B/L	BEF/LUF	39.2986	40.5332	40.6207	40.3399	40.3399	40.3399	–
DK	DKK	7.35934	7.48361	7.49930	7.43556	7.4538169	7.45207	7.43297
D	DEM	1.90954	1.96438	1.96913	1.95583	1.95583	1.95583	–
EL	GRD	305.546	309.355	330.731	325.763	336.630	340.750	–
E	ESP	160.748	165.887	167.184	166.386	166.386	166.386	–
F	FRF	6.49300	6.61260	6.60141	6.55957	6.55957	6.55957	–
IRL	IEP	0.793448	0.747516	0.786245	0.787564	0.787564	0.787564	–
I	ITL	1958.96	1929.30	1943.65	1936.27	1936.27	1936.27	–
NL	NLG	2.13973	2.21081	2.21967	2.20371	2.20371	2.20371	–
A	ATS	13.4345	13.8240	13.8545	13.7603	13.7603	13.7603	–
P	PTE	195.761	198.589	201.695	200.482	200.482	200.482	–
FIN	FIM	5.82817	5.88064	5.98251	5.94573	5.94573	5.94573	–
S	SEK	8.51472	8.65117	8.91593	8.80752	8.44519	9.25511	9.165246
UK	GBP	0.813798	0.692304	0.676434	0.658735	0.609478	0.621874	0.6172458
US	USD	1.26975	1.13404	1.12109	1.06578	0.923613	0.895630	0.8863928
JP	JPY	138.084	137.077	146.415	121.317	99.475	108.682	115.953

[1] The following currencies are fixed against the euro at the rates shown: BEF, LUF, DEM, ESP, FRF, IEP, ITL, NLG, ATS, PTE, FIM from 1999, GRD from 2001.
Source: Eurostat.

Table 7.1.2. Nominal effective exchange rate indices, annual averages (base 1995 = 100)

		1996	1997	1998	1999 (¹)	2000 (¹)	2001 (¹)	January to May 2002
EU-15	EUR	105.7	105.1	113.0	111.0	101.8	106.3	107.4
Euro-zone	EUR	102.2	95.6	98.5	96.1	88.0	90.8	91.3
B/L	BEF/LUF	98.3	94.2	95.0	94.1	91.0	92.2	92.6
DK	DKK	99.6	96.7	98.0	96.7	92.4	94.1	94.6
D	DEM	98.4	94.2	95.8	94.5	90.3	91.6	91.9
EL	GRD	99.6	98.7	94.9	95.9	90.6	91.9	92.3
E	ESP	101.4	97.1	97.7	96.7	93.8	95.0	95.3
F	FRF	100.7	97.2	98.9	97.5	93.4	94.8	95.0
IRL	IEP	102.7	104.8	100.3	97.5	92.1	93.0	93.2
I	ITL	110.5	111.4	112.8	111.1	106.7	108.2	108.5
NL	NLG	98.4	94.5	95.1	94.4	91.5	92.6	92.8
A	ATS	98.5	96.1	97.3	96.8	94.3	95.3	95.5
P	PTE	100.7	98.3	97.6	96.6	94.0	94.6	94.7
FIN	FIM	97.8	95.0	95.1	93.7	89.8	91.7	91.6
S	SEK	110.2	106.2	105.2	104.0	104.0	96.3	97.1
UK	GBP	102.2	119.3	124.9	125.3	129.1	128.2	129.6
US	USD	106.1	114.9	122.4	122.1	127.9	135.0	138.3
JP	JPY	87.5	82.8	78.4	91.8	103.0	93.7	87.1

(¹) The euro from 1999.
Source: DG ECFIN.

7.2. Interest rates

Interest rates are among the basic indicators for any analysis of a country's economic situation. The durability of convergence achieved by a Member State is reflected in the level of long-term interest rates (one of the Maastricht Treaty convergence criteria), as measured by government 10-year bond yields (see Table 7.2.1). Short-term interest rates (generally the day-to-day money rate, see Table 7.2.2) show the situation on the money market. The difference between these two representative rates determines the structural tendency of the yield curve (rising, falling or stable). This difference and changes over time can be used for forecasting analyses.

Long-term rates

The notable feature as regards long-term interest rates in the euro-zone at present is a parallel trend for national rates coupled with figures very close to the lowest (i.e. German) rate. For 2001, the largest gap was between the long-term Greek and German rates, and was only 50 basis points (bp). There was a difference of only 6bp between Luxembourg and Germany. In 2002, the differences between national rates are tending to shrink even further. In April, the gap between Greece and Germany had fallen by 14bp to 36bp and between Luxembourg and Germany it is only 4bp.

The start of 2002 was marked by the slight rise in interest rates which had begun in December 2001, following a fall in the previous few months. Thus the long-term rates in April 2002 were at roughly the same level as in May 2001: 5.3 %.

Long-term interest rates for EU-15 were at much the same level as in the euro-zone, although Sweden had a higher rate. Any comparison of these two values must take account of the differences in the methodology on which they are based. The EU-15 aggregate is an arithmetic mean of the national values weighted by GDP, whereas the euro-zone aggregate is an arithmetic mean calculated on the basis of representative government bond yields, with the mean weighted by bonds outstanding.

The United States' long-term rates are currently close to the European level and have been since December 2000, whereas the level of Japanese long-term rates is very different, at 1.45 % for the first few months of 2002, an extremely low level which is likely to persist throughout 2002.

Delving further into the past we see that the most spectacular change in long-term rates in the EU Member States was between 1996 and the end of 1998, during which period there were two interesting phenomena: a widespread fall in long-term yields in all EU countries to give an all-time low, and the fact that this drop led to an unprecedented convergence of rates. In January 1996, the Netherlands had the lowest

Table 7.2.1. Long-term interest rates (10-year government bond yields, period average, as a %)

	1996	1997	1998	1999	2000	2001	Jan. 2002	Feb. 2002	Mar. 2002	Apr. 2002
EU-15	7.47	6.25	4.91	4.73	5.42	5.00	5.00	5.06	5.30	5.30
Euro-zone	7.23	5.98	4.70	4.66	5.44	5.03	5.02	5.07	5.32	5.30
B	6.49	5.75	4.75	4.75	5.59	5.13	5.08	5.15	5.37	5.37
DK	7.19	6.26	4.94	4.91	5.64	5.08	5.08	5.15	5.40	5.40
D	6.22	5.64	4.57	4.50	5.26	4.80	4.86	4.92	5.16	5.15
EL	14.36	9.91	8.47	6.30	6.10	5.30	5.24	5.31	5.50	5.51
E	8.73	6.40	4.83	4.73	5.53	5.12	5.05	5.11	5.34	5.34
F	6.31	5.58	4.64	4.61	5.39	4.94	4.93	4.99	5.24	5.24
IRL	7.29	6.29	4.79	4.72	5.51	5.01	5.02	5.20	5.42	5.41
I	9.40	6.86	4.88	4.73	5.58	5.19	5.14	5.20	5.41	5.40
L	6.32	5.60	4.73	4.67	5.52	4.86	4.84	4.91	5.16	5.19
NL	6.15	5.58	4.63	4.63	5.40	4.96	4.97	5.03	5.27	5.25
A	6.32	5.68	4.71	4.68	5.56	5.07	5.08	5.06	5.35	5.38
P	8.56	6.36	4.87	4.79	5.60	5.16	5.06	5.14	5.31	5.36
FIN	7.07	5.96	4.79	4.73	5.48	5.04	5.05	5.10	5.33	5.32
S	8.02	6.62	4.99	4.99	5.37	5.11	5.27	5.36	5.63	5.69
UK	7.94	7.14	5.58	5.02	5.33	5.01	5.02	5.04	5.34	5.33
US	6.54	6.45	5.33	5.64	6.03	5.01	5.00	4.90	5.28	5.21
JP	3.04	2.15	1.29	1.75	1.76	1.34	1.42	1.52	1.45	1.39

Source: Eurostat.

rate and some countries — Spain (358bp), Greece (953bp), Italy (456bp) and Portugal (357bp) — were nowhere near it. By December 1998 the picture was very different. The gap between the lowest (German) rate and the others had narrowed considerably: Spain (21bp), Greece (331bp), Italy (14bp) and Portugal (26bp). The Greek long-term rates started off from such a high level that they took longer to match the other European rates, but by December 2000 the gap between the Greek and German rates had narrowed to 65bp.

After a slight rise between January and the end of October 1999, long-term interest rates in the euro-zone levelled out a little but did not remain slack for long, since yields then rose substantially to a peak in January 2000.

After that — and through most of 2001 — long-term yields in the euro-zone continued to fall, but that tendency was reversed in November 2001 and the new trend spilled over into the first quarter of 2002.

In the United States, long-term yields also tended to weaken during 2000 after strengthening throughout 1999.

In Japan, yields tended to rise at the start of 1999, but this tendency was short-lived, since Japanese bond yields started to fall during the first quarter of 1999 before becoming more stable in 2000.

Short-term rates

The reference rate for the euro-zone money market is the EONIA (Euro OverNight Index Average), which is a weighted average of overnight unsecured lending transactions calculated by the European Central Bank (ECB). As from January 1999, the EONIA has replaced national rates.

For a clearer understanding of how interest rates behave on the money market, information is needed on changes in official short-term rates fixed by the central banks. One important point for this analysis is that countries wishing to join the euro-zone from the outset had to have identical official interest rates on 31 December 1998.

For the 11 countries in question, this convergence was achieved as follows:

One group of countries — Belgium, Germany, France, Luxembourg, the Netherlands, Austria and Finland — had already had relatively low official interest rates for several years and maintained those rates at roughly the same level.

In contrast, countries such as Spain, Italy and Portugal, which had had higher official rates in the recent past, were obliged to reduce their rates steadily to make them converge with the level in force in the other countries.

Table 7.2.2. Short-term interest rates (day-to-day money rates, period average, as a %)

	1996	1997	1998	1999	2000	2001	Jan. 2002	Feb. 2002	Mar. 2002	Apr. 2002
EU-15	5.12	4.67	4.54	3.26	4.46	4.50	3.40	3.44	3.42	3.42
Euro-zone	:	:	:	2.74	4.12	4.38	3.29	3.28	3.26	3.32
B	3.21	3.36	3.51	–	–	–	–	–	–	–
DK	3.89	3.53	4.11	3.11	4.37	4.70	3.54	3.57	3.52	3.45
D	3.27	3.18	3.41	–	–	–	–	–	–	–
EL	13.31	12.93	12.58	10.41	8.20	–	–	–	–	—
E	7.65	5.49	4.34	–	–	–	–	–	–	–
F	3.73	3.24	3.36	–	–	–	–	–	–	–
IRL	5.22	6.08	5.78	–	–	–	–	–	–	–
I	9.10	7.02	5.23	–	–	–	–	–	–	–
NL	2.89	3.07	3.21	–	–	–	–	–	–	–
A	3.19	3.27	3.36	–	–	–	–	–	–	–
P	7.38	5.83	4.34	–	–	–	–	–	–	–
FIN	3.63	2.86	3.26	–	–	–	–	–	–	—
S	6.29	4.21	4.24	3.14	3.81	4.09	3.85	3.85	3.94	4.10
UK	5.88	6.53	7.24	5.23	5.85	5.04	3.79	4.06	4.02	3.75
US	5.30	5.46	5.35	4.97	6.24	3.89	1.73	1.74	1.73	1.75
JP	0.47	0.48	0.37	0.06	0.11	0.06	0.00	0.00	0.00	0.00

Source: Eurostat.

Ireland was different again, raising the official rates to 6.75 % in May 1997 before making several reductions during the final two months of 1998.

Since the 11 countries all had the same official rate on 31 December 1998, EMU could begin, with the key repo rate at 3 %. In April 1999, the European Central Bank (ECB) reduced its repo rate to 2.5 % before raising it to 3 % in the November of that year. This upward trend was reinforced in 2000 by several rate rises, to 4.75 % by the end of the year. Since May 2001, the repo rate has steadily fallen, to 3.3 % in April 2002.

The other EU countries have a somewhat different scenario. The official rates in Denmark and Sweden fell several times during 1999 before their central banks raised them during November. In 2000, both of these countries continued to raise their key rates, but the rise was steeper in Denmark than in Sweden. In October 2000, this trend was reversed in Denmark, and key rates have been falling since then. In April 2002, Denmark's repo rate was 3.55 %. In Sweden, the upward tendency continued, interrupted only by a fall in September 2001. At the start of May 2002, the Swedish repo rate stood at 4.25 %. The Bank of England raised its repo rate twice at the beginning of 2000 (from 5.5 to 6.0 %) and then left it unchanged for the rest of the year. Since February 2001, the rate has fallen steadily, to 4 % in April 2002.

Greece cut these key rates many times during 2000, with the repo rate falling from 10.75 to 4.75 %. By the end of December 2000, it was at the same level as in the euro-zone Member States, and Greece became the twelfth member.

In the United States, the Federal Reserve raised the federal funds rate from 5.5 to 6.00 % during the first half of 2000, and then left it unchanged for the rest of the year. Since January 2001, the "fed funds" rate has fallen steadily, from 6.50 to 1.75 % by April 2002.

In Japan, the discount rate fixed at 0.5 % since September 1995 was cut twice during the first quarter of 2001 to 0.25 %. In September 2001, there was a further fall and the rate is now at its lowest ever: 0.1 %.

The structural tendency in the yield curve is currently upwards for all countries under observation. However, the gap between the long-term and the short-term rates is much larger in the United States, and thus the American yield curve has a sharper slope than that of Japan or the European Union.

7.3. Consumer prices

Consumer price inflation is best compared at international level by the "harmonised indices of consumer prices" (HICPs). They are calculated in each Member State of the European Union, Iceland and Norway and also in most candidate countries. HICPs form the basis of the monetary union index of consumer prices (MUICP) for the euro-zone, the EICP for EU-15 and the EEAICP for the European economic area. HICPs are not intended to replace national consumer price indices (CPIs). Member States have continued so far to produce their national CPIs for domestic purposes.

HICPs and the MUICP are used by, among others, the European Central Bank for monitoring inflation in the economic and monetary union and the assessment of inflation convergence. As required by the Treaty, the maintenance of price stability is the primary objective of the European Central Bank (ECB). The ECB defined price stability "as a year-on-year increase in the harmonised index of consumer prices for the euro-zone of below 2 %, to be maintained over the medium term".

The MUICP was published for the first time for the 11 countries initially participating in the third stage of EMU with the release of the index for April 1998. At the beginning of 2001 Greece joined the euro-zone and the MUICP covers the 12 Member States now. The MUICP was chain-linked in December 2000 to include Greece starting with the January 2001 index, since the euro-zone is treated as an entity regardless of its composition.

Trends in consumer price inflation 1999-2002

The annual rate of change (m / m-12) is commonly used for analysing inflation trends. This measure is appropriate for short-term analysis, although it suffers from variability due to one-off effects (such as tax changes). Table 7.3.1 and Figure 7.3.1 show the annual rates of change in the HICPs, the MUICP and the EICP for every third month between January 1999 and April 2002.

The annual rates of change of the EICP illustrate an overall rising trend from 0.9 % in January 1999 to as high as 3.0 % in May 2001. This trend was reversed from June 2001 and the annual rate of change dropped to 1.8 % in November 2001. Since then, the annual rate of change of the EICP has risen somewhat. Since June 2000 the annual rate of change of

Table 7.3.1. Harmonised Indices of consumer prices (1999-2002), annual rates of change as a % (m/m–12)

	1999 Jan.	1999 Apr.	1999 Jul.	1999 Oct.	2000 Jan.	2000 Apr.	2000 Jul.	2000 Oct.	2001 Jan.	2001 Apr.	2001 Jul.	2001 Oct.	2002 Jan.	2002 Apr.
B	1.0	1.1	0.7	1.4	0.3	2.3	1.7	3.7	2.7	2.9	2.5	2.3	2.6	1.7
D	0.2	0.8	0.6	0.9	1.9	1.6	2.0	2.4	2.2	2.9	2.6	2.0	2.3	1.6
EL	3.3	2.6	1.6	1.7	2.4	2.1	2.6	3.8	3.2	3.7	4.2	3.2	4.8	4.1
E	1.5	2.3	2.1	2.4	2.9	3.0	3.7	4.0	3.8	4.0	2.4	2.5	3.1	3.7
F	0.3	0.5	0.4	0.8	1.7	1.4	2.0	2.1	1.4	2.0	2.2	1.8	2.4	2.1
IRL	2.1	2.0	1.9	2.8	4.4	5.0	5.9	6.0	3.9	4.3	4.0	3.8	5.2	5.0
I	1.5	1.3	1.7	1.9	2.2	2.4	2.6	2.7	2.7	3.0	2.4	2.4	2.4	2.5
L	– 1.4	1.3	– 0.3	1.9	3.5	3.2	4.7	4.3	2.9	2.7	2.4	1.7	2.1	1.9
NL	2.1	1.9	1.8	1.8	1.6	1.7	2.8	3.2	4.5	5.3	5.3	5.0	4.9	4.2
A	0.3	0.1	0.3	0.8	1.4	1.8	2.0	2.2	2.2	2.5	2.8	2.3	2.0	1.6
P	2.5	2.7	1.9	1.8	1.9	1.9	3.3	3.7	4.4	4.6	4.3	4.2	3.7	3.5
FIN	0.5	1.3	1.4	1.6	2.3	2.5	2.9	3.4	2.9	2.8	2.6	2.4	2.8	2.6
MUICP	0.8	1.1	1.1	1.4	1.9	1.9	2.3	2.7	2.4	2.9	2.6	2.3	2.7	2.4
DK	1.2	1.7	2.0	2.6	2.8	2.9	2.8	2.8	2.3	2.6	2.3	2.0	2.5	2.3
S	0.0	0.3	0.2	1.0	1.0	1.0	1.3	1.3	1.6	3.0	2.9	2.9	2.9	2.2
UK	1.6	1.5	1.3	1.2	0.8	0.6	1.0	1.0	0.9	1.1	1.4	1.2	1.6	1.3
EICP	0.9	1.2	1.1	1.3	1.8	1.7	2.1	2.4	2.2	2.6	2.5	2.2	2.5	2.2
US	1.7	2.3	2.1	2.6	2.8	3.1	3.7	3.4	3.7	3.3	2.7	2.1	1.1	1.6
JP	0.2	– 0.1	– 0.1	– 0.7	– 0.9	– 0.8	– 0.5	– 0.9	0.1	– 0.4	– 0.8	– 0.8	– 1.4	– 1.1

NB: m/m–12 is the price change between the current month and the same month in the previous year.
Please note that for the United States and Japan the national CPIs are given which are not strictly comparable with the HICPs.
Source: Eurostat.

MONEY, INTEREST RATES AND PRICES IN THE UNION

the MUICP has been significantly beyond the 2.0 % stability threshold defined by the ECB with a maximum of 3.3 % in May 2001. It could also be noted that the annual rates of change of the MUICP have been generally higher than those of the EICP since October 1999.

A more stable measure — the 12-month average change — is the average index for the latest 12 months compared with the average index for the previous 12 months. It is less sensitive to transient changes in prices but it requires a longer time series of indices. Nevertheless, similar trends to those described above may be noted, as shown in Table 7.3.2. In April 2002 the 12-month average rate of change is at 2.5 % for the MUICP. This is higher than the 2.0 % set by the ECB as a medium-term price stability threshold for the euro-zone. For the EICP the same rate was 2.3 %. The situation was the same one year ago.

The protocol on convergence criteria relating to Article 109(j)(1) of the Treaty requires that a Member State's rate of inflation "does not exceed by more than 1fi percentage points that of, at most, the three best performing Member States". Table 7.3.2 shows some summary data based on 12-month average changes. Reference values have been calculated using a simple arithmetic mean of "the three best performing EU Member States" and "the three best performing euro-zone Member States".

Since January 2000, Austria, France, Germany and later also Italy have been among the three best performing Member States in the euro-zone as shown in Table 7.3.2. France, Sweden, and the United Kingdom were among the three best performing Member States in the EU in 2000. From May 2001 to April 2002, the United Kingdom and France have been permanently among the three best performing EU Member States.

Table 7.3.2 also shows which Member States were above or below the reference values in each month. Ireland, Spain and Luxembourg were above both reference values during nearly all of 2000, and Ireland continued to do so up to August 2001. Since September 2001, the Netherlands has been continuously above the reference value. From the end of 2001 until April 2002 Portugal and Greece were also above the reference value. Finland, Greece, Spain and Luxembourg too were between the (present) lower EU reference value and the euro-zone reference value for nearly the whole of the year 2001. The average spread of inflation rates, which is shown in Figure 7.3.2, provides a useful tool for illustrating inflation convergence since the early stages of the EMU. The spread is calculated as the standard deviation of annual inflation rates of HICPs from the EICP taking country weights into account.

Household consumption patterns

The consumption patterns of households determine the relative importance (weight) of household monetary expenditure that is attached to each of the categories of goods and services covered by the HICP. The impact on the all-items index of any price change is proportional to the size of the corresponding weight.

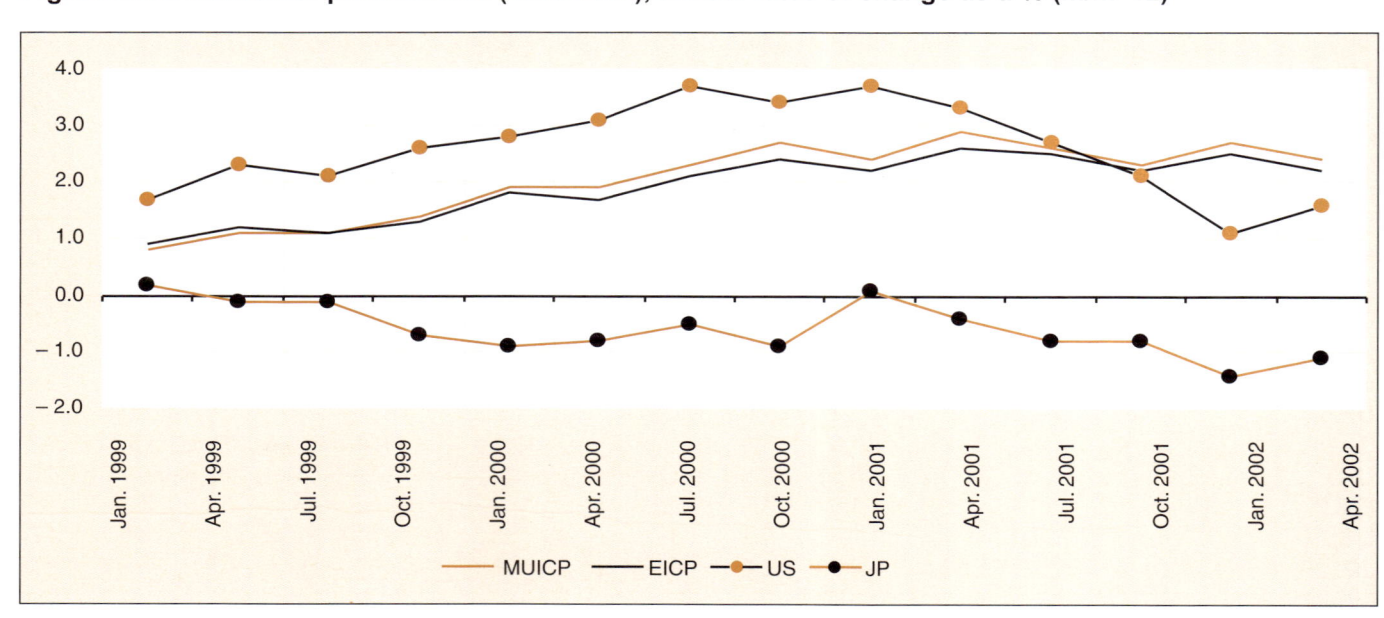

Figure 7.3.1. Consumer price indices (1999-2002), annual rates of change as a % (m/m–12)

NB: m/m–12 is the price change between the current month and the same month in the previous year.
Please note that for the United States and Japan the national CPIs are given which are not strictly comparable with the HICPs.
Source: Eurostat.

MONEY, INTEREST RATES AND PRICES IN THE UNION

Table 7.3.2. Harmonised indices of consumer prices (2000-02), 12-month average rate ([1])

	2000 Jan.		Mar.		May		Jul.		Sep.		Nov.	2001 Jan.		Mar.		May		Jun.
A	0.6	S	0.8	S	0.9	UK	0.9	UK	0.9	UK	0.8	UK	0.8	UK	0.8	UK	1.0	UK	1.0
S	0.6	F	0.9	UK	1.0	S	1.1	S	1.2	S	1.3	S	1.4	S	1.4	S	1.7	F	1.9
F	0.7	A	0.9	F	1.1	F	1.3	F	1.6	F	1.8	F	1.8	F	1.8	F	1.9	S	1.9
D	0.8	D	1.1	A	1.1	D	1.5	D	1.7	A	1.9	A	2.0	A	2.0	A	2.2	A	2.2
B	1.1	UK	1.2	D	1.2	A	1.5	A	1.7	D	2.0	D	2.1	D	2.2	EICP	2.3	EICP	2.4
MUICP	1.2	B	1.3	B	1.5	EICP	1.7	EICP	1.8	EICP	2.0	EICP	2.1	EICP	2.2	D	2.5	D	2.5
UK	1.3	MUICP	1.4	EICP	1.5	B	1.8	MUICP	2.0	NL	2.3	MUICP	2.4	MUICP	2.4	MUICP	2.6	DK	2.5
EICP	1.3	EICP	1.4	MUICP	1.6	MUICP	1.8	NL	2.1	MUICP	2.3	I	2.6	DK	2.6	DK	2.6	MUICP	2.6
L	1.4	L	1.8	NL	1.9	NL	2.0	B	2.2	I	2.5	NL	2.6	I	2.7	I	2.6	I	2.6
FIN	1.5	FIN	1.8	P	1.9	P	2.0	P	2.3	B	2.6	DK	2.7	RV (EU)	2.8	B	3.0	B	3.0
I	1.7	I	1.9	EL	2.0	EL	2.2	EL	2.4	P	2.6	RV (EU)	2.8	B	2.9	RV (EU)	3.0	FIN	3.0
NL	2.0	NL	1.9	FIN	2.0	I	2.2	I	2.4	EL	2.8	B	2.9	FIN	2.9	FIN	3.0	RV (EU)	3.1
EL	2.1	P	1.9	I	2.1	FIN	2.3	FIN	2.6	DK	2.8	EL	3.0	EL	3.1	EL	3.3	EL	3.5
P	2.1	EL	2.0	L	2.1	RV (EU)	2.6	RV (EU)	2.7	RV (EU)	2.8	P	3.0	NL	3.1	E	3.5	E	3.6
RV (EU)	2.1	RV (EU)	2.4	RV (EU)	2.5	DK	2.8	DK	2.8	FIN	2.9	FIN	3.0	RV (EMU)	3.5	RV (EMU)	3.7	L	3.6
DK	2.2	DK	2.4	DK	2.6	DK	2.8	E	3.1	E	3.4	RV (EMU)	3.5	P	3.6	L	3.8	RV (EMU)	3.7
RV (EMU)	2.2	RV (EMU)	2.5	RV (EMU)	2.6	E	2.9	RV (EMU)	3.2	RV (EMU)	3.4	E	3.6	E	3.7	NL	3.8	NL	4.0
E	2.4	E	2.5	E	2.7	RV (EMU)	2.9	L	3.2	L	3.6	L	3.7	L	3.8	P	4.0	P	4.2
IRL	2.7	IRL	3.1	IRL	3.6	IRL	4.2	IRL	4.7	IRL	5.2	IRL	5.2	IRL	5.1	IRL	4.9	IRL	4.8

	2001 Jul.		Aug.		Sep.		Oct.		Nov.		Dec.	2002 Jan.		Feb.		Mar.		Apr.
UK	1.1	UK	1.2	UK	1.2	UK	1.2	UK	1.2	UK	1.2	UK	1.3	UK	1.3	UK	1.4	UK	1.4
F	2.0	F	2.0	F	1.9	F	1.9	F	1.8	F	1.8	F	1.9	F	1.9	F	2.0	F	2.0
S	2.0	S	2.1	A	2.3	A	2.3	A	2.3	EICP	2.3	EICP	2.3	DK	2.3	L	2.2	L	2.1
A	2.3	A	2.3	S	2.3	EICP	2.4	DK	2.3	DK	2.3	DK	2.3	D	2.3	A	2.2	D	2.2
EICP	2.4	EICP	2.4	EICP	2.4	DK	2.4	EICP	2.3	I	2.3	I	2.3	L	2.3	D	2.3	A	2.2
DK	2.5	DK	2.5	DK	2.5	I	2.4	I	2.4	A	2.3	L	2.3	A	2.3	DK	2.3	EICP	2.3
D	2.6	I	2.5	I	2.5	S	2.4	B	2.5	B	2.4	A	2.3	EICP	2.4	EICP	2.4	DK	2.3
I	2.6	MUICP	2.7	MUICP	2.6	MUICP	2.6	D	2.5	D	2.4	B	2.4	B	2.4	B	2.5	B	2.4
MUICP	2.7	D	2.7	D	2.6	D	2.6	MUICP	2.5	L	2.4	D	2.4	I	2.4	I	2.5	I	2.4
FIN	3.0	B	3.0	B	2.8	B	2.7	S	2.5	MUICP	2.5	MUICP	2.5	MUICP	2.5	MUICP	2.6	MUICP	2.5
B	3.1	FIN	3.0	FIN	2.9	FIN	2.8	FIN	2.7	FIN	2.7	FIN	2.7	FIN	2.6	FIN	2.6	FIN	2.6
RV (EU)	3.2	RV (EU)	3.3	E	3.2	L	2.9	L	2.7	S	2.7	E	2.8	E	2.9	E	2.9	E	2.9
E	3.5	E	3.3	L	3.2	E	3.1	E	2.9	E	2.8	S	2.8	S	2.9	S	3.0	S	2.9
L	3.5	L	3.4	RV (EU)	3.3	RV (EU)	3.3	RV (EU)	3.3	RV (EU)	3.3	RV (EU)	3.3	RV (EU)	3.3	RV (EU)	3.4	RV (EU)	3.3
EL	3.6	RV (EMU)	3.7	RV (EMU)	3.7	RV (EMU)	3.7	RV (EMU)	3.7	RV (EMU)	3.6	RV (EMU)	3.7	RV (EMU)	3.7	RV (EMU)	3.6	RV (EMU)	3.6
RV (EMU)	3.8	EL	3.7	EL	3.8	EL	3.8	EL	3.7	EL	3.7	EL	3.8	EL	3.8	EL	3.9	EL	3.9
NL	4.2	P	4.3	P	4.3	IRL	4.2	IRL	4.0	IRL	4.0	IRL	4.1	IRL	4.2	P	4.1	P	4.0
P	4.2	NL	4.4	IRL	4.4	P	4.4	P	4.4	P	4.4	P	4.3	P	4.2	IRL	4.3	IRL	4.3
IRL	4.7	IRL	4.5	NL	4.6	NL	4.8	NL	4.9	NL	5.1	NL	5.1	NL	5.1	NL	5.0	NL	4.9

([1]) Average of the last 12 months compared to the average of the previous 12 months.
NB: RV (EU) = reference value defined as unweighted arithmetic mean of the three best-performing countries in the EU/+ 1.5.
RV (EMU) = reference value defined as unweighted arithmetic mean of the three best-performing countries in the EMU/+ 1.5.
Source: Eurostat.

There is no uniform basket applying to all Member States. The structure of the weights may vary considerably between the HICPs for individual Member States as well as between the HICP for an individual Member State and the average weighting structure according to the EICP or the MUICP. The index is computed as an annual chain-index allowing for weights to change each year.

Table 7.3.3 gives an overview of the weights used in the 15 Member States, the euro-zone (MUICP) and for the EU (EICP) in 2002.

For 2002, according to the weighting patterns for the MUICP and the EICP, the divisions food, housing and transport are the three categories with the largest weights when calculated as averages for the country groupings concerned. A weight of approximately one sixth of the MUICP and slightly over 15 % of the EICP is attached to food, a slightly lower weight for both indices is attached to transport, about the same as for housing. A weight of around one tenth for both indices is attached to recreation and culture, though it is a bit more important for the EICP than for the MUICP. Closely below are the weights for restaurants and hotels, again slightly higher for the EICP.

MONEY, INTEREST RATES AND PRICES IN THE UNION

Figure 7.3.2. Average spread of inflation rates (weighted standard deviation), EU 15, 1996-2002

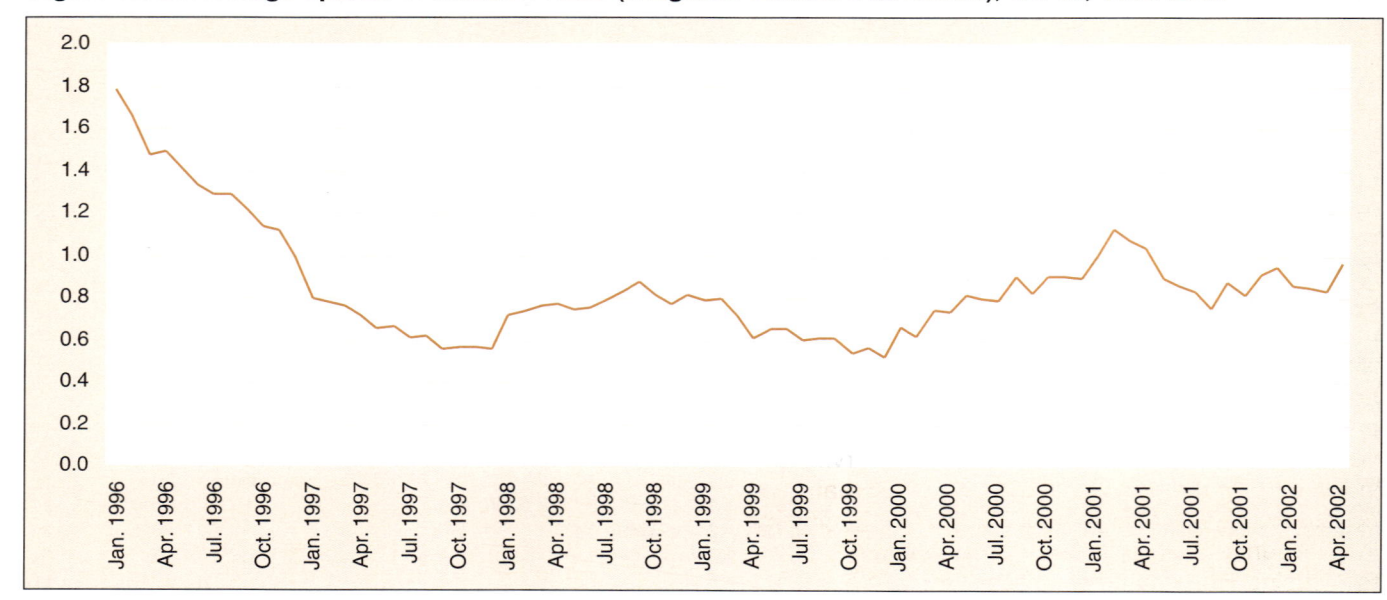

Source: Eurostat.

Table 7.3.3. Consumption weights in the EU, the EMU and the 15 Member States, as used in 2002 (‰)

	EICP	MUICP	B	DK	D	EL	E	F
Food and non-alcoholic beverages	156	164	171	161	141	186	216	170
Alcoholic beverages, tobacco and narcotics	42	40	31	59	46	49	32	40
Clothing and footwear	76	80	68	59	72	122	104	55
Housing, water, electricity, gas and other fuels	144	150	160	190	210	89	107	140
Furnishings, household equipment and routine maintenance of the house	77	79	77	69	74	73	62	69
Health	36	39	39	30	39	53	28	42
Transport	150	152	134	162	151	135	146	175
Communications	25	25	25	17	19	30	24	27
Recreation and culture	106	95	139	118	111	46	67	93
Education	11	9	5	9	7	19	17	5
Restaurants and hotels	97	90	83	55	50	141	149	88
Miscellaneous goods and services	80	77	68	72	81	57	47	96

	IRL	I	L	NL	A	P	FIN	S	UK
Food and non-alcoholic beverages	155	168	129	155	135	213	158	156	115
Alcoholic beverages, tobacco and narcotics	83	27	151	50	32	31	66	51	51
Clothing and footwear	56	114	62	63	69	66	56	74	61
Housing, water, electricity, gas and other fuels	81	96	91 93	197	142	90	142	188	107
Furnishings, household equipment and routine maintenance of the house	48	109	20	90	83	76	56	62	69
Health	28	37	176	44	42	57	48	30	23
Transport	138	138	17	127	146	204	163	140	140
Communications	21	34	83	17	30	17	38	35	24
Recreation and culture	119	79	4	111	113	38	116	119	159
Education	17	11	97	15	9	18	7	4	17
Restaurants and hotels	196	107	79	71	134	139	83	65	137
Miscellaneous goods and services	60	82		60	66	51	67	75	97

Source: Eurostat.

Within the national HICPs the weight for food varies between 11-15 % (the United Kingdom, Luxembourg, Austria and Germany) and 18-22 % (Greece, Portugal and Spain). For transport the weight varies between 12-14 % (the Netherlands, Belgium, Greece, Ireland and Italy) and 16-21 % (Denmark, France, Luxembourg and Portugal). In contrast, the weight for recreation and culture ranges between 4 % (Greece, Portugal) and 13-16 % (Belgium and the United Kingdom), and the weight for housing varies between 8-11 % (Ireland, Greece, Portugal, Italy and Luxembourg) and 18-21 % (Sweden, Denmark, the Netherlands and Germany). It should, however, be noted that HICPs capture only monetary expenditure and unlike national accounts or household budget surveys do not impute costs for the shelter service provided by owner occupied dwellings. This means that countries in which a larger proportion of the population lives in rented dwellings tend to have a larger weight for housing than countries in which a larger proportion of households lives in their own dwellings.

The weight of a Member State in the EMU or in the EU is its share of household final monetary consumption expenditure in the EMU or in the EU totals. The country weights used in 2002 are based on national accounts data for 2000 updated to December 2001 prices. For the EMU, weights in national currencies are converted into euro using the irrevocably locked exchange rates. For the EU, weights in national currencies are converted into purchasing power standards (PPS). The euro-zone country weight reflects its share in the EU total.

Table 7.3.4. Country weights (as a ‰) for 2002, price updated to December 2001 prices

	MUICP	EICP	EEAICP
B	33.97		
D	305.57		
EL	24.68		
E	103.43		
F	204.12		
IRL	12.08		
I	193.36		
L	2.56		
NL	52.00		
A	31.85		
P	20.45		
FIN	15.94		
MUICP	1 000.00	804.36	795.15
DK		13.73	13.58
S		18.41	18.20
UK		163.49	161.62
EICP		1 000.00	
IS			0.85
NO			10.60
EEAICP			1 000.00

NB: Due to rounding effects, the weights may not add up exactly to 1 000.
Source: Eurostat.

7.4. Purchasing power parities

Purchasing power parities and international volume comparisons

The differences in values of GDP expenditure between countries, even when revalued in a common currency using exchange rates, correspond not only to a "volume of goods and services" component but also to a "level of prices" component, which can sometimes assume sizeable proportions.

Exchange rates are determined by many factors, which reflect demand and supply on the currency markets, such as international trade and interest rate differentials. In other words, exchange rates usually reflect other elements than price differences alone. Therefore, the use of exchange rates as conversion factors in cross-country comparisons is not advisable.

To obtain a pure comparison of volumes, it is essential to use special conversion rates (spatial deflators) which remove the effect of price level differences between countries. Purchasing power parities (PPPs) are such currency conversion rates that convert economic indicators expressed in national currencies to an artificial common currency, called purchasing power standard (PPS), that equalises the purchasing power of different national currencies. In other words, PPPs are used to convert nominal final expenditures on product groups, aggregates and GDP of different countries into comparable expenditure volumes.

> **How are PPPs calculated and what is PPS?**
>
> In their simplest form, PPPs are a set of price relatives, which show the ratio of the prices in national currency of the same good or service in different countries (e.g. a loaf of bread costs EUR 1.87 in France, EUR 1.68 in Germany, GBP 0.95 in the United Kingdom, etc). For the price collections (see the box "International price and volume comparisons" at the end of this section), a basket of comparable goods and services is used which are selected to represent the whole range of goods and services, and to be representative of consumption patterns in the various countries.
>
> The simple price relatives at product level are subsequently aggregated (weighted together) to PPPs for groups of products, for total consumption and finally for GDP.

> To fix a *numéraire* for the numerical procedure of the PPP calculation, usually one country is used as a base country and set to equal 1. For the European Union the selection of a single country (currency) as a base seemed inappropriate. Therefore, PPS is the artificial common reference currency unit used in the European Union to express the volume of economic aggregates for the purpose of spatial comparisons in real terms. Economic volume aggregates in PPS are obtained by dividing their original value in national currency units by the respective PPPs. 1 PPS, therefore, buys the same given average volume of goods and services in all countries, whereas different amounts of national currency units are needed to buy this volume of goods and services, depending on the national price level.

Per capita GDP volume index

The per capita GDP volume indices shown in Figure 7.4.1 re calculated as real expenditure volumes (expenditure values in national currency, converted using PPPs) in per capita terms, expressed in relation to the European Union average. The data analysed here are preliminary and should, therefore, be interpreted with caution, as they are subject to revision. The final data for 2000 will be published in December 2002.

These indices are not intended to rank countries strictly. In fact, they only provide an indication of the comparative order of magnitude of the per capita GDP volumes in one country in relation to others. It is therefore preferable to use these indices for dividing countries into groups of a comparable level. The 2000 preliminary results presented here highlight in this respect the following groups of countries:

— Group I (> 125 % of the EU average): Norway and Luxembourg;
— Group II (> 110 % and <125 % of the EU average): the Netherlands, Austria, Iceland, Ireland, Denmark and Switzerland;
— Group III (> 90 % and <110 % of the EU average, i.e. close to the EU average): United Kingdom, France, Sweden, Finland, Germany, Italy and Belgium;
— Group IV (> 75 % — threshold for the Structural Funds ([1]) — and <90 % of the EU average): Cyprus and Spain;
— Group V (> 50 % and <75 % of the EU average): Hungary, the Czech Republic, Greece, Slovenia and Portugal;
— Group VI (<50 % of the EU average): Romania, Turkey, Bulgaria, Latvia, Lithuania, Estonia, Poland and Slovakia.

([1]) One of the particularly important uses of PPPs is for the European Commission to establish both the list of regions that could benefit from the EU Structural Funds as well as the amount of funds to be allocated to each region. One criterion for allocating these funds is based on PPP-converted GDP per capita being less than 75 % of the EU average. The aim of the Structural Funds is to gradually reduce economic disparities between and within EU Member States.

Figure 7.4.1. Per capita GDP volume indices, EU-15 = 100, 2000 preliminary results

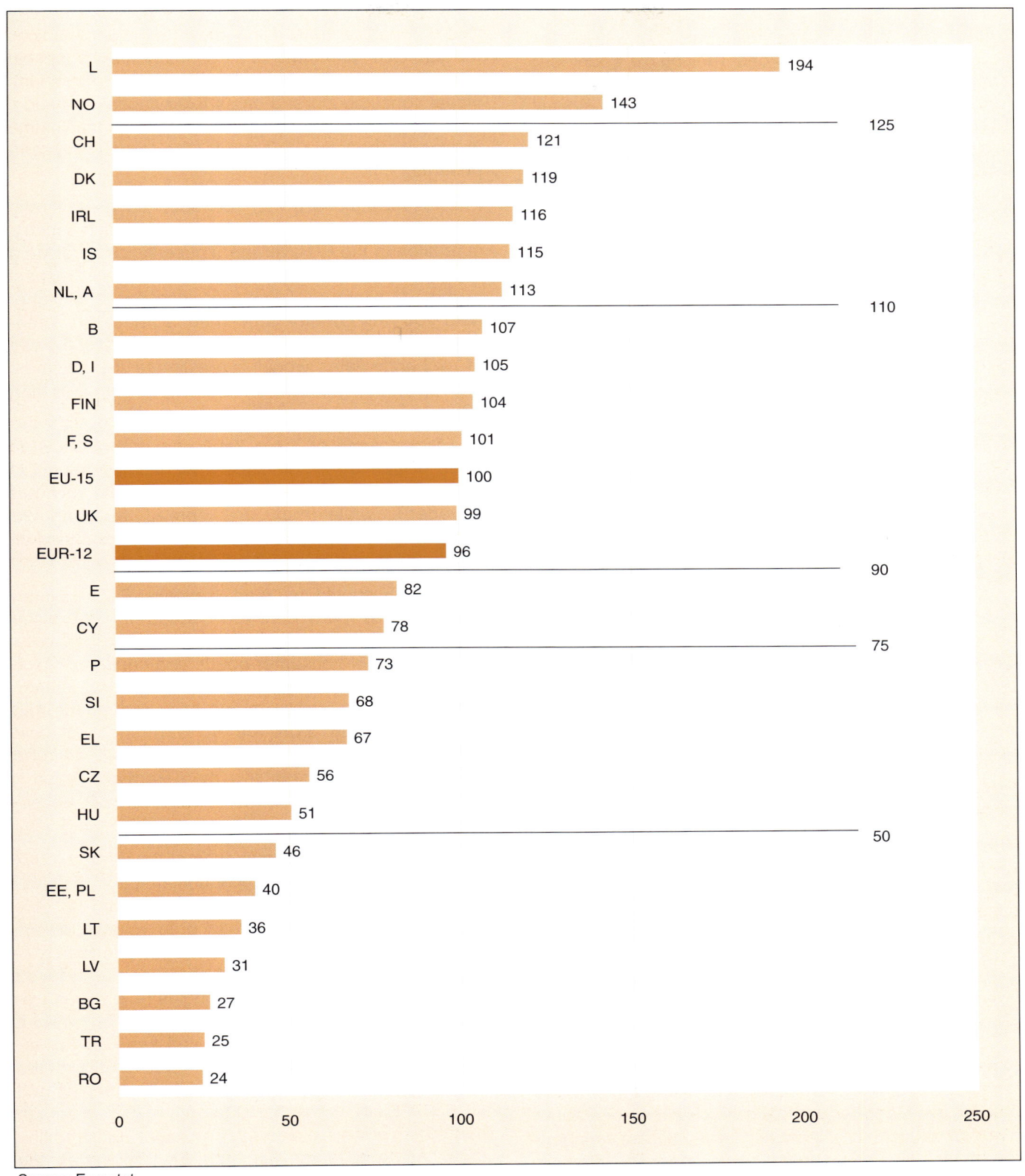

L	194
NO	143
CH	121
DK	119
IRL	116
IS	115
NL, A	113
B	107
D, I	105
FIN	104
F, S	101
EU-15	100
UK	99
EUR-12	96
E	82
CY	78
P	73
SI	68
EL	67
CZ	56
HU	51
SK	46
EE, PL	40
LT	36
LV	31
BG	27
TR	25
RO	24

Reference lines: 125, 110, 90, 75, 50

Source: Eurostat.

MONEY, INTEREST RATES AND PRICES IN THE UNION

> **Grouping of countries**
>
> As referred to above, GDP volume indices are presented in the form of country groups. This helps to focus attention on the broad ranking of countries rather than the precise results which are subject to a statistical margin of error. For example, a recent review of French construction prices, which has resulted in a significant change in construction prices compared with 1999, has not resulted in a significant change of the position of France relative to other countries at the level of GDP: it remains in a group, including Belgium, Germany, Italy, Finland, Sweden and the United Kingdom, close to the EU average.

> **Country specific comments**
>
> Per capita GDP is highest for Luxembourg and Norway. One of the reasons for Luxembourg's high GDP per capita index is the large share of cross-border workers in total employment that contribute to GDP. In addition, a non-negligible part of the expenditure on certain products on the Luxembourg territory is accounted for by cross-border shoppers. Regarding Norway, results are significantly influenced by oil price variations, due to its position as a large oil exporter.
>
> The data for Malta are not included in this chapter. Malta is currently undertaking a revision of its national accounts in order to adopt the European system of accounts, ESA 95.

Purchasing power parities for GDP and its components

The first two columns of Table 7.4.1 show the exchange rate to the euro and PPP at GDP level, respectively. In addition to PPPs at GDP level, Table 7.4.1 also presents PPPs for the three following components: household and NPISH final consumption expenditure, actual individual consumption and gross fixed capital formation. When analysing these PPPs, it appears that they are generally close to that of total GDP.

Nevertheless results for gross fixed capital formation reveal that the PPP for this component is lower than that for the other items for Nordic countries (Finland, Sweden and Iceland), whereas it is significantly higher for the majority of the candidate countries. The latter is clearly influenced by the fact that most candidate countries import a large share of their equipment goods, which implies higher relative prices (see Table 7.4.2).

Price level indices and per capita volume indices for GDP and its components

The first part of Table 7.4.2 shows price level indices for total GDP and three of its components: household and NPISH final consumption expenditure, actual individual consumption and gross fixed capital formation. In its second part, Table 7.4.2 shows per capita volume indices for the total GDP and for the same three components.

Price level indices (PLIs) are obtained as the ratio between PPP and the exchange rate for each country, in relation to the EU average. These indices provide a comparison of the countries' price levels with respect to the EU average: if the price level index is higher than 100, the country concerned is relatively expensive compared to the EU average. In this case, the use of exchange rates would overestimate the volumes; the opposite is true if the price level index is lower than 100.

The first column of Table 7.4.2 shows that, at GDP level, disparities in the price level index among EU Member States lie between 69 (Portugal) and 123 (Sweden), while they are spread between 28 (Bulgaria) and 133 (Switzerland) when considering all participating countries in the ECP.

Table 7.4.3 should be read vertically. Each column indicates how many euro are needed in each of the countries listed in the rows to buy the same representative basket of consumer goods and services, which costs EUR 100 in the country at the top of the column. For example, to buy the same basket of goods and services, costing EUR 100 in Germany, will cost EUR 136 in Switzerland. In other words, Switzerland is about 36 % more expensive than Germany when it comes to final consumption expenditure of households.

Interesting also is the comparison of the volume index for household and NPISH final consumption expenditure and the actual individual consumption in Table 7.4.2. The differences between both volume indices are, relative to the EU average, the goods and services which are provided free of charge or at reduced prices by the State to the households (e.g. for education and health). Denmark, as an example, when it comes to the volume of goods and services households and NPISH pay for, is to be found at 96 % of the EU average. When it comes to what households and NPISH actually consume, Denmark is 9 percentage points above the EU average. A similar redistribution effect can be observed within the EU for Sweden, the Netherlands and France. Among the EFTA countries it is noticeable for Iceland and Norway and among the candidate countries particularly for Slovakia, the Czech Republic and Hungary.

Table 7.4.1. Euro exchange rates and purchasing power parities, 2000

	Exchange rate to the euro	Purchasing power parity (1 PPS in national currency)			
		GDP	Household and NPISH final consumption expenditure (*)	Actual individual consumption (**)	Gross fixed capital formation
Belgium (B)	1	1.00286	1.00971	1.01238	0.979345
Denmark (DK)	7.45382	9.02100	9.09561	9.12526	9.06801
Germany (D)	1	1.03779	1.00708	1.01934	1.05754
Greece (EL)	1	0.761929	0.794643	0.765426	0.812811
Spain (E)	1	0.826580	0.833858	0.824188	0.849962
France (F)	1	1.03051	1.02886	1.02414	1.04514
Ireland (IRL)	1	1.04227	1.08504	1.05472	1.04017
Italy (I)	1	0.855137	0.857581	0.863153	0.823947
Luxembourg (L)	1	1.05963	0.969256	1.04097	1.04652
Netherlands (NL)	1	0.989246	0.981495	0.949356	1.10427
Austria (A)	1	0.993090	0.977113	0.991218	1.00036
Portugal (P)	1	0.694697	0.715635	0.694822	0.781023
Finland (FIN)	1	1.07832	1.16581	1.15316	0.920672
Sweden (S)	8.44519	10.3803	10.8351	10.7558	9.64564
United Kingdom (UK)	0.609478	0.705756	0.722574	0.717096	0.708222
EU-15	:	1	1	1	1
Iceland (IS)	72.5848	92.2076	95.1153	92.7169	85.3816
Norway (NO)	8.11292	9.85977	10.4824	10.3577	10.3228
Switzerland (CH)	1.55786	2.06968	2.13564	2.17482	1.82020
Bulgaria (BG)	1.94792	0.546603	0.592566	0.539236	0.813967
Cyprus (CY)	0.573924	0.466295	0.477550	0.476849	0.412696
Czech Republic (CZ)	35.5995	15.3100	16.2913	14.4068	20.6004
Estonia (EE)	15.6466	6.96111	7.18031	6.31985	12.1384
Hungary (HU)	260.045	114.820	117.774	104.436	169.418
Latvia (LV)	0.559227	0.262075	0.297445	0.253729	0.405895
Lithuania (LI)	3.69516	1.59412	1.73744	1.48782	2.73184
Poland (PL)	4.00817	1.98016	2.15012	1.93840	2.47369
Romania (RO)	19 921.8	6 530.19	7 565.89	6 523.24	9 041.91
Slovakia (SK)	42.6017	16.0588	17.0694	14.4183	25.6803
Slovenia (SI)	206.613	132.932	137.064	131.108	145.394
Turkey (TR)	574 816	328 671	376 013	343 155	377 647

(*) Household and non-profit institution serving households (NPISH) final consumption expenditure refers to consumption of goods and services which households and NPISH actually paid for.
(**) Actual individual consumption consists of household and NPISH final consumption expenditure plus goods and services for individual consumption provided by the government free of charge or at reduced prices, e.g. in education and health. The latter are goods and services that, while provided by government, are consumed individually by households and NPISH.
Source: Eurostat.

Table 7.4.3 provides an interesting cross comparison of price level indices for all ECP participants. Within the EU, when it comes to the basket of goods and services representing household consumption expenditure, Sweden (129 % of EU-15) is the most expensive country, followed by Denmark (122) and the United Kingdom (119). All three EFTA countries are generally more expensive than the EU Member States, with Norway being about the same price level as Sweden. All candidate countries are less expensive than the EU average, with Cyprus (83) coming closest to it. The least expensive country in the comparison is Bulgaria (31).

MONEY, INTEREST RATES AND PRICES IN THE UNION

Table 7.4.2. Price level indices and per capita volume indices for GDP and selected components, 2000

	Price level index, EU-15 = 100				Per capita volume index, EU-15 = 100			
	GDP	Household and NPISH final consumption expenditure (*)	Actual individual consumption (**)	Gross fixed capital formation	GDP	Household and NPISH final consumption expenditure (*)	Actual individual consumption (**)	Gross fixed capital formation
B	100	101	101	98	107	99	102	112
DK	121	122	122	122	119	96	109	124
D	104	101	102	106	105	109	106	108
EL	76	79	77	81	67	77	72	69
E	83	83	82	85	82	82	81	98
F	103	103	102	105	101	95	99	97
IRL	104	109	105	104	116	92	92	133
I	86	86	86	82	105	108	106	104
L	106	97	104	105	194	145	139	200
NL	99	98	95	110	113	97	104	111
A	99	98	99	100	113	112	111	128
P	69	72	69	78	73	75	77	90
FIN	108	117	115	92	104	82	87	114
S	123	128	127	114	101	84	96	91
UK	116	119	118	116	99	109	107	83
EUR-12	96	95	95	97	96	95	95	99
EU-15	100	100	100	100	100	100	100	100
IS	127	131	128	118	115	114	124	144
NO	122	129	128	127	143	98	107	131
CH	133	137	140	117	121	120	110	140
EFTA-3	128	134	135	121	129	112	109	137
BG	28	30	28	42	27	29	29	13
CY	81	83	83	72	78	90	84	76
CZ	43	46	40	58	56	49	55	57
EE	44	46	40	78	40	39	43	26
HU	44	45	40	65	51	44	50	40
LV	47	53	45	73	31	29	33	26
LT	43	47	40	74	36	36	43	19
MT	67	71	66	74	66	68	71	76
PL	49	54	48	62	40	41	43	38
RO	33	38	33	45	24	25	27	16
SK	38	40	34	60	46	39	46	41
SI	64	66	63	70	68	62	65	80
TR	57	65	60	66	25	27	26	23
CC-13	48	53	48	62	33	34	35	30

(*) Household and non-profit institution serving households (NPISH) final consumption expenditure refers to consumption of goods and services which households and NPISH actually paid for.
(**) Actual individual consumption consists of household and NPISH final consumption expenditure plus goods and services for individual consumption provided by the government free of charge or at reduced prices, e.g. in education and health. The latter are goods and services that, while provided by government, are consumed individually by households and NPISH.
Source: Eurostat.

Table 7.4.3. Cross table of price level indices for final consumption expenditure of households, 2000

	B	DK	D	EL	E	F	IRL	I	L	NL	A	P	FIN	S	UK	EU-15	IS	NO	CH	BG	CY	CZ	EE	HU	LV	LT	PL	RO	SK	SI	TR
B	**100**	83	101	126	121	98	93	118	105	102	104	140	86	79	85	101	77	78	74	328	121	218	217	220	187	212	186	261	248	151	153
DK	121	**100**	122	153	146	119	112	142	127	124	125	170	104	95	103	122	93	95	90	397	147	263	262	265	227	256	225	316	300	183	185
D	99	82	**100**	126	120	98	92	117	105	102	103	140	86	78	85	101	76	78	74	326	121	217	216	218	186	211	185	260	247	150	152
EL	79	65	79	**100**	96	78	73	93	83	81	82	111	68	62	67	80	61	62	59	259	96	172	172	174	148	168	147	207	196	120	121
E	83	68	83	105	**100**	81	77	97	87	85	86	116	71	65	70	84	64	65	61	272	100	180	180	182	155	175	154	216	206	125	126
F	102	84	103	129	123	**100**	95	120	107	105	106	143	88	80	87	103	78	80	76	335	124	222	221	224	191	216	190	266	253	154	156
IRL	108	89	108	136	130	106	**100**	127	113	110	112	151	93	85	92	109	83	84	80	353	130	235	234	236	202	228	200	281	268	163	165
I	85	70	85	107	103	83	79	**100**	89	87	88	119	73	67	72	86	65	66	63	279	103	185	184	187	159	180	158	222	211	129	130
L	95	79	96	120	115	93	88	112	**100**	97	98	133	82	75	81	96	73	74	70	312	115	207	206	208	178	201	176	248	236	144	145
NL	98	81	98	123	118	96	91	115	103	**100**	101	137	84	77	83	99	75	76	72	320	118	212	212	214	183	207	181	255	242	148	149
A	97	80	97	122	117	95	90	114	102	99	**100**	136	83	76	82	98	74	76	72	317	117	210	210	212	181	205	179	252	240	146	148
P	71	59	72	90	86	70	66	84	75	73	74	**100**	62	56	61	72	55	56	53	234	86	155	154	156	133	151	132	186	177	108	109
FIN	116	96	116	146	140	113	107	136	122	119	120	163	**100**	91	98	117	89	91	86	380	140	252	251	254	217	246	215	302	288	175	177
S	127	105	128	161	154	125	118	150	134	130	132	179	110	**100**	108	129	98	100	94	418	154	277	276	279	239	270	237	333	316	193	195
UK	118	97	118	149	142	115	109	138	124	120	122	165	102	92	**100**	119	90	92	87	386	142	256	255	258	220	249	218	307	292	178	180
EU-15	99	82	100	125	120	97	92	116	104	101	102	139	85	78	84	**100**	76	77	73	325	120	216	215	217	185	210	184	259	246	150	151
IS	130	108	131	165	157	128	121	153	137	133	135	183	112	102	111	131	**100**	102	97	427	158	283	282	286	244	276	242	340	323	197	199
NO	128	106	129	162	155	125	119	150	135	131	132	180	110	100	109	129	98	**100**	95	420	155	279	277	281	240	271	238	334	318	193	195
CH	135	111	136	171	163	132	125	159	142	138	140	189	116	106	115	136	104	105	**100**	442	163	294	292	296	253	286	250	352	335	204	206
BG	30	25	31	39	37	30	28	36	32	31	32	43	26	24	26	31	23	24	23	**100**	37	66	66	67	57	65	57	80	76	46	47
CY	83	68	83	104	100	81	77	97	87	85	85	116	71	65	70	83	63	65	61	271	**100**	180	179	181	155	175	153	216	205	125	126
CZ	46	38	46	58	55	45	43	54	48	47	48	64	40	36	39	46	35	36	34	151	56	**100**	100	101	86	97	85	120	114	69	70
EE	46	38	46	58	56	45	43	54	49	47	48	65	40	36	39	47	35	36	34	151	56	100	**100**	101	86	98	86	120	115	70	70
HU	46	38	46	58	55	45	42	54	48	47	47	64	39	36	39	46	35	36	34	149	55	99	99	**100**	85	97	85	119	113	69	70
LV	53	44	54	67	64	52	50	63	56	55	55	75	46	42	45	54	41	42	40	175	65	116	116	117	**100**	113	99	139	133	81	82
LT	47	39	47	60	57	46	44	55	50	48	49	66	41	37	40	48	36	37	35	155	57	103	102	103	88	**100**	88	123	117	71	72
PL	54	45	54	68	65	53	50	63	57	55	56	76	46	42	46	54	41	42	40	177	65	117	117	118	101	114	**100**	141	134	81	82
RO	38	32	38	48	46	38	36	45	40	39	40	54	33	30	33	39	29	30	28	126	46	83	83	84	72	81	71	**100**	95	58	58
SK	40	33	40	51	49	39	37	47	42	41	42	57	35	32	34	41	31	31	30	132	49	88	87	88	75	85	75	105	**100**	61	62
SI	66	55	66	84	80	65	61	78	70	68	68	93	57	52	56	67	51	52	49	217	80	144	143	145	124	140	123	173	164	**100**	101
TR	65	54	66	83	79	64	61	77	69	67	68	92	57	51	56	66	50	51	49	215	79	143	142	144	123	139	122	171	163	99	**100**

Source: Eurostat.

International price and volume comparisons

Eurostat participates in the "international comparison programme" (ICP), which has been running for 30 years. In Europe, Eurostat and the OECD cooperate in the framework of the "European comparison programme" (ECP), in which Eurostat annually establishes PPPs for the 15 EU Member States, the 13 EU candidate countries and three EFTA countries, Norway, Iceland and Switzerland. A rolling three-year survey cycle is used for consumer prices. About one third of the consumer goods is surveyed every year, and for the remaining two thirds, suitable consumer price indices are used for extrapolation in the intervening years. Capital goods prices, rents, and GDP weights are collected annually, as well as salaries in the government sector, which are used as proxy-PPPs for the respective part of this sector. For the remaining OECD member countries, the OECD follows the Eurostat survey cycle for consumer prices, whereas a benchmark-extrapolation approach is used for the other components, with PPP calculations every third year.

Symbols and abbreviations

EU	European Union
EUR-11	euro-zone before 1 January 2001 (Belgium, Germany, Spain, France, Ireland, Italy, Luxembourg, Netherlands, Austria, Portugal and Finland)
EUR-12	euro-zone after 1 January 2001 (EUR-11 and Greece)
EU-15	European Union of 15 Member States (EU-12 and Denmark, Sweden and the United Kingdom)
EEA	European Economic Area (EU-15 and Iceland, Liechtenstein and Norway)
EFTA	European Free Trade Association (Iceland, Liechtenstein, Norway and Switzerland)
OECD	Organisation for Economic Cooperation and Development
B	Belgium
DK	Denmark
D	Germany
EL	Greece
E	Spain
F	France
IRL	Ireland
I	Italy
L	Luxembourg
NL	Netherlands
A	Austria
P	Portugal
FIN	Finland
S	Sweden
UK	United Kingdom
CC	Candidate countries
BG	Bulgaria
CY	Cyprus
CZ	Czech Republic
EE	Estonia
HU	Hungary
LV	Latvia
LT	Lithuania
MT	Malta
PL	Poland
RO	Romania
SK	Slovak Republic
SI	Slovenia
TR	Turkey
IS	Iceland
NO	Norway
CH	Switzerland
US	United States of America
JP	Japan
EUR	euro
BEF	Belgian franc
DKK	Danish crown
DEM	German mark
GRD	Greek drachma
ESP	Spanish peseta
FRF	French franc
IEP	Irish pound
ITL	Italian lira

LUF	Luxembourgish franc
NLG	Dutch guilder
ATS	Austrian schilling
PTE	Portuguese escudo
FIM	Finnish mark
SEK	Swedish crown
GBP	Pound sterling
BGN	Bulgarian lev
CYP	Cyprus pound
CZK	Czech koruna
EEK	Estonian kroon
HUF	Hungarian forint
LVL	Latvian lat
LTL	Lithuanian litas
MTL	Maltese lira
PLN	Polish zloty
ROL	Romanian leu
SKK	Slovak koruna
SIT	Slovenian tolar
TRL	Turkish lira
USD	United States dollar
YEN	Japanese yen
billion	billion (thousand million)
:	data not available

European Commission

Economic portrait of the European Union 2002

Luxembourg: Office for Official Publications of the European Communities

2002 — 167 pp. — 21 x 29.7 cm

Theme 2: Economy and finance
Collection: Panorama of the European Union

ISSN 1680-1687
ISBN 92-894-3771-5

Price (excluding VAT) in Luxembourg: EUR 30

This publication is designed to set out in a single volume wide-ranging macroeconomic data on the European Union and its Member States and to provide an analysis of those data. The focus is put on economic structures, their temporal development and structural differences between Member States. After analysing the economy as a whole, dedicated chapters deal with enterprises, households and general government. While the data provided allow country-specific analysis, the central aim is to draw a profile of the Union and the euro-zone, comparing them, where possible, with their main trading partners.

.... Eurostat Data Shops

BELGIQUE/BELGIË
Eurostat Data Shop
Bruxelles/Brussel
Planistat Belgique
Rue du Commerce 124
Handelsstraat 124
B-1000 Bruxelles/Brussel
Tél. (32-2) 234 67 50
Fax (32-2) 234 67 51
E-mail: datashop@planistat.be
URL: http://www.datashop.org/

DANMARK
Danmarks Statistik
Bibliotek og Information
Eurostat Data Shop
Sejrøgade 11
DK-2100 København Ø
Tlf. (45) 39 17 30 30
Fax (45) 39 17 30 03
E-post: bib@dst.dk
URL:
http://www.dst.dk/bibliotek

DEUTSCHLAND
Statistisches Bundesamt
Eurostat Data Shop Berlin
Otto-Braun-Straße 70-72
(Eingang: Karl-Marx-Allee)
D-10178 Berlin
Tel. (49) 1888-644 94 27/28
Fax (49) 1888-644 94 30
E-Mail: datashop@destatis.de
URL:
http://www.eu-datashop.de/

ESPAÑA
INE
Eurostat Data Shop
Paseo de la Castellana, 183
Despacho 011B
Entrada por Estébanez
Calderón
E-28046 Madrid
Tel. (34) 91 583 91 67 /
91 583 95 00
Fax (34) 91 583 03 57
E-mail:
datashop.eurostat@ine.es
URL: http://www.datashop.org/
Member of the MIDAS Net

FRANCE
INSEE Info service
Eurostat Data Shop
195, rue de Bercy
Tour Gamma A
F-75582 Paris Cedex 12
Tél. (33) 1 53 17 88 44
Fax (33) 1 53 17 88 22
E-mail: datashop@insee.fr
Member of the MIDAS Net

ITALIA - ROMA
ISTAT
Centro di informazione
statistica — Sede di Roma
Eurostat Data Shop
Via Cesare Balbo, 11a
I-00184 Roma
Tel. (39) 06 46 73 31 02/06
Fax (39) 06 46 73 31 01/07
E-mail: dipdiff@istat.it
URL:
http://www.istat.it/Prodotti-e/
Allegati/Eurostatdatashop.html
Member of the MIDAS Net

ITALIA - MILANO
ISTAT
Ufficio regionale per la
Lombardia
Eurostat Data Shop
Via Fieno, 3
I-20123 Milano
Tel. (39) 02 80 61 32 460
Fax (39) 02 80 61 32 304
E-mail: mileuro@tin.it
URL:
http://www.istat.it/Prodotti-e/
Allegati/Eurostatdatashop.html
Member of the MIDAS Net

LUXEMBOURG
Eurostat Data Shop Luxembourg
46 A, avenue J. F. Kennedy
BP 1452
L-1014 Luxembourg
Tél. (352) 43 35-2251
Fax (352) 43 35-22221
E-mail:
dslux@eurostat.datashop.lu
URL: http://www.datashop.org/
Member of the MIDAS Net

NEDERLAND
Centraal Bureau voor de
Statistiek
Eurostat Data Shop — Voorburg
Postbus 4000
2270 JM Voorburg
Nederland
Tel. (31-70) 337 49 00
Fax (31-70) 337 59 84
E-mail: datashop@cbs.nl

PORTUGAL
Eurostat Data Shop Lisboa
INE/Serviço de Difusão
Av. António José de Almeida, 2
P-1000-043 Lisboa
Tel. (351) 21 842 61 00
Fax (351) 21 842 63 64
E-mail: data.shop@ine.pt

SUOMI/FINLAND
Statistics Finland
Eurostat DataShop Helsinki
Tilastokirjasto
PL 2B
FIN-00022 Tilastokeskus
Työpajakatu 13 B, 2. kerros,
Helsinki
P. (358-9) 17 34 22 21
F. (358-9) 17 34 22 79
Sähköposti: datashop@stat.fi
URL: http: //tilastokeskus.fi/tk/
kk/datashop/

SVERIGE
Statistics Sweden
Information service
Eurostat Data Shop
Karlavägen 100
Box 24 300
S-104 51 Stockholm
Tfn (46-8) 50 69 48 01
Fax (46-8) 50 69 48 99
E-post: infoservice@scb.se
URL: http://www.scb.se/tjanster/
datashop/datashop.asp

UNITED KINGDOM
Eurostat Data Shop
Office for National Statistics
Room 1.015
Cardiff Road
Newport NP10 8XG
South Wales
United Kingdom
Tel. (44-1633) 81 33 69
Fax (44-1633) 81 33 33
E-mail:
eurostat.datashop@ons.gov.uk

NORGE
Statistics Norway
Library and Information Centre
Eurostat Data Shop
Kongens gate 6
Boks 8131 Dep.
N-0033 Oslo
Tel. (47) 21 09 46 42/43
Fax (47) 21 09 45 04
E-mail: Datashop@ssb.no
URL: http://www.ssb.no/
biblioteket/datashop/

SCHWEIZ/SUISSE/SVIZZERA
Statistisches Amt des Kantons
Zürich
Eurostat Data Shop
Bleicherweg 5
CH-8090 Zürich
Tel. (41) 1 225 12 12
Fax (41) 1 225 12 99
E-Mail:
datashop@statistik.zh.ch
URL: http://www.statistik.zh.ch

USA
Haver Analytics
Eurostat Data Shop
60 East 42nd Street
Suite 3310
New York, NY 10165
Tel. (1-212) 986 93 00
Fax (1-212) 986 69 81
E-mail: eurodata@haver.com
URL: http://www.haver.com/

EUROSTAT HOME PAGE
www.europa.eu.int/comm/eurostat/

MEDIA SUPPORT EUROSTAT
(only for professional journalists)
Postal address:
Jean Monnet building
L-2920 Luxembourg
Office: BECH A4/017 —
5, rue Alphonse Weicker
L-2721 Luxembourg
Tel. (352) 43 01-33408
Fax (352) 43 01-35349
E-mail:
eurostat-mediasupport@cec.eu.int